The Journal of Our Journey:
Five Years with Doc and Cindy Blackmore

By: Cindy Blackmore

The Journal of Our Journey: Five Years with Doc and Cindy Blackmore
by Cindy Blackmore

Printed in the United States of America

ISBN 9781613790090

www.xulonpress.com

One of my husband's favorite quotes was "The quality of life is
so much more important than the quantity of life." This book
is dedicated to everyone that supported us and allowed us to
have the quality we sought during these five years. A special
dedication goes out to all of those that participated
and shared these five years with us.

If you enjoy this journey, don't miss the *"rest of the story."*

You will find it in the book titled

<u>**Remember to Laugh...**</u>
<u>**The Story of Doc and Cindy Blackmore**</u>

Prelude

What a wonderful day Saturday, September 11th, 2004, was. My husband, Darwin (known as Doc to many of his friends), was on a hunting trip in Colorado with my brothers and my cousin. It was opening day and they had perfect weather! Towards the end of the day, they had downed a large elk. They decided to go back to camp and track it the next day as dusk was falling quickly. They were on bicycles about six miles up an old mountain service road. They had chosen to go hunting in a part of the state that did not allow motorized vehicles so they decided to use bikes.

As they started down the mountain, they swerved on some loose gravel and Doc's bike ended up traveling a little bit off the beaten path and it hit a ditch. When it did, the bike folded and Doc went flying over the handlebars, landing on his neck. He broke his neck and was instantly paralyzed from about the chin down and he was not able to breathe on his own. My brother, Lloyd, knew CPR and assisted breathing but he also was the only one that knew where they were at to seek help. So he gave my cousin, Mike, a crash course in assisted breathing/CPR and left to get help. My other two brothers, Eric and Mike, were hunting in a different location and were not with them.

They were around 12,000' of elevation and the air was thin but Doc was not afraid. Mike was breathing for him and God arrived to give him peace. God told Doc that he was not going to let him die on that mountain because he had something he wanted him to do. Doc often said it was the most peaceful feeling that he ever experienced and it was indescribable. God sat with him and Doc often told the story of feeling the physical presence of God sitting beside him. Of the beautiful night and the way the breezes were blowing the tree tops. The beauty of the moon as it rose into the sky. He never lost consciousness and even though Mike had never done assisted breathing before, he managed to continue to administer it for over two hours...until help could arrive.

When the ambulance arrived, they were surprised to not only find Doc alive but in very good physical condition. They were actually on a body pickup as they did not think they would find him still living. Doc said that the physical presence of God left him at this time but he left him with the peace. Before they transported him, they gave him something to put him to sleep and that is all Doc remembers until he woke up at the hospital.

I had spent the day in St. Louis, Missouri, shopping with my cousin Tammy and we too, had a great day! The weather was perfect for us and we were just settling down for a quiet evening of pizza and a movie when the phone rang. The message was that something had happened in the mountains to Doc and he was hurt bad. They were trying to get him to the hospital but I should prepare myself for the worse. I immediately started praying and called others to pray with me.

Several hours later, I finally received a call from the hospital telling me that Doc was there and that his injuries involved a spinal cord injury which had left him paralyzed. I wasn't familiar with paralysis and I suddenly knew that I was going to enter a world completely new to us and that things might never be the same. We called the airport but I could not get a flight to Colorado until the next morning.

Our son met up with me and flew out first thing the next morning. Before we flew out, we made calls to churches to ask for prayers. I called my boss to let him know that I was not going to be at work on Monday and I called Doc's place of employment to let them know he had been injured and probably would not be returning to work… at least not for a long time. There was still hope in the back of my mind that somehow this would all be ok and things would once again be like they used to be. That was not to be. Things were never the same. In some ways, it was hard but in others, we learned lessons of great value and our faith grew stronger than I ever imagined it could be. It doesn't do any good to play the what-if game so I have never gone there and I do not plan to ever play that game. It is what it is.

That is how we lived our life. The best way we could. As Doc used to say, "we played the hand we were dealt." We made the most of it.

Of course, it took several months of medical care and then rehabilitation care to stabilize Doc and then to teach us how to live in our world with our new disabilities. It wasn't easy and the road was rough but Doc kept a smile on his face and never lost his sense of humor. Our love supported each other on hard days and God supported us on all days!

I have written a book of the experiences, titled 'Remember to Laugh... The Story of Doc and Cindy Blackmore', but it seems like it would not be complete unless I make these following pages available in a second book to accompany it. The following chapters are e-mails that I sent out during the years. I started them directly after I received a laptop from my place of employment that gave me the opportunity to stay in touch. During the first few days after the accident, I was staying in contact through phone messages and even after I received the laptop on the 13th or 14th, I was still doing it one person at a time. After a day or two of that, I started a mass e-mail list that grew long over the next five years but it became an important lifeline. For me and for those that read them and waited for them each month! It changed people's lives and I want to make sure you understand that it wasn't through any talents of mine. It was through the grace of God and the words that he gave me as I kept everyone up-to-date. The first book that I wrote contains the story of how our life changed and the miraculous things we witnessed. The pages in this book are a journal of how we lived our life and the adventures that we had. You will find some spelling errors and some grammatical errors but I left them just they way they were when I sent them out because it didn't seem right to change them. They were already a piece of history and if I was tired or in a hurry when I typed them and missed something, maybe God wanted imperfections in them!

To give you an overview of the first three days, Doc had surgery and his spinal cord was not severed but badly bruised. Only time would tell if he would recover any or all of his body movement or feeling back. It would be a long and tedious journey no matter what the future held. That was all we were told because no one really had the answers. My brothers stayed with me until the 13th, which happened to be my birthday. My son and cousin flew back to Missouri on the 14th. Soon it was just Doc & I fighting a battle that we never thought we would be fighting. We never felt alone though because our family, friends and even strangers were with us every step of the way. Most important of all was that God was driving our bus and we were never in doubt of that! This is the journey of the next five years.

September 15-2004 (a.m.)
The first of our e-mail updates…

Words will NEVER, and mean NEVER, be able to express what your share of thoughts, giving, and praying is doing for us! I received the Orscheln care package yesterday and it was amazing. One thing after another came out of the boxes that uplifted me! The pictures of all of you were the greatest! I have them on Doc's wall and he has asked (by blinking) several times to bring them closer so he can look at them too! He blinks once for no and twice for yes and then a bunch of times when he wants to say something and then I go into a guessing game until I figure it out. It is sorta entertaining for both of us.

He has been in good spirits most of the time although yesterday he had a down day. It didn't stay down long though because your care package had several items that we read and looked at that made him smile. Then the paramedic that rescued him came to visit and told him 9 years ago, he did the same thing and broke his neck. 18 months later he was walking again and now is back to normal so I think that gave Doc a bunch of hope too. The paramedic told him that he has to stay focused on going all the way and not stopping… he is going to visit him once or week or so while we are here. I think he feels a real bond with Doc so I think his support is going to be great!

So far, Doc is kicking butt at what they thought he would be able to do!! That is the good thing. He is officially still paralyzed from the shoulders down but he has signs of things trying to mend which are all positive things. I really feel like prayers are making the difference so keep them up. He can shrug his shoulders, feel his shoulders, feel part way down his left arm, feel all his right arm and now he has feeling in his right hand (as of this morning), and then his chest has some feeling. He can't move any of that but he can move his left leg and his left foot/toes but he can't feel those. Some things come and go but the nurses tell me that is normal in a trauma and in a spinal cord injury. The good news is that there are things happening and for up to a year, we can only improve! The greatest news of all is that they are trying to take him off the ventilator and let him breath on his own. It appears that his chest breathing muscles are not going to be paralyzed and it might be as soon as tomorrow that they will have the tubes out and he will be doing his own breathing. They turned the machine off for an hour this morning and he actually had better vital signs than when the machine was working for him. If they can pull this off, he will be able to start talking as soon as they take the tubes out. They are pretty hopeful that there isn't any damage to his vocal cords and I can't wait to here his voice!!!! I think he can't wait to talk either!!! He is probably really tired of just listening to me jabber (and I know many of you are thinking, "so what's different about that?"). I was quiet for a little bit this morning because I asked him if he wanted me to shut up and just sit still for a minute and I got a two blinker! I am setting little goals and he is so far checking them off one by one. After they take the tubes out, they are going to run some tests on his swallow muscles and if they are in tack, he gets to start eating. He told me(after a ton of guessing!!!) that the first thing he wants is a bottled water!

You only have to visit with others in the ICU to know that we are some of the lucky ones! Life can throw you some curves but a working brain is the most important thing of all and we have that. He has his personality and his quirky sense of humor and it is all still very much active. We have been entertaining each other in some pretty unique ways! He has promised to beat me at a game of trivia pursuit as soon as he can talk! We will see if I can let him win! Hehe

I hope you can tell that while he has sustained some serious injuries and the future is going to be a challenge, we are still so hopeful and uplifted because of the grace of God and the things that each of you have done and continue to do! Someone here made the comment that it is sad that I am so far from home and alone but they were wrong because I do not feel alone. I feel like every one of you is standing out in the hall waiting for an update along with all the rest of Doc's co-workers and our family and friends from around the country!

There are signs every day that God is pulling off some amazing stuff and I have to sit back and just let him do his thing. I am not much for not being in control but I am going to step aside in this and let him work! A prayer is much like a smile…you give one out and get one back because even though I have been saying a ton of prayers for Doc too, I also stop frequently to thank him for family and friends like you guys! So your prayers are coming back in your direction and Doc & I will remember for the rest of out lives the outpouring of affection that we have gotten so far and I am positive will continue to get. It is my prayer that we look back on this in a year or so and remember that we only made it through it all because of all this support! I have tried hard not to waste tears on things that I can't change but I can tell you that I have wasted a few on the acts of kindness that continue to spew from Missouri! The nurses and other families in this hospital waiting room continue to be open mouthed at the number of calls and acts of kindness that they are witnessing!

Please make sure that the persons are the floor and in maintenance get to see this and I know they don't have e-mail! They are all a part of this!

I will keep you up to date on changes and things as they happen (and I know in my heart there are going to be changes)!

I know this is a little long winded but you probably didn't expect anything less from me! To each of you we send our LOVE!

Cindy and Doc

September 15-2004

Before you share too much of it, some of it has already changed. Please read the update below and know that I am praying it is just a 2nd opinion from someone that wants to be better safe than sorry and that all these things they are implementing are just temporary. It felt a little like one step forward and 2 steps back but I think they are just trying to do this right!

The doctor is telling me that even though Doc apparently is breathing on his own, she doesn't know how long he could do that without permanent strain to the body so she is wanting to put him on a ventilator regardless of the results of the test. Once she is convinced that he really is capable of doing that, she will remove it. She cannot put the trek into the neck until his surgery wound heals and that will not be until later next week so that means that he cannot talk to me until then. I have explained that to him and he is cool with it so I am going to chill with him. Then they are going to put a feeding tube into his stomach because until they are convinced he can actually swallow, they need to feed him. If it works out the muscles in that area are ok, they will remove the feeding tube at that time and let him eat. I asked when that would be and I sorta got the "nothing is going to happen overnight and I need to dig my heals in for the long haul" speech. She is telling me that there are good signs that he has the possibility of some long range improvements. She said that they are unlimited because only time and God know what they are but that they will take at least a year to see but that in the meantime, they will do what they need to do to keep him healthy.

So based on this, I back up a little bit, take a big breathe and jump in again. As long as Doc hangs in there with a positive attitude, I will be ok.

Keep the prayers coming. I still can feel God's promise in my heart though that this going to work out!

Thanks for all the notes and love that you guys are sharing with me!

Cindy

September 16-2004

An update for all that would like to know....

Well, one dr still said doc was doing good and if he continued to breathe well on his own, they would take him off the respirator and let him take over. Another dr. (we are naming her Dr. Party Pooper), still wants to put in a trach and keep the respirator on whether he needs it or not for a few months. The 1st doctor looks like he is winning out though and they are talking about seeing how today goes and then taking out his tubing tomorrow or Saturday. Then he could talk to me.

He has additional feeling in his left arm all the way to the wrist, which is an improvement.

The neuro surgeon was impressed enough with what he has doing on that he has ordered re-hab to go ahead and start today to try to improve what he already has going for him. They are letting me know that they are hesitant to put a ton of promise into these things but that they are positive things that are happening and that for the extent of his injuries, it is pretty amazing. I just know in my heart that God is taking care of his injuries and I just have to keep taking care of his other needs for awhile.

The next step after the breathing issue is resolved is whether his swallow muscles and feeding tubes are paralyzed. If so, they will have to feed him by a stomach tube until or if they mend, but if not, they can feed him regular. That is our next hurdle. One race at a time!

I feel like this is a soap opera and I am giving each of you the "Days in Grand Junction with Cindy and Doc". One only wonders what exciting things will happen tomorrow! Stayed tuned.................

September 20-2004

Just want to let everyone know that we are still thanking you for and asking for continued prayers. We are certain they can and will be the difference. There isn't going to be any miraculous changes in the next few weeks but rather continued little baby steps. They have moved Doc out of ICU and he is now in room 319 on a regular floor. It isn't completely regular because he still has a nurse that doesn't have a full wing to take care of-he is just one of 4 patients that they have. He had a rough day on the day they moved him but he is settling in now.

We still have 2 versions on trach or no trach. The man that makes the decision though is the one that wants to try to take him off the respirator without a trach so I think that is the way we are heading for now. They have been taking him off the respirator for the past 4 days and now they are going to keep him off the respirator night and day to see how he holds up. If good, they will pull the plugs and see how he does. In worse case, he starts to struggle and then they will have to add an emergency trach. They are not wanting too put one in right now because it would lay right on his surgery wound and they are afraid of infection in the injury. The neuro surgeon came in this morning and said that Doc continues to move in the right direction and that it is simply time that is going to give us the answers to our questions on what he can and cannot do in the future. I think we are looking at 4-5 weeks more here and then I am hoping to transfer him back to Missouri. We are concentrating on the breathing issue first. Then they are starting physical therapy to keep his muscles and bones in good working order. I am happy to say that I have been trained and passed the test so that I am able to do it for him once a day and then they come do it once a day. I think Doc is nervous about me getting my hands on him in any medical form at all but he is stuck with me! We do understand that no matter what comes back from the swelling, it won't be everything and we will be relying on the mending process for the main stuff. I also understand that even if some motion or feeling comes back during the swelling stage, he won't be able to do much with it until re-hab. They will actually have to teach him how to use things again or how to adapt.

His digestive system is working well and as soon as they can get the tubes out they are going to test his swallow muscles but the neurologists is not suspecting any problems. They are pretty optimistic that he will soon be eating and drinking on his own. He is definitely ready for some food and especially (after we played 20 questions) his bottle of water!

He is blinking this morning that he is totally bored so I am heading back to my room to pick up some pictures. He wants to look at something other than tv, walls, and ceilings.

We continue to communicate with blinks and we will both be glad when we can talk. They are going to move him to an electric chair today and let him sit up for awhile. He is blinking that he is going to like that. I think he is ready for anything that will get him moving a little bit! It is not like Doc to be immobile. Maybe God is teaching him patience and me compassion!

I am still staying in the hospitality house but if I have to leave because Doc is out of ICU, there has been this wonderful angel, name Teresa, that is a respiratory specialist in the hospital that has opened her home and family to me during my stay here. She is turning out to be a great friend. She has even offered me a vehicle to use if I need one to get back and forth to the hospital. Some people have very huge hearts and I am meeting some of them in Grand Junction!

Doc has a rotating, air filled bed that keeps his body moving in all directions now so they don't have to flip him all the time. I think he is liking that too! He reads every e-mail that comes to him because I can turn the lap top around for him to see. He also reads every card that is sent to him and I think he enjoys them. I don't know if he likes reading on his back or if he likes telling me with a blink that he is ready for me to open the card to read more but that will all come in good time!

I will keep you updated of any news in the near future but in the meantime, we are just playing a waiting game. Thanks for your continued support and prayers and know that it is our opinion that no one in the world could have more support from family, friends and co-workers than we have. I hope God blesses each and every one of you!

Cindy and Doc

P.S. As soon as Doc gets his voice, I will let him dictate me a note to send to you on his own. He blinks that he has things to say!

September 23-2004

I have been putting off updating everyone on the wonderful days in grand junction because things looked very close to pulling Doc off the respirator and his breathing on his own. I thought if this happened it would be great news and a good time for an update. Things kept happening though to put it off each day and now I just thought I would go ahead and let everyone know what is going on. Things are not going in the right direction right now. I know there are going to be ups and downs but there seems to have been quite a few down days in a row.

A couple of days ago Doc started losing some of the motion that he had earlier in the week but no one seemed to concern because things come and go during the swelling stage. Yesterday, though, he had pretty much lost all movement so the Neuro doctor ordered an MRI. During the MRI last night, Doc had what they call a vegal nerve reaction which amounts to his heart slowing down to the point of the patient passing out. It isn't uncommon but the patient is usually out for just a few minutes and Doc was out for much longer than that. To the point that they rushed him for a cat scan to see what brain activity was happening. On the way down to the cat scan, he came back to us and seemed to be as alert as ever. Because of the trauma though, they made the decision to hook him back up to the respirator and let him rest overnight. (just for the record the cat scan was clear).

When they came in this morning the neuro surgeon said that the MRI showed an abnormally amount of swelling on the spinal cord for this long after surgery which is probably why he is losing some of what he had. They also tried to start weining him from the machine again but when they switched him over, he cannot breathe on his own at all today. He is not able to cough anymore either which was a strong thing he had in his favor. They have tried to trigger the cough but it is not responding. They don't know why he is swelling or why he quit breathing on his own and even if they did, they cannot operate on a spinal cord. So they are giving him medicine to dissolve blood clots in case that is the problem and they are also giving him a heavy dose of some type of medicine that reduces swelling. We are praying that the swelling is what is paralyzing his chest muscles and cutting off what nerves that appeared to be transmitting signals. So, they will continue this treatment for the next 3 days and see where it takes us. I think the doctors are as baffled as I am.

In the meantime, they have decided for sure to add a trach to be on the safe side in case they fix the problem and something like this happens again. I think they are trying to stabilize him because the trach will be a surgery and they are talking about trying to schedule it for this weekend.

The bright side of all of this is that Doc remains alert and is communicating with our ever popular blinking program. We even have progressed to be able to spell out words so that we are not limited to yes and no. This has eliminated the need for some of my guessing skills. I think he is a little scared at the turn of events too but remains positive. We both feel like God is still in this with us so we are trying to trust in what his plan is and ride the ride!

He received over 80 cards today and over 200 for the week. The ladies delivering the mail said they have never seen anything like it. He reads each and every one and is enjoying them all! Please continue to pray and hopefully, the next update will have a little more positive news!

At this current minute, he is sleeping peacefully so I am going to take the opportunity to grab a sandwich and stop by the chapel to do what I ask each of you do to do and that is to keep praying.

Thanks so much.

Love, Cindy and Dar

September 24-2004

I have titled this weekend a "Plateau Weekend" because we are just passing time. It was wonderful that nothing to cause more worries happened but it was disappointing not to be making strides forward. We did have a tiny flicker of hope yesterday morning when Doc wiggled one toe on his left foot. It is his 2nd toe and Jaymi (our oldest daughter) has been trying hard to figure out how you can wiggle one toe without the others moving. We have both been smiling to vision her sticking her foot out and trying to figure it out. You can all try it if you want too but it is impossible! (except for Doc!).

I had a wonderful nurse named Dane in ICU and he and his wife were the ones that shared their vehicle with me. He has been up here a couple of times this weekend to say hi. Teresa, the respiratory therapist that offered her family and home to me, also comes up frequently to say hi. Mark and Carol Cunningham came up on Friday and stayed until Sunday and it was wonderful to have familiar faces here with us. Mark stayed with Doc for awhile and Carol and I ran to Wal Mart. (I imagine Wal Mart has really been missing me!). I bought a game there called Crap or Fact and we have been playing that all weekend. Doc thinks he is really good at it but I really think we are about tied in victories! He can make some pouty faces that almost makes you want to let him win but I am seeing through it! I have gone from reading blinks to reading lips and I cannot wait until my ears can do the listening work again.

He continues to have wonderful nurses and doctors all working for the common cause of helping him make progress. My prayers are with them too!

They put the trach in his throat on Friday so his mouth is free to form words (although we can't vocalize them yet), brush his teeth, and pucker for kisses! (He is a good puckerer!) He keeps telling me to go get him something to eat and not just something…he has specific requests-cheeseburgers, ham w/baby carrots, ice cream, coffee, cookies, ect…! He remains on a feeding tube however, that they have inserted into his stomach. In about a week, they will trade out trachs and if he can get some power in his diaphragm, he will be able to make sounds and start to learn how to form words.

Doc currently cannot feel anything or move anything much below the chin. The doctors remain optimistic that this is all just a temporary set back and that as soon as some of the additional swelling (that swelled up out of the blue—inserting a pun!) goes down, he will get back everything he had going for him and then we can start heading in the right direction again. I am trying not to be impatient but this waiting game is hard! I asked the doctor this morning if he could give me any idea on a timeframe for the swelling and he just smiled at me and put his hand on my shoulder and said "time". They still think he will breath on his own and the trach will come out and then he will eat on his own the feeding tube will come out. "time"….I always knew it was precious but I never knew how slow it could move when you wanted it to march on.

Always, in the past, it has flown by! It is like everyday is a Monday at work (you know the days that last forever!!).

I picked up Ellen Smothers from the airport yesterday morning and she is staying with me until Wednesday night. Then 2 of our 3 kids are flying out on Friday morning (thanks to all of you who donated frequent flyer miles to make this possible). We are both really excited to have them coming and they get to stay until Monday evening! It is good to have a friend sit with me and to eat with. As I am typing this and visiting with Doc, she is doing my laundry for me! I am still able to stay at the hospitality house and she is staying with me there. We even took a walk yesterday while Doc was taking an afternoon nap and getting a bath. The weather was beautiful as it is again today! It is a beautiful city, sitting in like a bowl surrounded by mesa's.

Cairo School sent a wonderful care package and lots of love with Mark and Carol and we had fun going through the treasures as we did with all the packages, pictures and cards that we have received from all of you! Jennifer (Doc's co-worker and partner in crime) sent some homemade cookies which he is slobbering over and I am eating! At least I let him pick out which kind to eat each time I have one! AECI also sent many hello's and messages to Doc through Mark.

My morning still starts with a visit to the chapel and my day ends with a visit to the chapel. I can feel that I have the prayers and faith of each of you with me and that in the end, this is all going to turn out to be an experience in which we have gotten to know the love and compassion of our family and friends and a renewed bonding with God that he is always with us! It has opened my eyes to the joys of sharing and caring for others. This is not to say this hasn't been a hard experience and I am sure will remain so until the end! However, I have met so many other wonderful patients and their families in the hospital and my prayer list grows longer with each passing day as does my list of friends! Thanks to all of you for your continued support and prayers and I will keep you updated on the "Days in Grand Junction".

Love to each of you
Cindy and Doc

September 29-2004

First off, I want to say THANK YOU loud enough for all of you to hear it from Colorado to Missouri! I know that Doc thinks that my voice is loud enough to carry that far too! What I am extending my thank you for is to each of you that worked or ate at Golden Corral last night to support us coming home! I heard it was like a miracle how everyone pitched in and it was fun to hear that it sounded like it was an enjoyable time too! For any of you who have not heard, enough money was raised to bring Doc back as soon as he is well enough to travel. What a prayer that has been answered!

Now for the latest update:

Dr. Griffith (Doc's neuro surgeon) is back. He was impressed at what Doc had done in the first week and he is pretty sure he knows why he lost it all. He is saying that he noticed Doc's sodium levels dropped to a dangerously low point on the day before he lost everything. He said that keeping your sodium level up is very important and without good sodium, injuries tend to do some major swelling (which explains the swelling). His test from yesterday still shows the swelling. The doctor is optimistic that this is a chemically/drug treatable ailment. He is starting him on some drugs today that he hopes will help. He is telling us that there is nothing that surgery will help but just drugs and time. He said that we have to know that this might be a permanent thing but he would hope not and that he would be hopeful that this is just temporary. He reminded us again that it might take up to a year to know for sure if this is all going to work out. So now we are going to do the drug thing and keep praying!

After the little speech on taking up to a year, I figured it wasn't the time to ask how long it would take for the drugs to kick in. I also didn't ask how long before we could transport him because you can tell he isn't stable enough to move yet. They are going to try and do all they can to get the swelling down before they move him to see if can start weining him and breathing on his own again. His system does seem to be adapting better to the respirator. Earlier in the week, the machine was having to give him 90% of his oxygen to keep his vital signs good but as the week is going on, he keeps being able to improve on that. As of this morning, he is at 45% and holding his own. The lung doctor was excited about that and he was very hopeful that these drugs will assist in the swelling/spinal cord injury and that we will soon be back on the road to improvements!

I brushed Doc's teeth this morning and his smile is adding the sunshine to the room even though it is a rainy day outside! We continue to be optimistic and prayerful that this is all going to work out. There is no way that it cannot with all the love, prayers and support that we are getting. That in itself if powerful medicine!

We also were told this morning that it might be possible in the next day or two that Doc will have a different trach inserted so that he can start to make some sounds with his vocal cords. That means I have to share the talk time~!

If anyone is keeping record on the game side of things, I beat Doc at "Fact or Crap" last night but I am sure we will have to have a re-match today! I will say that Doc beat Ellen (our friend that is visiting) though if anyone is interested! As you can tell, even though some minutes in our days are very hard, most of them are full of hope and we try to add a smile here and there! We added a ton of smiles yesterday when we received a vcr tape that the community had put together with different persons all sending us messages of hope and cheer. That was fun to watch and we enjoyed the ball-games and smiling faces! We have looked it over and over and it is like bringing part of Missouri into our room! We also continue to receive cards by the bundles and they are appreciated! We still are amazed at how many persons that we know and how many that really care!

Please make sure that this is posted so the persons that work in the plant at Orscheln Products all know that I am thinking of them too!

Thanks to all of you for everything and remember to pray hard that these drugs kick in and do the trick!

You are all in our prayers too,
Cindy and Doc

October 4-2004

Well, it has been awhile since we updated everyone on Grand Junction so I thought I would take a minute and say hi! Doc and I are still hanging in there but progress is really slow. Right now we are just trying to hang on and get healthy so we can start working on the injury. It is a constant battle just trying to keep all those things with your body working correctly. It seems like you fix one thing and another thing breaks (we used to have cars like that and after a little bit you trade them in…I'm not planning on trading Doc in though so I guess I will just keep fixing him up!)

We still aren't breathing on our own BUT his system is making oxygen at a better level than he was. I think the respirator is only supplying him 50% which is an improvement. If we can keep him at that and start moving down from that, it would be a first step! They are still thinking that it is the swelling that is cutting off his breathing muscles but they won't guarantee it so it is still a waiting game (and he reminded me again that this waiting game is at least a year long). Dr Griffith, the neuro doctor, said that your spinal cord nerves can do 3 things..work, be alive but not work, or die. He said that Docs are alive but not working. That means they can heal (which is what he said they are currently trying to do) or not heal and that is what the next year will tell us. They are also starting some physical therapy on his swallow muscles and they are hopeful that they can start working on a program to start working toward eating and drinking some regular food/drinks. I think that would be very exciting for him. He told us earlier in the week that he wants to breath, eat and then talk. It looks like eating might come first but they will have to run some tests. I have been cheating though and bringing him up some ice cream from the cafeteria and then letting him taste it and move it around on his tongue before I suction it out and shove some more in. I am glad that I don't have to be a full time nurse but Doc is tolerating me. (I know nurses probably don't use words like shove).

Friday morning, he moved his left and right feet slighty and wiggled his toes on his right foot. He did it for the neuro surgeon and he said that was a small but good sign. Unfortunately, he can only do it off and on. The doctor said that the swelling is throbbing though so it will go on and off and it isn't anything to be concerned about but that is still a waiting game. They remain optimistic that some of his earlier progress will come back with time. In the meantime, they are just trying to keep him healthy.

He ran a 104 degree temperature this weekend and I was frightened that it might be the pneumonia they warned me about but it wasn't. They think it is associated with his lungs but it isn't pneumonia. They asked the neuro surgeon if they can start sitting him and up and moving him around more because they are thinking that will really help and he said yes.

Dr. Kelley, his main doctor, told me yesterday that all this stuff is normal and that I could probably expect another couple of weeks before some of this illness stuff takes care of itself. After we get all the stuff taken care of that is making him not feel good like infections and fevers, we can start concentrating on the re-hab. That means that we can't come home for at least 2 weeks and then they said we would just have to look at his condition at that time. I can tell that he is not ready to move to re-hab yet and we will just have to be patient for that day. For a couple that really loves Colorado, we sure are anxious to get back to Missouri.

I continue to run Doc through his exercises every morning and afternoon and I can't say he is any Cindy Crawford or anything but he does all right. I like the way his legs look anyway!

Adam and Jaymi (our 2 oldest kids) came out this weekend and it was so much fun to have them here. They got here Friday morning and they have to leave at 5 tonight. Saturday, Adam and Doc watched the Missouri game while Jaymi and I went to the mall for a little bit and that was enjoyable to spend a couple of hours there with her. Then yesterday, Jaymi chilled with Doc and Adam & I took a road trip up to the Colorado Monument Ridge Drive and did a little hiking. It felt good to be out in the mountains and sunshine! I kept thinking how much Doc would like to do that so I have plans on doing this again with him some day!

Janice and Robert Austin (fellow Cairolites!) stopped by on their way to California last night and it was so nice to get some Cairo hugs again! She even wore her Cardinal shirt for Doc and he really enjoyed that! He is ready for this play off stuff (and by the way.... Tom and Brad...so sorry the Cubs didn't win the wildcard-NOT). I probably need to get him a Cardinal shirt and cut it up to fit around his traction stuff so he can be a pure supporter. I have figured out how to fix shirts to fit over the traction outfit and they are telling me in another week or two, we can start dressing him up in regular clothes.

The kids are trying to make me fat because it seems like they are always ready to eat. Last night they even treated me to a meal at the Texas Roadhouse and that was fun. (I think you know that your kids are finally adults when they pick up a tab. It felt different having them pay but not a bad different.)

I had to leave the Rose Hill House but we just got a motel room for the past 3 nights because of the kids being here. I am supposed to check back with them today to see if they have something opening up but if not, I think I am going to take Teresa (the nurse that offered a bed) on her offer and stay with her family. She has 4 little kids and I am really looking forward to meeting them. Kids are so fun!

For the Cairo School that sent Doc his Cardinal blanket....he has really enjoyed it and on the nights when he gets chilly, that is what the nurses are using to cover him up!

He continues to read his cards and ask me to check e-mails and read all them to him. Some of you are quite entertaining!

Oh yeah, an update on the crap or fact tournament. Doc and I are currently tied on victories and we are embarrassed to say that since Jaymi and Adam have been here, Doc has won once and Jaymi (our dingy blond) has won all the rest of the games! I guess it is true that you can have more luck than sense! (P.S. Jaymi wanted me to point out that Adam didn't win a single game.)

Thanks so much for all the thoughts, hugs, love, prayers, and messages that all of you continue to send our way. I will continue to say thank you for these things on all our e-mails because they are so important to us. Even though this seems like it is the same thank you over and over, it is a new thank you each time! It is still an awesome feeling to feel inside that God is right beside us and a year from now, we are going to look back on this and be amazed at what is going to happen in the next 11-12 months!

I will keep you posted because even though we aren't feeling/ moving a lot more yet again, we are starting to work on other things that might start us in the right direction again.

Cindy and Doc (ps.. it is warmer here than at home and it is also beautiful and sunny!)

p.s. I wanted also to say thanks for those of you that make sure I don't leave anyone off the distribution list. I know that several of you forward this on to others that want an update and I wanted to thank you for doing this. I get a lot of messages that say that they read these because someone else has forwarded it to them.

October 11-2004

Oct 11th and it is hard to believe that as of tonight, we will have been here for an entire month already. It seems like the days are long but then you turn around and a whole month is gone!

What a beautiful week we had last week in Grand Junction. Every day was beautiful, sunny and in the mid-70's. The sun rises so pretty over the mesas that surround the city and then when it sets, the mesa glows in the colors. The best news about all of this is that Doc got to finally witness it. They started with getting him into a chair on Wednesday and Thursday. On Friday (and Saturday), they loaded him using sling type equipment into a wheelchair and outside into the sunshine we went. They told him they would try do this everyday!

There is a really nice waterfall in front of the hospital and he asked if we could take our picture in front of it so we did. I don't think the camera broke or anything but the film isn't developed yet so we aren't sure! Thanks to the Orscheln crew for the cameras!

Jennie, Doc's sister, came to visit on Friday and she is staying until tomorrow. We have enjoyed her visit and with her being here, I have gotten to get out and get a few things done that I needed to do too.

The most exciting news that I have is that on Wednesday he had some feeling in his right shoulder and chest. That was exciting but then it disappeared on Wednesday night and hasn't returned yet. Again, the usual response is that they don't really know why and that we just have to bide our time to see what he regains and keeps. The doctor gave us some hope because on Thursday he told us that he expects that the day Doc starts going forward again is going to be the day that things start happening quickly! I think he is excited to think of what the future could hold for us and so I am clinging to his excitement! He said he has had a lot of patients in Doc's condition and the ones that get better are the ones with the positive attitude. He said that Doc has the most positive attitude of anyone that he has ever had and he is laying odds that he can lick this!

Doc took a swallowing test last week to see if he could swallow food and get it to go down the correct pipe but he failed with flying colors so we are working on some re-hab therapy for the throat. I think he likes doing the exercises because it is something that he can do for himself. He has been doing them all day long, every day. They really think he is going to have to get some diaphragm muscles back though, in order to put in a different trach before he will be able to swallow correctly. When they do that, we will probably be able to start talking, eating, drinking, and will be assisting the respirator. That will be the biggest step we will take and so that is the first thing we are praying for to come back. I know Doc is really, really wanting some food and drink.

To all our AECI buddies....I wanted to tell you that we got the golf hats this week and Doc has been showing them off. They sit up on a shelf that he can see and every once in awhile, he asks me to get them down for him. He also got his book in the mail with pictures of all of you and he really, really was excited about that-we look at it several times every day....GREAT IDEA! I also want to say thank you for the money that you raised from the golf club raffle and to thank everyone that participated.

To our Cairo crowd, I have heard about the cake/ice cream social and the hot air balloon raffle and we wanted to say thank you to all that helped and participated in that! We have also looked at your video several times. It was good to see your smiling faces and feel like we had a little bit of home in our room! Your pictures of the things from home were great too and we look at those often.

This next little bit is for all the young people that have taken the time to send Doc and I a note or card. I know that when you are in your teens and/or early twenties, life can be really busy and I don't think I knew at that age how much kind words meant to someone that was in our position but you guys are awesome! Thanks to all those out there that are friends to our kids that have taken the time to tell us how much you love us too!

We can only play Fact or Crap when we have a visitor or two so we didn't play it much last week. Doc and Jennie have played a couple of times and are tied! Someone (and I don't know who but thank you!) sent us a really cool Missouri Trivia book. Doc and I have made a game out of that also and I almost hate to report that he has won every game that we have played with that! I might have to cheat to beat him at that by reading ahead! hehe

All of your support has been great and when we are ready for re-hab it is sounding like we will need it. I have explored all our choices but it appears that if we want quality spinal cord re-hab, we need to hope to get into Rusk (Columbia) or Craig (Denver). We really want to come back to Missouri but our case worker is telling us that Rusk currently does not have a room available for at least a month. Craig does, but we really don't want to be so far from home with months and months of re-hab ahead of us. We could start at Craig and then transfer to Rusk but the expense is going to be much greater than if we just head to Rusk right off and the doctors really do not want us making 2 moves. I talked to one of the doctors and he wants us to hold out here until something opens up at Rusk. He feels that it is important to get close to home and not to make the 2 moves. He also said that as long as we keep getting him up and working him out that putting off rehab an extra week or two is not going to hurt anything. He even said that who knows, he might even be breathing again by that time! I know the nurses are thinking that re-hab is coming quickly and we are going to have to make some decisions. I will probably try to get more answers this week. It has seemed like God has taken all the rest of the past 3 weeks into his hands so I am just going to let him take this problem too. Everything has a way of working its way out and so I am not stressing on this.

We continue to receive signs that our angels are working right beside us and we continue to have faith that in time, all this will work out. It is amazing how easy it is to handle this. If you had asked what we would have done in a situation like this before we actually experienced it, I wouldn't have guessed like we are. I would have thought we would have been all messed up and confused and scared but we are not. We both feel like it is just going to take time and faith to be able to look back on this and actually call it one of our great experiences. That is mostly due to the outpouring of prayers, thoughts, cards, gifts, support, and messages that we receive daily. I hear of stories that warm the heart as many of you gather together to make our days easier. I hear you telling how neat it is to be part of something bigger than yourselves and I understand because that is how I feel. Every one of you that take the time to read these e-mails, pass them on because someone else wants to read them, or answers them are so special to us. The neatest thing is when someone tells me they want to help or they are praying daily, I know they mean it from the bottom of their heart and it is more than words. It is called caring!

I heard on the news just now that Christopher Reeves died last night and my heart goes out to his family because I know how hard it was to battle through this injury and then to lose him to heart failure. I know that all spinal cord injuries are different but it still hit home!

I am not sure what the future holds but I know that Doc & I are not alone. I know I have a plethora (big word for me but I think it means a bunch!) of help just waiting for the word. I am not sure how many more weeks we are looking at in Grand Junction and then where we are going from here but you can be sure that I will let each of you know as soon as I know. In the meantime, keep praying, stay safe and I will be in touch! I will try to send out a weekly update because I hate to do such a mass e-mail more than once a week...I know you all have work to do....BUT if something great or not so great happens, I will pass it on!

In our thoughts,
Cindy and Doc chilling in Grand Junction.

PS...**Go Cardinals**! We have been cheering them on and we spread our rally Cardinal blanket out with each game! Doc has several wagers going on with the nurses and until Saturday night, he was cleaning up...things like ice chips, suckers, and special treats! Saturday night, he ended up owing some of them some things but they all involve us coming back here in a year or two when Doc is much better and taking them out! I think we can do that! He also has converted several of them into cheering for the Cardinals!

October 17-2004

Good morning everyone! Another week gone by and winter is getting closer. I heard that Missouri had some cool, damp weather last week. We had picture perfect fall weather in Grand Junction with the sun shining and the temps in the mid-70's all week except Sunday was little cloudy/windy/cool. Doc was able to go out and sit in it several days. They take him out every day unless they get too busy. Everyone enjoys the outings (including the nurses)!

We had another slow week but we did have a moment or two of good things this week. I think it is just going to be really, really slow going! Wednesday, his room was freezing (like always) because all week long he kept running this ridiculous high fever and they keep the air on low, low, low and the fan running so it is cold! (For those of you who know how I hate to be cold, this is ironic!) Anyway, back to the story…I wanted to warm up my frozen hands and I figured that laying them on Doc's warm legs and arms would be ok because he was hot and I thought they might act like ice packs! I put one on his forearm and one on his thigh and he looked at me and said, "did you put your hand on my arm because it is really cold?" That was exciting because it was his first sensation since he lost what he had-OR else my hand was REALLY cold. The doctors are telling me that hot/cold sensation is different from feeling sensation because Doc could not feel me touching him, just the coldness. That being said, he couldn't feel it the next day so once again, it was a come and go thing but at least it was a sensation! The 2nd exciting thing to happen was that on Thursday, he told me that it felt like his diaphragm was trying to work on and off. Then on Friday, he was able to exhale some air from his mouth! He is a long way from breathing on his own but this might be the first step towards it! Time will tell! The doctor said that he is not inhaling yet. Our final bit of good news is that even though he continues to run his high fever on and off, they still can't find any infection or reason for it. I am just grateful that we haven't run into the dreaded pneumonia bit that they warned me about. The neuro doctor came in and said that it is still probably the sodium and swelling holding up progress and it is not unusual after this amount of time to still be in limbo. He still says he wouldn't make any predictions about the future but not to give it up!

I will be really glad when he can talk again because my lip reading skills leave something to be desired. Poor Doc usually starts to try to tell me something and before I can figure it out, he is telling me "never mind-it isn't important"—which just makes me more determined to find out what he is saying and then after I work through it all, he was right, it wasn't important!

Dr Kelly said that he thinks Doc is ready to move back to Missouri as soon as Rusk gets an opening so we are waiting to hear from them. The case worker up here is contacting them on a regular basis trying to get a date but so far, we don't have a date. I am getting the impression that we are looking at 3 to 4 weeks out yet. In the meantime, we are working his muscles out and keeping them ready for rehab. Dr. Griffith, the neuro surgeon, said that he is actually glad Doc is still here for a few weeks because he thinks it will do him good to have a little more healing time before rehab.

His swallowing exercises are going good and even though he isn't ready to eat yet, the speech therapist says that he is getting closer to that day! He can spit a little bit (he says like a llama) and now that he can exhale air at a pretty good rate, he can blow in my ear now! He told me today that if he could eat right now, he would want some raisin bran. It changes from day to day but today he wants cereal!

We still are able to move our toes and feet just a little bit and it has been the one constant in all of this even if it is a little inconsistent on which toe or how much or when!

Kevin Dale, an old Cairo schoolmate, came by with his parents to visit us Friday and that was a nice surprise! It is always good to see someone from home! They were getting ready to go hunting for a week. Also, I have a cousin that doesn't live too far from here and her family comes out at least once a week to visit with us! This week, Monty, her husband, brought Doc a Bronco's hat...I think this is a sign we have been in Colorado for too long! Anyway, Doc laughed and said that as soon as we get back to Missouri, we are sending him a Cardinal hat!

Carrissa (our youngest daughter) is coming out this weekend and we are ready for that visit! I think she is ready to say hi to dad too!

We continue to get cards, e-mails, calls, and offers of prayers and help! Many of you already know that we are taking you up on your offers of help and we wanted to thank all of you for doing whatever it is that we ask! It is making it much easier to just concentrate on getting Doc back to Missouri. There is going to be the need for many more things once we get back to Missouri and we are planning on taking some of you up on your offers of help so be prepared!

We have been playing Missouri Trivia and I am sad to report that Doc is still victorious and I have only won one game. I told him I was going to cheat and read ahead one night after he falls asleep...I don't think he is too frightened though!

Our highlight during the past couple of weeks has been cheering the Cardinals on! We have enjoyed watching them as they work their way to the World Series! Hopefully, they can hold Houston off for a couple more games.

This waiting game continues to drag out for us but on the flip side of it, we know we are part of a bigger plan and Doc told me this week that he feels certain that God wants him to tell his story someday. We aren't sure of how it all goes yet, but one day we will be able to share it all from start to finish! Being part of a story is harder than reading a story. When I read a story, I sometimes flip to the end just to see what happens and in this case, we have to actually live it day by day. The funny thing is that most of you are part of this story and you have to wait with us to see how it all ends too even though many of you are characters in it! I have been keeping a journal so I don't forget many of the things that happen to enforce our faith. Some of these things people might say are coincidental but if you saw as much as we have, you know that these are more than coincidental happenings. They are messages to hang in there and be patient! There will be a day that we will share many of these stories with all of you! Some of you will be surprised to find out that you are actually God's angels working on earth and you didn't even know what an important role you played in all of this!

Doc and I both are getting the feeling that we are in this waiting game and God is telling us to be patient. It was funny but last night, I had a dream that Doc rolled over in his hospital bed and the nurses were all amazed at that he just started moving. I was telling the nurses about my dream and after they left the room, Doc looked up at me and said that he had the same dream last night! Another coincidence? These are the things that just make me wonder! How does 2 people have the same dream on the same night?

As always, we will stay in touch if anything changes during the coming week. We ask that you continue to pray for us and look forward to the message that I send out that says that we are coming home!

Days in Grand Junction,
Cindy and Doc

October 19-2004

This has been a little bit of a bumpy day because we found out that going home isn't going to happen very quickly. We found out this morning that Rusk does not have room for Doc and will not give an estimate of when they would have room and as the insurance does not want to keep him in the hospital any longer, we have no choice except to find another place to rehab. Craig is the closest, located in Denver, and that is where they would like Doc to go for rehab. So it looks like our stay in Colorado is going to be extended by a few months.

Our next step is to apply for a spot at Craig and then wait for them to review it. After they review it, they have to tentatively accept Doc as a patient and then they send a team of doctors here to meet with Doc and review his case before they officially accept him. Then they will move us to Denver. I asked the case worker what would happen if they deny us too but she didn't think Craig would do that so hopefully, all that will work out. We are concentrating on the fact that Craig is known to be the best spinal cord injury rehab in the nation and we probably should be rejoicing that we have the chance of using their facilities! They also have family housing so I will be able to stay with him through the rehab and actually help participate in most of it.

I have to admit that when they first unloaded it on us this morning, it was pretty disappointing! I was so looking forward to being back home, in our own house, close to family and friends so I had to take a moment or two to overcome that disappointment. After we (actually I, because Doc was already prepared for wherever we ended up) regrouped though and remembered that our prayer was for God to lead us where he needed too, we are focused on just the next phase of this journey!

So now we pray that Craig does have a room for him and that we continue to move in the direction of getting better! I know that right now, months can seem like a long time but in the scope of a lifetime, a few months aren't too much. Dr. Griffith said that if Doc does really well, it can be as short of a stay as 3 months. After Craig is completed, they will let him come home and give him a new team of Doctors in Columbia that will continue his outpatient rehab. We continue to pray for improvements as his injury heals but in the meantime, we have to learn to deal with things as they are.

Doc does have a small bronchitis infection but they are giving him antibiotics for that and it shouldn't be anything too major. They are thinking that might be part of his fever problem although he has had the fever for over a week and this infection just showed up yesterday. I know that there are things that baffle doctors as much as us sometimes!

Doc continues to have the most amazing "it will be ok" outlook and he even told me that he is strong enough for both of us so I can lean on him if things get heavy. I can only say that I am glad that if we had to go through this, I am thankful he is the patient because I would never be able to be as strong as he is. He maintains his smile on his face for everyone that enters the room and he is truly going through each day waiting for the day when things start to change for the good.

The good news in this week is that our daughter Carrissa and my brother Lloyd will be here the day after tomorrow for a visit (and I need someone at AECI to please convey our thanks to Kenneth Clarkson for donating his frequent flyer miles to get them out here! Doc has said 3 times this morning how nice that was and I agree!). We are looking forward to their visit.

I will keep you posted on our location as soon as I know what is going on but I got the feeling that things could start moving pretty quickly now,

Still in Grand Junction for now,
Cindy and Doc

October 21-2004

Just wanted to say good morning to everyone! Yesterday we found out that we have been accepted for the first step at Craig. We have passed the paperwork part and they are sending out a representative to interview Doc & I on Friday morning. If we pass the interview (and the nurses tell us that they don't think we will have a problem with that), then they send out a team of doctors next week to review his case and talk to his doctors. If that goes well, they will try to find us a place at Craig! The closer we get to moving to Craig, the more we feel like this is what we are supposed to be doing! It is always amazing how things work out.

Last night while we were watching the Cardinal game, I was taking Doc through his range of motion exercises that we do 2 or 3 times a day and for the first time, I noticed a very little movement in his right hand when I asked him to try and move it. It was so little that I had him stop and the movement stopped and then I had him move it and it came back and I did that several times to make sure I wasn't imagining it but every time it was in the same spot and every time when I told him to stop, it stopped so I think we have a little movement in the right hand. We didn't even have that after surgery so this is the first time we have had any movement in that part. That was a bright spot! Then the Cardinals won and that was GREAT! Now they just have to do it again tonight!

Lloyd and Carrissa will be here in less than 4 hours and I cannot wait! I think Carrissa and I are going to run some errands this afternoon while Lloyd entertains Doc.

Other than that, they have a church service in the chapel every morning at 6:30 and I like to attend that so I had better get off here and get myself cleaned up! I just wanted to let everyone know what was going on!

Hoping that we are staying in your prayers and
knowing that you are in ours,
Cindy and Doc

October 24-2004

As the World Turns in Grand Junction… This one is a little long but I had a lot to report plus I am known for being a little windy!

Since the last time that I checked in with everyone, we have had some snow in the mountains but it didn't reach the valley. It was wonderful to watch though! I think I like snow that doesn't actually reach me! The weather in the valley stayed a little overcast because of the snow clouds but the sun broke through occasionally and the temperature stayed mild. We have never snow skied but one of the nurses here teaches at a ski resort and she asked us if we would like to ski because there is a quad ski chair that allows persons in Doc's situation to ski if he would like to try it. He wasn't too sure about it but I think he is tossing it around! Hopefully, we will get past needing that chair before we want to try it!

Doc was still able to get outside most days! He is getting better because even if he can't get outside, he asks if he can just sit by a window or something. When they get him up, he is sitting up longer without getting so tired looking.

We have enjoyed my brother and our youngest daughter being out here! Carrissa & I have gotten away to run some errands while Lloyd has sat with Doc. As our move away from the hospital gets close, there is a bunch of stuff that I have to figure out how to move from here to wherever.

Doc hasn't moved anything new but it appears that his gag muscles **might** be coming back (he gagged 3 times yesterday) and he is occasionally exhaling more air (consistently for about 7 hours yesterday) than the respirator gives him which the therapist told me **might** be the first sign of his diaphragm starting to kick in…that would be my greatest wish! We are not giving up hope that more is coming! Doc is constantly smiling and saying "give it time"! We still mess with a temperature every now and then but Doc is getting stronger and healthier every day!

Our interview with the Craig representative went really well. Her name was Sue and I have to admit that she was very straight forward and honest with us. She asked us to tell her about our situation from the day of the accident to now and we updated her through all of that and then she said that based on her 29 years of experience, she was going to be honest with us and tell us that if Doc hadn't gotten his diaphragm back by now, she would be very doubtful that he will. She said that not to give up because she has seen faith and prayers do miraculous things but that usually swelling goes down in 3 or 4 days and he has had no diaphragm for close to 4 weeks now. So, just going off her experience, she would say we would be treated as a patient expecting a lifetime on the ventilator. The rest of what Doc is experiencing though that is coming and going, she was excited about. She said that those were good signs that he could make some type of recovery in the physical sense. After the interview, she told us that she was going to recommend us for Craig and she would review his medical records and then come back and talk to us. After she came back, she back-tracked a little bit because she said that in her 29 years, she has never seen a case like Doc's. After looking at how much he had for 10 days and then the reasons why he lost it (sodium levels) and looking at the huge amount of swelling on the MRI (which she said extended high into the brain stem even), she was going to change her mind. She said that there is still swelling and that based on Doc still having sodium issues with his body, she would say that his diaphragm might have a good chance at kicking in again! Sue was more optimistic after reviewing the medical records and that made us feel better. She also said that she was very confident that his throat muscles were already kicking in and she would guess that he would be able to eat/drink/talk/and gag and hopefully that isn't too far out! Just to answer a few of your questions that you might have, I am going to outline our interview with you:

- IF Craig accepts us, Doc will be up and out of bed every morning and will be on a busy schedule. They will be taking him places (even Bronco football games—too bad it won't be baseball season!) and keeping him busy. They will teach him how to use a mouth activated wheelchair so he can do as much for himself as possible. They will take him to the gym each day and teach him how to play sports with special equipment (there is even a fishing pole that he can cast out and reel his own fish in that is totally mouth activated). A guy in Nebraska used it and was even the state fishing tournament champion!

- They will be taking us both through extensive ventilator training so we will know what to do in any type of emergency with the ventilator.

- They will cover any type of special equipment requirements with us and teach us how to use them, including vans with special wheelchair ramps installed. (which wasn't as bad as I thought because she told us that we would have to buy a van- which one is based on head room for his size wheelchair- and then it is customized with the ramp and special seat belts and electric plug ins for the wheelchair/ventilator batteries and the customization usually would run about $5,000. I thought it might even be higher than that!)

- IF he has to be on a ventilator, he is going to require someone with him ALL the time! This is where all of you family and friends would come in when we get home! Even if I have to mow the grass or run to the store, I will need someone to sit with Doc. They said it doesn't have to be anyone technical or anything because they just have to be able to hear the ventilator alarm and then do the proper thing if it goes off and Doc & I will be very prepared to show them what that is and that is very easy to do. It will take 2-3 people to get him up every morning and 2-3 people to put him to bed every night so I am going to need help! I know that many of you would be willing to do this and to be honest, I am hoping that some of the neighbors can do the morning/night stuff so that we are not having anyone too far from home to dash over for a few minutes. I will have to hire someone to stay with him during the day while I am at work and even though insurance might cover this for the very beginning, Sue did not think they would cover it for very long.

- We will not be confined to the house and they will teach me how easy it is to get Doc out of the house and to find things to do. I will make sure that we have the same active life that we have always had because that is going to be our quality of life until if/when we get back to what we think is normal! So when we get home and you get our answering machine, do not be surprised! Hehe!

- IF Doc gets any diaphragm muscles back, they guarantee me that they can rehab those muscles to help him breathe (at least part of every day on his own!). If he gets as much back as he had in the beginning, Sue was almost positive that he would be off the ventilator completely. BUT this being said, we need to pray really hard for the diaphragm to start working soon! Sue said that every day that goes by without him using it creates more of a chance that it won't come back.

- She told us that she would recommend that we go ahead and start building the ramps as soon as possible and that we have to have ramps into 2 of our doors because of fire hazards. She gave me the specs of how much slope based on how high we have to build the ramps. Several of the guys that Doc works with have volunteered to do this.

- She said that we might have to make other changes but that if she were us, she would not make any more changes to our house or even think about the van or any special equipment for at least 2 months because Doc could really make some recovery that would make all of this unnecessary. There is still the chance in the coming year or two that he can recover up to all of his functions. We just need to be prepared for that not to happen and how to deal with the current situation until it does happen.

- IF we are in a wheelchair when we come home, it can have special tires on it that allows us to take walks (even on the gravel roads) with no problems.

- Sue said that many of the things that we were going to need would not be covered by insurance. She recommended that all the fund raisers that you guys have done and are doing for us be deposited into a trust fund just for Doc's equipment/ medical needs and that we do not have our names on it but rather turn it over to a bank to pay the appropriate bills. I am getting ready to talk to someone about that.

- I can stay in an apartment complex right across the road from Craig for free for the first month and then after that, it will cost $700/month but at least I will be close to Craig.

- I can be at as much of Doc's rehab that I want to participate in and can come and go as I please.
- Doc can have other guests but Sue told us to remember that he is sharing a room with another person so we have to be considerate of them. Visiting hours are in the evenings during the week, after 11 a.m. on Saturday, and then all day on Sundays.
- After Doc passes his wheelchair tests and we both pass the ventilator training, he will be allowed to leave Craig and come across the road to visit me in my apartment.
- Doc will be at Craig approx. 3 months if he doesn't get any diaphragm back and 4 months if they are able to rehab his diaphragm. So even though I am REALLY, REALLY ready to come home, I hope it is 4 months! I am planning on making some trips back and forth though once things get settled a little bit.
- We have to have a discharge plan established by the time we leave that proves to Craig that we have family/friend support at home that is going to help us. We have to prove that our house is capable of supporting Doc's needs. We have to have a Missouri plan to support further medical/rehab requirements. Craig will help us put this plan together but without some of you guys, I will never be able to complete this and so I am going to say thank you far in advanced to all of those that I call and ask for help that say yes! Without this plan, we had to agree that Doc would go to a nursing home when he is dis-

missed from Craig instead of going home. Sue felt confident that we wouldn't have to do this but we still had to promise.

- I had to promise that I would not do anything for Doc that they thought he should be doing for himself. (Sue said that in our short meeting, she didn't think I had that kind of personality anyway. I guess that is good but she is right, I will be pushing Doc to be as self sufficient as anyone!)

- When we are discharged, Craig will send 2 representatives home with us and they will spend a night or two in our house with us before they leave us alone so they know that we are ok.

As you can read, all of this is sorta like a dose of reality and there are a lot of IF's but it is comforting to know what you have to do to cope with a situation. This doesn't mean that this is permanent (and she even said there is a good chance that much of it won't be because Doc's damage was so incomplete and you never know!). It is hard to look at reality when you feel deep down that you have this promise from someone higher up that it is going to be ok and you know you need to hold on to that faith! Doc and I both feel like somehow this is all going to come together in the next few months and it is both exciting and scary to think how it is going to end or when it is going to end. We have to remember that this could be a long, slow healing process and we are looking at possibly a year or two before we know where we are going to end up. I think Doc and

I both feel like something great is going to happen well before that but we aren't in on the whole plan so we don't know for sure when or what.

Craig called Friday afternoon to tell our case worker that they were reviewing the recommendation but they would not be able to give us an answer until Monday morning. They also told her that IF they accepted us, to be ready to transport Doc either Monday afternoon or Tuesday. So based on that, our case worker told us that she felt pretty confident that the answer was going to be yes but to still remember that no promises have been made. I will let all of you know as soon as we know! I will let you know the new addresses and numbers so you can continue to contact with us and as always, I will continue to e-mail. I am going to have to fly to Denver separate from Doc but United Airlines is working with my return flight ticket from coming out here and they are letting me split the trip home without any additional charge.

I will also point out that Sue said that the medical and physical therapy that Craig provides will take us to a certain point but the faith and prayers of all of you can and does miraculous things because she has seen it happen! So we continue to ask you to pray and we thank you for every one of them!

I continue to get cards and e-mails asking me what many of you can do to help and as you can tell, I am going to need it and I will be asking! There is a song out there that says that it is hard to be humble and it is right. We have always had a sense of pride at being self sufficient and all of a sudden, we are no longer self sufficient. We are even being told that we probably will not go home until we can prove we are not self sufficient! So I humbly thank each of you for the fund raising efforts and the physical time and labor that many of you have provided and will provide to us in the future that allows us to continue to live in our community and in our house! I hope and pray that this is only a temporary situation but if that is not the plan for us, we will learn how to cope with it along with all of you helping us! I know we will never be able to repay many of you for that help but I can promise you that if there is anyway in the future for us to pay it forward to someone else in need, we will! So what you guys share with us, we can promise that it will go forward if at all possible and hopefully, it will continue to go forward from there and years from now, it will be continually growing into someone helping someone!

And last but not least, keep cheering for those Cardinals! Doc wears his rally hat on top his halo for every game and keeps his Cardinal blanket on the bed (funny isn't it? That Doc has a halo? BUT that is what they call the traction suit he is in!).

Keeping you posted from Grand Junction and
hopefully soon from Denver,
Cindy and Doc

October 25-2004

We just found out about 5 minutes ago that we are for sure accepted and approved to go to Craig. We will be flying out of Grand Junction at 8:30 in the morning. They came and asked me how much I weighed and then they came back and said that I could fly with Doc. So that makes me feel good—good thing I went on the diet last year (hehe). I took my luggage to UPS and they are going to ship it out today and it should be there tomorrow for me and then all I have is this lap top and a little carry on. I hope that is ok because I didn't ask!

I am taking Lloyd and Carrissa to the airport to catch their flight in about 45 minutes. I will hate to see them go but I have some friends that are coming out this weekend so that will be good to look forward to.

Our prayer was answered that Craig would take us and now we concentrate on praying for some action from the diaphragm. That would be the next exciting thing to happen!

Will keep you updated,
Cindy and Doc

Oh yeah, the address is:

Craig Hospital
3425 South Clarkson
Englewood, CO 80113

I don't have a room # or phone # yet but I will try to include that in my next e-mail!

October 26-2004

Just to let you guys know, we are in Craig and we are getting settled in. They changed our flight time to 6:30 so we were up early and on the plane! They aren't doing too much today except admitting us and getting us settled. I haven't been to my apartment yet but I will check that out in a little bit. Doc is in a room with 2 other people but each area has its own curtained walls. They sound like this is going to be a good facility to rehab in. The nurses have been really nice so far and the Dr. seems pretty nice too. Doc will have his own team of doctors and they will meet as a team each week to make decisions as a team. I think he has 6 different doctors along with rehab personal.

They are not going to get him up today but they will start tomorrow. Today, they are just filling out paperwork and maybe taking some x-rays. Tomorrow they are taking mri's and cat scans and doing lots of other types of bloodwork. They said they want to do all their own testing so there will be a lot of that. It will probably be closer to next week before we start actual rehab.

The dr. gave him a really good going over and told us that they usually try to determine whether a break is complete or incomplete (and by complete, they just don't mean severed but it could mean bruised-like Doc's-with little chance for recovery). After he looked Doc over, he said that he wasn't going to make a determination yet. He said he was going to ride the fence and let time make the call. In the meantime, they have to rehab him as a complete because he can't do anything else at this time. He said that we are going to rehab for the worse and hope for the best! He said that they will do a MRI to know for sure but he is in agreement with St. Mary's doctors that the swelling is still there. He said that we have to be aware of the chance of nothing coming back but that we can remain hopeful that things will too!

In the meantime, we are going to start rehab next week and then in a couple of weeks or so, we will be able to go on group field trips to the zoo, bronco games, museums, ect.... Whatever Doc wants to sign up for. Then as soon as I finish a class on ventilators and Doc is getting around good with his wheelchair, they will give Doc & I passes to leave the premises by ourselves and we can do anything or go anywhere we want! That will be exciting! We might take a walk around the block in the snow!

They are going to start working on this throat first thing because they want to get him to talking and eating as our first goal. That will be a good thing. They are also going to start testing his diaphragm today to see if there is anything for them to work with. If not, they will test it regularly and jump into it as soon as they see something but if they see anything today, they will start that rehab this week! If nothing comes back, then we will be prepared with the knowledge of ventilators and what we need to do to cope.

I have an address and a phone #. The phone will ring at the nurses station and then they will call our room…if I am in here, they will transfer the call but if I am not in here, they will either take a message or they will send someone down to help Doc when he can talk.

The phone # is 303-789-8271

Address is

Craig Hospital

3425 South Clarkson

Englewood, CO 80113

Doc is in Room 301C

I think that is all for now,

Cindy and Doc

October 31-2004

Good morning to all from Denver (winter is here! We had the biggest snow last night!). We are getting settled into Craig but we haven't gotten to start much rehab yet. Since we got here, they have been running tests and finding stuff that has to be fixed before we can rehab.

They found several infections, which could have been the cause of the fevers for the past few weeks. They are treating those with antibiotics. They found a blood clot in his upper right arm so they had him on blood thinner and bed rest for 72 hours, which expired Saturday evening. They also found out he was dehydrated and his sodium level is still really low. Then they found a problem on the cat scan because one of the screws that was inserted into his spinal column to hold it in place is backing out. They had to contact their neuro surgeon to see if he thinks it is ok to continue to move Doc or if it is too unstable. If it is too risky, they will have to do another surgery to fix that spot. The good news is that they are finding these things and fixing them. It is also good news that none of this has made his injury worse. The spinal column is still all lined up correctly and looks good. Dr Falci (the neuro surgeon) came in on Saturday and we didn't see him but he looked at Doc's cat scan and told the nurse that he would consult with Dr. Ripley (Doc's dr.) on Monday but he thinks the screw is not a big deal and will not require a 2nd surgery. In the meantime, Doc stays on bedrest with the hope that he can be up and rehabbing on Monday!

They also are going to start on Monday putting Doc through some swallowing tests and seeing if they can trade the trach out for a different one that would allow him to talk and eat. If he passes the test, that milestone could be in the next day or two! Maybe by the next e-mail that you get from me, I will tell you Doc is preaching to me!

They have moved Doc from 301C to room 301B. It is a much better room because he has windows all around him and he can see out. We can even see the mountains!

I also wanted to say thank you to all the staff at St. Mary's. They are a group of caring persons and they took good care of us. They continue to think of us and pray for us! They have called and e-mailed us this week to keep up and we appreciate their thoughtfulness! We will never forget them and we look forward to the day when we can walk back in and say hi!!

Doc is getting pretty bored with all the bed stuff because he was really enjoying getting up and getting outside and now he has been in bed for a week! He is still in good spirits though and continues to remind me that no matter what they find or what they say, we cannot give up faith that this is all going to work out in the end. It is easy to feed off of him when he is so certain that we are going to be ok.

We have already found several new friends in the Denver area and we continue to meet persons that are helping us…here and in Missouri!

Howard and Ellen Smothers visited us this weekend and it was good medicine for both Doc & I to have them with us for a couple of days! I have to admit that while we were listening to a wonderful Christian CD that Linda Taylor sent us, we were playing poker with Doc. And for those that are keeping track, Doc won! We get pretty inventive when it comes to games. Howard built Doc a card rack and he just indicates which cards he wants to discard and we plug away!

I had to wait to get into my apartment because they had to do some repair work before it was ready for me. I had to stay in a motel until they fixed it up and even though they had a shuttle, it was usually an hour trip to get from place to place. I am glad that I am finally settled in across the street. (I got to move in on Saturday!). Howard and Ellen helped me drag all my junk over there. It is a handicapped type apartment so I got to get several ideas on how to do a handicap bathroom (if we need too) but that is still several months out and we are going to stayed focused on not having that need!

I know that the weeks are starting to drag out (it is actually a couple of days past 7 weeks now!) and we just wanted to say that you guys are really sticking this out with us! We continue to get phone calls, e-mails, packages, support, and cards daily! What a great group of family, community, friends, and co-workers that we have!

We haven't even thought about the injury this week (as far as what movement or feeling that we have or don't have) because we have been so busy thinking about just fixing the stuff that they found. What they need to do to work on that the injury is like an afterthought right now. It is amazing, though, at some of the stories that you hear from others in the same condition though and some of their remarkable improvements! We met one guy that has been here for a couple of months and has made miraculous recovery in just the past 2 weeks! We remain hopeful that as they work through making Doc healthier and the swelling starts to go down that we can expect some recovery. In the meantime, we will learn what we need to do to survive until that day arrives!

Please continue with the prayers and I will continue to keep you updated through the next few months (we are here for 3-4 months). Some of the updates might be pretty short because I think many of the weeks will start to run together with the same things happening each week and I don't want to bore you with the same stories!

I continue to maintain a journal and someday, we are going to tell this story in total with an ending and that is the day that we look most forward to! It is right ahead of coming home! That will also be a wonderful day! We miss all of you!

In our prayers,
Cindy and Doc

November 7-2004

Greetings from the wonderful world of Denver! We have had the most beautiful fall weather last week but I haven't gotten to see much of it except when I cross the street from the apartment to the hospital. There is an enclosed bridge that crosses the street on the 3rd floor and when you are on that looking south, you can see Pike's Peak. It is a pretty picture.

This has been a real up and down week so we have good news and bad news. The doctors are telling us that this will be normal for the next year or two.

Doc has been getting up in a wheelchair all week and each day he sits up a little longer. We lasted over 5 hours by the end of the week. We usually get up right after noon time and stay up until evening. Starting on Tuesday, we are supposed to have a puffer wheelchair that will allow Doc to get around on his own and do his own weight shifts. (A weight shift is what you have to do when you don't have any natural feeling or circulation in your body and you have to force the blood to flow around some of your prominent boney parts to avoid pressure sores.) Doc does 20 minutes upright and then 2 minutes on his back. He has to wear a timer and when it goes off, he switches positions. I will be really glad when he gets a chair to do this for him because even though he has lost a bunch of weight, he is still heavy when I have to lift him up and down every 20 minutes. I even have blisters and calluses on my hands now like a real farm girl-my brothers would be proud!

They found out this week that the screw that I wrote about last week was never really secured and the plate that it was supposed to be holding in bent out and penetrated the back of Doc's throat. A throat surgeon looked at it and told us that unless we do surgery, Doc will never swallow, breathe, or talk again. At least it didn't do any permanent damage and they can fix it. A neuro surgeon will also have to do part of the surgery because the bottom of the plate is still attached to the spinal column. They are going to take the plate out because it looks like the bones are healing well enough to not need the plate anymore. After they take the plate out, they stitch up the throat and then in about a week or so, we can try the swallow test and talking stuff. Maybe by Thanksgiving we will be eating and talking! That is our goal anyway! They currently have the surgery scheduled for this coming Friday at 10 a.m.. The bad news in all of this is that Doc will have to stay in his traction and halo gear for at least another 8 weeks past this surgery so he will be in that for a long time before he can get rid of it!

We had a couple of other problems this week as Doc's arms, hands, legs and feet swelled up really big. They are still swollen but it is a common thing with high level spinal injuries and wheelchairs when you first start getting up so no one seems too concerned but me! I try to feed off the doctors and nurses so if they say it's ok, I have to believe them. His sodium level is still low but it was higher towards the end of the week so the doctors are thinking they were giving him too much fluids and that maybe cutting those back will help. They are also testing his bones, his kidneys and his bladder this week to make sure the spinal cord injury isn't causing any problems with those items. I think they have him scheduled for one test per day.

The good news is that Doc is almost done with all his antibiotics and there doesn't appear to be anymore infection. His lungs are looking healthier and he is tolerating a very high level of tidal volume off the ventilator which they tell me is a good thing. He fever has either been gone or low-grade for several days so I am hoping that is behind us too!

No matter what they throw at us, Doc just keeps smiling and telling me it is just another bump and it will be ok. He tells me every morning that no matter what happens today or what anyone says, do not give up the faith! We remember that every morning and it makes us feel like soldiers getting ready for the battle. And each day does feel like a battle! I am not sure if we have actually won any of them yet but we for sure aren't defeated! If I ever feel like I am losing the war, most of you are only a telephone call or e-mail away and it doesn't take much to turn me around and send me out with more ammunition! On top of that, I continue to gather more stories on the signs that come from someone much greater than us to remind me that this isn't something that we are controlling anyway.

Doc & I often discuss how powerful all this is and how glad we are that if this had to happen to us or to someone we knew, we are glad it was us. I see others here that are younger, that have small children, that have no community support, that have no family with them at all, and the list goes on that are going through the same things and it is harder for them.

We have been playing cards, listening to music, reading books, and watching movies to pass the time. We can take some walks when Doc is in his wheelchair but until I pass my suctioning and ventilator classes we can't leave the nurses station by more than 50 yards. That doesn't give us much freedom! I can take the suctioning class on Tuesday at 6 p.m. but they haven't told me when I can take my ventilator classes though so I am not sure how long we are going to be confined to the hallway!

At 1 p.m. (mtn time) on Monday, we have a conference with the whole team of doctors that we have and they are going to give us their analysis of the injury and what they think the future holds BUT as our doctors in Grand Junction reminded us as we walked out the door, no matter what anyone says, no one can know for sure what the next year or two holds. Only time and God will make that call!

I wanted to tell you that Doc and I look at the pictures that our work places and the Cairo community sent to us almost every day and we have to smile when we see all of you smiling at us! Thoughts of all of you are in our minds all day long!

We are never sure what tomorrow holds but we will remain prayerful that it will be good stuff! One of these days, tomorrow is going to be a GREAT day!

It is amazing how I think the week is so boring and nothing happened but then when I start to type it out, I end up with a novel for you all to read! See, this is proof that you can make something out of nothing!

Well, I will close for now and I would be remiss not to remember to continue to say thanks for the prayers and all the rest of the support that we are getting! If that GREAT tomorrow arrives this week, I will be sure to let each of you know! Until then, pray for it and I will write again next week!

Cindy and Doc

November 14-2004

Our meeting with the doctors went really well last week although they didn't have a ton of good news for us. They were very thorough about explaining everything and showing us the results of all the testing they had been doing. What is boiled down to was that they could see that the swelling that Doc had going on was very extensive and that it actually did some damage above the point of injury-probably more than the injury itself. It appears to have killed some nerves off and at one time, this was considered to be permanent but now they are saying that sometimes, although unlikely, these nerves that are damaged due to swelling can regenerate themselves. So they are leaving us some hope that down the road there can be recovery of some type. They said probably nothing for 3-6 months though before we see anything even starting to heal. As usual, it was the same old "give it time and put it in God's hands" and we will see what happens. We figured that was some good hands to have it in.

Most of our tests that we had going on this week came out clean except the bone test. They told us that Doc has what they call HO. It amounts to bone growing in the joints where it shouldn't be growing. They found it in his hips and in his knees. They can't fix it but they can put him on medication to stop it from getting worse. He will be on that medicine for 3-6 months. They took some x-rays to see how progressed it was but we haven't heard back on them yet.

He finally got fitted for his puff and sip wheelchair. They were trying to teach him to drive it and you have to puff hard once to engage it. Well, Doc puffed hard, it engaged and off he went like a shooting bullet! The therapist had the speed set wrong and Doc was laying rubber!!! The therapist was running after him trying to catch him but there was no way! Then Doc hit a doorway and crashed and burnt! It didn't appear to hurt him but the chair is sorta bent up! After I saw that he wasn't hurt, I had to laugh at the scene it presented! It sure looked like something that would happen to the 3 stooges or something. Now this week, I am supposed to learn to drive it and Doc is telling the therapist that he wants to watch! I think he wants to see me crash and burn too but I am not planning on doing that!

Surgery went really well on Friday (although it lasted 5 hours). The little hole that they thought was there turned out to be a 2" tear and they were shocked at how big it was. On top of that, there was a lot of saliva that had gone through the tear and it was built up in his neck and around the spinal column. They did some testing on it to check for infection and the initial results are that there is infection in it. They are hoping to have the type of bacteria it is analyzed by tomorrow and then they will get him on the appropriate antibiotics for it. Doc gets to take his halo/traction off in only 4 weeks instead of the predicted 8 more weeks. He will have to wear a neck brace until he gets some muscles back in the neck but that will be better than this whole traction getup! The only negative information that we received from the surgery was that his bones are not fusing quite as good as they would hope in his neck. If they aren't better in 4 weeks, they will have to do yet another surgery from the back side of his neck and graft his spinal column again but they would be able to still use a neck brace vs. the whole halo/traction getup. I think the thing that made me the most excited was that the surgeons got together (throat and neuro) and they told us there might (and I say might) be a chance that the fact that the plate had completely cut off Doc's airway 100% could have been the reason he stopped breathing on his own instead of the injury and diaphragm causing the problem. They are going to run some tests on his diaphragm (don't know when) and see if there is any chance of getting him off the ventilator (at least part of each day). They warned us that it still might not be possible but they were both hopeful that this was part of Doc's problem. Again, time will tell because we have to let the throat heal and run the tests before we will know.

Pat and Mark (my sister and brother in law) came out this weekend and we were really glad they could visit. I have to tell you that we played Fact or Crap with them and Doc won. I won't tell you who lost BUT Pat said that she was going to rename it "I Lose". We also watched several good movies because Doc just wasn't up to getting up after surgery and doing much else. It was still really good to have them here this weekend.

We also had some of our Grand Junction friends that came to Denver and stopped to visit. They are and will be some of our dearest friends and it is always good to see them and know that they are thinking of us! I wanted to say thanks to all of them! Making new friends has been one of the best things that has coming out of all of this!

I finished my respiratory classes and my training. I had to pass the suctioning section, the ventilator section, and the bagging section. Now that I have passed that, Doc will get more freedom. They said that after he feels better from surgery, we can go anywhere we want in the hospital and we can start signing up for the field trips that they take. I think we are close to having to pick out a ventilator too. I thought we would have a big selection to choose from but there are only 2 available to us. One is a big old yucky green thing with knobs and dials all over it. It is a huge size for a portable. The other is a nice sleek laptop sized ventilator with digital readouts BUT it is noisier than the other one and the battery only last about 4 hours when the other one lasts 8 hours. Doc & I talked it over (and as usual, he told me not to worry about it because he didn't think he would need one anyway by the time we go home) and we haven't decided which one to go with yet but I am leaning toward the smaller, digital one although I don't like how noisy it is or how short the battery life is. Of course, insurance might make our minds up for us!

We are also signed up for van classes and we have to learn how to maneuver a wheelchair onto a van lift and get locked down once we get in. Then we have to start discussing what our needs are there and getting something rolling on that. I think we go to that class on the 24th. They are also supposed to start meeting with us to go over what they want us to do for the house (when we find that all out, several of you that have volunteered to help are going to be called to the front line! And we are grateful to each of you!).

Sometimes, all this education is overwhelming but I know it is their job to get us prepared as quickly as possible to go home. AND we are ready to go home! We are both getting more homesick with each passing day but feel like we are where we need to be for now though.

Last week I had several e-mails telling me that my e-mail told about Doc's progress but not much about me. So for all of you that might be worried about me I will tell you that I am plugging along and keeping myself healthy. I know that letting myself wear down or not eating right is not going to help Doc or me. I would be lying to say that this isn't hard or that I don't get scared or that I don't cry. I probably shed at least a tear or two once or twice a day. Some of you know that I shed more than a tear or two sometimes because I make those calls to unload occasionally. I have to admit that I toggle from the reality of today to the hope of tomorrow all day long! In the long run though, I am really doing well and I know that someday I am going to look back on this as a rough time but will know that my faith grew by leaps and bounds. There is always a silver lining to everything and I spend part of my days just looking for it. Many times, you guys supply my silver linings! Doc spends much more time worrying about me than he does for himself. I told him that he didn't have to worry about me so much because I had so many of you that sent e-mails last week to check on me and that caused him an emotional moment. I think it was his way of saying thanks to all of you that are taking care of me during all of this too!

We both continue to pray hard for recovery and for each of you! I have to admit that I have moments where I waver but I have not seen Doc waver for even an instant that this is all going to be ok. I can only know that in order for him to be that certain and that strong, he has to have something pretty great filling him with that kind of strength! That is what I feed off of.

For those of you that are mighty deer hunters, I am thinking of you and wishing you luck! Doc is sure missing it! Just stay healthy and safe! IF any of you get that big one, we want a picture and the story! (Actually, to be truthful I don't but Doc would enjoy it!).

Continue the prayers because I am hopeful that now that we have repaired some major problems with the surgery and they are attacking all these other problems that they have found, we will be moving forward and hopefully, quickly! Thanks for hanging in there with us!

Cindy and Doc

November 21-2004

We were lucky enough to have a bunch of company this week. It was nice to see familiar faces. Fred and Irene (friends we met in Grand Junction) that live in Colorado Springs came to visit on Tuesday and that was wonderful. Then we met a new friend, Patty, that is the sister to our dear friend, Shelly (from Grand Junction), who came to visit and bring me some made up food that I can microwave. There is an interesting story about meeting Patty that I will share will all of you one day! God truly sent her as a message to us! I especially was grateful to Patty for helping me find a church within walking distance that I attended on Sunday. It felt wonderful to be back in church! Then my cousin Marvin and his family were able to stop by for a visit on their way to Glenwood Springs. On Friday afternoon, some Cairo friends (Mutters, Haydens, and Sanders) surprised us walking into the room for the weekend! All of these smiling faces and hugs were welcomed!

Saturday was a wonderful day because it was probably the most "normal" day we have had since all this started. We set up some tables in the therapy room and played pitch with our Cairo friends all morning and most of the afternoon. Doc and I had a wonderful time!! Now I have to admit that Doc and Don (Mutter) were the reigning pitch champions although I think Lori (Hayden) and I had them shaking in their shoes every time they had to play us! (We did win the first game against them which was enough! I think they just under-estimated us!). After Doc got tired, he went to bed for some napping and football. The guys took off to see the mountains and the girls went shopping at Cherry Creek Mall. It is an outside type mall and they had greenery around the lampposts and Christmas lights everywhere. Christmas music was playing and the snow was falling and I finally remembered why I love the season so much! It was a totally enjoyable evening with a sense of peace enveloping me as I finally realized that no matter what happens in the future, life goes on and you always have those things you love that take up special places in your heart! Just like in nature, human life adapts to what is thrown at it! Anyway, it was a great time of kinship, complete with snowball fights and good food. Then we went back to visit Doc with an armful of Applebee balloons and shared some laughs. I think we were all laughing with tears in our eyes at a special "balloon" story! It was especially joyful to watch Doc trying so hard to laugh even though the halo he is in was preventing him from having a hearty one, he had a good one!

Now that I have tempted all of you with what in the world a "balloon" story could be, I guess I had better finish it even though we sort of made a pact with our friends that what happens in Colorado, stays in Colorado. We tied the balloons to Doc's bed and Don came over to show Doc a wonderful, witty shirt that he bought and one of the balloons floated right over into his face! No matter how hard Don worked to get the balloon out of his face, it kept floating back. Finally, it attached itself to Don's nose. (more than once). Don was swatting at it and at last decided to just move. However, the balloon just followed him! It wasn't until he got VERY far away that the balloon lost interest! We know it wasn't static in his hair causing it…………….(Don, if you are reading this, I meant because you had a hat on, not because you don't have any hair! Hehe).

They brought me a Christmas music CD, much to Doc's delight (hehe) and starting this weekend, I will officially be able to listen to it as much as I want!! (at least until after Christmas). My mom sent a beautiful little Christmas tree with them and it is just waiting to go up this week!

Now to back up to the beginning of the week, we had a real scare on Tuesday because Doc's vital signs went awry and they rushed him to the hospital next door because they thought he had a blood clot travel to his lungs. It ended up not being the case though and everything worked out. (thank you to my dear friend, Mike Schmidt, as he got me through that one!) They made the decision to go ahead and get him back on the blood thinner so they didn't have to worry about that anymore. I think they were wanting to wait until longer after the surgery but it was a case of which was the worse chance to take. They found another infection in the bone they took out of his neck during surgery which makes a total of 4. As soon as they knew which antibiotics would work on each of those infections, they got him started on them.

By Wednesday, Doc was feeling better and his fever had gone down. He was able to get up and stay up for 6 hours. He also got to go to wheelchair driving class again! They have the speed on his wheelchair set so low now that I think I can blow him down the hall faster than he can drive but at least he isn't having anymore crashes. For the whole week, we had to drive with a permit as we weren't allowed to go anywhere with Doc driving unless we had a therapist (licensed driver) walking with us! When the therapist left, I had to put in neutral (actually there aren't any gears on it) and push it. When Doc actually passed the driving test, we were free to drive it without the therapist. I now remember what it was like when you couldn't do anything for yourself until your mom and dad knew you weren't going to get hurt trying it by yourself! Just like back then, I think I am ready long before mom and dad (Craig) does! Anyway, Doc is begging for more speed and they have promised on Monday that they might give him a little more juice!

Speaking of the crash, I finally put 2 and 2 together (only 4 days went by-pretty quick response for me!) and asked the doctor if it is possible that the reason Doc's left foot swelled up was due to the crash and not to HO or blood clots. The doctor looked at me and said it sure could have been and no one had ever told him about the crash. He looked at the wheelchair condition, seen the badly bent legs, and immediately ordered x-rays. Anyway, there weren't any breaks but he did stretch some ligaments which amounted to a sprained ankle. He said that as Doc isn't running any marathons in the next few days, we weren't going to worry about it because it would heal in time. He just told him "NO MORE CRASHES!"

Continue the prayers because this week might be a big week in regards to talking and eating! They are starting Doc on ice chips for eating and working up to other foods if it works out. If that goes well, they can reduce the cuff on the trach, allowing Doc to talk.

I understand that the Cairo Booster Club sponsored a Spaghetti dinner for us on Friday night and I wanted to thank everyone who participated in that. Craig is just starting to give us lists of things that they think we are going to need and it doesn't seem to be coming to an end anytime soon.

We are also starting to meet with the proper people to go over what we need to do to the house. As soon as we get everything ironed out so that we know exactly what we need, we will start asking people to help us out there so we can come home! This week is going to be busy talking about the house, the van, and all the equipment! I think we have at least 2 classes every day along with our scheduled therapy classes. We get Thanksgiving off and then I am taking part of the day after Thanksgiving off to take the shuttle shopping! I have already warned Doc that he is on his own for a few hours!

As this is Thanksgiving week, I wanted to tell everyone that there is one thing that I pray especially hard for this holiday but there is a HUGE list of things that I pray thankful prayers for! All of you are right at the top of that list! Remember to find your thankful things this week and everyone have a VERY safe holiday. I think my most thankful prayer is that I have been able to love and be loved! I have found out how much the past couple of months and for that, I have been blessed!

I think Eric (my brother) and Kim are going to try and visit this weekend so even though I shed a tear when one friend leaves, it is heartwarming to know that I have another hug right behind them! All of you are like the fuel that keep my engine running! Thanks!!!

Now my smile for the day is something that happened last Thursday. They had just gotten Doc up in the wheelchair and I had combed his hair and he looked really good so I just told him that I thought he was so handsome. Doc just looked at me with a tear in his eye and told me that I must be a saint. Imagine that, Saint Cindy… who knew? AND NO, he is NOT on pain medication!

Have a wonderful Thanksgiving, Cindy and Dar from Denver

November 28-2004

Hello to all our family and friends once more from Denver! Already another week has flown by! It seems like the days are long and then I turn around and it is already time to drop you all another line! It is almost December and it looks like it! We are getting quite the snowstorm! I am glad I am only walking in it and not driving!

I have to be honest and say that this week was probably one of our hardest weeks yet. We had to address a lot of reality stuff and I think Doc & I both are getting impatient with the lack of improvement and how slow everything is progressing! (we were warned about it taking months and months and being slow and having ups and downs — but we must have heard it in Spanish because we didn't comprehend it!). We have talked (well, without vocalization) about it though and it isn't that either of us have given up the faith that God still has this under control because we truly believes that he does! We are just not having the amount of patience that he wants us to have. Maybe this is just one of the lessons that we are supposed to be learning! At least we have each other to lean on and that makes it a little easier. We still have the smiles on our faces and they are never very hard to find!

We met with the throat surgeon and he wasn't too optimistic about Doc's chances of talking or eating at this time. He put us off until this Wednesday and then he is going to re-evaluate but at this time, he doesn't see enough muscle working to even warrant a swallow test. He said it is all connected to the injury and we will just have to wait it out and see what happens. So we are taking that step one week at a time! It was disappointing though because we thought we were close to those 2 steps.

We had to order Doc's power and manual wheelchair this week. It was hard putting the sip and puff style on paper and it was even harder when Doc asked what would happen when he got his arms back and didn't need the mouth driven mechanism anymore. Not so hard that he still was thinking that this is going to come to past but hard because the therapist writing the order didn't have the faith that this was going to happen (although she never said so but you could tell). Then while we were ordering the manual wheelchair as a backup, the therapist let us know that while we were talking about how to load it in a car or how to fold it etc...that we weren't thinking along the lines they wanted us to. The manual wheelchair was only a backup for the power wheelchair breaking and that we wouldn't find it a good method of getting around in. He pretty much warned us that getting anywhere without the power chair and van would almost be impossible. He thought that unless Doc made improvement he would ever ride in a truck or car again. He also went over transferring methods and that was when we found out that transferring Doc out of his wheelchair and unto the couch was pretty much impossible too. What it came down to was that he would be dependent on the ventilator, wheelchair and van. That was the extent of his mobility and I think it finally hit us at how challenging this could all be without improvements! That being said, we just had to refocus ourselves out of the bucket of reality and back into the bucket of faith! We made it through that afternoon and moved on! You might smile at one of the points during this though because Doc had to choose a color for his wheelchair out of the "way cool", "way hot", or "contemporary" groupings and I think the therapist was expecting Doc to be a contemporary type of guy but she was surprised to find out he was a "way cool" guy with the choice of Sunkist Orange! I already knew that though (that he was a way cool guy!).

What we moved on to next was the transportation class and what was going to be required for that. That was a financial set back because I don't know what I was expecting but when they told us Doc was going to need the big van because of his size and the size/weight of his wheelchair, my first thought was that I was going to have to drive that big old thing! But then when they said that we could pick one up for $50,000 or a little more, I changed my train of thought from driving it to paying for it! They dropped that out like I had it in my billfold and I could just pull it out. Anyway, the bottom line is that hopefully, we can find a good used van that will work and we will be able to afford it! I have put everything else into God's hands and it has worked out so I have no doubt that this one will work itself out too! He is going to have to work pretty quickly though because we have to have one by the discharge date and they have tentatively set that for mid-January.

Speaking of that, I think we are both nervous and excited about coming home. That seems so close to us and we seem to have so much to do and learn before that date! I have a feeling that the classes are going to start in earnest. It is all so overwhelming when they start throwing things at you that you have to learn and they are things that someone's life depends on you learning correctly!

Our family services person is telling us the main things that have to be done in order for Doc not to be sent to a nursing home is the ramps to the house have to be completed, the entryway into our living room and bedroom has to be assessable to his wheelchair, we have to have a van for transportation, a generator for power back up in place, our equipment has to be in place (which is Craig's responsibility), and we have to have our help defined during the day to assist Doc while I am at work. I am going to have start researching his home care. Maybe I can find some retired nurses or someone with kids that wanted to stay home that might want some part-time work that I could share the days with several different persons even!

We had a bad day on Thanksgiving because Doc spiked a fever and his vision turned blurry so they took him over to the hospital to run some tests and they found that during the initial injury he lost one of his arteries that runs up through the spinal column to the brain. We have two of them and his right one is not working. The good news was that on the whole, his left one is compensating by running a larger flow of blood to the brain but any type of blood pressure changes, it can't handle it, thus causing blurry vision. As long as Doc is reclined immediately, there isn't a problem though so we have a fix. They also increased his blood thinner because that is a dangerous spot to get a blood clot. They also said that time will tell but it is possible for that to heal also.

Since that though, Doc is doing much better! He is feeling and looking better and I think we might be back on track. We are just riding out the road and there have been a bunch of bumps on it! Speaking of driving, Doc has gotten a little more speed in forward and reverse and I am happy to report that he has had no more accidents! He even popped his nephew on his lap this weekend during a visit and gave him a spin around the hospital. I think he was having a good time with that! His nephew was amazed that he could drive it all by just the thing in his mouth! The therapist said he was the fastest learner she has ever had!

We had a wonderful visit from Eric and Kim (my brother and his family) and my mom. Eric and Kyle stayed with Doc one afternoon while the girls did a little Christmas shopping and I think we all had a good time. Then we played some cards and watched a movie or two. Eric even went grocery shopping and cooked me an omelet for breakfast! I have to tell you that I did not know my brother could cook but I know now that he can handle an awesome bacon & cheese omelet! When I came back from the hospital, Eric and Kim had added a pretty, purple cd player to my apartment and I had Christmas music and that was wonderful! They actually added some other stuff for Christmas too and it was a nice home away from home Christmas feeling! We are hopeful that Doc will get an off campus pass this week and he can start spending some time over here with me in the evenings! We are looking forward to that! I have some stuff for the kids and we are going to wrap it and do some decorating while he is here! He has a pretty big smile pasted on his face when we talk about that! I think it is a wonderful thing that our kids are getting to join us for the holidays!!! Thanks to those that made that possible! You should know that it is the BEST Christmas present Doc & I have ever had!!

Then we have this Friday to look forward to because we are taking our first field trip out of the hospital. They are transporting the patients and their families to the mall for a Christmas shopping outing. (I can only imagine the stories I will have to write about next week after this outing!) Each family gets a nurse or therapist to help them so we aren't so scared on our first adventure out. Then after the a.m. shopping, we have a choice of more p.m. shopping or a movie. Guess what Doc chose? I would imagine that you all got this answer right if you said movie! He wants to see the Polar Express so I hope that is playing!

We got our AECI Christmas party invitation in the mail and we noticed that they are having a comedian this year instead of a dj or band. Doc said that was probably because we couldn't be there to dance! Maybe next year!!! Anyway, please have a wonderful time and know that we wish we were there too! Doc misses you guys a bunch!

We continue to get a bundle of cards and prayers daily and we especially got a bunch from our Immaculate Conception friends out of Macon this week! Thanks to all of you for continuing to remember us!

I was thinking how I wanted to close this week and I noticed that there is a Christmas classic on tv tonight called "It's a Wonderful Life". The main character is a George Bailey and he finds out his life is wonderful because of all the friends he has and through the renewal of his faith. He didn't realize how many he had or how much they thought of him. They all sent up prayers for him and they were answered. That is exactly how we feel! We feel like Darwin is our Missouri George Bailey. We have so many friends and so many prayers going up that we are certain God is listening. We were watching another show this week and there was a line in it that said, "Seeing isn't believing but Believing is seeing!" We are hoping that Doc gets better and we are praying that Doc gets better but even more importantly, we believe that Doc is going to get better!

Have a wonderful week and I will keep you posted if anything wonderful happens in our "wonderful life" and thanks to all of you for adding the "wonderful" in it!

Cindy and Doc

December 5-2004

December is officially here and Christmas season is in full swing! You can see and hear it as you walk through the halls here! Craig likes Christmas as much as we do! They even changed the florescent lights in the ceiling to red and green (every other one). Even I never thought of doing that!

I have to say that this week was easier. We still had a ton of stuff to make decisions on and we seem to be in class from early in the morning until late in the afternoon. Not much time to hardly break for lunch but all of it is just getting us prepared to be back with all of you! I prayed for strength to do what we need to do until that day when we get our miracle! I can only tell you that we know in our hearts that it is coming! As long as I concentrate on that, the rest of this is just a passing stage in our life and we are learning to deal with it for as long as God wants us to.

We talked to the neurologist Thursday night and he has been reviewing Doc's records because of the problem with the artery they found last week and he feels even more certain that it was not the swelling/sodium that caused Doc to lose functions. He thinks when that artery messed up, it threw a blood clot into the brain and that it blocked the flow of blood down to the spinal cord. He still wants to do a MRI after Doc gets the halo off because if there is a blood clot there, Doc will need to stay on blood thinner indefinitely. There is a possibility it will never go away and then there is a chance that it will dissolve and then anything is possible! Do you know how we will know what it will do? The same answer we always get…TIME! He said there is no way to predict what the future holds if he finds a blood clot. He said the flow of the blood clot could explain of how Doc lost his functions that he had. He also is pretty certain that is also the problem inhibiting Doc from swallowing, thus preventing him from eating and talking. We will see what the MRI shows! In the meantime, he is talking about running a hearing test to see how fast Doc's brain processes signals. (I hope he doesn't put a whole lot of stock into that test because I KNOW Doc has selective hearing and it doesn't have anything to do with a blood clot! Nothing personal guys, but I think that is a male thing!)

I have to write that many of you have again been used as God's angels on earth because many of the things that I wrote you about last week that were starting to stress me out, have been taken care of/or are in the process of being taken care of. Thanks to a couple of you working hard for me, a van is being located and modified for Doc's specific requirements and it is over ½ cheaper than what Craig originally quoted us!! Craig's transportation dept was a little hesitant about what we found because they thought it might be too good to be true but then they made some calls and came up and gave us the green light. They said they were ready to sign off on it so we are set to go. We also now have a generator being installed! I have some of the changes on the house already happening thanks to many of you! Then one of the biggest moments of hope this week was that we were told that they had some equipment that was donated because someone that was in Doc's condition a few months ago has completely recovered and he donated his equipment to Craig to distribute to patients needing it. (the best part of this story was the recovery of the young man though!). Doc and I told the therapist that when Doc recovers we plan on bringing his equipment back here and doing the same thing with it!

I would like to say thank you to each of you by name for the stuff that is happening but then you already know who all of you are and trying to list everyone that is helping would only create the chance that I would leave someone out and I would hate to do that! All along many of you have been asking what you could do to help and now that I can actually start asking, you are all doing it! I will continue to ask for help from different persons as different needs arise and I will again say thanks in advance! For many of you, the help will come as we come home and we need your support and muscle!

I have been listening to Christmas music and I never realized how many songs refer to "home" in the lyrics! What I am finding out is that home is really where your heart is! My home is with Doc and the kids (which will be here in less than 2 weeks) and with each of our dear friends— and I visit with all of you every week and many more of you more than that! We love the cards, phone calls, e-mails and prayers! The nurses all comment on how many we get each day and they just keep coming! They said they've never seen anything like it!

We received a wonderful tape of a Thanksgiving mass from our St. Pius friends and the St. Pius kids sent us a special hello along with a special blessing from Father Mike! That was GREAT! Thanks to all of you and for all the perpetual adoration prayers and cards that we receive! We cannot wait to join you again!

We also got a package from my cousins in the St. Louis area and they had a Texas Hold 'em Tournament/Benefit for us which was a neat idea and I only wish I could have been there! I'm not much of a poker player but I would have had fun anyway! The package had some really fun pictures of the evening and it was so nice to feel like we experienced it! Thanks to all who planned that and participated in that! I also wanted to say thanks to the Creed family and those that helped or participated in the rummage sale the Cairo community had for us! All of this is helping us get the things we need to get Doc (and me) home!

Our meeting with the throat doctor on Wednesday confirmed that Doc is not ready for the swallowing test or deflating the cuff in his trach for vocalization so we continue to wait and pray for those 2 things! We will meet with this doctor sometime in January before we head home. In the meantime, there is a speech therapist working with Doc to help him strengthen the muscles that it is going to take to perform these activities! If she sees a bunch of improvement that would lead her to believe that Doc is ready for a test, they will look at it and try to rehab it before we leave!

We got our first off campus pass for just the 2 of us on Tuesday afternoon so we buzzed over to my apartment. Unfortunately, we only got an hour because the ventilator ran out of juice and the AC adapter they sent with me had a broken plug! It was a bad thing but then again, it was a good experience for me. I found out that I didn't panic but figured out what to do to keep the ventilator operational until I could get him back to the hospital and get him plugged in again with a good cord. I don't know if Doc was scared or not but he at least pretended to have faith in me and that helped a bunch! (Of course he can't talk and I was working from behind his wheelchair so I am only assuming he wasn't afraid!). We could both hear the alarm going off but I was the one reading the message of battery low and then battery lost! Then we tried it again Thursday night and had a little better luck! We wrapped presents, listened to Christmas music and did our advent wreath! If Doc could have eaten cookies, I would have made some! (although he still has a standing offer of homemade cookies from some of the nurses at St. Mary's and they are just waiting for the day he eats to send him some! He hasn't forgotten!)

Then on Friday, we had our first outing in a van as we were signed up to go Christmas shopping in the mall and then to a movie (Polar Express). That was a good time! Doc's physical therapist is Chuck! Doc really likes him and he told him he wanted to bring him home with us when we go home! However, I put my foot down because they just talk about sports, sports, sports and then when they are done with that, they talk about sports! Well, I am writing this because Chuck was supposed to be our "spotter" on the shopping outing and as Doc was excited about having this opportunity to buy me a Christmas gift, I could only imagine what Chuck and Doc would come up with. Luckily, they changed our "spotter" to Doc's occupational therapist and HER name is Gail! I feel better about what is going to pop out of the box on Christmas Day now! After the day was over, I asked Doc if it was good or bad. I didn't know if it would put emphasis on the wheelchair and how hard it is to get around or if it would have a degree of something normal about that would bring comfort that we can still do some of the same things we did. He said it was a good day and it was just good to do something normal! I was glad that was what he took away from it!

I always try to read these updates to Doc before I send them out so he can add anything he wants to say or things that I forget about but this next part, I will not read aloud to him. His brother, Owen, who lives in Texas is surprising him with a visit tonight and staying until Wednesday. He will really enjoy that!

We had the nicest compliment from one of the nurses here. She said that she loves to have us because every time she walks into our room there is such a sense of peacefulness and love that she leaves feeling like a new person! We had several nurses that shared that with us during our stay in St. Mary's too so I have to think that God is really sitting with us to make others feel that feeling! It makes me happy to know that!

We continue to meet so many wonderful persons here that we are creating friendships with. When we first got here we met a young man named Collin who is in the same condition as Doc with the exception that he can talk and eat but on the down side, his injury is complete and he is unlikely to have the chance to get much better. He is only 19 and he was injured while jumping out of tree into a pile of leaves he & a friend had raked up. We felt a bond with him and his family right off and then we found out this week that he and Doc are on the same team. They team up 2 patients to go through training for living at home and then they get to go on outings that they plan together. I am glad they got each other because you can tell they are going to be good friends! They even did a flower arrangement class together and whenever you can get 2 guys to discuss which color flowers they want to put together into a vase you have to know they are BORED! Our families have been much help to each other though and I run into them in the halls at Craig, the elevator at the apartments, the stores and when I go to church! I guess God is throwing our paths across each other repeatedly for a reason!

We have another conference with our team of doctors/therapists/ and nurses Monday afternoon. I think they are planning on giving us a specific dismissal date at that time and go over any problems or medical matters that we need to be made aware of although they are so good about keeping us informed as we go through each day that there aren't usually any surprises. Then if it stays on schedule, Doc will get his halo and traction off sometime within the next week. Doc will then be in a neck brace for another month. The biggest thing about that is whether his spinal column fused together or whether he is going to have to go through another surgery. I have been praying hard for him not to have to go through another surgery! 3 should be enough for anyone!

I was sitting here looking around my apartment thinking of how do I close this letter this week, when I saw the pile of gifts that I have in the corner waiting on the kids to get here. I thought of how many gifts that we have that we cannot see or wrap. If we could wrap every kind thing that each of you have done or offered, the prayers each of you have said, the number of cards and e-mails you have sent, and/or the calls that you have made, into little packages with bows on them, a person would probably think we were Santa Claus to have that many gifts in one place! They all have "To Doc and Cindy" on them and we have unwrapped each of them with joy and a grateful heart!

Until next week,
Your friends,
Cindy and Doc

December 12-2004

I am not sure how the weather is in Missouri but in Denver, Colorado, it is almost fall-like instead of winter! The temperatures have been up in the 60's and sunny almost everyday. It has been nice for Doc though because they have been taking him out and practicing driving around in his wheelchair in an outdoor terrain.

This week was again spent mostly talking about things we need to have in place to go home. Equipment and taking care of needs were the hot topics. We even went over air travel and I have to tell you that by the time you go through what you have to go through to get on an airplane in Doc's condition, I would almost rather walk! However, when we come home, they are telling us it has to be commercial air so I guess we are going to have to weather it once anyway! From now on though, until Doc gets better, we are driving!

Speaking of driving, it looks like we might have the van situation worked out! Thanks to Tara Head for calling me and letting me know of where we could find a van already equipped that was close to what Doc was needing. With a few adjustments (that Mark Cooley and Gregg Jacques are researching for me), I think it is going to work out! (And for all our Cairo friends, I think it is black and gold!-Imagine that!)

Our conference went really well this week. They continue to tell us that things are moving along and it is just going to take time to tell how Doc will progress. They are unwilling to call him a complete or incomplete but most of the patients that we meet here are complete so just having that uncertainty among the doctors is enough to give us extra hope! Our team of therapists and doctors continue to be amazed at what all of you are doing for us at home! They call you our army! We have a tentative discharge date of January 19th but they called it a movable target because it depends on whether the equipment is all in place and if Doc has anymore progress that they would need to rehab, then they could extend it. (like talking or eating or breathing or anything else that would pop up!)

Now, about our army! Things are moving along well in Missouri. They are working on house modifications, ramps, laying a better area for the van to load/unload Doc so there won't be so much slope, getting the van, installing the generator and arranging for home care. All these things seem to be falling into place and I am sure that even though most of it is through the elbow grease of many of you, it is really through the grace of God that it is falling into place so easily. We wanted to say a special thanks to all of you though, because we know this a really, really busy time of year and trying to fit our needs in, isn't easy!

We continue to be blessed with signs and assurances that all of this is going to come to pass. I have to be honest and tell each of you that it is not because we were so strong in our faith before the accident (I thought we were but it isn't anything to what we know now!) but something is giving us the strength to make this all relatively easy to know that it is all part of a great plan. Doesn't mean that there aren't tough spots in each day but in the whole picture, it gives us courage to wait it out!

We grabbed on to that courage on Tuesday because we hit another bump in the road. The bones in Doc's neck did not fuse so they have to do another major surgery to pull bone out of his hips and then fuse it into his neck. They have it scheduled for 7:30 mtn time on Tuesday morning. So we will be getting over that hurdle this week. Doc said that it is just good that they think they can fix it. We also are excited because when they take him in for surgery, they are going to remove the halo/traction and after surgery, he will just have a heavy neck brace to wear for 12 weeks. Even though it is another 12 weeks, at least it is not the halo/traction! It is going to be a fairly long surgery but they are telling us that after it is over, they will move him straight back to Craig. Then he will be on bedrest for Wednesday and up and in therapy again on Thursday. On Friday, Doc & his team (Collin) and their families (that means me) are heading the Museum of Natural History for an outing. We can either do the museum or the imax. Doc wants to do the imax and I think it is on lions so it will be ok! Then when we get back from that, they are hosting a Christmas buffet for the Craig patients, employees, and families. (Doc cannot eat yet so I guess I will have to just eat an extra piece of pie for him!). He will still attend though!

We took a field trip on Tuesday after classes and went to the movies to see "Christmas with the Kranks" and we both really enjoyed the outing. It feels good to do normal stuff once in awhile.

We have been spending the evenings in my apartment now that we have the pass to leave the hospital and that is nice because I can do some work on the computer and Doc reads all the e-mails that everyone sends him. It is nice to be able to watch a television show or talk (in our silent movies type way!) without a nurse popping in for something!

Friday was an exciting day because we had to go to this wheelchair driving clinic and it consisted of 3 guys that were around 20 years old and then Doc! Their mission was to go on a scavenger hunt for things from the basement to the 3rd floor on both the East and West sides of the hospital. The first one back with all the right answers won. It was supposed to be for driving exercise because you had to apply a little speed and then you had to use the elevators a lot too. To make an exciting story short, Doc was the first guy back with all the right answers (he moves pretty good for an "old" man)! Joel also made it back with all the right answers but it took it a lot longer. So they both won! They get to go to the gift shop with a gift certificate on Monday to make a purchase. I think I am actually going to come out the winner in this though because I have been to the gift shop and it has a bunch of stuff that I liked but nothing that I could see Doc wanting so I am smelling a treat for me! (now I will add for those that don't know Doc that well, he really did not find the scavenger hunt that big of a deal! I think he would have rather been doing something else! He is about tired of making flower arrangements, decorating miniature Christmas tress, scavenger hunts, etc...

He does like the movie outings though) (PS: I haven't told him yet that I signed him up to make fleece scarves and pillows this week! Ooolala!)

We had a wonderful visit with Doc's brother Owen this week. Doc was totally surprised! He knew someone was coming but he didn't know who! It was a good visit and Owen joined us on our outing to the movie. We also had a call from the Driskell family (Doc's mom's side of the family) who were having their annual Christmas party and it was nice to hear from all of them! Thanks to all that took a moment to say hi!

Friday night, we went to a Christmas party and dance that Craig put on for patients and their families. They had some pizza, music and karaoke (sp?). I have chaperoned a bunch of after-prom parties with the karaoke and I have heard a bunch of bad singing BUT it was nothing to how bad this was! It was so bad that Doc & I were in stitches just trying to sit through it. I know it wasn't kind to laugh but it was either that or cry! It was a nice evening though and Santa even had a small gift for all the patients that came (Doc must have been a good boy because he got a nice CD case-which worked out nicely because he has gotten a few really nice cd's sent to him!).

Now for all you guys out there, you might be a little jealous because on Saturday, the Denver Bronco Cheerleaders came in and did a dance routine and then visited with all the patients and even though it is December, their Christmas outfits were pretty short! I was teasing Doc that I didn't care if he looked because he wasn't going to chase any of them very far anyway. After I told him that, I thought he mouthed that "I have something more special", which was going to get him a big brownie point but he said I had it wrong... I finally figured out that he said, "I have some more speed!" (which he did because his therapist had bumped his wheelchair speed up just an hour earlier). Needless to say, he lost a brownie point on that remark! He was a hit though because they all gathered together (37 of them) and he got his picture taken with them. After that broke up, they all came over to sign a calendar of themselves (clothed even more skimpily, I might add!) and tell him what an awesome smile he has! It was a good thing for them to do and you could tell it meant a lot to the patients!

The girls are going to be here this coming Sunday and then Adam will follow early on Monday morning. I cannot tell you how excited we are that they are coming! We can hardly wait!

We continue to be flooded with Christmas, Get Well, and thinking of you cards! We love every one of them and it is so good to hear about stuff going on at home! Thanks for thinking of us and praying for us! Even though Doc's progress seems slow now, I am going to tell each of you to continue to pray because we "know" that this is all going to work out some day! It is just not a feeling of hope but one of knowing! It comes from something much greater than ourselves! Thanks to all of you for being a part of it!

Have a great week,

Your friends in Colorado,

Cindy and Doc!

December 19-2004

Hello from Denver!! I caught myself calling the hospital home this week! That is a for sure sign that we have been here too long!

Doc had his 4th surgery on Tuesday and it took about 5 hours but it was successful. The doctor was really excited about how well it went. They took some bone out of Doc's hip and fused it into the spinal column along with a small wire. (he has about a 6" incision on his lower back for the hip bone and about a 10" incision on the back of his head & neck). The halo came off and we have a small neck brace on. I haven't decided yet whether Doc loses his angel status with the loss of the halo or not. I will keep you posted but even though he is a heck of a nice guy, he was never an angel. (Of course, you might have to be one to recognize one and I've never claimed to be one either). I thought the neck brace would be a big and bulky thing but it isn't too bad and I can take off the front of it to shave him and stuff. Plus they think that surgery went so well that he only has to wear the brace for 8 weeks instead of 12 and then he won't have to wear any type of neck brace. Now we are ready for a haircut! I told him that last time I saw his hair this long (with the little curl in the back of it) was in the 70's! That was a long time ago!

Wednesday was a lazy day because he was bedridden and I took some film in to be developed with Doc and all the cheerleaders on it! I think I will have some fun pictures if they come out! Even though I am glad that I don't have all my camera equipment out here, I am really missing it and I am pretty tired of disposable cameras! Those of you who know me, know that I rarely go anywhere without my camera and to have not taken a picture in over 3 months, is a long time for me! (the pictures I take with the disposable cameras just don't count!)

I spent some time really fixing Doc's room up while he was over at the hospital for some tests on Tuesday afternoon! If there were a Christmas decorating contest, Doc's room would stand to be in the finals! It is really Christmasy (a made up Cindy word) in his room with tons of lights, greenery, and everything else that makes it Christmas, including music!

We received a couple of wonderful things this week that really brightened our days! First we received a wonderful package full of cards from the Immaculate Conception School children and they were so fun to read and look at! We cherished every one of them! They all had wonderful messages and beautiful pictures!

Secondly, we received a video of the AECI Christmas Party! I thought it was nice that they had thought to tape it but then we started to watch and realized that "We were home for Christmas, if only in their dreams!" They actually included us in the evening, the meal blessing, and in the entertainment! What a wonderful family that we have there! Thanks to all of you that participated that evening in praying for us and remembering us! I hope the memories of us brought smiles and not sadness! We were smiling (and laughing) the whole time we watched it except for a tear or two that we shed but only because the kind things that was said and done! It was great seeing all your familiar faces! We are just so glad that Doc is still with us for this Christmas and we dream of those ahead of us being better! As for "Mr. Kahuna", Doc said to tell you that what happens on the golf course, stays on the golf course! (he will talk again so beware!). Anyway, we just wanted to say thanks to all of our family at AECI for that evening! I wasn't sure of how to put it into words how much it meant to us and I am not sure that I have yet but just know that this might be one of those things that just leaves me speechless (and that is saying a lot!)…Oh yeah, Doc wanted me to especially write that he was glad that Tom was in the shot with his hat on because he loved that hat! He even had me rewind that part to see it again! Becca, you did a great job taping it!

Those were both great ways to spend our lazy day! Then Thursday, we were back up and back in classes and therapy. No chance to get too lazy!!

Then Friday, we were out on the town again as we went to the Museum of Wildlife and attended an Imax show on lions. When we returned they had a complimentary buffet set up for all the patients and their families and I only wish Doc could have eaten because it was an awesome display of food! I am not getting skinny out here (especially at this time of year!).

Saturday morning, Doc had a MRI to see if has that blood clot in his brain that they think is there. We haven't heard the results of that yet. Then that night we went to the Reindeer Races in the rec room. That was fun and Doc did a fantastic job at picking the winning reindeers! I think he picked 4 winners in 6 races! He won some wonderful things like a t-shirt, a cooler bag, a bottle of shampoo and a tube of chapstick! I only picked a 2nd place winner in just one race and I won a bottle of hairspray!

We met a new friend this week whom is a cousin to our new neighbors at home. She is wonderfully kind person who is picking up the girls for us from the airport and bringing them to the hospital. She and her church have also volunteered to make a Christmas dinner for our family and deliver it to the apartment on Christmas evening! I am more convinced with each passing day that this world is busting at the seams with wonderful people! I personally think that heaven it going to be much more crowded than I thought it was going to be!

There is going to be a non-denominational service at 3 p.m. on Christmas Eve and the hospital chaplin asked if my kids would help him in that and they were glad to. He also asked if we would share our story as part of the message he wants to give, which we feel like we are supposed to do. Doc is really glad that they are having some type of service that he can attend. Then the kids and I are going to "midnight" mass at a local church at 10 p.m.. I know that Father Mike, St. Pius, often laughs when someone asks him what time midnight mass is but I actually have it in writing in the local church bulletin that midnight mass here is 10 p.m.. I know Colorado is an hour behind Missouri but I didn't know it was two hours

I have held off sharing this next little bit because Doc & I weren't sure exactly what it means, if anything and we don't want to make a mountain out of a molehill, but if there was one Christmas gift we could share with each of you, it would be the good news of improvement through your prayers, so for what it is worth (keeping in mind that we are even nervous about it lasting), this is what has been happening in the past week or so….Doc got his sense of smell back, he can feel full pressure in his seat and in his lower back when in a wheelchair (which is good news according to the doctors as it might be a sign of more recovery to come!), he felt a shot in his stomach but only one time so far and he said that HURT, he felt pressure in his arm when they took his blood pressure, he felt an iv that they put in his right foot for surgery, he has his gag muscle back when suctioning his trach (which the doctor says is the first step toward reducing the cuff in order for him to talk. We are only waiting on the cough to follow but in the meantime, they have decided to recheck his swallowing muscles this Wednesday because there is an outside chance that he might be better) and finally he can occasionally feel pressure as I touch his shoulders and chest. It is enough for his team to be re-evaluting his discharge date because if he continues to make improvements, they are thinking of pushing it back to see what else they can re-hab! We continue to feel that in God's time we are going to have our miracle and if it happens to be a Christmas miracle, rest assured that all you will know the split second after I do!!!

We are both so thankful for the continued communication from all of you (including those that we haven't even gotten to meet yet) that continues to flow to us! Everyday when they deliver the mail, they tell us that Doc always wins the most mail contest! The wonderful Christmas and Get Well cards (most of them with handwritten inspiring messages!), the e-mails, the phone calls, and the packages! I know that even back in September and October I was referring to all of you as our "angels" but as angel season is really here....we just wanted to say that even though your halo's may not be shining or your wings flapping, we know what you are!!

By the next time I write, our kids will have arrived and Christmas will have come and gone! Isn't it amazing how fast time flies? So this is going to have to be the e-mail in which we wish every single one of you the most Blessed of all Christmases! For those that are struggling financially, we pray for monetary relief...for those that are struggling with illness, we pray for health...for those that are struggling with relationships (especially marital or family stress), we pray for healing in spirit...for those that have loved ones away from you through the holidays, we pray for love...for those that are missing loved ones that are no longer with us on earth, we pray for peace...We pray every night for all of you even if we don't know a specific need...Everyone of us has crosses to bear and some are heavier than others but when we share them, they are all lighter!

Merry, Blessed Christmas to each and every one of you

with our love,

Cindy and Darwin Blackmore and in the holiday season, Adam, Jaymi and Carrissa!

December 26-2004

I hope everyone had a wonderful week with a joyful Christmas since the last time I wrote! We had a white Christmas but only because of leftover snow from Thursday! It was still pretty and white though!

The girls arrived late Sunday night and Adam arrived early Monday morning so it was a joyful beginning of the week! Doc had a rough night Sunday night and woke up with a 102 temperature Monday morning. That was his first temperature for a long time. They worked hard at bringing it down and they finally had it under control by 11:30 and then he could get up! They thought it was due to him being so excited about the kids coming but they ended up running a bunch of tests anyway to be sure so the first day they were here, we spent most of the day hopping from class to class and test to test but they just tagged along on all of it! We did get to leave the hospital and come over to the apartment in order to eat some supper and play one game of pitch and one game of Kings Corner (Doc won both of them!).

Tuesday was Carrissa's birthday so I left her with Doc for a little while Jaymi, Adam and I ran to the grocery store and got a birthday cake for her! Then we had a special supper at the apartment for her!

We had a wonderful call from our AECI buddies and Doc's union brothers/sisters that they had done a fund raiser for Doc and a fellow co-employee that is going through a different type of medical tragedy. They had supported a raffle and then made a deposit into our account and called to wish us a Merry Christmas. We also had a nice Christmas Gift from CBG North County out of Florissant that was greatly appreciated! I cannot list all the individuals that have helped us but know that we have appreciated everything that you have done and continue to do to help us with everything we need! With all the help of many of you out there, we are pretty certain that we are going to be able to buy the van and make modifications to the home without selling Doc's truck! That makes me feel so good because that truck meant a lot to him and I am POSITIVE that he is going to drive it again some day-not only because of my faith, but because Doc tells me so! In the meantime, I will be the caretaker of Doc and his truck! We also got a box from AECI with a bunch of VHS tapes in it and I don't know how they did it but they picked out movies that we didn't have and haven't seen. I thought we already had a pile in our room but they managed to add a bunch more to it. The selection in the hospital is very weak so we have been sharing ours with the other patients and this is just more entertainment for all of us! That is what we spend most of our free time doing (watching movies). Then I also wanted to say thanks to all of you that baked Christmas goodies and sent them to us! We had a lot of enjoyment eating the cheeseballs, candies, and cookies (although I am not sure how much enjoyment it is going to be when I try to zip up my jeans next week!). We also had plants, balloons, and other little treasures sent this week and we wanted to say thanks to all of those that sent those too! I guess in general, just to make sure we don't leave anyone off, thanks to all of you for making our Christmas brighter!!!

Wednesday was a busy, busy day! I think they were trying to get everything they could out of us before the holidays got here! Doc had an appointment with the throat doctor and we got mixed news. He said that he had some swallowing muscles again which was great news but that Doc was forcing them to work instead of the nerves automatically triggering it. There was also a lot of swelling and he thinks it is from the surgery that he had last week. So based on his examination, he felt more comfortable in saying that Doc probably would be able to talk and eat again but probably not for at least another month or so. Last time, he wouldn't even tell us if he thought it would ever come back! Then we had all our regular classes like occupational therapy, physical therapy, speech therapy, and "living in the real world" classes. After those were over, Doc had a hearing test (which he passed with flying colors! Now I know he can hear if he wants to!). Finally, we ended the day with some video of persons training on Doc. Human Relations was making a tape of Craig and they needed some footage of a person on a ventilator with people learning how to operate the equipment. I guess you could say that Doc was either a "movie star" or a "dummy". When we finished that, we all filed over to the apartment for supper and cards! We played poker with Cheez-its and Jaymi lost and Doc won…I think it was because Jaymi was eating all her "wagers" and Doc couldn't eat! It was a wonderful evening!

Our kids are real troopers! They have followed us around all week and have taken in everything they can learn in a week! I think they all know the respiratory stuff now, how to drive the wheelchair (which I haven't even attempted yet!), all about his medications, range of motion exercises, his lungs, etc... They go from class to class asking all kinds of questions and getting right in there to experience what they can for themselves. They have even all sat in the lift and let each other lift them in and out of bed! I am so glad that we have them because they are a wonderful extension of Doc & I! They truly have been our Christmas gift this week!

Christmas Eve was a great day and we watched a movie in the morning and had a great time reading a HUGE package of homemade Christmas cards from the St. Pius school (which they should be very proud of because they were great!), went to a non-denominational service, where Doc and I told our story of what happened and how God played a role in it that day to a crowd for the first time! Then we went to a Christmas Eve dinner at Craig. After that, we went over to the apartment for some family time and we made a call to my moms on a speaker phone to listen and talk to all of my family because that is when we usually have Christmas with them! Later in the evening, the kids and I went to "midnight" mass at 10 p.m. while Doc got his first real shower since the 1st week of September. That had to feel good! On Christmas morning, we slept in a little bit, had a family lunch in the cafeteria that the hospital sponsored, came over to the apartment (after the nurses gave Doc all his meds and iv's as their Christmas gifts!), and opened our gifts which was so much fun! Then our neighbor at home, Derek's, cousin (that lives in Denver) brought us a Christmas supper to the apartment around 5. All of us enjoyed the entire day but we knew in our minds of how close that we came to not having Doc with us this Christmas so that was the greatest gift of the day!

Doc got a wonderful Christmas present on Christmas Eve because one of his roommates was from Greece and they couldn't speak any English. His wife came over every morning at 6 a.m. to start rambling in Greek at the top of her lungs and didn't stop until he went to sleep at night! It was pretty much driving everyone crazy and they finally found a room to move him to that would make everyone happier! We didn't complain but I think they noticed that it was an aggravating situation! Doc was smiling ear to ear as they wheeled his stuff out of the room—and he thought I talked a lot! He has a whole new respect for my quantity and volume!

Adam had to leave for the airport at 3:45 a.m. on Sunday morning and it was hard to say good-bye to him but I know his fiancé (Laura) will be glad to have him back so they can have a little Christmas time together too. The girls will have to leave that early on Thursday morning and I am sure that it will be here way before I want it to be!

They told us on Thursday that they aren't sure about the discharge date now because of the equipment situation. The one piece of equipment that has to be here and fitted to Doc before they can send him home is his power wheelchair and when they called about it, insurance hadn't approved it yet so it is not even ordered. They were told it will take 4-6 weeks after it is ordered for Doc to receive it and than another week or two with him having it here before they would be comfortable in the discharge date. We are going to find out more next week so we are sort of in limbo right now (but we are comfortable in the limbo stage so it isn't a big deal!). Somehow everything that has happened to us in the past 3 months has been for a reason and just part of our path so this must be too! Maybe we are waiting those extra weeks because that will be when the breathing kicks in and we will be in the right place to re-hab it! You never know!

I know that I always write thanks for the calls, cards and e-mails but I really do mean it! Everyone of them is appreciated and loved!! I continue to know that God is working through each of you and some of you know it too now! Some of the e-mails that I get have the most awesome stories in them about what some of you are experiencing while in prayer for Doc! All I can say is that is how we know our miracle is coming! Thanks to all of those that believe in our miracle without any reason to and for those that have a reason to and have shared it with us! We continue to know to know in our hearts that it is on its way.

In closing, I just realized that before I send our next e-mail that it will be 2005! Wow! Anyway, I hope all of you have a fun and safe New Year's Eve and New Year's Day!

Your friends in Denver,
Doc and Cindy

January 1 2005

This past week flew by, as we knew it would! The kids were a joy to have with us and we miss them but it felt good to know they had things to do and persons waiting for them when they got home too!

It was a lax week here with everything still in the holiday mode. There were several persons on vacation, including Doc's doctor, physical therapist and occupational therapist so he didn't have a very hectic schedule. We were scheduled for two outings. One was on Monday and it was to the movies. The girls went with us and we saw Oceans Twelve, which we all enjoyed! I usually don't pig out on buttered popcorn but I used the girls being with us as an excuse to splurge and needless to say, I was almost oinking by the time we left! It was good but when you aren't used to eating buttered pop-corn, it doesn't sit in your stomach the way it used to!

Then Tuesday was not such a good day. Doc woke up feeling puny and stayed that way until late in the day. He finally kept his eyes open for more than an hour around 5 p.m. The girls and I chilled with him most of the day but when he was on his 10th nap for the day (it was hard to keep track of them because you couldn't tell when one nap ended and another one started!), we decided to take a walk and do a little after Christmas shopping! It was a good break and we weren't gone long. When we got back, he was feeling better so we ventured over to the apartment for supper and cards. He stayed awake and managed to win (AGAIN!). It is embarrassing at how he keeps pulling out the wins because we should be able to pull one off now and then!

Wednesday morning the girls went over in the morning and helped Doc get ready so I could do a little work. It felt good to have a little break and know he was in good hands. They called me after they got there though because for some reason, he had an appointment set up with Dr. Reed, the throat doctor. I thought when we left Dr. Reed last week that our next appointment wasn't supposed to be for 4 weeks. It wasn't on the schedule until that morning, and even the nurses didn't know how it got scheduled or why. Anyhow, after we got there, Dr. Reed did another examination on his throat and told us that he thought Doc might finally be ready for the swallow test. He said he wasn't sure that Doc would pass it or that he was necessarily ready to talk and/or eat but he was really close. He wants to test it and see for sure where we are at. He said he is really surprised at how rapidly Doc is mending in that area. He said most persons that he sees in Doc's original condition take at least a year to get to where Doc is now and sometimes they never get there. So even though it is slow to us, it sounds like Doc is speeding along! His test is set up for 11 a.m. on Monday so an extra prayer around noon from you couldn't hurt! They said talking should come before eating so if we aren't good across the board, we might at least get to do a little talking! I know we have been hopeful in this area before so I am trying not to get my hopes up too much but it is still exciting to think that it might be close at hand! If we are really close, they might push out our discharge date to rehab these things but I think we would have to be very, very close if not already in process! We have been practicing for 3 months on what his first 3 words should be and I think he has them memorized!

Mike (my brother) and his family arrived Wednesday night and stayed until Saturday so they got to go with us on the 2nd outing of the week. Luckily, for Mike, it was a trip to the mall Thursday evening and I know how much he enjoyed that (hehe)! I am sure it was fine with Tracie and Kelsie though! It was a great visit and the timing helped me with the girls leaving at 3:30 am on Thursday morning because it wasn't quite so sad. They also brought a big enough vehicle to haul boxes (and I mean boxes!) of stuff home with them that I was going to have to ship so that was helpful too!

Mike and Jeana (my cousins from the St. Louis area) arrived for a visit on Saturday morning and it was wonderful seeing them too! It is amazing at how many visitors we have been blessed with being so far from home! All of them have been a sight for sore eyes! Plus, I have to admit that I have enjoyed the hugs too!!

They are still telling us that our discharge date is tentatively set for January 19th so in less than 3 weeks we should be home unless something changes! The wheelchair issue seems to be resolved and they are telling us that it should be here in time for modifications before we head home. They have cut the lead time from 6 weeks to 2 weeks! (I think the wheelchair mfg'r was responsible for losing the quote so insurance is putting some pressure on them to get that wheelchair to us fast!) If not, that will push us out. We have finalized the van situation and within the week, it should be modified for Doc and then we will have that option to consider for coming home. We are hoping to bring the van out here and go home in it rather than go through everything we would have to go through to fly home. I think we almost have them convinced here to let us do that! (I am putting my debating skills to test! Between my arguments and Doc's pitiful, pouting faces, (which he can pull off very well!) we might win this battle!).

It sounds like things are happening at home and I get updates daily to keep us informed! What a team we have working for us there! I am glad to hear the house stuff is coming along because I have been mostly concentrating on what I need to learn and taking care of the equipment. I have been just leaving the house/ramps and/or the van situation to most of you but it is all so important!

I continue to hope that God has me completely prepared for everything that I need to know by the time I go home but he still has to free up a bunch of brain space for me to take more in! He has done a fine job so far so I will just continue to go with the flow. Everything has been falling into place and I feel confident that it will continue to do so!

Doc has had a little more sensation in his feet and his back this week but no motion yet. We wait for that day because then they will have more re-hab options! In the meantime, we are glad that he has some things happening because a little bit is better than nothing! I continue to pray especially for breathing! Every morning when I see him, I ask him if I still take his breath away and he just smiles! One of these days he is going to say no! (but he better add that I could!).

I celebrated the New Year with Mike and his family in New York time and Missouri time (the most important!) with a call to each of my kids and then finally in Denver time curled up in bed with a good movie on tv! Doc missed it all but 2005 came anyway! Mike even brought a bottle of bubbly so I even had a toast! I can look back on 2004 and think it was the hardest year of my life but then again, I would rather look back on it and think how blessed and lucky I was! As Doc says, we only have 2 options and we have to make a choice! I would rather pick the one that makes me smile.

I cannot tell you how important it is that we continue to pray because I think it is the most important part in all of this! Thanks to all of you for your continued support in that area!

Hoping your 2005 is wonderful,
Cindy and Doc

PS: I'm not complaining (ok, maybe a little bit!) but has anyone noticed how television is overloaded with football games at this time of year? And they call it a HOLIDAY! I did let Doc watch all the games he wanted but he had to pay me 5 kisses for every game!

January 3, 2005

I thought I would send a picture of all of us from the kid's Christmas visit! AND I wanted to update you on Doc's swallowing test today. It went very well and even though they don't think he is ready for solid foods, they thought he would be able to handle some liquids and possibly some ice chips. They also did not see anything go down the windpipe so that might clear him for some cuff deflation allowing him to do some talking. All of this was per the radiologist and the speech therapist and it has to finalized through Dr. Reed and his analysis of the test but things are looking good.

Based on that, they have talked to us about moving Doc's discharge date back but they have to put a plan together with a detailed layout of what they expect to do for Doc in those areas and how long they think it will take. I am getting the indication that they are possibly thinking another month. As much as I want to be home, I am excited about going home with Doc eating and talking again so I will wait it out a little longer!

Nothing is for sure yet but we are keeping our fingers crossed that the doctor agrees with the therapist and we might be talking and/or drinking by the end of the week! I will keep you posted!

Thanks for the prayers and thoughts!
Cindy and Doc

The Blackmore Family, 2005

January 9-2005

This has been a good week! We finally have a week that we are making some strides! It seems like 4 months was a long time ago and sometimes it seems like yesterday! I can hardly remember what life was like outside the hospital but I am anxious to rediscover it.

I already updated all of you with the good news of the results of the swallowing test that Doc took on Monday. That was exciting for us and we were impatient for the doctor to finally give us his blessing that it would be ok to try eating some ice chips. Then to finally get to deflate the cuff in order to make a few words was awesome! On Wednesday, Doc got to say his first words in 4 months and it was wonderful-He did indeed say those 3 magic words, "I love you". They did 30 minutes of therapy and it was more like a loud whisper but they said that was normal and that it would get stronger until it was finally his voice again. Now they do three 15 minutes sessions a day and will increase that this coming week. Thursday they started the ice chips which will lead to drinking and eating someday. The someday varies which each patient so they won't say how long they think it will take but at least we are heading in the right direction. I am not sure that I actually had permission to keep shoving ice chips down him all weekend but I did! I figured I would increase it by a couple each day and so far we are doing great!

They are putting together a plan to submit to insurance to justify a request for more rehabilitation. It sounds like discharge will be pushed out a little bit and there is a chance I can take Doc home eating and/or talking! That would be great! In the meantime, maybe there is even more to this than meets the eye and we will also be in the right place for the diaphragm to kick in and then they can start to wein him off the ventilator and help him to learn to breath on his own again. All of this would be great and I think it is just a matter of timing!

We talked to the neurologist this week and based on all the testing they have run on Doc since his halo came off, he has concluded that the damage that set Doc back was indeed due to the damaged artery in his neck and he thinks it was injured initially and then he suffered a small stroke at the base of his brain due to the blood supply being deminished. When he suffered the stroke, things started to shut down because that caused more injury above the initial spot. He was excited at what Doc has going on as far as sensations and swallowing goes because he said that is very hopeful. It is an injury that can or cannot mend….just takes a lot of time! In the meantime, he has to take an aspirin a day for 6 months! At least he won't have any headaches for awhile!

Besides the talking and swallowing exercises, Doc continues to have sensation in his shoulders, chest, and back. Along with that, he continues to feel his muscles in his legs and he has feeling in his feet. Occasionally, he feels them taking blood pressure in his arm. He also has pretty consistent sensation on his lower stomach muscles. There still isn't any movement and the sensations still come and go BUT it all is sooooo much more than we had 3 weeks ago that we celebrate all of it as heading in the right direction! We have to remember that they told us it would take at least a year to see what the recovery would be and we have just been at it 4 months!

Now I have to slip in something that was pretty nice for me.... Doc had a tech one day (Jim) that was giving out back and neck massages (that he used to do for a living while on the armed forces medical team) in exchange for the nurses helping him with his duties (like making beds and stuff). Anyway, they were all doing "tech" work and telling me why when I happened to mention that I had never had a professional massage. Within minutes, Jim was being dragged into the room to give me my first professional massage! The first thing he asked me do was remove my sweater (I did have a shirt on under it) and you should have seen Doc's eyes! Jim must have caught the look because he told Doc not to worry because he knew what he was doing and Doc could watch him to make sure he was on the up and up! Doc kept an eye on him, which I am glad of because when he gets his arms and hands back, I am hoping he remembers how to do it because it was wonderful!!! I had a shoulder that had been hurting for a week or two and it hasn't hurt since!

On Tuesday morning, we had our final surgery in the series of what he needed for inserting tubes and stuff and I am glad that we are past all those. For the past 2 months, I have been wearing his wedding band on a chain because they didn't want it on his finger with impending surgeries. They can't have any jewelry on during surgeries & his ring was too tight to take on and off. So I have been wearing it around my neck so he can see it each day but I am so afraid that I am going to break the chain or something and lose it. We will both be glad to have it back on his finger! I am just waiting on some swelling to go down so I can slide it back on!

On Tuesday afternoon, we went to wheelchair maintenance class. The things that I know now! I call learning about bearings and batteries BORING! I made Doc pay close attention because it was more up his alley than mine! If something goes wrong, he will just have to help me fix it. Now after we left there is a "rest of the story". Todd, the guy that took us through the training, had just told us how people put things on the wheelchair that don't go on it and then they forget and sometimes things get smashed or leak water and then the wheelchair has problems. We went upstairs right after this class was over and I reclined Doc's chair for his weight shift and completely forgot that I had thrown an extra battery on the back of the chair because it was too heavy to carry. Needless to say, I smashed the battery into a motor box which caused the motor to start to grind and as it wasn't able to move, it started to smoke and smell! No matter how hard I tried to bring the chair upright, it was STUCK! I even laid on the ground and tried to pry it up with my feet...about this time, Todd walks in the room and asks what in the world I am doing...I have to tell him the story and he proceeds to laugh and while I am pushing the back of the chair up, he manages to release the battery. Everything ended up being ok except that I was pretty embarrassed. Then, yes there is more, we head over to the apartment and I unlock the door, throw my purse and key on the bed and hold the door open for Doc to wheel in. About the time he reaches the end of the hall, I hear his vent alarm go off so I think I should check it out. Needless to say, I allow the door to shut behind me and we are locked out (with the message on the vent being "low battery"! So we have to venture down to the lobby and call security to come over and unlock the door (in time to get him plugged in and all is well!). All Doc was said that he figured something like this would happen. I am not sure what he meant but I think he implied that he was just waiting for me to do something silly....I am just really glad that I did not disappoint him!! I am also glad that I fit it all into one evening so that I don't have on-going days like that one!

Friday night was one of the scariest moments of my life! We were sitting the apartment, watching some golf on tv, and Doc did a weight shift when the bracket broke on his vent tray and if fell off the back of his chair. It started to sound an alarm but that was ok at first because I thought it just needed some of the usual attention but I could not find the problem and I could tell that it was not giving Doc any air. Doc was telling me that he wasn't breathing and then he passed out on me! All the time I was desperately trying to figure out why the stupid vent wasn't working! I finally gave up on trying to fix the problem and I grabbed the manual air bag and started pumping air into Doc's lungs. He rolled his eyes around and focused them on me and pasted his usual smile on pretty quickly! I was so scared that I was going to lose him in my apartment after all we had been through! I should have known better! Anyway, in between squeezing the air bag, I managed to get my cellphone (thanks to all of you that are taking care of that because it really was a life saver that night!) and called the hospital. (I now have a greater respect for what the guys did that night on the mountain!) They sent over some nurses right off and between the 3 of us, we kept Doc bagged while we pushed him back to the hospital. Once there, they hooked him up to his regular ventilator in the room and all was well. They took the portable one and ran a test on it and found out it had two problems (both of them undetectable by just looking at it...so at least I was relieved that it wasn't something that I had done! (my track record is not always good!) Doc seemed to have no problems with the incident but I told him that I either needed to find a corner to cry my eyes out in or I needed to call a friend. Luckily, I found a friend (thanks Carol!) that talked with me for a little while and then I was fine! God has too big of a plan in store for us than to have let a little problem with a vent interfere! I wasn't thinking clear enough to remember that at the time though!

We did have some fun moments this week. On Thursday night we went to the movies and then on Saturday we went to another museum and it was a good day!

I guess there have been some on-going parties happening at our house! Thanks to all of you that helped with the cleaning and remodeling! I did get an e-mail from one of my brothers that said that every time a group gathers in our house, it rings with laughter as they move my junk from room to room and recollect all the memories that my "junk" reminds them of. He wrote that Doc had to be a saint or blind in love to let a wife buy and/or keep that much junk and set it around! I say that if it makes people smile, then it isn't just "junk"! I say that it is very "special stuff"! I did read his e-mail to Doc and Doc just said he was "blind in love". I think this means that I can keep buying and/or saving my special stuff!

So far 2005 has treated us pretty good and I hope it has been a good start for all of you! I will keep you posted with our discharge date when I know it. The last I heard, they have tentatively moved our discharge date to the end of the month but haven't specified a specific day yet. We found out this week that almost every piece of our equipment has not even been ordered yet. It would be hard to go home without equipment! Especially some of it! Combine that with the fact that we are making some forward progress, I think we are here for a little while longer!

I do have to say thank you to a lot of you on the discharge issue too! Craig usually sends a couple of persons home with the discharged patients to make sure that their home environment and homecare meets their expectations before they officially discharge the patient. Our team met with the supervisors of the various departments and it was decided that after knowing us, seeing the amount of mail and visitors that we have been getting and watching what we have learned, they are not going to send anyone home with us. (this reminds me, we had to go to a "social class" this week to talk about socializing after we are discharged and the therapists were laughing about us having to go to that because they have been watching our family and friends come & go and they are sure that we don't have a socializing problem!)—I think they are right! Anyway, they feel like we have the appropriate support at home and they will make Doc's discharge effective upon leaving (although they told me this before my experiences Thursday and Friday! Hehe!) AND they are going to let me bring Doc home in the van so we don't have to fly. I will just have to pray for good weather on the day that we leave. (unlike this week…we had a huge snowstorm on the same day that I think Missouri was having a huge ice storm!—I would rather have the snow but I don't want to drive home in either one!).

We continue to pray every night and every morning for courage to face whatever we are supposed to deal with for the day. We don't even look to tomorrow anymore but take each day as it comes! I have found life to be much easier that way! We also include all of you in our nightly prayers too! Thanks to all of you that are praying for us! It feels good to share our good news with you this week because you have stayed right with us through the bad weeks too!

Your Friends in Denver,
Cindy and Doc

January 16-2005

And the adventure continues....it is amazing how one little word can make you look at something differently. We had a friend that answered our update from last week on how she looks forward to reading our adventures. To me an adventure is a wonderful trip or discovery into something. (that being a fun or exciting time!). I never thought of our current situation as being an adventure but it really is! Everyday, something happens that causes us to laugh or cry or worry or celebrate! Life for each of us in an adventure with different settings! That put a different light on the situation so now every morning, I think of what is going to happen in our adventure today! It makes it sounds like a temporary trip that will come to pass which is what it really is. We will not be stuck in Denver or the hospital forever! That adventure will be over in the near future and then we can start another one! So, now that I have typed that, I bet you are dying to know what adventures we had this week!

It was a very busy week of classes and rehabilitation stuff. Doc continued to work on eating those ice chips and deflating the cuff and working those vocal cords (we are up to 30 minutes/time, 3 times a day). I think we started each day with a class at 9 a.m. (which is early because we have to start getting up at least an hour before we have to be up—it takes awhile to get dressed and moved into the chair!). When he can actually eat breakfast, we are going to have to start even earlier than that! Then we didn't finish most days until after 5 p.m.. I know that is a normal "working" day but somehow these type of days seem longer and harder than work ever seemed. By the end of them, we are both emotionally and physically drained! Our normal day ends by getting Doc ready to take a shower around 8:30 or 9:00 and then he usually gets to bed around 9:30 or 10. I usually head back after I am sure he has made it to the shower. Then I finish up some work on the computer and take care of the mail and stuff and am ready for bed by 11 or so.

On Tuesday we had our monthly review meeting with our whole team and they informed us that our newest formal dismissal date is February 11th. They also told us that they thought Doc was making great strides with his talking and swallowing but that they did not think he would be eating or talking before we go home. They didn't want to take away from the fact that he is on the road to achieving that and that they thought he would even be much closer by that date but they also wanted us to know that it wasn't in the plan to be completed before we come home. It might be possible but it would be a slim chance. They also told us Doc was short on blood again. They gave him a blood transfusion on Wednesday and then they had a blood doctor look at him to evaluate why he keeps losing it but Doc & I were of the same opinion! We think it is all the blood with-drawals they take. It is sort of like a bank account…you can't keep taking and not giving without eventually running out! They didn't pay much attention to us but that's our story and we are sticking to it! (sounds like a good line to use in a song, doesn't it?)

Then Tuesday evening, we came over to the apartment and we had our usual "if it can go wrong at the apartment, it will" adventure! Doc was turning into the doorway when his wheelchair went into a really fast gear and stuck! He went flying across the room and he spit the sip & puff control out of his mouth, which is supposed to stop it but it didn't. Then I grabbed the control which is supposed to be the emergency stop and it didn't work either. So Doc hits the wall and then his wheelchair actually starts to climb the wall and his chair is quickly standing on its back wheels! I was scared that it was going to flip him and I can tell you that it is hard to hold a 420 lb chair from doing what it wants to do! I tried though! Anyway, I found the switch to his control box and flipped it off and that seemed to work (stopping him in midair). I pulled the chair back into the middle of the room and slowly turned everything on preparing for it to take off again but it didn't. If Doc wasn't there to see the same possessed chair that I did, I would have thought I imagined it all! Anyway, it didn't do it anymore since so I am not sure what happened but again, we made it through it. I bet the people in the hospital sometimes think we make up these stories!

Wednesday evening, Doc actually talked on the telephone to a few persons while his cuff was deflated. He said it was challenging trying to time the conversation with the flow of air through the trach and his voice is still more like a whisper but I think those that talked to him were just glad to hear him making noise!

Thursday was a big day because Doc had hunting and fishing lessons with puff and sip guns and fishing poles. Amazing technology involved! Fishing was the sport he was most interested in and we have our name on a waiting list to buy one. Craig actually has the design on this and they haven't patented it yet because they really want someone else to do it so they just hand out the design and hopefully, patients can find engineers to put it together for them. It is a pretty neat project actually! There are 2 engineers in the Denver area though that donate their time and I met one of them (Peter) and he said he really likes putting them together and trying to improve the design! He is currently almost done with 12 of them and all his labor is free so if I can purchase one of them for Doc, I think I am going to invest in it and then someday, if Doc doesn't need it anymore, I can donate it to Rusk and let someone else enjoy it. Otherwise, I will grab a copy of the design and talk one of my buddies at work into helping me make sense of it! Who knows, maybe we will be able to patent it! The biggest problem with it is that the parts are $500 and unless it isn't produced like prototypes, the cost would be too high! Doc was the patient they chose to demonstrate the sip and puff gun they had and that was neat to watch. They had a target set up at the end of the gym and Doc positioned the gun using his head and then you sip to pull the trigger. He had twelve shots and hit the bullseye with 8 of them! He has the target taped to his wall! That little treasure of a hobby starts at $600 and the guy that invented it does have a patent on it but he still hands out his design for free for anyone that wants to make their own or they can purchase it complete from him. Then later in the day Doc got to drink some apple juice (well, not actually drink because they gave it to him a teaspoon at a time!). His taste buds enjoyed that! They will continue to increase the consistency of things until he moves up to food. (they are hopeful that within the next week or two he will move up to sherbert or something like it!). Starting on Monday, he can have anything he wants as long as it is a thin liquid (just for the few of you that might be thinking beer, that excludes alchohol!). He has requested me to make sure we have some diet mountain dew and citrus v-8 on hand! He really wants some coffee but he said he doesn't want that until he can have a whole cup…he doesn't want to stop with just a teaspoon or two of coffee! (I personally think that even a teaspoon of coffee is too much!)

We had a visit from Ted and Theresa Sander this week and it was like a breath of fresh air to get some visitors from home! I think it had been exactly 12 days since our last Missouri guests! Anyway, it was short visit but I still stole my hugs before they left!

Friday we had an outing with a trip to the "stock show"…. Now this was a real adventure….who would think of combining hunting, livestock, farm equipment, Dodge trucks and a rodeo into one event? I would have to guess either Tim Myers (a friend and co-worker of mine) or one of my brothers! But, believe it or not, I think it was actually someone else's idea of a perfect day (and it must be a good one because it draws over 600,000 people and makes Denver over $80,000,000)! Needless to say, for those of you that can't read between the lines, it wasn't exactly the mall! They did some interesting booths though and some of it was pretty neat to look at! It was really crowded and not easy to get a wheelchair around in though! The rodeo was entertaining too! (did you notice that I left off the livestock, equipment and hunting stuff?) Now if Doc was typing this, you probably would have gotten a different perspective because I think he got more out of it than I did. (I was typing that last line and I have to smile because I got to thinking that I probably meant literally because I only had two feet to track the manure home with and he had 4 wheels!) The best part of it was that we finally had a day off from classes because the van left at 11 a.m. and did not get back until after 5 p.m.. Doc was wiped out though… it was a lot of sipping and puffing for the day!

We could have signed up for a leather craft session and a tye dye class this week but Doc passed up the opportunity! Imagine that! I think after that fleece scarf and pillow session, I have squeezed in my last craft class! We did go to the "horse" races though on Saturday night (for just a little bit though because the Rams were playing!-badly, I might add!). They have wooden horses with numbers on them that run a race with throws of the dice. Doc enjoys trying to pick the winning horses! Then when you win and you walk away with a bottle of shampoo or something, you just feel sooooo GOOD!

The biggest down side to the week for me was a stupid cold! I have been so glad that I have been blessed with good health through all this that I know I shouldn't complain about a cold but I will be glad when I feel good again! It is hard to keep up with our pace when you feel under the weather plus I worry being around the patients because I would hate to pass it along! I managed to squeeze a couple of hours to myself on Wednesday morning and I dashed to Wal Mart to load up with cold medicines and they helped. Then when I got back, Doc's doctor had noticed that I was under the weather and he left a prescription for an antibiotic on Doc's bed for me to get filled. I thought that was pretty thoughtful of him! Anyway, it is getting better so I guess something is working! For a while there I was competing with Doc on which of us could talk the loudest and I am not sure who was winning!

I know that several of you are praying for us (if not all of you!) and I have written in the past how we pray every night for all of you also! I have to tell you, though, Thursday night a great prayer was said because when they deflated Doc's cuff so he could talk with me a little bit, they actually left us alone and I asked Doc if he would like to say the prayer for us that night instead of me for a change. He wanted to and so we bowed our heads and Doc's weak, whisper of a voice sounded out our prayer and it was like music from heaven! The uplifting thing about it was the longer he went on with the prayer, the stronger his voice became until at the end of it, he was almost talking! We both felt the special blessing of that prayer and it ended with a special thanks that Doc was able to be the one saying it! What a wonderful couple of minutes!! I think it was the most special part of my week!

I am not sure if they will move our discharge date out again or not but I am going to assume that we are going to be home in 25 days from today but who's counting! Until then, know that we think of all our family and friends by the minute and can't wait to see you!

Cindy and Doc, Reporting live from Denver

January 23-2005

This was probably the most quiet week we have had since we got here. Well, not actually, because my talking has been cut by 35+ hours/week and Doc is getting to have his share of the time and then some! He continues to make progress by having longer and longer periods of time with his cuff deflated and his vocal cords working. His voice is getting stronger and stronger. His pulmonary doctor talked to us on Monday and he told us this Wednesday, they are going to make a decision on whether to change his trach out for one that would allow him to talk 24 hours/day or one that would allow him to talk all day and then put the cuff up at night (I don't think he is ready for the 24/7 one yet so I am betting on the other one!). Either one will give him a more normal voice because more air can flow through the vocal cords with them. I enjoy listening to him and I doubt that I will ever tire of him talking! (even if that means that I am being quiet!). He has been entertaining everyone and when other patients know that he is going to have his cuff down, they come to visit. Everyone enjoys his wonderful sense of humor and even Doctor Ripley asked him if he has always been this funny or if it is something new! I just tell everyone that it is the same Doc that I have loved for almost 27 years! If laughter is good medicine, you can find it in our room 3 times a day! Dr. Ripley calls him the hospital "sit down" comedian (in reference to the non-stand up ability!). *(just for information, for those of you that don't understand what taking the cuff down means, I will try to explain it as I understand it...there is a small balloon, called a cuff, in the trach that runs down to Doc's lungs. That balloon is kept up with air in order to keep things from falling into the lungs causing infections. As they determined that Doc is able to control what falls down the stomach tube vs. the lungs, they decided that it is safe to keep the tube open to the lungs. The cuff is above the vocal cords so that is why they can't work until the cuff is deflated. When the cuff is deflated, the air flows through the vocal cords and Doc can make vocal noises. They have to wein him up gradually because it has been 4 months since he used them and he has to build up stamina but he is doing great with it! He cannot breathe on his own at all yet, though, so keep in mind if you talk to him that he can only make words when the air is exhaling so he can only make part of sentence and then he has to wait for the ventilator to give him some more air before he can make more words. It is hard to get used to but we are getting there!)*

Back to my first sentence, the reason I said it was quiet was because we didn't have many classes. I think they have taught us most of what they can and we are just waiting on the speaking and eating rehab to continue while we wait on our equipment to come in. They have been working on teaching Doc how to use his mouth more, though, using a stick! As far as everything else goes, I think they have taught us everything they can until Doc gets some motion back in his muscles! We still have the same sensations but are still waiting on the motor skills! There will also be some additional training on the equipment but not until it comes in! I do have to add a little note here…until this week, Doc could not turn his head at all and his muscles in his neck seemed to not be working. This week for the first time, he turned his head slightly (and I mean slightly) to the left which was promising. Chuck, Doc's physical therapist, had an official name for the muscles but then he clarified it for me by calling it the shaving muscles (because that is the muscle that men tighten to shave their necks). I tried to flex those muscles in my neck but I only achieved making Doc laugh! I couldn't do it….I asked Chuck if only men had them because I don't shave and he at first he looked speechless and then he just told Doc he sure felt sorry for him! I never did get a straight answer! (I think it must be one of the 7 great mysteries in life!). I also told Chuck that it was ok if only men had them because as women, we shave under our arms so we must have some extra muscles there! Anyway, "speechless" Chuck is going to start working on the "shaving muscle" to try to strengthen it. It will be helpful to Doc using his "stick" if he could get a little head rotation!

In the meantime, we are just trying to get back into the real world. Our doctor has given us more liberties. We now have permission to leave the hospital campus without hospital personal (although we still have to have signed permission for each outing). We can still sign up for the hospital outings but we also have the liberty to schedule a courtesy van with a volunteer driver that doesn't work for the hospital but just volunteers to drive the van to wherever we want to go or to take a walk within walking distance of the hospital. Doc immediately asked me out on a date! (Doc asked me if he could drive instead of looking for a volunteer!) I told him that I have always thought his driving skills left something to be desired even before the accident and I was pretty sure that no legs and no hands would only make it worse but he said that he has always driven on our dates! He has been telling anyone that will listen that I won't let him drive us on our date Sunday! I asked him where we were going and he said he wanted to take me to the movies to see 'Racing Stripes'! So that was our first solo adventure that we drove to (although we were back in time to watch the all-important football games!). We also took a walk this week to Safeway to pick him up some things that he can eat now (smoothies, yogurt, and sherbert). It was about 7 blocks away and as the weather was sunny and 70, it was a beautiful walk! Then there is a division II basketball team in town that is the only division II basketball team in the nation to be undefeated (Metro College). Chuck is a good friend of the coach so it sounds like we are going to get some good tickets to one of their games the first week of February! I would rather be cheering for the Bearcats but until I can do that, I will at least be keeping up my cheering skills!

We were also moved from the 301B to a suite (room 323). They call it moving from the West side to the East side (at least that is the direction of home). The rooms are tiny but at least we are together (& without 2 other roommates). It has a microwave, apartment fridge, tv/vhs, and a fold out couch in the living area for me to sleep on and a bed in the bedroom area for Doc and a private bathroom/ shower. We have much more privacy and I have an opportunity to practice taking care of him with help only call away for a couple of weeks before we head home (although I have already been doing a lot of that!)! We also are saving the $30/night that we were paying on the apartment! It will be nice to have "our" own place again! It has only been a couple of nights but we are both really enjoying it!

Speaking of "our" place, I think our house is almost completely ready for us to come home! Thanks one last time (well, maybe not the last...) to EVERYONE that helped in getting it ready!!! We appreciated it all, from the driveway and pad that was poured for the van to unload the chair, to the ramps, to the construction, plumbing, electrical work, phone lines, painting, flooring and general cleaning that everyone donated so much time to! I probably will not ever know all of it! I am so excited to get home! I think Doc is too! We are in countdown mode! (only 18 more days!)

We are almost ready to bring the van out! Thanks to whoever ends up bringing that out (I think it is going to be Steve Wood)... (actually, thanks to several of you because we had more volunteers to do that that we had vans!). We also are hoping to have someone follow in a pick up truck to bring the van driver home and to haul home some of our accumulated "special stuff" or "junk" (as my brother would call it) and some of our equipment that Doc is going to need that we are getting donated to us! I am planning on sending home as much as I can with the truck so I don't have to worry about fitting it all into the van! I have a feeling just the basics, us, and Doc's chair are going to fill it up on the way home! It will be good to have the van out here for a little bit to allow us to practice loading into it and getting settled with how everything works. Then my brother is going to fly out (with donated frequent flyer miles-thank you) to drive us home. I think my sister-in-law is putting together these plans for us. I also have a friend (Ellen) that is flying out on the week we go home to go through some respiratory training and assist me on the way home. Doc is looking forward to having both of us to entertain him on the way home! (take my word for it!).

We did have an adventure last week that I neglected to write about but I thought with this being a slow week that I might throw it out there and let you all smile a little bit. We had to go to re-entry classes as they call them every day and for two days, it was on sex education I and II. It basically was to discover or re-discover that part of our world with our new situation. The problem was that it was like group stuff and we had 14 patients in there..2 of them women…12 of them men…out of the 12 men, 9 of them were under 20 years old and most of them had their parents in there with them. Needless to say, they really wanted us to ask questions and most of them, like myself, to be honest, had questions but didn't want group therapy on the issues! Anyway, it was pretty quiet during the first class and most of the young kids that were in the class had the best time after it was over teasing me that I probably was going to have a boring time of it after we got home because they noticed that

Doc had slept through almost the entire hour! I told Doc that was totally embarrassing to have him show so little interest and that he had better stay awake the next day ! So the next day we attend class and they want to start it out with questions and like the day before, no one wants to be the one to ask! With no questions being asked, they hand out a quiz with questions on it about what we covered the day before. Every time that you got a question right, you got a snickers candy bar. I am happy to report that my husband had a whole lapful of snicker candy bars by the time the quiz was over and after the class was over, he shared all his candy bars with all those young boys that were teasing us the day before (he couldn't eat candy bars anyway or he might have kept them)! I told them now I knew why my husband slept through the class....he already knew it all! Hehe Honestly, it has been a joy getting to know those young men and they will always hold a special place in our hearts! We have always loved young people and it was like a gift to have so many of them here with us even though it broke my heart to see such young persons struggling with what we are AND the fact that almost all of them resulted from auto accidents involving no seat belts and alcohol! They are a special bunch of boys and have been good medicine for Doc and I both! Almost all of them went home this week though and we will miss them! We will also miss our dear friends, Richard and Judy, because Richard and Doc had their accidents on the same day and have been with us through St. Mary's and Craig but we are glad for them to have gotten to go home. I know they are happy to be there!

Besides all of this, we also took a hospital outing to the movies on Thursday night to see 'Coach Carter'. Then on Friday night, we got to go to our first professional basketball game to watch the Nuggets. It was supposed to be a patient only outing but they had 2 patients that had to back out so they asked me if I would like to go. I was really happy to get to go..both to make sure Doc was ok (although I am sure he would have been) and because I have never been to a professional basketball game. It was really entertaining! On Saturday, he was up and at it early again because we were on another hospital outing to the mall. We wanted to window shop because we don't need anything else to haul home but I found out that I don't know how to do that. Doc says that I just know how to shop (no window to it!). We were sitting in our room one night and thinking about one of our days and I told Doc we had made another good memory. He eyes got a little watery and he said that at least we can still have fun! We do too! Life is what you make it and I told him I thought we would have "fun" until our dying day and hopefully, even that time should be rejoiceful! I remember sitting on a grassy knoll on the evening of Jerry Orscheln's funeral and watching a wonderful fireworks display and thinking of all the persons that were enjoying it and hoping that I would have that many smiles on the day they buried me!

I was also talking to Doc one night this week and I told him that I know everything is moving so slowly (at least to us it is-the doctors and therapists think we are making great strides!) but I still know in my heart that he will walk again and I was 99.9% sure of it! He just looked at me and said he was 100% sure of it! I won't explain all of the reasons why we think so but we have the faith that what we are going through right now will come to pass and then we will have another mission in store for us. So many things have happened to let us know this but the human side of us wonder occasionally if it is wishful thinking and then it is like something much more powerful than us reminds us that it will come to be! That is going to be the exciting part of it.

We did have a couple of visitors this week from some of our new Colorado friends and it was fun! Thanks for the company and the food! It will be great to go home with so many new friends. That has been one of the good things to come of all of this! Then my cousins Marvin and Alicia and their family stopped by to see us Friday and spent the morning with us! That was great!

On Sunday, I had to work with a nurse for awhile so she could explain all the supplies that we would need when we get home. They were making the first order for us but it will last about a week. It is amazing at how much stuff is on the list! Not only to see the list of supplies but to learn how to use them all! I continue to feel over-whelmed on some days at what I still need to know but I am hoping that once I get thrown out into the middle of the lake, I learn how to swim!

I can't think of anything else to add to this except that we are a little further east with our room change and a week closer to being home. Hopefully, the equipment issue will resolve itself because other than the diaphragm kicking in and being able to rehab the breathing (which would be GREAT!), the equipment issues will be what stalls us out on coming home. Just for the record, I didn't know that the power wheelchair was going to be delivered in pieces but it is. So far, we have 2 armrests and a headrest. If the rest of it makes it, we will be set (at least we will be if I don't have to be the one that puts it all together!). I am still waiting on the respirator equipment too because that will be pretty essential! We have the bed and a lift in hand so far and a shower chair on order. We are still waiting to find out if insurance will cover a back up manual wheelchair that we appealed and what respiratory equipment they approved.

Praying that everyone that reads this e-mail this week has a wonderful week and that you all slip in a prayer for us again when you think of us!

From a Spring like Denver (because the weather has been awesome!), Cindy and Doc

January 30-2005

We started out the week on Monday with one of those bumps in the road! The bump was that one of the spots that Doc had some minor surgery on has tested positive for some type of infection. (they call it VRE but that didn't mean anything to me!). Anyway, the infectious disease doctors have decided to treat it with 3 antibiotics for 10 days (at least they are through his stomach tube and not IV) and they are pretty sure that will take care of it. Until it clears up, everyone that comes in physical contact with him, in his room, has to wear a gown and gloves and the whole nine yards! It is just a precautionary measure to make sure that it doesn't get spread to other patients because it is highly contagious! He can still socialize with others and go to classes and stuff but no one is supposed to touch him without a gown if they are in his room. Out of his room, it doesn't matter....I know that it doesn't make sense but those are the rules!

They came in Monday afternoon and wanted to know if we would talk to Craig's Board and tell them our story on Thursday afternoon. They always pick 4 patients and ask them to share their story and their experiences at Craig & how they came to be at Craig. Then the board asks them some questions. I think they use it as a forum to see what is going on in the hospital. Anyway, at first we weren't sure if we wanted to do it or not but then we decided that sometimes you do things that you don't really want to because they might help someone else. It ended up being a good thing and we were both glad that we took the time to do it!

I always think there isn't much happening and then before I know it, we have packed our week full of activities! We even passed up making leather projects, guitar lessons, making miniature indoor gardens and facials. We did play Bingo on Friday night but I think Doc would have rather been watching basketball or something! He won 3 games though and I didn't win any so he should have been the one having a good time! I like to get out of the room occasionally and do other things and he just tags along. The suite is working out great though! It is nice to have a room to ourselves and Doc says that he really likes his new roommate! It is tempting to go back to your room after classes and watch tv or movies and just settle in for the night but I think it is important to get out and do things. I always try to get Doc out and make a tour of the 3rd floor to visit with some of the patients and tell them good night. You wouldn't believe how many of them don't have any family here with them and seem lonely! The bad part of that is that by the time we get our shower and meds in when we get back, it is usually close to midnight or after and we have taken a bite out of our night! The good part is that you feel like you might have brightened up someone's evening just a little bit.

After all the tons of education that we have already gone through, nursing has jumped into the picture now. As soon as we moved over to the East side, here come the nurses with all their stuff! Some of it is really helpful and pertains to actually taking care of Doc's needs. Some of it, however, it totally off base and is driving me crazy! They even have given us a 13 page test that we have to pass before we can be discharged and so much of it seems so irrelevant to me. It has diagrams that we have to identify body parts on and I feel like I am back in high school science class. I am not sure why it is necessary to know where all the internal body parts are located and what all their purposes are but they seem to think it is important. Maybe I am going to save us some money and become Doc's surgeon or something! That is scary!! I figured I just need to know what to look for to alert me that something isn't right and then a doctor would know a whole lot more than me. I think a better question would be 'what is your doctor's phone #?'! I told the nurses that I didn't mind knowing how to help take care of Doc but that I just want to be his wife…not his nurse or doctor! Anyway, Doc said to suck it up and finish the stupid test if that is one of the steps to getting discharged so we will! BUT I don't have to be happy about it! ☹

Tuesday was a HUGE day! We finished our classes at noon so we headed out in the beautiful Denver weather on a walk to Safeway to buy Doc some more assorted soft foods (and a cream puff for me.. yummm) (Doc especially wanted tapioca pudding). We found out that on Wednesday he was going to get mashed potatoes and gravy and on Thursday, he was going to get scrambled eggs and milk. A little bit later, they came in and told us they were removing his tube feeding altogether and letting dietary take over his diet (mostly with pureed food-yum yum) and let him start some serious eating. He was nervous about it but I don't think they are going to let him waste away! When they are sure that he can sustain himself, they will pull the tube out of his stomach and let that heal up! About an hour after that, they come in and tell us that they moved out our discharge date again. It is now scheduled for 2/24. They said that they are pretty sure that if we move it out until then, he will come home without a feeding tube in his stomach, with a trach that at a minimum would allow him to talk all day and possibly even 24/7, and as he gets his collar off on 2/8, they are pretty sure they can start working his neck muscles and get them strong enough to support his head and possibly even get some turning radius out of it. On the top of that, it will allow more time for his wheelchair to get in and allow us some time to make sure that it is in good working condition. In the meantime, we continue to pray for the breathing muscles to kick in also and then we could be working on that! We are happy with all the little steps though and we are glad to be working toward positive things! Our thankful prayer list is getting longer and longer!

Well, pureed food is everything we thought it would be. On Wednesday, Doc had mashed potatoes, peaches, orange cake, mixed vegetables, and cauliflower soup. I think the only thing that he liked a little bit even was the peaches. He did enjoy his chocolate pudding that I had stashed away for him though! I think I added that he actually ate only 500 of his required 1500 calories but then they brought him a power shake that is fortified with a ton a calories to make up the difference. He said it was better than the baby food vegetables and soup! As the week went on, the food got better. They started to find things that were real food that he liked better that they didn't have puree.

Our visit with the throat doctor on Wednesday morning went really well and he could see all of Doc's throat muscles, including the vocal cords for the first time since we got here. The doctor was really excited. He said everything was working with the right side being normal and the left side being a little weak but the main thing was that it was all working! He recommended staying with the trach that Doc has now and then when he can go all day with the cuff deflated in this one, changing to a smaller size. So now we wait until we can go all day without deflating the cuff. We are up to 2-4 hours sessions and later in the week they are going to try to do a straight 8 hours, moving up an hour at a time from there! It will nice to have him talking more often (especially on outings!). On top of that, I have officially been cleared to do the cuff deflations myself so we don't have to wait on respiratory when we want to go up or down with the cuff. (or up with the cuff as the case may be…I bet Doc would like to be able to take a small syringe once in awhile and close up my vocals too…but alas, that isn't an option-lucky for me!)

Speaking of outings, after our board meeting presentation on Thursday afternoon, we departed for Cherry Creek Mall. That was an enjoyable outing. I think it might be our last mall outing before we go home though, because like the little craft classes, I have dragged Doc through his last shopping trip! Darn the luck! Plus, he has bonded with so many of the Rec. Dept. people (including Joe, the manager) that they set up most of the February outings with things that they had Doc in mind for. So, that means that I am going to get to participate in some awesome outings like target shooting at the local shooting range with a puff & sip gun, going to an arena football game, going to fishing classes, a wheelchair basketball game, an actual hunting trip on the 20th and finally last but not least, attending a game between the Wings and Rockies (and we don't even know what the game is...Doc says it is too early to be baseball so I don't even know what it is...All I know is that it is some type of sport! Yippee!). Now I have to be honest and tell you that Doc told me that we could sign up for a movie outing too so he was generous enough to think of me on one day of next month! We are also signed up for a pancake dinner on the 10th and as he is scheduled to have pancakes on Tuesday, I think that will be a go! I will keep you posted on all of these EXCITING adventures that we will be partaking of in the next 3 weeks! I know a bunch of you women out there are really jealous that I am getting to do those thing and that some of you men out there are wondering how Doc has lasted through this many malls and craft classes! See what happens when he gets a voice?

Oh Yeah, the Rockies....The team came to Craig to meet with some patients and Doc visited with the shortstop, center fielder, and 3rd baseman. They gave him an autographed hat and he just smiled at them and asked them if they ever heard of Larry Walker because he is on "our" team now! He is a character and I am glad those 3 guys had a good sense of humor!

We found out about mid-week that they had an outing on Friday scheduled for bowling. They wanted us to sign up for that and Doc said he thought it might be hard to grip the ball but they told him they had a way for him to bowl using a special piece of equipment that slides on his chair. So he decided he wanted to go and we were all set to leave the room on Friday morning when they came in and said they had canceled the outing for us because Doc's lab work came back saying his blood was too thin. They were afraid that if there was an accident on the way that it would be critical so we ended up missing out on that. We ended up chilling in the room for the day and watching movies. He had a little spell where he was pretty mixed up during the afternoon so I was glad that we were in a hospital and not a bowling alley. Doc was disappointed not to bowl but it just wasn't a healthy day!

We received a call Saturday night telling us that the fundraiser that was held at Heartland for us was a huge success. We were speechless and once again, I am saying thanks to all of those that supported that evening and I hope everyone had a good time! We wish we could have been there! A special thank you to Heartland for donating the food and to those of you that put a lot of effort into planning it! It is amazing at how every single time we get a bill on something insurance doesn't cover or notice that we have to purchase something, almost the exact amount of money needed just shows up! I know it is being heavenly sent to us through all of you! But even more endearing to us than the money raised, was the mass amount of family and friends that we had that came out to support it! You will NEVER know how much it warmed our hearts to hear of the huge turnout! It is especially heart warming to know that we have so many that are still in there with us even though we are pushing on the 5 month anniversary of the accident! Thanks for hanging in there with us!

We had a wonderful visit from a friend and co-worker of Doc's on Sunday. Jesse Burton and his wife, Barb, stopped by and passed some time with us. I wanted to leave this next part off but Doc wouldn't let me. Their story is that we played pitch and that Doc and Jesse won. So they wanted everyone to know that "A" shift can still play pitch! Our story is that we tied 11-11 (we aren't talking about the 2nd game!) and they came up with the bidder wins in a tie! Imagine that...I thought that rule only applied when it worked for me! Anyway, they left in the afternoon and were nice enough to haul home some of our stuff that we would want to make sure to keep dry and not have on the back of a truck. Now, we are looking forward to a visit from some more of the guys that Doc works with that are dear friends to him that are bringing out the van and then hauling back our bed on a truck! They will be here very late on Wednesday night but we will get to visit with them on Thursday for a while! Doc is really looking forward to that and we are hoping that therapy will work with us and give us the morning off to visit with them!

I know that my high school and college math teachers are going to wonder how I can take the number of days until we get to come home from last week's e-mail and subtract another week and end up with a higher number but that was what happened this week. With the new date, we now have a count down of 24 days until we come home! MAYBE…because Doc is telling everyone that he is going to start breathing on the 20th and then we are going to have to stay longer! As much as I want to get home, I like his plan!

We continue to know in our hearts that prayers are making a difference so we continue to ask for them! Someday, Doc is going to 'stand' up and we will be telling our story of how it happened (through the power of prayer!). It is easy to go through this knowing that!

Thanks to all of you,
Cindy and Doc

PS: This is for Janet…Doc says your cookies are going to be much longer for the waiting and he is planning on eating them someday so be ready to bake!

February 2-2005

This e-mail is going to be an extra e-mail this week with a special thank you to all of you that have done something special and we haven't said thank you! If this is a repeat thank you, it's ok because I don't think we could ever say it enough! I continue to hear about things like, "did you hear what so and so did?", or "did you know what so and so donated?" and so on and so on! I try very hard to thank every one of you for any of the special things but just in case I left any of you off because I either forgot to say thanks or I just don't know what you did yet, I am saying thanks! I've probably made a mistake in trying to list them all but here goes.....

- To my cousin Tammy for her solid support on the night that it happened (and since then!) and for getting me & Adam on the plane to get here! And then to her family for paying for the tickets!
- For my brothers and Mike S for keeping Doc alive until the ambulance could get there!
- For my cousins in Colorado and how wonderful they have been in supporting us while we were here (even providing Doc with a Bronco hat!-a definite sign that we have been here too long!).
- This thank you includes all the special things that were done on the house modifications, generator and the driveway. (too many involved to name all of you..but especially Devenport

Construction, Orscheln Properties, Orscheln Products, Co-Workers, Friends, Barry, Charlie and my family)

- To Macon REA for helping with the water heater and the rest of their support!
- To Missouri Western and East Central Colleges for the support that they have given our kids when they knew we weren't there to help if they needed it! (especially Dr. Neil and Jay Merhoff)
- For the offices of Dr. Maddox and Dr. Furhman and all of their kindness.
- For all of the churches that added Doc to their prayer list! I truly am amazed out how non-denominational prayer is! Which religion we choose to worship under does not stop us from praying for the same things!
- the van (including the buying of it, modifying it, the licensing of it, detailing it, and delivering it to us) (Thanks Tara for calling us!)
- to Doug Sharpe for keeping our heat pump filter cleaned and for letting us use his truck to haul a bed home
- for those that gave money to the gang that brought the van out for gas and their expenses
- for those that mowed our grass when it needed it
- the fund raisers (those that organized them, participated in them, donated things to them, attended them)

- the deposits made straight to our account that we don't even know where they come from
- the phone calls just to say and hi and check on us! Especially those that called on a frequent basis to check on us (Brenda, Lori, Pam, Carolyn & several of Doc's buddies!) It is especially good now that Doc can talk!
- the e-mails from so many of you! Many of them giving me great inspiration or a hug when I need it!
- For the care packages that came from Missouri that added some "home" atmosphere to my apartment and Doc's room! (I will never forget the initial care boxes from Orscheln the first week that this happened and I wondered how would I need all that? Now I know…I have used everything!)
- the countless visits from all of you that made the trip to Colorado or for those of you in Colorado; the trip to the hospital
- the donated frequent flyer miles that allowed our kids to visit (twice) and will bring my brother out here when it is time to drive us home.
- the special letters and cards (especially I wanted to say thanks to Marge Gibson and Bill for keeping us updated on the Cairo activities…it is wonderful at how you keep us in contact with HOME with so many cards and letters, and to Martha Link for all the weekly church bulletins and updates from that area of our lives. Thanks to the Cairo/Jacksonville church for

sending us the bulletin keeping us updated with that part of our world and to all the videos and cards from our St. Pius and Immaculate Conception families!) Also, there are those that have diligently sent us a card every week just to let us know they were still praying and thinking of us (The Chism family especially comes to mind!)—that adds up to at least 22 cards so far! I would call that dedication!

- I also wanted to say thanks to Sandy Henderson because barely a day goes by that I don't get an e-mail that just says hi!

- For our kids and their wonderful support to their parents! For growing up and handling so many of your problems on your own! We are proud of you!

- To my cousin Lisa, for her wonderful jokes that Doc is still waiting on to be funny! :)

- To our new Colorado friends that bring me food at the hospital and give us company. (there are several of you but especially Ditta, Patty, and Catherine).

- To our good friends that we met through St. Mary's (Shelly, Fred, Irene and Fred) for all their prayers and support! They have become like family to us! Especially a heartfelt tear goes out to Kenessa who lost her battle to hold on to John but knows he is in a wonderful place now.

- To our St. Mary friends and their continued support, including beautiful poems that Terri sends to us, calls & songs from Mary, and special notes from Corene, Pam and Dena! To the coat that Chris donated to us so Doc would be warm when his halo was on and we wouldn't have to cut up his good one! To the cookies that Janet promised Doc that he will be able to eat soon. To all of our caretakers while we were there because they were awesome! A special thanks to Teresa and Dane for their wonderful gestures of caring!

- To other Craig patients and their families that have become our friends: I hope we have given you has much inspiration as you have given us. (Richard /Judy; Mike/Lynelle; Collin/ Judy/Ed; Shawn/Trudy!)

- To Orscheln Products for sending me a laptop that has allowed me to continue to do a little work (a good release for me) and for staying in contact with all of you! That has been a lifeline for me!

- To our wonderful co-workers and all they are doing to make this as easy as possible. Including the payroll deduction that the AECI co-workers are participating in and those at Orscheln that are taking care of our cellphone (that literally helped save a life one night!). And for all the things and time that many of our co-workers and places of employment have donated and volunteered to do.

- For everyone that sent something that made Christmas a wonderful time for us!

- On top of all of this, we need so say an extra special thanks to our family! I can absolutely tell you that they are WONDERFUL!

We are very proud of our families! This includes all of you!!!! We love you!

- For the Cairo School community and all that the kids and faculty have done there to make sure that we have not been forgotten!

- To our fellow square dancers and Friday night golfers! Thanks!

- And then there are those that have allowed me to call them and cry if I needed to and were just there when I needed them. (including those that gave up precious vacation days just to visit when I called and said I needed them!). (Ellen took care of most of these calls but there were a few others that gave me a shoulder once and awhile too!)

- There are all the persons that have written to volunteer to help and really meant it—if you haven't gotten to help, just know that asking was enough and there is still going to be many needs when we get home and I remembered those that offered!

- For all those that volunteered to help with Doc when we get home and get him transferred into bed, out of bed, and to spend some time with him during the day! For those that are helping me find others to help care for him while I am at work.

- I know that the floor was put into our house this past weekend and for all that worked on that, thanks!

- I know the ramps were put in this weekend and we wanted to say thanks to AECI for the material and then to all that welded them, painted them, and installed them.

- For all the help that I have been getting from those that pick up and forward our mail (Kim), help us with insurance problems (Kent, Jennifer, and Connie), send e-mails to make sure that Doc has all his paperwork in line through work for whatever issues come up, and for those that are helping cover my share of work at Orscheln's while I am not there! (Mike, Lin and Brad)

- To Tom and Sue Bisch for taking over our adoration hour at St. Pius until we can get back! I am glad that it was you!

- We wanted to say a special thanks to Father Mike and to Father Plough for everything that they have done for us! You have given us many blessings!

- To Craig hospital and all that they have donated to us as far as equipment goes and in helping Doc recover some independence and giving us a chance at some good times until things can be more normal! Also to those that went the extra mile and took time out of their personal lives to bring something home cooked to Doc or by treating Doc to something special like coffee and banana splits!

- Something else that we are REALLY thankful for are the prayers and **especially thankful** for those that are praying that have told me in the past that they aren't sure if there is a reason to pray! I also wanted to say thank you for those that share the faith that this is going to come to pass with us! Sometimes, it is hard to believe but that is what faith is all about!

I am sure that I am still leaving off all kinds of things and I guess the whole purpose of this to let you know that even if we don't know what you did or we haven't said thanks, we appreciate it all and will be eternally grateful for all the kindness that has been spread our way! I know that I listed a few by name and yet there are a ton of you out there that called, sent me a book or a letter or whatever that I would want to say a personal thanks to but then this would just be an unending e-mail! Know that each of your names are swimming around in my head as I type this! I also wanted all of you to see what has all been happening even if you think you haven't done very much! I want you to see how important each of you have been and how vast this entire experience has been so far and it's not even over yet...*even if it is just that you look forward to reading the e-mails so I have a reason to write them*! I typed this list partly to say thanks and partly so that some day I can look back and never forget all that happened!

I had an e-mail this past weekend that said that they have never seen anything like the way our community is rallying around us to help us get home and I just wrote her back that I think our community should be an example to our country at how family and friends can and do support each other in times of need! That is going to be a great part of our story someday! Pretty overwhelming isn't it? I know that I did not cover everything but when you read this, you have to think, *wow*..... I know we do! I have never questioned why this had to happen to us but I have questioned why we would be so worthy as to be chosen to go down this path...maybe it is because we have such wonderful family and friends to support us! Thanks to all of you! Love, Cindy and Doc

February 6-2005

This week started out with a trip to the Swedish Hospital Coffee Shoppe and Amy, our Occupational Therapist, treated Doc to his first flavored coffee since the accident. You could see on his face how much he enjoyed that! It also started with a solid meal of green beans, baked potato, and ribs....NOT PUREED. Doc handled all of it well so they gave him waffles the next day. That went well too, so they upgraded him to what they call soft mechanical. That is "real" food! Dietary told him to stay off the tube feeding, he would have to eat ½ of the stuff on his trays. He struggled with that because it took so much effort to chew and swallow but he was working through it. Doc thought that it would be great to be able to eat again and I think it was, but it was also a lot more work than he thought it would be! If you haven't caught on yet, I am talking in past tense because Friday night we hit a snag! All day on Friday Doc had a pretty good fever and by evening, you could tell he wasn't feeling well at all. They started running blood work on him again looking for infections and stuff. Then they gave him some medicine (which they had changed to him swallowing so they could get away from the feeding tube). The medicine immediately started draining down his chest as it was seeping through the hole in his throat for his trach! I am not a nurse or doctor (yet) but I knew that was not a good sign! I called the nurse and she came in to look at it and you could tell she was more than a little concerned. She got on the phone to the doctor and they are afraid that Doc has aspirated some of the food to his lungs and that is what is causing the fever (they are running tests on Monday for pneumonia). They aren't sure of the how or why and won't be until they finish the testing but in the meantime, his cuff is back up and he isn't allowed to talk. They have taken him off his food diet and have hooked up the tube feeding again. The doctors are hopeful that it is just a temporary set back but was disappointing to us both! They said that first they need to figure out what the problem is to fix the fever, find out what caused it, and then start taking steps in the right direction again! One step forward and then two back....sometimes it is hard to understand why the path has to be so bumpy but as long as we make it to the end of it someday, we won't care how bumpy it was!!! We will just be glad to have made it to the end!!!

There were many highlights in our week. Jen, our speech therapist, took Doc & I to an ice cream shoppe on Tuesday night and bought us a banana split for supper (it was HUGE and I am glad we shared it!). You should have seen the look on Doc's face...it was seeing a little of heaven! I really enjoyed watching him. It is funny how many times I have found reasons to take pictures! All the little accomplishments are like doing it for the first time again and they are all "Kodak" moments!

I snuck out early on Wednesday morning to do a little Wal Mart shopping (I have some nieces having some birthdays this month so there is some important stuff to take care of). Plus there are a couple of kids that are here that we have grown close to that have their dad here and we wanted to get them something for Valentine's Day.

Anyway, I was hoping they would get Doc up and going but they didn't do a very good job. When I got back, close to 10, he was still in bed and hadn't had breakfast. He was really bummed because Jess & Barb Burton had stopped by to tell him good bye before they headed back to Missouri and he had to spend that time just getting up! It all worked out though and we ended up being a little late for a technical class but we still made it.

They tried to get some software to work on the computer that Doc's voice would activate but they couldn't get it to recognize Doc's voice. Either they were having a problem with the software or Doc's voice is still too weak. They are going to work on it and get back with us sometime before we go home. I hope they can figure it out because it is a pretty cool tool.

The Infectious Disease doctor came by on Wednesday night and told Doc that he would have the VRE infection for quite awhile but it would have to be something that his body would just work through. As far as any other infections that he had, they are all cleared up and he was going to sign Doc off as being completed from his end. That was before our Friday disaster! Now he is back on our team and looking for reasons that Doc has a fever again! He has found them in the past so I hope he can find it again! As I said earlier, they are almost certain that it centers around the lungs this time!

We passed up the opportunity to make homemade Valentine Day cards (I didn't even mind missing this one!), clay class, and making masks for the Mardi Gras celebration that they are having later this month! (I actually didn't mind missing any of these!).

We cleared Thursday morning and Doc was almost feisty the way he was telling his nurses that they better not schedule any tests for Thursday morning because he wouldn't go! He had some friends visiting from Missouri and he would not be available until after lunch! I enjoyed watching him in action because he is usually so laid back that I think they were surprised! He had four of his friends/ co-workers (Woody, Harland, Victor, and Bear) that made the trip and it was everything that Doc thought it would be. They had to head out at noon though and I think Doc wanted to just keep them here until the 24th! (At least that was what he told Jesse and Barb!). Anyway, we loaded up the bed and several boxes and they made a good haul back to Missouri in Doug Sharpe's truck! I still have a bundle of stuff here but with almost 3 weeks still left (and possibly more if Doc would pull off that breathing thing!), I had to hold on to more than I would have if we had kept our 2/11 date.

They left us with our van and it was nice to finally see it! We both thought it was beautiful! Again, a big thanks to ALL that helped with getting that here (from calling to tell us about it, taking care of the license, modifications, detailing it (Cottingham's), the fund raisers that paid for it, and for getting it here!). It took a great deal of work from several persons and I just wanted to let you know that we appreciated it! Thursday afternoon, we experimented getting in and out of it and it was a little tight but we will get better with more and more practice. We know it will work and now we just have to use it! Before we know it, we will be burning some of the rubber off the new tires as we drive it back across Kansas!

Our speaking was coming along. Doc had gotten up to almost 7 hours without any breaks before they put a hold on it. Hopefully, as I already wrote, the problem won't be serious and he will be free to talk to me again soon. After we have had a taste of it, I will really miss it! We loved our time to talk and to be able to make phone calls and tell others hi!

Thursday night, Craig offered free 15 minute professional messages to family members only. I wasn't going to do it but Doc talked me into it so I gave it a shot! I have to admit that I was pretty relaxed by the time the massage was done and bed sounded good. Being relaxed and going to sleep must have something in common! Unfortunately, I had to wait another 3 hours before I made it to bed but it was still a good feeling!

Friday was our biggest adventure for the week. They almost canceled it on us because of Doc's fever but when he threatened to go AWOL, they gave him a little slack and turned their heads on his fever and let him go. We went to a shooting range and Doc had a good time shooting targets! Everyone there was so anxious to help him and they didn't charge us anything-the owner said that he would rather have a million Doc's having the courage to get back into hunting after his ordeal than a million paying customers-I think he meant it too! You could tell that Doc just wasn't feeling well though so it didn't take long for him to give up but he got his target to take home with him and he made 4 of 4 good shots! After we got back, he was pretty much done in and that is when the sad part of our adventure started!

Jason Watkins had come by to eat some pizza with me on Thursday evening though so I was glad to have someone to sit and watch a movie with us as we went through all our ordeals! It was good to see him! He still introduces himself to the nurses as one of our neighbors so living in Denver doesn't change that! I think we both think of him still just being across the field!

I guess for me, it was a hard week just because we worked so hard all week to accomplish our eating and talking skills and then everything just collapsed! As usual though, someone was watching over me because I had several e-mails that had a nice note in them just for me! All of them combined to give me a huge hug and the stamina to keep going! You just do what you have to do to get through each day but sometimes it takes a little boost from someone and some of you knew the exact moment I needed that!

Now I have something for you to chuckle at...Remember last week when I was complaining about our wonderful adventures that we have in store for February? Remember when I said something about going to the Wings over the Rockies and I thought it was some sort of sport? Well, in reality, I found out that it was actually an air show. It is a show of airplanes flying with the Rockies in the background. Not that I am saying that I am going to get a whole lot more out of watching airplanes than a sporting event but I have to be honest and tell you that there is a little more diversity in our outings than I thought!

On Saturday, we had the opportunity to go to the arena football game but Doc & I knew that Trudy and Shawn (our newest friends from Arkansas) wanted to have a "date" to the game. (It worked out anyway because Doc was too sick to go anywhere on Saturday but we had volunteered to watch the kids!) Shawn is injured like Doc but is in a little different shape. He has most of his upper body and can breath but his vocal cords are damaged so he cannot talk or eat yet either. Anyway, they have 2 small children and are trying to go through many of the same things that we are while trying to keep up with homework and raising the kids in the apartment. You could tell that Trudy really was excited about having some time with just her and Shawn. Plus, we really like their kids. Patrick and Megan practically live in our room anyway! Most of the nurses here already think they are ours. They are 7 and 9 and are little chatterboxes! They fit right in our room….hehe (I mean with all the talking that Doc does you know!). They usually bring their math homework with them because mom doesn't know much about math and I don't mind it. In return, I think Trudy has made it her mission in life to fatten me up! She makes homemade meals in the apartment every evening and always brings me a plate. On top of that, there are many mornings that she is knocking on our door with breakfast for me on her way down the hall to Shawn's room. She is a nice person and is turning into a good friend! The kids and I played cards all afternoon and watched a movie. Doc slept through his share of the "babysitting" but he had a good excuse!

I had a good time driving the van to church Saturday night and then to Wal Mart to get a couple of things that I forgot earlier in the week. It felt good to have a vehicle to pile into instead of carting it all the way back. I also swung by KFC for a bite to eat before I headed back to the room. That was good too! Felt like I had a little freedom. Since the girls left, I don't think that I have been away from the hospital except on our "outings" and to go to church for an hour on the weekends (and that trip to Wal Mart earlier this week). I get the feeling that the nurses aren't very comfortable with a vent dependent patient on this wing. I can tell that most of them have very little experience with it and they rely pretty heavily on what I know.... sad isn't it? Doc dependent completely on what I know? He doesn't show any panic though...he only shows confidence and that helps!

Sunday, Doc felt a little better and it was good to see him smiling again. He watched the superbowl and I watched the commercials! They had a big party downstairs but Doc was hooked up to 3 IV's and we just didn't feel like dragging all that around with us! Plus, we had a relaxing time in the room together because for a change the nurses were leaving us alone! (they were probably all watching the game too!)

Only 17 days left until we cross the Missouri border. I feel like putting a sign on our door that says "Missouri or Bust!" I want to play that advent calendar thing that you do at Christmas and mark off a day each morning when I get up so I can see how close it is getting! As a matter of fact, I think I will!! Speaking of advent, we were here for that entire season and now we are already entering Lenten season with this Wednesday being Ash Wednesday! I just want to make sure that I am home before the end of this one!

In the meantime, there has been more stuff happening this week with Doc but none of it has been consistent enough to write about it. Most of it comes and goes but it is stuff that hasn't happened since September so please keep praying because something is working! I will tell you that the speech therapist and throat doctor both told us that what we have seen as far as Doc talking and eating is something like a miracle in itself and that they have never seen anything like it! (at least I hope that we continue along that path)! So I will pray that we get enough consistency with some of the other improvements that I feel like I can share them with you next week! By the time you read this, we will probably know for sure what is going on with the throat but go ahead and say that extra prayer if you don't mind because even if they identify it as not good, that doesn't mean that it can't go in the right direction again just as quickly!

Holding on to our faith and hope in Colorado,
Your friends,
Cindy and Doc

February 13-2005

Hello to all! I always was under the impression that Denver would have harder winters than Missouri and I was wrong. Denver has wonderful winters and every time I hear about how snowy, icy, gray, and cold it is there, I look out our window and see some wonderful sunny skies and the temperature rarely requires more than a jacket! I think Denver averages as many winter gray days as we do sunny days! I hope we drag this weather home with us next week!

Monday started out with a bunch of tests but only to find out what type of antibiotics that were needed to get rid of Doc's fever and attack the problem. They identified the problem as a form of pneumonia. They also put in a new feeding tube because the doctor said that even if Doc was eating a full diet, he still was planning on us going home with the feeding tube intact. He said that 3 months from now something could happen and that he would rather us have it and not need it than to need it and not have it. He also said that we will have to come back here in 6 months for a re-eval visit and if we haven't used it for awhile, it will be the first thing he pulls! That is our plan!

Then after Doc's afternoon IV, we headed to the movies for an outing. It felt good to get out of the hospital with Doc because he hadn't left his room in 3 days. Doc was ready to get out and do something! We didn't even know what movie we were going to go see but we didn't care. It ended up being "In Good Company" and we both enjoyed it although it was one of those that once you see it, it is enough…it's not a repeat type movie!

Tuesday, they started running tests to find out what caused the problem but the big test came on Wednesday. That was the day they ran the swallow test and as they had kept a hold on the eating and talking until after the results of that, we were anxious. Doc failed the swallow test because it showed food aspirating into the lungs (although they termed it a "trace") which surprised a bunch of persons. They don't know why he passed one and since then has gone backwards. I guess it is just one of those things. So the cuff is up, no more eating for awhile and he is back full-time on the tube feeding! That was disappointing to both of us! There is a new treatment, though, that they have just put into practice that is proven to have positive results! It isn't long term and they started it on Wednesday afternoon! The treatment is done once a day for an hour at a time. After 10-14 days of treatment, the patients that were close to having a good swallow usually make it over that hump. They say that Doc is a prime candidate for this and they are hopeful that this will make the difference. I am not sure about the timing because it is going to take us right up to our current discharge date. As if this didn't bum us out enough, we also found out when we got back to the room that they were waiting to tell us that Doc has a couple of bladder infections and one of them is very hard to treat. Our cross was heavy on Wednesday but I know there has to be a reason for the set back. As Doc said, take each day one at a time and don't give up! We are definitely becoming each others strength like never before! One of the nurses this week told us that over 90% of marriages end in divorce when a spinal cord injury occurs…if she is right it is an amazing statistic! It takes both of us to keep going each day and I praise God that our marriage is so blessed. We have always had the blessing of a good marriage and I am finding out every day how great that blessing really is!

The Wednesday morning news was probably the biggest downer that we had so far and I would have to say that if there was a day when we both hit bottom, that was it! As the day went on though, we had enough good things happening that I soon bounced back and refocused! I just thought that we should be thankful that they have a treatment to try that they have confidence in and that we are looking at only 10-14 days for possible results! Then later in the day, Doc went to physical therapy and he had gotten more range in his neck. Hopefully, the collar will come off in the next day or two and we can start building up the strength too! After that, the pulmonary doctor (Dr. Mountain-how appropriate!) came in to tell us that because the aspiration was just a "trace", he thought we could continue with the cuff deflations and talking. We just need to make sure we do a good suction before we lower the cuff and that we don't keep it down for too long! At least we can still visit. The infectious disease doctor came in to explain that while Doc has the potential in his bladder for the serious infection that I mentioned above, it hadn't activated. It is just lying dormant. He said that they are still working on trying to find an antibiotic that will work on it just in case it activates but we might not even have to be concerned about it. So if you do a count… we had two things to be bummed about and 4 things to be excited about. As usual, if you look for it, the good outweighs the bad!

Tuesday night was Fat Tuesday and they had a big Mardi Gras party in the Rec Room downstairs so Doc and I attended that for a little bit. We got some pretty awesome beads…but don't worry, we didn't have to do anything to earn them except just show up for the party! They served a bunch of New Orleans type food and it was pretty festive. The couple that hosted it was from New Orleans and she was a patient here last year and was disappointed that they didn't have a Mardi Gras celebration, so this year they came back and threw it themselves. She left in a halo and in a wheelchair and returned this year walking and 4 months pregnant. Pretty neat story! Anyway, they cooked all the food and rec department did a bunch of work to make sure the decorations were bright purple and green! It was neat although Doc was disappointed that he couldn't eat the crawfish! (I did not eat any for him either! I stuck with the jambalaya, which was good! I also got a naked baby in my bread pudding. I just thought all of them had a naked baby in it but then I found out later that there is just one in the cake and the person that gets it is supposed to be the one that does the cake next year! At least it wasn't what Doc thought it meant—I will leave that up to you to figure out!).

Thursday was national pancake day and again, we missed that party because Doc couldn't eat! He loves pancakes and I wasn't going to go and make him look at them! It is amazing how many of our activities centers around food! As a society, food plays a big part in almost everything we do!

Friday was another bowling outing. We signed up again to try it because we missed it last time due to Doc's blood being so thin. This time we got to go and I think Doc had more fun on this outing than any other. They have this cool piece of equipment that straps to his chair and it allows him to drive his wheelchair to the lane and with a quick stop, he can release the ball. It was fun to watch him having a good time but he wore me out! I played 4 games with him but on each turn, I had to load his ball on his equipment so it was like picking the ball up and down for 8 games for me! Then he wanted to play again so I let him play one more but I just helped him...I didn't play my ball! Doc scored over 100 every time and you could see as the games went on, he was learning where and how to release the ball better. He might someday get back to his old 170 average (or not!). We did have a bet and to be honest, I won but even on a good day he would have had trouble beating me because I had a 161 game which is really unusual for me. So now he owes me a Valentine dinner at the local ice-cream corner café. I wish he could eat with me but it doesn't sound like it will happen by Monday! He told me he was planning on taking me out to eat anyway and that is about the only place that I will let him "drive" to besides the hospital cafeteria and how romantic can that be? Plus, if we go to the ice-cream shoppe, he promised to buy me a double scooper for dessert!

By Thursday, the antibiotics seemed to be working and as of today, we have gone 4 days without a fever so I am hoping that is a sign that we have the infections under control (I am knocking on wood (my head) as I am typing this!) They told us that they would talk to us on Monday about how long he would have to stay on it but it sounded like if everything goes good, he is really close to coming off the antibiotics!

Now for the news that I held back last week....I think it is exciting but as usual, it is a seemingly slow process but Doc is wiggling his fingers and thumb on both hands AND his toes on both feet. I probably shouldn't use the verb "wiggling" because it is more like very small flickers of movement. The main thing is that he controls it and any controlled movement is great! You have to start somewhere and as this is our first signs of movement south of the neck since September, we will take it! The sensations that I have written about before continue to get a little bit stronger and it continues to move into other areas. He is getting more pressure sensation in his upper arms. The story of how I found out about that goes like this......We were walking across the bridge that goes over the road and it is enclosed in glass. In looking down, I saw a Volkswagen so I proceeded to "slug bug" Doc in the arm. Our PT said that was just plain mean...hitting a quad like that...but I don't think of Doc as a quad...plus, I owe him about a jillion "slug bugs"! Anyway, after I slugged him, he told me he could feel it. And for the record, I didn't hit him that hard!!!!! So then I told him that if he could feel his upper arms, maybe he could shrug his shoulders and he did it. The left side was stronger than the right side but he did shrug both of them. Since then, he hasn't had that ability but the therapists here tell us that is not unusual. When muscles start coming back, they are very weak and they will only function on and off for awhile because it is the body's natural tendency to shut them down if they get tired and they get tired quickly. They told us to keep working them as things came back but to be careful not to overwork them. They also thought that if something started to flicker to life again that it might take awhile but that eventually, the things that are happening will happen more often and become stronger. Hopefully, this is a sign that we are starting to heal and head in the right direction. If we can get Doc healthy again and get him to start eating again, this can quickly be going in an exciting direction!

Doc's orange power chair is here and he gets fitted into it on Monday and Tuesday from 10-12. Hopefully, it will go without any snags and before you know it, we can ditch our Craig possessed chair and have our own (hopefully, it will not be possessed too)! We are anxious to see it! I think most of the rest of our equipment is coming together too. We are only waiting on a rotating mattress at this time. We have some equipment to buy that insurance is not going to cover and we appreciate all that everyone did to help us obtain it!

Speaking of that, we especially wanted to send a special thank you to the Little Dixie Square Dance Club that organized and sponsored a bake sale/dance/auction for us on Saturday night! I told them that I hope everyone danced their shoes off because we would have! I also told them to save some yellow rocks for us which is square dance language for hugs! Thanks to everyone that participated in that!

This e-mail, as this week's many adventures, ended up being full of ups and downs just like our original doctor in Grand Junction told us our year would be full of! I guess he was right! He told us not to believe anything that anyone told us because no one knows for sure what the future holds for Doc except one and we have to just wait it out! Based on that, we pray for the bad times to get better and give thanks for the good! We pray for more of the good and hope for less of the bad! Friday was our 5 month anniversary of the accident so we have a long time to go if we are going to work through a year or two of this! We continue to remember each of you and thank you for remembering us!

Hopefully, we are only approximately 11 days from coming home! As it gets closer, I am more and more ready! Our PT told us this week that he thought we really need to get home. He said the longer you stay here, the more they find wrong and sometimes you just have to go home to get better! He told us there is a lot to be said for the love of family and friends and I think he is right! All of you are the medicine that we both need right now!

Missing all of you,
Cindy and Doc

February 20-2005

ONLY 4 MORE DAYS! We are marking the days off the calendar each morning and we are getting really close to the 24th... the day with the HOME written on it! I cannot tell you how excited we are. Eric (brother) and Ellen (friend) are flying out on Tuesday and going through some respiratory classes and then they will help us drive home on Thursday. It will be a long trip but there will be a huge reward at the end of it!

This next paragraph might sound crazy but when I left home on the 10th of September to go shopping with my cousin, I had painted my toenails! Since that day, I looked at those toes every time I took a shower and I have watched the nail polish wear off a little bit each week. This week, when I took a shower, there was just a trace of it left and I thought of how weird it was to compare how long I have been away from home by how much nail polish was left on the toes! It has been something that has stayed with me through all these months. Every time I looked at it, I remembered how when I put it on, I never in a million years thought that I would be going through what we have gone through during its duration. I also think how strange it is that the week that it would literally be finally worn off is the week that we are heading home! (almost just in time for sandals and toenail polish again!) I might call this another one of those coincidences that have just been part of our life in the past months but I think that polish was a comforting connection to home, as strange as that sounds, and now that I don't need it anymore, it is gone! I am not sure exactly why I am even sharing this but to me, it was a part of the past 5 ½ months!

Doc was cleared as on Monday to take his collar off so that is a step in the right direction. He said he can't feel too much difference because the trach collar is still wrapped around his throat but I can sure tell! It looks good to see the head, neck and shoulders when you look at him. He finally got to see himself in the elevator mirror and he said that he looked different, even to himself! He thought his neck looked skinny and it does somewhat. His neck is really weak and it is going to take some time to build up enough muscles to support his head again. In the meantime, we use a collar in transfers to and from the wheelchair. We leave it off when he is in bed and in the wheelchair but we have to tilt the wheelchair a little bit in order for his head not to fall forward. They have been working on some range in turning his head so that when he does get muscle back, he will be able to look from side to side. He can turn it to the left a little bit but he has a long way to go on turning it to the right. I am sure this will get better with time but as usual, we are ready for it to be better right now!

Monday was a CRAZY day! I was trying to get last minute answers to questions and get everything lined up for coming home this week and no one wanted to answer the questions. Everyone was throwing it over to someone else and the circle never ends! There were a lot of unanswered questions that I needed answered with our discharge date zooming up on us! By the end of Tuesday, a lot of it started to come together. I just had to remember that I was not in charge and I finally found the right persons with the answers. Sometimes it takes me a little bit to remember that I don't have control but after 5 months of practicing, it is getting easier! It was amazing at how frustrated I was Monday night and yet after I remembered to let go of it, it all started working out!

I hope everyone had a wonderful Valentine's Day! Doc took me out to eat and we had a nice time (at least I did...poor Doc just watched me chew and swallow). I let him drive but he didn't let me ride! What good is a wheelchair if I can't sit in his lap and go for a ride? One of these days I might get one of those! We tried another swallow test on Friday because they were really hoping to get Doc back on food before we left but it didn't work out. They said he had improved but not enough to take a chance on eating yet. He still had small amounts aspirating to his lungs so we are going to be on hold for eating for awhile yet. The main thing is to keep Doc healthy until he can swallow and if that takes tube feeding, then that is ok. We were really disappointed but we are trying to roll with the punches! The plan is to maybe look at continuing the throat therapy at Rusk 3 days a week for a couple of more weeks and then see where we are at. If we do that, it will be better until just waiting for a month or two and then just running a test to see if he is better. For us, at least it is a plan and we are still striving to be able to eat as soon as possible! We are supposed to line that up on Monday.

To offset our disappointing news on Friday, the infectious disease doctor stopped by to tell us that he is surprised the VRE infection appears to have already disappeared. They are going to run one more test before we go home but if it is negative again, he is clearing that off our chart! I think that is a really good thing!

Doc also got his "really cool" orange wheelchair Friday. I have to say that I think the color is cool too but everyone tells us how neat the new wheelchair is and to be honest, neither Doc nor I think wheelchairs are cool! But if you have to have one, it is nice to have the technology that we have that enables him to drive it and feel comfortable in it. So far, we have had a small list of problems that we have run into with it over the weekend but no climbing the walls or anything! Hopefully, they will get us all fixed up before we leave! I am NOT a wheelchair mechanic! (AND do not want to be!).

I spent some time this week packing up and starting to load up the van. So far, everything is fitting pretty well and I haven't overloaded it yet. I still have several boxes of stuff in the room. I am sure that all my camping packing experiences are coming in handy! You learn how to pack a lot in little places when you take 3 kids camping with you for a week at a time! The main thing is that I still have room for Doc (and for those that might be wondering, yes...he has asked if he can drive home....no, he cannot....yes, he pouted....I think it will be a game that we play until the day he does drive again!).

We have our doctor appointment set up for next week in Columbia and that will be the beginning of finding out what we will need to do as we readapt to Missouri. All the rehab and medical needs will start to be identified after that. In the meantime, insurance has been wonderful enough to supply nursing support, although it is really limited! For the first few weeks, we will be able to have nursing assistance for 2 mornings a week and then after that, we will probably get it one morning a week. I am looking at other home health care options to use after we get home and combine that with persons who have asked to assist in Doc's care when we get home. It is all coming together and hopefully, it will all be temporary! We continue to have faith that Doc will recover from this, we just don't know when.

Sandy Henderson substituted a 2nd grade class one day and they had some wonderful messages to send us and we really enjoyed them. One of them stuck out to us and it was pretty simple. It simply said "cep triing" with a heart on the bottom of it. I think that is 2nd grade language for "keep trying". It made Doc and I both smile and Doc just said "always".

Thursday was the day that almost all the equipment was delivered! I felt like I was dizzy (dizzier than normal anyway) by the end of the day! They brought in 3 huge boxes with respiratory equipment in it and we had to go through and learn what everything was and how to use it and check it off the inventory list. Then the shower commode chair was delivered and the manual wheelchair. The shower commode is new but the manual chair was a donated one that we can use until we appeal our insurance's decision for denial. They are going to ship both of those home for us because after I saw the boxes with respiratory equipment, I wonder if I am going to have room for Doc now! Heck, I wonder even about me because Eric is driving so I don't even have that security! He will have the keys! Hehe!

After going through all the equipment and attending a fishing class we also had a home mods class to attend at 6 p.m. That was more food for the brain and as my brain was already stuffed, so it was hard to take more in. As our discharge date gets closer, they are looming like buzzards outside the door all waiting to cram more into our heads and to be honest, I don't think there is room to cram much more. There are days that I want to lock the door and say "out for the day!".

We didn't have too many exciting adventurous outings to write about. We were so busy tying up lose ends and packing that we didn't spend too much time in the recreation department. We did go to that fishing class on Thursday night so Doc could spend a little more time learning about the sip and puff fishing pole. We went outside to practice it and as there is not a lake in the parking lot, Doc only caught a bush and a doorway! We continue to be a waiting list to purchase one of them but they can't give us any timing on it yet. Hopefully, we will have one by summer or as always, there might be a reason that one isn't available yet....maybe we won't need it!

Sunday, was Doc's biggest adventure for the week. They took him pheasant hunting and we were out all day. We left at 9:45 a.m. and didn't get back until almost 6. It was an experience and although I am not a hunter and don't understand the joys in it, I did enjoy being out in the country and watching the hunt! They started us out with a nice lunch of baked pheasant, fried pheasant, pheasant casserole, along with an array of other foods. We were served in an old hunting shed filled with horns, antlers, and feathers! Doc was just sitting and looking around with the biggest smile on his face! He looked at me and said couldn't I just imagine having a place like that at home during whitetail season. Well, to be honest, NO! Why would anyone want to be an musty building with a bunch of dead animal heads and feathers, a dusty floor, an old kitchen, 7 tables with 50 unmatching chairs, and a big screen tv & a pile of hunting videos? I think Doc would be comfortable living in that environment but I will hold out for my house! After we ate, they took us out to watch the dogs learning how to point and that was interesting. Then they took us to this huge corn field and they shot some clay pigeons for awhile and then they let go of some pheasants and turned the dogs loose to find them. They have ATV's modified for paralyzed persons that they load them on and if necessary, the guns are mounted to the ATV. Doc wasn't able to actually hunt on this trip because if your break is less than 6 months old or if you are on blood thinner, they don't consider you healthy enough to bounce across the field on an ATV. (imagine that) It was fun just to watch the dogs and the other guys though! The guy that owns the pheasant hunting resort told Doc that he was invited back anytime he wanted to come and they would get him on a hunt in the future. He said that it would always be a freebie for him! It is amazing at how many nice people there are in this world!

I remember when my dad had cancer (a long time ago) and we visited him in the cancer hospital. We saw a lot of people who were aware that without a miracle their days were numbered. You would think that it would be a depressing place. At least I did...I wasn't very old and I couldn't understand how all those patients had so many smiles on their faces and so much faith. The feeling of not quite understanding why you would be so happy in a bad situation stuck with me for a long time but somewhere along life's path, I figured it out. This place is a different type of situation but the same type of message. Most of the patients here don't necessarily have numbered days but they are aware that their life has changed and they possibly will never walk or live life the way they used to. For those that have severed their spinal cords, they almost know that for sure. However, when you walk the halls here, you will always find a smiling face and very few tears. There is faith in the halls similar to what I remember from the cancer hospital but the feeling that lingers the most in the conversations is hope. Hope that things will get better or hope that someone will make an exciting discovery on how to mend the spinal cord or hope for that miracle of healing! The best part of this is that almost weekly, you meet someone that has had that happen to them and they can tell you the most amazing stories of what happened to them and then how they got better. Doc & I share that faith and hope that someday we can share our story and give inspiration to someone else so they can believe that "it can happen". All of your prayers are playing into that plan so thank you for them!

I know that we are planning on being home and the next e-mail that I send out will be from Missouri and not Colorado. I have had several persons asking me to take the time to continue to update you on our progress and to keep in touch. I don't want to wear out the situation by dragging out these e-mails too far but I will let everyone know how this week goes and how our first weekend at home goes. After that, I don't want to bore you all with real life! We will just be settling into our new life and trying to adjust to the new world we will be living in. We won't have any exciting Craig adventures but you can rest assured that if I have anything to say about it, Doc and I will still have lots of fun adventures! I wanted to remind you again that during our journey, you all played a major part and continue to do so. We are eternally grateful for your support while we were out of town and for your support as we get home! We ask for your continued prayers because, as I have written before, recovery from this type of injury can take years! So if I don't end up sending out a "Days in Colorado" type update every Monday, you are welcome to e-mail me at any time and I will write back. Otherwise, I will continue to update you all on major things and hopefully, one day, I can tell you exciting news!

Until next week,
Cindy and Doc

February 27-2005

Well, we made it (although a day late-I'll explain further down) and it is wonderful to be home with family and friends. They say home is where the heart is and even though we were really excited about coming home to Missouri, it was also hard leaving Colorado because part of our hearts now belong in Colorado with all of our new friends that we met through St. Marys and Craig. We want all of you to know that we think of you often, will not forget you, and will do our best to stay in touch! We wanted to say thank you again to all the doctors, nurses, therapists, and techs that all did their part to get us home healthy!

Monday started out really busy and stayed that way all day! Doc's orange chair had some stuff to fix on it so they took him out of it and he never made it back into it. As the day went on, they found more problems and so it finally went to the shop to be worked on with a promise that it would be back in time for the trip home! We continued to be educated but it wasn't as stressful as Friday because we had the weekend to regroup and I was able to hang in there a little better!

Monday afternoon, we met the New Jersey Net's mascot, Sky Fox. That was fun! They took a pretty cool picture and left Doc with a neat NBA All Star t-shirt. Sky Fox left me with a huge hug! I think I got the better end of the deal! We also had our last family conference and it went well. I think our whole team knew it was time for the next step but we will miss them and they will miss us! We do have a re-evaluation scheduled for August 28th, so we will be seeing them before we know it! Hopefully, we continue to pray that things will start to happen and we can go back much improved in regards to the injury!

As Monday started to run down, I had a wild adventure to report! I started at 5:30 to walk to the corner ice-cream store for a turkey sandwich. I get there and they tell me that they weren't very busy so they shut the kitchen down early and they can't fix me a sandwich. No big deal, I just walk back to the room and tell Doc that I am going to run a roll of film by wal mart and I will pick up a sandwich while I am out. I go down to the van and the battery is dead. So I come back in a little confused at what to do and then I think about the hospital security. I call them and they do jumps so they meet me in the parking lot and give me a jump start. He tells me to make sure to drive it to recharge it and it should be ok. I decide to go ahead and get a sandwich when I pull out of the parking lot and the rearview mirror falls off and bounces across the dash! Needless to say, I sat there and had a good laugh! I was thinking that I couldn't even make up this story! I go ahead and drive to wal mart and they have an automotive department. They are getting ready to close it up BUT they ask me what I needed and I told them about the battery and that I am afraid to turn off the engine in case it doesn't start again. They tell me, no problem, they can do that before they close up! They tested the battery to make sure it was dead. Then they see my mirror problem and offer to fix that too! They were so nice!! Anyway, I had to buy a little $2 tube of rearview mirror glue (amazing that they sell a tube of glue just for a rearview mirror but they really do!) and a battery but I am ready to go again! Nothing was going to keep us from driving across Kansas on Thursday (or Friday). After I finally get that taken care of, I run by Sonic and get a sandwich and head back to the hospital. I end up eating a cheeseburger at 8:30 when I started out for a turkey sandwich at 5:30. Now this is the not the end of this little story....They hung the bracket for the mirror but I had to wait 24 hours to put the mirror on it....I go out the next day to hang the mirror with my new tools and wal mart has glued the bracket on the window upside down! Some things in life just make you smile. Anyway, I waited until Eric got here and he saved the day! (Not that we needed the mirror anyway because I had the van so full with stuff that you couldn't see out of it!).

Tuesday wasn't any better than Monday and they continued to wait in line (literally) to give me equipment and/or advice. The wheelchair issue grew a little bigger and they hinted that they might not be able to have Doc's chair done in time for a Thursday dismissal. They identified more problems and came up with some solutions so parts were ordered for over night delivery and we hoped that it would all work out. Eric and Ellen arrived later in the afternoon and we glad to see them! We warned them that they might not be going home when they thought they would but they were wonderful enough to be as flexible as we needed them to be. I told them I hoped they weren't caught in the same current that we were in because at times, it seemed like we would never see Missouri again!

The worse part of Tuesday came at 5 pm, because our supplier of equipment/supplies made a couple of calls to the hospital to tell them not to discharge us because our insurance had decided to go with a new supplier and that they were going to collect their equipment from us and start over. Needless to say, it didn't make sense and although I couldn't help to stress a little of the thought of how long that would take, I knew that it was unlikely. Anyway, our insurance case worker called first thing the next morning and it was all straightened out. No one had made a call and everyone seemed confused as to where our supplier had gotten his information. When we found out that we were still going with the same supplier (although I would have like to pull the tail of the sales rep that pulled the wrong chains!), we found out the supplier had to go out to the house to do an inspection and approve our house for the equipment/supplies. I was a little confused at why it would be their business to go to our house. If insurance orders and pays for the equipment, my environment shouldn't be their business. I told them that if I want to buy a dress at Wal Mart, they don't run to my house to make sure my closet has room in it before they sell it to me (if they did, I would be in trouble!). Anyway, to make a short story out of this, they came out and signed off that everything was ok! Thanks to all of you that made it possible! They even made the comment that they would like to use the bathroom as a "model" example to those that are building them! Good job to the bathroom workers!

Tuesday evening, Eric and Ellen attended a respiratory class so they could learn how to help with Doc's care. My brother Mike also went through it while he was here so between all of us and those that we train, Doc will be in good hands. At least I hope so…Eric and Ellen came back and said that if they had to grade themselves, they would have given themselves a "C". I am not sure that made Doc feel cozy! Anyway, they continued to practice and then started applying their skills to the real deal and as Doc survived, they upped their grade to a "B". I feel confident that they will soon be earning an "A". They also had a crash course in a bunch of the rest of his care but they are passing with flying colors as I am sure that all of our family and friends that jump in will! I am just REALLY glad to have the support and to be able to share some of the care! THANKS!

Wednesday was just like a carbon copy of the rest of the week! There was someone wanting something almost every minute of the day and at times, they were waiting 3 deep. I had Eric and Ellen to help though so it was nice to hand off some of it and/or at least share it! We also knew by mid-morning that we weren't going home on Thursday and we started to hope for Friday and fear for Saturday! We went to bed on Wednesday night still not having an orange wheelchair.

Wednesday night, Patrick turned nine. We all went to his birthday party and it was a good time! I will miss them! As a matter of fact, I am going to miss several of our new friends! It was hard to tell them good bye! After the party was over, we played some 4 point pitch and as usual, I have to report that Doc pulled it out in the end. BUT, even though Doc had his cuff up and could not vocalize, I caught him talking across the table and that is CHEATING! I called him on it and all he did was put this innocent face on and then he got the cocky grin on his face and I knew I was in trouble!

I helped Meagan with her 5th grade math homework on Wednesday night (when 6 nurses couldn't figure it out!-ouch!) but when Patrick came looking for math help on Thursday night, I wasn't in the room. I am happy to report that Ellen was able to assist in 3rd grade math and he left all happy!

Doc continues to improve a little bit each week. He can move his neck a little bit better and is starting to support his head better although he has a long way to go. His fingers and toes still have a little twitching to them but he can't feel them yet. He is healthier and I hope that we are on a better road. We have had so many bumps that it would be nice to have a smooth road for a little while!

They came in on Thursday morning and said that they were working hard to get the wheelchair done but they weren't sure on the timing. They wanted to know if they got it done by 11, if we would take it out and load it in the van, go to a movie or something and then come back. They wanted us to work it out and see how it rode in the van and how it drove outside the hospital halls. If there was a problem or if we didn't get it by 11, then they wanted us to try it out on Friday and stay until Saturday. We kept our fingers crossed and sure enough, the wheelchair came sneaking in the room around 10:30. So we headed off for the parking lot and between Ellen, Eric, and I we got Doc loaded but if someone was watching us, we probably didn't look very smooth and I would go so far as to report that we were probably looking a little bit like the 3 stooges loading Doc! We headed off for the movie theater and watched "Hitch". (for those that are wondering about the movie, we all thought it was very funny and entertaining! Two thumbs up!). Then we loaded back up and it went much, much better the 2nd time! I think we are going to get good at it eventually! When we got back, there were a few minor things to take care of on the chair and we also wrapped up a home call system so that if Doc needs me in the middle of the night or if he needs one of his caretakers and they happen to be in another room, he can press something with his chin that would let us know and/or wake us up! One of these days, I know he will able to just yell out but that day just isn't here yet! Then we started our massive round of good-byes, supper, and final round of packing!

I was busy with medicines and paperwork to complete the discharge until about 11:30 Thursday night and then they came in at 4:30 a.m. to take some blood from Doc so that last night was short. Doc's blood was a little thin on Thursday so they were testing it to make sure that it hadn't gotten worse. I was so afraid that it might be and then we would be stuck another day or two but it wasn't any worse so it was all good! We went ahead and got up at 5 and started our morning care. We were done and out of the hospital by 7. It took us awhile in the parking lot, not because of loading Doc this time, but because we had a huge pile of stuff on a luggage cart to fit into an already stuffed van. I don't think Eric had much confidence in my packing skills but we loaded it all in and had lots of room to spare. I even told him that there was this awesome mall that I had found and that I hadn't gone back to because I didn't want to have too much to haul home but we could go now that I knew I still had room. He just said get in the van and the next stop was Missouri! Fine with me (well, sorta, because the next stop was actually Limon, CO and it was lucky for Eric that he stopped!) hehe! There were a few more stops along the way but Doc never got out until we got home. He just did his weight shifts in the van and we continued to head east! Eric even let me to listen to some good music along the way….Of course, I had to listen to come country too! We had beautiful weather and it almost perfect! I was concerned about traveling across Kansas in February but as usual, someone was taking care of us and cleared the path for smooth sailing all the way home! The van worked like a charm and it was a smooth ride! Doc was excited to finally ride in something that didn't bounce him around like jello! Again, thanks to everyone that helped us in obtaining it! It worked great!

We are going to have another modified swallowing test in Columbia on Monday (so they can set a baseline) and we have a doctor appointment with our doctor in Columbia on Wednesday. That will start to get us in the mode for outpatient care. I am not sure what it is all going to entail but we are anxious to get into a routine and start living again! Carrissa (our youngest) is starting her college softball games this week and we are hoping to get to several of them! We missed her whole fall season and we aren't planning on missing the spring season. Adam (our son) is getting married in 2 months and it will feel good to be able to jump into more of the wedding plans and attend their bridal showers. Speaking of the wedding, I want you to know that Doc has been practicing dancing with his wheelchair and we are getting better. By the time it gets here, we might even have a few "steps" down. Jaymi (our oldest daughter) is graduating in May and it will good to be able to help her as she moves on with job opportunities and graduation plans. Just to start thinking about other things is wonderful. Speaking of our kids, they all took off work and came home to help with Doc for a few days. Adam gets to stay until the end of the week and he will be a huge help!

We have nursing care on Monday and Thursday mornings and I am working with home health care to establish a plan for the rest of the week. My agenda for the next week or two is to get my feet back on the ground finding a routine that works for Doc & I, training the persons that have asked to spend some time with him while I am at work, hire the professional help that Doc will require, work through some of the issues at the house and get our taxes (yippy) done (can't even imagine what it is going to take to gather all the information and paperwork together but I am sure it will come together!) After

I get a handle on it, I am anxious to get back to work. I hope I remember how to do it....they have crammed so much new stuff in my brain in the past 6 months that I hope they haven't shoved out things that I needed to retain! They say that we all have a bunch of brain power that we never use but I am not sure how much I have left! I know do know one thing, when they start

cramming more into the brain than it can handle, it seeps out through the eyes.

I can never, never tell you how good it feels to be home! How special it was to see all the cars lined up on our gravel road with persons standing outside of them waving us home! Just like the whole situation seemed surreal as we went through it, finally being home seems surreal too! The house, driveway, and all the welcoming touches were wonderful! Someday, I think our community (and extended communities) and the way this whole situation bonded all of us together will be an awesome story to share in big fashion. To our family—mom, sisters, brothers, cousins, uncles & aunts, grandma, and friends—we love you and we have thanked God that we have you every night! We met some patients at Craig that said they feel like the quality of life is gone being paralyzed and I do agree that it does seem to loose a little of the quality but you just have to find a way to put the "quality" back into it. Having family and friends like all of you has helped us put some "quality" back into it and I know it will only get better now that we are really home! I know that a ton of you have written or called that you want to come by and visit as soon as we catch our breath! I have told all of you that we are anxious to see you too. I wanted you to know that as soon as Doc gets over his "jet lag" and we get settled, you will all be invited to a "coming home" party and all of you will be invited! We would love to say a personal thank you to each and every one of you! (Plus, I have a bunch of hugs to catch up on!). I have to tell you that Eric says that when we have this party that I might have to say a few words to all of you. I am already practicing because you all know how short of words I usually am! I will be ready though!

In the meantime, we will continue to stay in touch when we have things to write about but it probably will not be every week. I will keep you posted though because I know we have some exciting things in our future and I cannot wait for the day to share the whole story. In the meantime, if you would remember us in prayer once and awhile, we would be eternally grateful and as always, we will return the favor right back at you! It has been a pleasure writing these e-mails and it helped immensely in keeping my sanity! So many of you told us how much these e-mails have come to mean and how they have helped you too! Knowing that good is coming out of this is comforting. Thanks for the kind things that all of you said about the e-mails (especially those of you who call me "windy"-who knows where that comes from?) and for the encouragement to keep writing them through the whole ordeal.

I am going to end this with how we ended our stay at Craig. The therapy gym on the 3rd floor where we had physical and occupational therapy has a plethora (great word, huh?...before you go look it up...it means a lot!) of banners hanging from the ceiling! Every patient is invited to add theirs at discharge with their name, date, and a message on it if they would like. Even though there was a plethora of them, there wasn't a St. Louis Cardinal banner so we left a little bit of Missouri and Doc asked them to hang it in a prominent place so it is the first banner you see as you walk into the East side of the gym. The message that Doc wrote on the back of it is how I am going to close this e-mail. It was "Remember to Laugh!"

From home in Missouri,

Cindy and Doc Blackmore

March 7-2005

I know I said that I wasn't going to update you every week but I cannot believe how many of you are still calling, sending cards & e-mails, and praying for us! As you haven't forgotten us, how can I forget you? I got to thinking that even though I am in our house (and it feels VERY good, I might add!), we are still not out there circulating very much so you are probably wondering what in the world is going on in our world!

I don't know what I was expecting when I got home but I wasn't expecting to be even busier than they kept us at Craig. I thought that was impossible but that is what is happening! We are still going to speech therapy working on trying to get over that hump and be able to eat again. It is taking 3 visits a week to Columbia for therapy and it appears to be going well. Doc passed his initial swallow test when we got home but not quite good enough for them to just turn him loose eating! It was good progress although we had been down that road once before and ended up with pneumonia so we are taking it much slower this time to make sure we are ready to eat before we start full time! Doc is eating just a little bit of soft foods each day for about an hour to work his swallow muscles and so far everything appears to be heading into the stomach and not the lungs. We have had tomato soup, pudding, and yogurt. They are going to do another swallow test next Wednesday and those results will tell us whether we continue with speech therapy or proceed with eating and start working with a dietitian.

We have also had a doctor appointment with our primary doctor in Columbia to get Doc's medicine refilled. They cannot fill a prescription at a Missouri pharmacy from a Colorado physician so we had to get them all rewritten (there is a total of about 16 prescriptions but we only needed 10 of them initially refilled!) ONLY! It is like a huge ordeal each week just to put the pills in the pill box so we know what to take when. Then I have to put them in a pill crusher and dissolve them in water to give them to Doc through his feeding tube. When he eats again, he can start taking them orally. Although, on this note, I have to write that the primary doctor is against any oral eating. He wants to play it safe and stay on the feeding tube indefinitely unless Doc makes major improvements. Doc said that he would rather take an outside chance on getting pneumonia again than to never try to eat again.

It is taking me about 2 hours each morning to get him up and going. It takes some time to go through the whole morning program. I keep thinking of ways that I might improve the timing but I haven't figured out any shortcuts yet. Then in the evening, things are a little faster but it still takes about 1.5 hours to put him down. There is so much to do that I never thought about before the accident! They say women take a long time to get ready but it only takes me about 15 minutes.....

We currently have a nurse coming out from Boone Home Health on Mondays and Thursdays from 7-11 but they need almost complete training in Doc's care. They are completely inexperienced with anything to do with his injury. With only 4 hours with each visit and the fact that it is a different nurse almost every time, I am finding it hard to get one trained to the point that I can leave her to do it alone. Then in April, insurance cuts it back to one visit per week. I am working with the home health care in Moberly trying to hire someone to help with the morning program for the rest of the week but again, I am running into snags. I need someone that would be able to work from 6-8 so I could be at work at a decent time and they don't have anyone that wants those hours. Even if they find someone, it would be more of an assistant type help so I am not convinced how much that is going to worth to me. I might just throw in the towel on that issue and plan on doing the care myself and then after I get Doc in his chair each morning, finding someone to pass the day with him because it gets much easier after he is up and ready. I already have 3 days covered and I am working on the other day and half. I was stressing about it earlier this week because I am anxious to get back to work and let my mind focus on other things again but on the other hand, I am like a nervous mother wanting to make sure that Doc has the appropriate care. As I have written before, I finally remember to sit back and take a big breath and turn it over to a higher power. God has taken care of us every step of the way and I have no doubt that when the time is right, he will show me what I need to do on Doc's care and I will know it is time to go back to work. It just must not be time yet.

We have had many persons helping us drive the van to Columbia for doctor visits because we have 3-4 a week. They have all been so helpful! Just having the company is reassuring to me but they also provide a little muscle that never hurts!

Everything in the house is working great! There was a small problem with the drain in the shower but that has been fixed and it is working great! (Thanks Fred and Randy!). My brother and brother-in-law came out and hung a tv in our room so Doc can watch something while he is in bed. That was nice! Then my sister and my nephews helped me uncover the trash cans in the garage and it was good to have that cleaned up too! The biggest challenge so far is just cleaning up the piles of remodeling materials and the piles of stuff that was shifted from the downstairs rooms to wherever an empty spot was found. Now there are NO empty spots in the house and it has been a scavenger hunt to find most everything! I am amazed at how much stuff fits into closets and cabinets! And I am also amazed out how I have everything in the closets except the one thing I need. My brother was right, I had a bunch of junk!

Today is Wednesday and we have officially been home 12 days and I finally got 2 rooms and 2 closets cleaned up and that felt really good. Just to be getting a handle on part of it is wonderful. I also finally made it through 2 weeks of mail and sorted through all the insurance paperwork. There was a fairy tale that I read when I was younger about something that no matter how much you used of it, the same amount was always there. That is how I feel like the insurance paperwork is. No matter how much time I spend on cleaning it up, the pile never seems to go down! Like magic (but black magic-yuck!).

I have been working on training family and friends on the vent and the trach. I think they are getting more comfortable and I know how scary it can be at first but it gets better and it isn't very hard. Everyone is so good about asking questions and diving right in with Doc's care. It sure makes things easier on me and I can never tell you how much it means to be able to share some of the load. It will especially be nice when I can actually leave Doc for awhile and get a haircut or something. I think we are getting close to having some persons comfortable enough to go ahead and head out for a little bit.

There have been several persons that brought food out to me and how thoughtful was that! It is difficult right now to get out and get grocery shopping done and it was really nice of all of you that thought about those little touches like bread and milk and frozen meals! At first, the phone was ringing off the hook with doctors, hospitals, therapists, equipment resources, supply resources, and insurance. It has slowed down a little bit and I am glad. I have more important calls that need to get through from those that love us!

We took our first solo adventure today on our own and we made it home in one piece! Our friend, Dallas Wheeler passed away and we wanted to go to his visitation. We will miss him. We also heard that Russ Evans, another friend of ours, passed away this week and we were sorry not to be able to make that visitation. Our next adventure is going to be on Saturday when we head to Union, Missouri, to watch our daughter play softball. We are praying for some pretty weather!

Doc has been laughing at me because I hit my head on the tv that they hung off our wall about 4 or 5 times every morning and then when I am loading and unloading him in the van, I hit my head on the roof another 4 or 5 times. I think he thinks I am doing it on purpose but I promise I am not. I am not that stupid because it hurts! Those things just keep getting in my way. I make him kiss all my booboos though so it isn't all bad!

We loved being back in church together again! I think that was the best part about being home! Our church family was so welcoming that it brought more than one tear to our eye! Our goal is that after we are settled that we visit several churches in the area that have had us on their prayer list because we would like to testify to our story to date. I still think there is more to it than has happened so far but we are ready to share our experience so far with the promise that we have for a tomorrow that is yet to arrive!

Doc is doing much better with his talking and appears to be building up more stamina with that every day. We are back up to around 5 hours with his cuff down so he can speak and we are working at increasing that each day. You can tell he is getting more comfortable with the speaking time. Our shoulders are moving more each day although it is super slow. He is getting more sensations in the shoulders also. Again it is slow, but at least we see positive things happening. He is still twitching his fingers and toes but no feeling yet. The best part is that he is sleeping really well since he has been home.

Our one funny adventure happened in out-patient speech clinic at Boone Hospital. It involved his wheelchair and a wall that has a big hole in it now. He sorta ran into the wall as he was coming out of the room and proceeded to try to drive through it. The therapist told him not to worry about it because they were talking about tearing it all out soon and remodeling it all anyway. If they keep having Doc come 3 times a week, they might not even have to hire a demolition team. Doc said that maybe he can work off his therapy cost by doing the demolition work for them! I don't think they bought into that!

The one moment that sticks in my mind the most is that one day this week, it was 2:30 in the afternoon and Doc asked me if he had told me he loved me yet that day. I told him I didn't think so and he said he didn't think so either. He said shame on him for waiting until that late in the day to tell me that and that he should be spanked. (although until he can feel it, it is easy for him to asked to be spanked!). Anyway, I was tickled at him! He is pretty special!

We continue to believe in the power of prayer and ask that you keep Doc on your list. There will be a day that we can all celebrate great things to come but in the meantime, we are planning on celebrating the great things that have already happened-things like being alive and being home. I think they are looking at hosting an open house party with finger foods and sandwiches on April 2nd, from 2-5 at the Cairo Christian Church activity center. All of you are welcome to drop by, share a hug and let us tell you thank you! If something happens where this changes at all, I will drop you another line but as far as I know, this is the plan. It was going to be later in the day but there is some type of major turkey thing happening in Moberly that my brothers and Doc are planning on attending that evening…I have been invited and you can tell that I am really having trouble sleeping with the excitement of that thought!

Life is good and we are so thankful to be home and to have so many wonderful friends and family members! Thanks to all of you again for being so supportive! We look forward to seeing all of you at the open house if it is possible for you to make it. In the meantime, I will continue to try and update you so you aren't just hanging wondering what is happening. It probably won't be that once a week e-mail but at least it will be communication!

From the Blackmore house,
Doc and Cindy

March 17-2005

Yesterday they had a benefit pulled pork dinner for us and I heard the turnout was tremendous but I am sorry to write that it was short a couple of persons that intended to be there! That would be me and Doc! We really wanted to be there to tell all of you that supported it thanks (not to mention that I was looking forward to Carl's pork!) Unfortunately, we were in the emergency room at Boone Hospital. Doc's oxygen levels had dropped to point that I had to put him back on oxygen and we hadn't been at that point for a couple of months. Then by the time we got him to Columbia, he was running a 103 degree fever. They ran a bunch of tests and there was a nice sized infection in his blood so they are working on finding out where it is coming from. They saw signs of pneumonia in his lungs but his urine also showed some infection. That means it could be coming from either one or both! Our luck is both! Another bump in the road! Anyway, they hooked him up to some IV's to start a battle against it until they could define the actual problem, which usually takes 24-48 hours to see what starts growing after they take the specimens. They wanted to admit him so that if it got worse, he would be close at hand for additional treatment but we really did not want to be back in the hospital! So, after I made sure Doc wanted to come home, I went to battle with my debating skills and finally won. I figured he had a better nurse at home…at least one that was trained to his specific needs (plus she kisses him in between his care)! He would get in trouble if that happened in the hospital!! On top of that, all his equipment at home is targeted for a quad and we were afraid that the hospital would be back to turning him every 2 hours all night instead of letting him sleep on a rotating bed. Doc just sat in the emergency room apologizing for something that he had no control of. I might add that it was nice to see Mike and Beth Nelson. They stopped by in the midst of the diagnosis to say hi as they were down there to see their new baby grandson for the first time! How exciting that would be!

In the end it all worked out and Doc is doing better this morning. His temperature has dropped to 100 and his oxygen level is getting stronger all the time with less oxygen from the tank. As soon as we get him on his antibiotic for a few days, he should be off of it again! Then we will be ready to rock and roll once more!

Lucky for us, Jaymi and Joey were here for the week on spring break. They were with me at the hospital yesterday and then they have done all my errands this morning, including picking up the prescription for the antibiotic. Later today, we have a serious card game scheduled!

We were able to attend our daughter's, Carrissa, softball games last Saturday and that was a blast! It ended up being a little cool and windy (and I hope that wasn't what caused our problems......) but we both felt like we were in the right spot. It was the first time we got to see her play college ball and it was fun. They won both their games and they look like they have a good team! We will be back on the road again at the next home game if at all possible!

Our home care issues are slowly being resolved. I think we have all the hours of the week and the morning care program identified and now we are just in the scheduling and training mode. In a week or two, I might be actually be back and work and feeling good about the care Doc is getting! I know we have to take each day one at a time but it sure will feel good to get pass some of these major hurdles! I wanted to say a special thanks to Linda Taylor and my mom for all their efforts.

Doc continues to improve (other than this little set back). They are really small steps but in the course of a week, it can be pretty amazing! His neck is getting much, much stronger and he can lift it forward and slowly but surely, he is pulling it back better each day. Then his motion to the left continues to strengthen and starting this week, there is a slight pull back to the right. I am working on the up and down first because that "yes" motion always gets him further than that "no" motion.

I am excited about this weekend because my future daughter in law is having a bridal shower in St. Joe and I think I am going to get to go. Howard & Ellen Smothers and Eric & Kim Gittemeier are going to come over and spend the day with Doc. (I have been teasing Doc that it takes 4 to replace me but I think any of them could handle it on their own!) It will be good to have a day out and to be part of the wedding excitement though! I haven't been much like a mother of the groom so far but I am working on it now that we are home. I even have a dress to wear and a hair appointment for the big day! I have to find a time to take a little gray out of it before then though. Someone has been creeping into our room at night and dying more of them gray every night!

I have a friend, Lori Hayden, that is coming to spend part of next week us and I am really excited about that! She is going to help me go through the piles of "junk" that was piled upstairs in the remodeling of the house. It will feel good to be able to see the floor of upstairs again plus it will be wonderful to have her to visit with!

We have also been working on some "honey-do" lists for when he is better. We have had a good time listing things that we both want him to do. Somehow, he keeps moving his stuff to the top of the list in priority but when the time gets here, it will change…I promise!

Well, based on my "honey-do" list today, I had better get off this computer and start them or they won't get done. I am trying to clear the evening because we have Brandon and Amanda Bailey coming over to play with us tonight and eat El Valquero's. (or at least some of their food!)

Thanks again to everyone that ate pulled pork yesterday and know that we wished we could have been there! We also wanted to say thanks to everyone that has stopped by to visit us so far! I know that many more of you are spacing it out and plan to visit in the future and we are looking forward to all of them!

Your friends,
Cindy and Doc

March 24-2005

I wish I had some exciting stories to share with you but I don't. As Doc has been sick, we haven't had many adventures so there wasn't much opportunity for Doc to give me any material. As a matter of fact, I don't have much to write about but I wanted to say hi! Doc is feeling much better. His fever is gone and his stats are doing better. They never called to verify the exact problem but I figured that whatever it was, they were happy with the antibiotic they first put him on because they never called to change it and it seems to be working. I am most worried about a skin sore that he has on his backbone that looks pretty nasty but we have a doctor appointment today with a wound doctor so we will soon know what to do about that! Those skin sores scare me!

We haven't had a bunch more improvement on anything else but Doc said that he hasn't really had time to concentrate on anything except just trying to breathe. It is amazing at how much thinking is involved in this injury. He says that there are days that he thinks about every single breath the vent gives him!

I was wearing out and I didn't even realize it until the day I got my break! I had my brother and sister-in-law (Eric & Kim) and a couple of friends (Howard & Ellen) come over last Saturday to sit with Doc so I could travel to St. Joe and go to my future daughter-in-law's bridal shower. It was the first full day that I was away from Doc since September and I have to tell you that it felt so good to be thinking about something else! They took really good care of

Doc and I came home refreshed and ready to go again. Things have been much easier this week! They also put up a beautiful railing on my front porch and I so delighted with it! I missed how my porch used to look and it made me feel good to have it looking nice again. Then Billy Scroggins (I hope I spelled his name correctly but if not, I know he knows who he is) came out while I was gone and put up some motion lights for us so we have lights when we pull up with the van and you can see the whole ramp. That was really helpful!! On top of that, Howard also did several "honey-do" jobs for me while I was gone and I was tickled pink!!

It is amazing how little bitty things mean so much. A couple of weeks ago, Ed Boeding and Tim Myers were out for lunch and I happened to mention how I missed my water pressure in the kitchen sink. In like 5 minutes, they had figured out the problem and I have awesome pressure there now! Not to say that I enjoy washing dishes but it is much better and I am really enjoying turning on the faucet and having good water. There are so many little things that I took for granted and as they are fixed, I celebrate at their working properly and I give thanks for the wonderful friends that we have that continue to help us out!

Speaking of being thankful for persons…I have to tell you that when Jaymi and Joey were home for spring break, Brandon and Amanda Bailey came over to visit and when I had all 4 of them helping me put Doc down at night, it took only about 15 minutes. It was amazing. I had gotten a routine down and was able to do it on my own and it didn't seem important to ask someone to come over to help but I totally enjoyed the help and the company as they assisted. Then Brandon has come back several nights and helped.

Another great friend, (Lori Hayden), came to visit us for a few days this week and she has been great company. She brought her scissors with her and gave my hair its trim job that it needed so badly. Then she helped me clean out an upstairs room so we could see the carpet again! She also is going with us today to help me transport Doc to his doctor appointments today.

We continue to have so much to be thankful for! At church this week the message was that there is nothing that God gives us that we cannot handle and if it gets too heavy, he sends "Simons" to help us just as Simon stepped out to help Jesus with his cross. We have had so many Simons since September that I can't even list them all but every one of them are embedded in our minds and hearts and we will NEVER forget any of them!

Our exciting news this week doesn't have to do with Doc but with our daughter, Jaymi. Joey proposed to her and she accepted so now we have another wedding in the works. They did it while they were home over spring break and I have to tell you how special it was that Joey brought that moment home to us and shared it with us. For 6 months we have been living through the hospital and everything that happened in our kids lives seemed to be so long distance. It felt good to be part of something so special as it happened! We are happy for both of them and grateful for Joey's wonderful family!

Now Doc has another reason to work on getting out of this chair… he has a daughter to walk down the aisle! Whatever happens though, we know we have to be patient to understand what is planned for us.

Speaking of that, it was pretty awesome how we were sitting in our living room and talking about how hard some days were one afternoon and how we wondered what we were supposed to be doing with our trial and then the phone rang. At first we were both irritated with the "stupid" phone because it seems to ring all the time but then when I answered it, it was someone from the church wanting us to testify at a dinner that they were sponsoring on Holy Saturday. I hung up the phone and told Doc that we were going to do that, and he just smiled and said that at least we know what we are supposed to be doing! Talk about having a prayer answered within the second it was asked!

Home health care is moving along. Starting Tuesday morning, I started training 3 more persons and I think I am finished with new people! It will take a few days to get enough training under everyone's belts to feel comfortable in leaving Doc alone with them but we are at least getting it narrowed down to a schedule and a set group of persons! I think Doc is going to have some wonderful care and we are fortunate to have the variety that we have. I have discovered that it is not easy to secure good home care but I think we are to be blessed with it! It will feel wonderful to be back at work and get into a routine again!

We continue to have some wonderful visits with family and friends and we thank all of you that take the time to call or stop by. It is good to hear from each of you! We wanted to wish you a very Joyful Easter! For the first time since we had kids, we aren't going to have any of them home for Easter. Carrissa is going to playing in Mississippi in a softball tournament and in a different situation, you can bet we would be there cheering her team on, Adam has to work and Jaymi is going to Joey's family. On a happy note, they are all going to be home the next weekend because Laura (Adam's fiancé) is having a wedding shower and we are hosting the open house to say thanks to all of you at the Christian Church in Cairo on the 2nd. It will be good to have all the kids together again since we haven't had that since Christmas (and we were missing Laura and Joey then).

Thanks for keeping us in your prayers because we are still in great need of them as Doc's recovery is in God's hands (but it is a great place to be!). We continue to remember each of you in return! Hopefully, Doc's health will continue to improve and the weather will turn off into some spring type temperatures because Carrissa has several softball games next week and we are hoping to get to a few of them in between doctor appointments and home health training!

Cindy and Doc

March 2005

I hope everyone had a wonderful Easter holiday. Easter has always been my most favorite holiday! It has always left my soul feeling like it was refreshed! There is something renewing about the whole season!

The doctor's appointment with the wound doctor went well and she felt like the sore on Doc's back would heal in time. She gave me some special covering for it that I change out every 3 days. Hopefully, in a week or two we will see some improvements. The doctor did not recommend a follow up visit so she was either confident that the stuff was going to work or else she was trying to avoid more holes in the walls! (although, Doc made it through this visit without anymore demo work!)

After the doctor appointment, Doc went with Lori and I out to eat. We went to Garfield's and even though Doc couldn't eat, he was sitting in front of a tv with golf on the channel so he was happy! Then we went shopping for some jewelry for my dress for the wedding and that was fun! Just ask Doc. He did say that it was enjoyable to be out...REALLY!

Doc and I ventured out on Saturday and went grocery shopping together. Doc said that the thought of a trip to Wal Mart was leaving him stoked! Hehe! We had a good time though because as usual, a trip to Moberly Wal Mart is like a family reunion! We saw a ton of our friends and it was good to visit! We finally made it through the crowd and got everything on the list and headed home. We managed to do it without any calls over the intercom like, "clean up in aisle 3" or anything. Doc did a fantastic job of avoiding the displays and the people!

On Easter, we went to my sister's house and even though our kids weren't able to come home, we had a good time with all our nieces and nephews! Our kids will all be home this weekend for a wedding shower for Laura and Adam and then our open house to say thanks to all of you will be hosted from 2-5 at the Christian Church in Cairo. Please try to drop by and let us treat you to a sandwich luncheon and a piece of cake as we tell you how glad it is to see you and say thanks for everything that all of you did! Doc has been keeping his cuff down so he can talk for several hours each day. Yesterday, we went for 7 hours and he did great! He is practicing so he can talk the whole time on Saturday! I think he has a lot to say or something!

Please pass this on because we are only spreading the message on the open house around through this e-mail and by word of mouth. For anyone that doesn't know, Cairo is on hwy 63 about 5 miles north of Moberly and once you enter Cairo, it is hard to get lost! You will find 2 churches in Cairo and we are hosting this at the Christian Church Activity Center which is connected to the Christian church. It is located about a block south of the main road through Cairo. I know there will be a bunch of persons there and it will be hard to sit and visit with each of you one on one for extended amounts of time but it will be a great time of fellowship! I have found that we should all take more time for that!

On Monday, the equipment company came by to put the correct wheels on Doc's chair. They are a little larger and have better tread so now he can really go! One can only wonder at what wonderful adventures we have to tell as we get used to these wheels! I can only tell you that I will be walking behind the wheelchair for a few days instead of in front of it!

This week is busy trying to finish up on all the home health care training because starting next week, I am planning on being back at work. I am a little nervous about leaving Doc but I am excited about being back at work! I am sure there is a little nervousness on the part of those spending the days with Doc too but I am sure they will adapt quickly and all will be well!

The weather is looking promising for a few days this week so we are hopeful to be able to catch a couple of Carrissa's softball games in the afternoon after the doctor appointments are done. We have a few of those this week! I think we are getting most of the initial doctor visits done and after this week, we will just have the monthly visits to take care of unless Doc gets sick. AND we pray that doesn't happen anymore!

This Wednesday we are going to a presentation for my brother, Lloyd. He is getting an award from the state for using his cpr training to save Doc's life. I don't know if he wants all the fuss but I am glad that we get a chance to officially say thanks!

As always, I continue to thank you for your prayers and know that they are making a difference! There is no doubt in my mind that there will be a day that we will be dancing for joy at Doc walking again. There is also no doubt in my mind that God is using us to do some special things for him, now and in the future! You might add a prayer that we do it right!

I continue to say thanks to all that continue to help us through the weeks….remind you to stop by for a sandwich on April 2nd if you can….tell my co-workers that I will see them next week….and Doc says that there better be some AECI guys eating a sandwich with him on the 2nd…..(we want to say thanks for the Cardinal brick-he shows that certificate off to everyone that visits!)

Your friends on this beautiful Monday morning!
Cindy and Doc

April 10-2005

I'm sitting here thinking of what adventures happened since the last time that I updated you and there actually have been a few. Some of them were good and some not so good.

First, Doc finished his round of antibiotics and then about 3 days later, he got back all his symptoms of the infections that he had. This time, I think I caught it in time to prevent it from getting bad; at least we managed to avoid the necessity of oxygen. He was given another round of medicine (or good drugs as he likes to put it!) and he finished it yesterday. Now, we are keeping our fingers crossed that this round worked and we will continue to progress in a healthier fashion.

The sore on his back it still there and it isn't looking any better but if you want to look at it from the cup ½ full version, it isn't looking any worse either. The wound doctor told me to keep using this duroderm bandage that stays on for 3 days at a time so I only get to peek at it every 3 days. I always keep my fingers crossed that it works but so far, it hasn't been the miracle bandaid that I think it should be because each piece of covering is $10. That is an expensive bandaid!

Laura and Adam's wedding shower went really well. The got so many nice things but the best part of it all was the visiting that I got in. I left Doc with my brother and Brandon Bailey and I think he had a good time with them. They watched sports on tv and that was much better for them than a wedding shower. Later in the morning they loaded him up and hauled him up to the church so that we could start our open house! He came speeding into the door and across the room with the biggest grin on his face! He looked like a kid on Christmas morning with all the anticipation of knowing great things were coming his way! They did too! The open house was a great success and we wanted to say thanks to all that took a minute to come by and let us tell you thanks! We had almost 150 persons stop by to say hi and we were thrilled! I know there were many more out there that wanted to come and things didn't allow it but we appreciated the thoughts and we still say thanks to all of you! Laura and Joey (our 2 newest additions to the family) were able to join us with their parents and they were thrilled with the wonderful community we live in and the people they were able to meet and visit with! We already knew we loved them all but it was nice to share them! Doc really enjoyed his co-workers, although not many of the AECI group were able to join us because they are in outage and many of them were working. Doc wants to find out if the vent will be ok in his work setting because if it is ok, he is wanting to make a trip up to see all of his buddies and say hi first hand! We will check it out!

By the end of the day, Doc was pretty tuckered out and we didn't do much that evening except watch a couple of the college basketball games! At least, he was playing the 'tuckered out, can't do anything except watch ESPN' act out very well! I fell for it!

On Monday, I left Doc in the shower with another woman and went to work. I told him that I few months ago that would have gotten him in trouble but I was actually feeling good about it! It was so nice to see all my co-workers and friends again and get back into a groove of some sort! It didn't take too long to remember the job and get back on track. The hardest part was getting in the hours. Doc had 3 appointments in Columbia and even when I make them for 5, I still have to leave at 3:30 to get home, get him loaded and to Columbia in time. In time, though, these appointments will decline and we won't have so many to go to. This coming week brings 3 new visits to Columbia but they are scheduled for the first 3 days, so we will get them over with and then be done with it. Our home health care worked out fairly well. I want to take our hat off to the Moberly Home Health Agency because the help we are getting through them is fantastic! We have really gotten good care! Then my mom and Linda Taylor did an excellent job of taking care of Doc during the day. They were a little nervous about it and I think they both lost a night or two of sleep over worrying about it but once they experienced it, it wasn't such a big deal. I hope they don't skip any sleep over it this week! Our only hiccup came on the last two days of the week and our planned home care help had a death in the family and we had to work around that. You can't ever plan for that and we made it. Brandon Bailey came out and played poker with Doc on Thursday and then even helped us on one of our dr. appointments that evening. He was a lifesaver (cherry flavor because that is my favorite!). Then on Friday, I worked from home, which wasn't a bad thing because I was able to do that mostly uninterrupted! All in all, it was a great week and I think it went very smoothly. I am looking forward to this week at work too!

Our latest wheelchair adventure was that we leaked some tube feeding out of the tube and into the motor cable under the chair. If you don't know, doing that will cause the cable to be defective and if you have a defective cable, the chair doesn't move! If the chair doesn't move, it is very hard to push! Our equipment company picked it up and had to keep it for a couple of days but they got it running again and brought it back. We had a manual wheelchair to fall back on but we were really glad to get our powerchair back. The manual wheelchair was much harder to do weight shifts in and Doc doesn't fit into it really good. Good enough for a donated chair but not one that you would want to sit in very long. The story that paints the funniest picture on this whole adventure is probably my mom and I trying to push Doc and his defective 450 lb chair up the front ramp by myself. I thought that it would be hard but not impossible. I got him about ½ way up the ramp and then when I couldn't push it further, I got in trouble when it decided to roll backwards. Luckily my mom was there and between two of us we got it all the way up! I had thought that if I couldn't do it, I would yell at our neighbor for some help but I didn't take into consideration that Doc wouldn't just stay where he stopped! I didn't figure in that backwards stuff!

Doc's progress is slow (like a turtle) but he was always pretty laid back and slow to move anyway! I don't know why this should be any different. The good news is that it is still going forward! He has had all types of things happen but they are always different and they always come & go. He has feeling, although weak, about ½ way down his chest now. During therapies, he has felt his elbow moving, his knees moving, his quad muscles, his groin area, rotation in his shoulders and his Achilles. The only feeling that he feels every time during therapy, though, is his shoulder rotation. He is starting to feel more than just pressure in his bottom area. He does more weight shifts because he gets tired of sitting. He calls it "bleacher butt". He had one night that we were working him out and he actually moved all his toes on his left foot. When I say move, I meant move. He bent them all really well upon request and it was much more than a twitch, which is what I am used to seeing. Again, that only happened one night and we usually get a little twitch in the fingers and toes but no significant movement. He is able to move his head forward and control it backwards (unless he goes too far and then it ends up on his chest and he is begging for someone to give it a shove back). I usually do it for the usual fee of a kiss! I, being the slave driver that I am, take him through all the workouts every day and make sure that he knows that there is more to do in the day than watch tv.

Speech therapy continues to move along and he is getting very good at lengthy amounts of time with his cuff down. We have been eating all types of soft foods and nothing appears to be going down to the lungs. I make sure that I feed him things with red, green, and chocolate coloring so I can tell when I suction him if any of the color shows up. So far, we have gone a couple of weeks and his swallow muscles continue to feel stronger to him. The therapist told us that she is leaving it up to Doc on when he wants to run another swallow test but he wants to wait for a little longer. I think we have been down that road so many times that he wants to feel more certain about it before we make the commitment to start on the dietary side of things. I am not sure that he is really ready to handle a full diet but we are definitely on the right track! We just hope it holds! Then the voice is up to more than 6 hours a day. Many days, he has his voice for 6 hours straight and it feels so good to sit and talk with him! I will never take that for granted again!

Yesterday, we headed up to Trenton to watch Carrissa play softball. Adam & Laura and Jaymi & Joey were able to meet us over there. We had a blast and the only drawback was the wind was blowing the dust off the field right onto us at about 30 miles an hour. We used mom's purple flowered scarf to cover up Doc's nose and mouth and try to keep the dust off the trach area. He asked if he looked good in it. I love purple so I thought so. I am not sure he would have agreed if could have seen himself though. Laura told him he looked like a bank robber with the scarf over his face like that! Might work but he can't point his fingers and say "stick them up". I teased him that he looked like pigpen off Charlie Brown by the end of the day because he was covered completely in brown dust! We had a great supper out and Doc even had a few bites of jello off the salad bar!

We continue to have persons come over to help us with all sort of things. I had someone come to help me look at adding a screen door to the back so I can open up our backdoor and let some air in. We had my brother come over and mow my grass for the first time this year with many, many more of you asking to help with that. I have had many persons call and pick out a night to help me put Doc into bed and every single night during the week is spoken for. I think if weeks were 14 days long, I would still have them spoken for! Thanks for all of you that do that every single week! Most importantly though, is all the cards and e-mails that we continue to get that let us know that prayers are still being said. Two words, faith and believe, still continue to pop up over and over! We have not lost either one of them and we thank all of you that haven't either!

I don't know when I will send out our next update because I have a huge list of to-do things as Adam's wedding is less than 2 weeks away and now we are already diving into planning Jaymi's wedding (set for Oct 22) but I will keep you updated on our adventures! I used to type these updates to let everyone in Missouri know what was going on in Colorado and now I feel like I am sending it to Colorado to let our newest friends there know what is going on in Missouri (although many of our Missouri family and friends don't know all our adventures either!). We wanted to close with a special hello to each of our new friends we met in Colorado and let you know that we have you in our thoughts and prayers daily!

Your friends,

Cindy and Doc

April 27, 2005

They say that time flies when you are having a good time so we must be having a blast! I cannot believe that we have been home for 2 months now!

I had several e-mails this week wanting to know how the wedding went and how Doc was getting along so I thought I would take a minute to jot a few words. I know my uncle is laughing at the word "few" because when I saw him this weekend at the wedding, he told me that even though it seemed like every e-mail was 13 pages long, he enjoyed them. He also told me that I must have come into this world talking to be so wordy. Doc really got into some hot water when he piped up with "I believe that!".

I will start with the wedding......it was beautiful, elegant, fun, and probably one of the most favorite weekends of my life! When we got into the van on Friday morning, I told Doc that I was sorta sad that we weren't piling into the car and heading out for the wedding as if things were like they used to be but I was also very happy to be driving the van and heading to the wedding with Doc smiling, healthy and still with us! So I threw out the sad thought and clung to the happy thought! My adventure began about Brookfield when I ran into this big windy, pouring thunderstorm. The van was rocking like a boat and if I had time to think about it, I might have gotten seasick but I was just trying hard to hold it on the road and keep the wipers running fast enough to see it! I was never a fan of driving in storms and Doc always seemed to thrive on the challenge so I would have loved to turn the wheel over to him but when I looked into the review mirror to tell him so, he was counting sheep! The storm lasted an hour of my driving time and Doc slept through every minute of it! Imagine

We arrived at the hall and helped what we could with decorating and flowers but Laura's family did almost all of it. They did a great job at making it look wonderful! Around 4:30 we headed over to the motel so we could get signed in and head back for the 6 pm rehearsal. Brandon and Amanda Bailey had followed us in our truck loaded with the equipment that we needed for the weekend (amazing how much there was but we had the lift, the mattress, and the shower chair…not to mention battery charges, supplies, clothes, and the list went on…). Brandon met us at the motel to unload the stuff but upon arrival we discovered they had given their only roll-in shower/handicap room away and moved our reservation to a plain handicap room which wasn't large enough for anything! So then I thought we were in a real pickle but before I panicked too much, they found another motel that did have a roll in shower room available and we loaded Doc back up and headed down the road. We arrived there to find everything in working order so after we unloaded and cleaned up, we headed back for the rehearsal and rehearsal dinner. Doc managed to keep his wheelchair in control and we didn't leave any mementoes in the church walls or at the rehearsal dinner. Laura's dad took good care of us in making sure that everywhere we needed to get into had accessible ramps and it felt good to be able to go in and out of homes as visitors like we used to.

After that, we met up with Trisha. She was a tech from Craig that we really became good friends with and as always, God placed her in the right place at the right time. She had moved back home to St. Joe to go back to school just a few weeks before we were heading to St. Joe and she was wonderful enough to volunteer to help us with Doc over the weekend. I don't know how hard it would have been without her but it was sure easy with her! She helped me every morning and every night to get him up and put him to bed. She watched him while I ran errands and while I did some visiting/dancing at the wedding. We finally got her up on the dance floor later in the evening and we were glad to see her have a few minutes of fun too! We got to take Adam out to eat lunch on Saturday and that was different that what I thought it was going to be!! I thought it was going to be Doc and me along with Adam & Trish. Then along came Travis, Joey, Jaymi, TJ, Carrissa, Brandon, Amanda, Matthew, and Dale. I have to admit that we had the most enjoyable, noisy lunch I can ever remember! Doc kept trying to order ribs but was having a huge problem getting the waitress to bring them to him—plus he wanted an order of baked beans and a piece of apple pie. Probably had something to do with Travis telling her he can't have them! Joey was sitting by him though and feeding him some scrumptious strawberry yogurt so I am not sure why he was complaining…hehe! It was a special hour!

Then came the moment of getting ready for the evening and getting our pictures taken a million times! While I am on the picture thing, I wanted to thank Mark Cunningham for taking wonderful pictures for us at the wedding and for putting them on a disc for me to share some of them with all of you. He wanted to make sure that his & Doc's fellow workers notice how good Doc can clean up! It was a wonderful time of visiting with family and friends and all I can say is that 1 a.m. arrived way too soon and it was all over! Doc did the dollar dance with Laura and she climbed up in his lap while he twirled her around in the chair. She was a little apprehensive at first but she told him it ended up being fun! I also got in a couple of slow dances myself and then each of the girls had to have one too. We had him sipping and puffing all night, keeping his chair moving! Doc still can dance like crazy though and you don't even have to worry about your toes getting stepped on anymore!

Sunday came and we watched the kids open their gifts and then headed home. We stopped at Brenda and Joe Evans (Jaymi's future mother and father –in-law) for a bar-b-q on the way and that was nice to visit with them for a little while. Both Adam and Jaymi are lucky to have found such wonderful families to accompany their partners. We got home around 9 and Joey & Jaymi came home with us so they were there to help me get Doc to bed and wrap up the weekend.

Yesterday we went to speech therapy and Doc was eating better than ever. They are ready to turn him loose on a more regular diet and see how things go. I am going to start working on weaning him off some of his tube food and onto a puree diet this week and see how things go. I will have to count calories and maybe we will be able to only have to be on the tube feeding at night time. We will see how things go. He ate an entire smoothie and a piece of cheesecake in the therapy though and had Nicole (therapist) dancing around the room! She was pretty excited. Then tonight we went out and I shared an order of alfredo with him which he had been waiting for a long time. I think he REALLY enjoyed it! It was just good to not be eating alone.

Speaking of being excited, there is hardly a day that goes by without us celebrating a new sensation. It is still all so slow and so hit & miss but it continues to change every day. Doc is experiencing all types of feeling…he had worms crawling on his bottom one day and then tingling all over his back the next day. He has had tingling in his hips and down his sides so hopefully that means good things and it will continue to improve. His toes and fingers continue to move a little bit and occasionally we have significant movement in them. He can feel several of the joints and muscles in his body as we do range of motion and he has touch sensation almost to the belly button now. We will have to continue to wait and see what time has in store for us but we are excited at anything new that happens, and like Nicole, we dance around the room celebrating little things! We continue to pray that the diaphragm kicks in and lets him gain independence from the vent but we aren't there yet.

We ask for your continued prayers and thank all of you for your continued support! Our road has been rough but it has been paved with a smooth surface through many of you! Thanks for the prayers, cards, visits, help with chores and the "Doc" sitting that so many of you are doing for us! I cannot imagine life without it and we do not take it for granted. Doc still wants to get up to the power plant and do some visiting but we aren't sure if the vent is safe in that setting. I e-mailed Craig hospital to ask that question and if I get the all clear, I will try to get him up there to visit soon. I also e-mailed Craig to find out about the all-important fishing pole because Doc is ready to fish and we aren't sure if we are going to be able to purchase one or if we are going to have to build it. We made our stop in at the new Bass Pro store last week and I think that really gave him the fever!

We are now looking forward to a fund raiser that they are working on for May 8th. They are going to have a country/western show in Moberly at the Municipal Auditorium in the afternoon. We are looking forward to that and I think that might be Doc's mother's day treat for me! As usual, there is something almost every weekend in May between that and Carrissa's ballgames, graduations, and our ever famous Orscheln Golf Tournament. On top of that, we have several weddings coming up that we get to keep practicing our dancing skills at getting prepared for Jaymi's big day in October.

Until the next update…your friends,
Doc & Cindy Blackmore

Cindy and Doc at Adam's Wedding

Adam, Laura and Doc

Cindy and Doc dancing at Adam's Wedding

May 19-2005

I have had so many persons asking for an update that I thought I would check it out and see when I sent last one out. It was almost a month ago so I thought I would catch everyone up on our many adventures! We have had some this month too!

I don't let Doc sit home much. We are on the go so much that when we do have an entire day at home, he always comments how good it feels to be home for the whole day. But then on the flip side of that, if he is home for very long, he always makes the comment that it feels good to get out, even if it is just for therapy! See? It is true what they say about the grass being greener on the other side of fence! The story of all of our lives!

May was really busy though! Carrissa ended up her softball season with Regionals in Columbia. I took part of the day off and Doc & I traveled down there. I wrote that in one sentence but that was a great adventure! First off, I headed home to pick Doc up to make it to the games on time and we were even ahead of schedule when I finally got him loaded and bolted down. Then I turned the key and I got a little clicking noise and that was it! I looked in the rearview mirror and asked Doc "what do I do now?". Well he walked me through how to jump a battery (and just so you know that I actually learnt it, red to red, black to black and DO NOT let them touch each other!). Anyway, I jumped my first vehicle and it started but it wouldn't stay started. That's when I found out that sometimes it is not the battery. Sometimes it is that yucky bluish/whitish corrosion stuff that is sticking to the battery posts. Then you have to get a wire brush, take off the battery cables and brush like heck! After I did that, we started up and stayed started so off we were! We finally made it to the ballfields and I was in the middle of unloading Doc from the van when the lift stopped ½ way down. There was Doc suspended in mid-air and the ramp wasn't working. How could 2 things not work in the same day? So I found the little handle under the seat and manually pumped the ramp down to the ground to let Doc off. That's when my husband told me that I probably didn't clean the post good enough because the ramp runs off the battery and it wasn't getting a good connection. About that time, I thought I had another use for that pumping handle...hehe! Actually, I thought he was wrong and I just smiled and said ok! My mind was just on getting to the softball game before it was over! So I locked up the van and we proceeded to cross the parking lot when his wheelchair stopped and it said there was a right brake cable error. So I got down and wiggled all the cables, turned his chair off and on and then we were off again. We went about 3 feet and it stopped again and this time the error message said the left brake cable had an error! The temperature seemed to be getting hotter by the minute but I crawled around on the pavement again and wiggled and turned everything off and on one more time. All Doc said was that this was going to be a great story to add to our adventures! We finally made it to the game and we didn't miss too much because it was 0-0 and they had to play 3 extra innings before the other team finally scored and we lost! It was an exciting, well played game though. So now, we are heading back to the van to take Carrissa out to eat lunch before the next game starts and do you remember a few sentences back when I said I thought Doc was wrong? Well, he was indeed right because when I got back into the van and turned the key (after pumping him up by hand with the ramp handle), I just got a clicking noise once more. I popped the hood and was starring at some more of that powdering looking substance. I had all my tools though so I wire-brushed some more and tightened things up once again and low and behold...the van finally started! We ate lunch, watched another game and finally made it home late in the night. I think I impressed Doc because he told me several times that he was really proud of how I handled the day! I guess he underestimated my power under the hood!

Mothers day followed that and they had a country western show fund raiser for us at the Municipal Auditorium. Those that donated their time to perform for us did a great job and I will always remember how special the day was. I think all those that attended were treated to a real special show but we still wanted to say thanks for those that came and for all those that helped put it together! Jaymi and Carrissa surprised me and came home for the day which made it very special! Then they surprised us once again and the "million dollar band" (we named it!) played a special tune just for us in honor of our anniversary and Doc & I danced to the words of a very special love song! I was wanting something to make this year special and it was given to us in the form of a gift of music!

Then the following Monday, I took off ½ day and Doc & I headed down to St. Louis to attend a dinner they were having for the softball team and their parents. It felt good to be able to support Carrissa and even though it was a long trip for an hour of pizza, it was good to have been able to do it.

The next day was our 25th wedding anniversary and I really wanted to do something special so that the day would be memorable. I came up with the idea of heading to Columbia for a lunch/picnic of frozen custard (something Doc had been wanting-with butterscotch topping) (cherries for me!) & he ate the whole thing. Then we drove to Blue Springs to go through an antique mall that we have always loved. Doc liked that idea because he said that he wanted to pick out something really special for me and didn't know how to shop for it but this would be great! He could look around all afternoon and then pick it out himself and it would be his gift to me! We started down the first aisle and he stopped me and asked me "how much is that stuffed mink?", then as the day went on it was "how much is that mauve birdcage?", "how much is that skunk salt & pepper shaker set?", "how much is that fencing mask?", "how much are those ceramic ducks?", and I could go on and on but not once did he ask me to price anything that I really liked! By the end of the day, he had me laughing so hard I had tears running down my cheeks. I think they were tears of laughter…I might have been crying at the thought of what I was going to be taking home! Anyway, when it was all said and done, he picked out a beautiful oak curio cabinet and an Italian amber colored glass cordial set to put on top of it! I thought of my brother right off and wondered what he would say about us bringing more stuff (junk) home and especially another piece of furniture to store it in. (the best part about it is that I still have 2 shelves empty just waiting on another adventure out to find something to put on them!). Doc did really, really good and I was excited! We loaded it up in the van and then headed out to supper. We stopped at the restaurant that we have always liked across from the Odessa outlet mall. They made us feel so welcome and it was a special dinner. Doc ate some bean & ham soup with crackers and then some mashed potatoes/gravy and some applebutter. They surprised us because they brought a beautiful decorated mini cake to the table with "Happy 25th Anniversary" and yellow roses on it. That was neat because Doc usually gives me yellow roses so I still got them…I just ate them this time! He ate a bite of that with me too. We both really, really liked the day and we will never forget it.

I finally was able to go to the dentist and finish a root canal that I started the week of Doc's accident. I have been hanging on to a temporary crown for almost 8 months and it really did not want to come out. I was thinking it was stuck there forever when Dr. Furhman finally worked it off! I wanted to say a special thanks to him and to all that work in his office for all their support during all of this and especially for their prayers! They are like another extended part of our family. It seems like we have a lot of those! It is a good thing!

The weather and Doc's health finally both worked together to allow us to attend a Cairo baseball game and our welcome there meant a lot to both of us! We live in a wonderful community and our friends are immeasurable! It felt like really being home when we finally sat and watched a baseball game with them! (which they won by the way and now we have the game winning ball in our living room!)

Doc had a couple of days to regroup before we were on the way to St. Joe to watch Jaymi graduate. That was a great day! Then all my brothers and some friends headed over to Jaymi's apartment and loaded her up to bring her home for awhile. Doc was teasing her fiancé and asked him that if this was only temporary. Her fiancé promised him it was just until October! Doc has enjoyed holding that over Jaymi's head all week! She has been a wonderful help and great company. The worse part is that we put Doc down to sleep and then stay up another couple of hours talking every night. That will probably catch up to me!

We still have our wonderful help coming in the evenings to assist in putting Doc down and when Jaymi can help, we are flying through it now! I think we are all getting better at it and then with the extra hands, he can be settled into bed in 20 minutes now! Much better than our original 2 hours!

As far as Doc's progress goes..we are making progress. It continues to be very slow and we have no promises from anyone as to what the future holds except the faith in our hearts but we remain optimistic! Doc can feel a light touching sensation in both thighs and it is a sensation that seems to there permanently, unlike some other things that come and go. He continues to experience zapping like sensations throughout his entire body and some are stronger than others but he never has a day go by without experiencing several of these! (we even made up a song called "butt zaps" but Jaymi wasn't impressed with it!) Our neck muscles are slowly getting stronger but he is still only able to barely support the head or turn it. He hasn't taken any breaths on his own yet but on the other side of things, he remains oxygen free and is doing great with his sats and temperatures. We still are messing with a couple of ugly sores but they aren't getting any worse, they just aren't going away either. There are days that he can really get some action in the hands and feet areas and then other days we just get little flickers. The best part is that he is talking almost all day long and his voice is getting stronger and stronger! He is eating 3 times a day and even though he isn't eating full meals yet, we are starting to get into the routine of "meal time" again. We are eating more quickly and more of it but we still aren't up to portion sizes. I am always ready to try to give him something new and more challenging to chew and he is always up to the challenge! I have been counting his calories and as soon as I can get him to close to a consistent 800 or more, I will cut his tube feeding off during the day and only run it at night. It always feels good to eliminate one more thing.

Oh yeah, I wanted to remember to tell you that we named the van! Doc started calling it Porky because he says that it reminds him of a fat pig. So the name has stuck and mom even found a lovely pig magnet that sits on the dash and we lovingly refer to our wheels as "Porky" now! So I guess if you see a van heading down the highway that looks like a pig, you can wave knowing that it is probably us!

As soon as the outage is over at AECI (where Doc works) we are planning a visit to say hi! He is excited about that I think those that work with him are ready too! Don't ever say that you can't wait to retire because I think we have discovered that you will miss it more than you think!

If you are wondering what Doc spends most of his time doing, it is cheering on his Cardinals! And they are worth cheering for most of the time! We won't talk about the game they played today though.

We wanted to say thanks for all the help that we are still getting in the way of yard mowing and whatever else everyone it doing to make our lives easier! We continue to ask for continued prayers and know in our hearts that they are making a difference. We have a list of churches that we are starting to schedule visits to in order to share our experiences and express our thanks! We are both looking forward to those visits and know that it is part of what we are sup-posed to be doing. We have great stories to share and some day we both know there is an ending to all of this that will be amazing! You cannot have an amazing story without an amazing ending!

Until the next update,

Your friends,

Cindy and Doc Blackmore

June 2005

You can always tell when about a month has gone by because I start having persons wondering how things are going since the last time they heard anything. The problem with typing up an e-mail once a month versus one a week though, it that I forget what I wrote last time so I hope you don't get any old news!

We celebrated Christmas in June this month because we missed part of it while in Colorado! We have some friends that we usually have a big, grand, hillbilly Christmas with where we exchange the most wonderful, valuable gifts imaginable. The kind that you find on the clearance tables or in the dollar stores! We always have a day of shopping before the big event and the ladies shop for the men and vice versa. We often laugh at what the shop clerks must think when they check us out and we are buying all the same useless, wonderful, they never thought anyone would buy, type merchandise. It's like there is suddenly a run on it or something! The guys always buy us the most lovely jewelry from Claire's and again I laugh at what the store clerks think when they check out our husbands buying these things and them making out how excited their wives are going to be to open it! I wonder what they say about them when they leave the store all excited with their purchases? I thought the women had out-shopped the men this year until we opened our 4' reindeer with turkey legs all made out of metal/nuts/bolts with a heavy duty spring as a neck and painted a beautiful bronze gold to create the greatest of all bobbing head things that I have ever seen! I had to give in graciously and admit we had been out-shopped! Oh yeah, we also got a frog with bouncy legs that has a lady bug on its tongue and everything wiggles when the wind blows! I almost forgot about that. It now sticks out of the ground about 3' in front of our house. We had about ½ dozen other 'special' gifts and I don't want to take away from them but I just am not going to list them all! On the big day of the party, I put up a tree and decorated the house a little (although not to the extent that I do in December), lit a Christmas tree smelling candle and we had a grand, warm Christmas party!

We continue to explore things to do in wheelchairs and we have found quite a few unique things that we are enjoying. We went on a hike that we found in one of our state parks and even though there was a bridge that had about a 5" lip that gave us some concern, we made it (with the help of Joey and Jaymi) and Doc & I felt good to be back in the woods! It was a beautiful day! We found an outdoor play production in Columbia and that was fun to attend also. Then we still are able to enjoy the movies and the mall (of course!). Then there are a multitude of softball and baseball games to watch to support our nieces and nephews!

There was a motorcycle show fund raiser for us in Moberly which we attended this month. We had a really good time there visiting with old friends and meeting new! Doc was slobbering over some of the bikes and planning the day when he might own one. He told them that he might be able to enter his own next year. We wanted to say a special thanks to those that put a lot of work into it and those that came and supported it. One of those working so hard that day also had a wedding to attend…..where he was the groom! A special wish for a wonderful marriage from us to him! The weather wasn't picture perfect that day and we appreciated the turn out! The trophy that they presented Doc with that day (a Budweiser beer can with a motorcycle on top of it) proudly sits on a shelf in our living room. It doesn't quite blend in with the outdoor theme of the room but Doc likes to look at it so it stays for awhile!

Doc "graduated" from speech/swallowing therapy so now he is free to try new foods and see how they chew up and go down the throat. He continues to try new things every day and I don't think he has had too much trouble with anything he has tried. Of course, we haven't tried steak or anything but we are making progress in that direction! We are able to go to restaurants and order off the menu and actually eat a portion of it so that is exciting for both of us. I wish you didn't have to be under 12 to order off the kids menu because that is usually more than he can eat……….If our taste buds were the same, we could share a meal but we have never ordered the same things when we gone out. He actually did have a Happy Meal from McDonalds and made it through about ½ of it so that gives you an idea of the volume that he can handle at one sitting. BUT it was hamburger and fries and not pudding, so we are making progress.

Last month we had the adventure with the battery on "Porky"(the van) and this month "Porky" had a flat tire. As I have lost my handyman for a little while, we had joined AAA and so it wasn't like I have to write you how I learnt how to change a tire this month–because I didn't even try! I just called AAA and they came and changed it and then I drove it to the repair shop and had it fixed! One wonders what "Porky" might do next month???

We did have one funny adventure, although it was scary at the time. We were in Dillards looking for candlelighter dresses for Jaymi's wedding and Doc took a corner too sharply and caught his arm in between the wheelchair arm rest and glass display case. The wheelchair continued to try to go forward and it went back on its tipper wheels and then started jerking. Jaymi and I were trying to get Doc to stop the wheelchair and all he kept saying was that he would after his head spasms stopped. The way the wheelchair was jerking was causing his head to jerk around and he thought it was spasms (although he had never had one before so I don't know why he thought that?) We finally got around to the clutches and threw them off and pulled him back manually and amazingly the head spasms stopped! Then we took a look at the damage and at first I was pretty scared because his arm was as flat as a pancake and you could see the shape of his bone in the forearm through the skin but it felt like it was all still in tact. I waited a couple of hours (while we continued to shop for dresses because the shopping had to go on you know!) and the muscle rebounded back and it wasn't too long before we had some shape back to it. It took a couple of days for the mark to go away but it did! Now I laugh at it

Doc made his own adventure with one of our many trips to Hobby Lobby. With the upcoming wedding plans under way, poor Doc has to go with us on all our shopping adventures and I cannot even find the words to tell you how much he looks forward to looking at flowers, netting, and candles. (He continues to ask Jaymi if she is sure that there isn't anything that she needed for the wedding from Bass Pro and I know it is hard to believe but we can't think of anything we need from Bass Pro!) There are times that we will park him and his wheelchair close by and then start down the aisles looking for various items on our list. One of these days we left the shopping cart in front of him and he became bored with sitting still so the next thing Jaymi and I knew was that he had pushed the cart, using his wheelchair, down the aisle and around to where we were. He was very proud of himself because I think it must have been challenging to keep the cart heading in the right direction without crashing into things. The only down side to that was that when we put him down that night we noticed that the cart had rubbed a bare spot on his leg over 7" long and the along the top of that mark was another one going the other direction about 4" long. I think that was there the bottom of the cart met the legs. He gave us a sheepish grin when we held up his leg to show him but I still think he thought it was worth it. Lucky for him it has healed nicely and other than a little scar, we didn't have any problems with it.

Father's Day was a good day as both the girls and Joey were home to help him celebrate. Adam and Laura were able to surprise him Friday night with a visit and some cards so he got to see all the kids and that was the only thing he said he really wanted. We are planning a big 3 day weekend in July where all of us are going to travel to St. Louis to do some fun things. We are going to a comedy club, the zoo, horseracing, and the Cardinal/Cubs game. That sounds like a full weekend to me and we are hoping all the kids will be able to join us! I call them kids but I made the mistake of saying that when I was trying to find a hotel room for all of us and they quickly reminded me that none of them count as kids. I told them they were my kids and they always would be...I really wasn't trying to get that "kids eat free" deal or anything!

Speaking of the Cardinals, Doc watches almost every single game and is enjoying that! Then I gave him some tickets for a game the last weekend in June and we braved a trip to the stadium (with the help of my sister, Pat, and her husband, Mark) and figured out how to make it to a game and get into the stadium. Now that we tried it once, it will not be so scary in the future! I am sure there will be many more Busch Stadium visits! I could tell that it meant more to Doc than I even thought it would! I think it was a very special moment for him when he looked across that field!

We had fun cheering the Cairo Boys Baseball team through the final four in state this year! It was an exciting time for out whole community and we were really proud of the boys!

Doc & I attended the Cairo Baptist Church one Sunday and were able to share our thanks and our story with them and it was a wonderful feeling. After it was over and we were on our way home, Doc said, "Talk about feeling like you just did the right thing…" We both know that this story isn't over but we both feel like it is important to share it so that others know that there is a purpose in everything and sometimes the worse situations can turn out to be great blessings! We have a mission and we are looking forward to continuing it in the days ahead! So many persons have touched our hearts and it feels good to reach back to others! Our next scheduled visit is with Oak Grove Baptist Church, north of Holiday on July 17th and if you can join us there, I think you will be welcomed! Several have asked of a list of churches that we are visiting and there are several that we are planning on visiting but other than this next one, we haven't set any solid dates yet. I will keep those posted that want to know though because I am sure we will be doing this for awhile!

We finally made our trip up to AECI to visit with all of Doc's working buddies and he felt good to be able to be there and tell everyone hi! It had been a long time since he had been to work! I am not sure if he did any more than he used to do while he was there but he tells me he used to work hard! Really! We just want all of those we got to see and all those that we missed to know that you all are close to our hearts and we have appreciated everything you have done and continue to do for us!

We continue to have persons coming by the house to visit, play cards, helping get Doc down at night, sitting with him during the day, mowing our yard, fixing stuff (which helps keep Doc's honey-do list under control because it continues to grow with each passing day but he is aware of it so it isn't going to be a huge surprise when one day he can do those things), sending e-mails and letters, and the many, many other things that make our world so wonderful! Thanks to all of you! I continue to believe that after faith, friends and family are two of the most perfect treasures a person can have!

Doc's progress remains slow but still heading in the right direction. He continues to feel sensations in new areas, continues to be able to get some movement out of the feet/toes/fingers, and continues to feel the 'zaps' as he likes to call them. He is keeping his oxygen level up without the use of oxygen and he rarely gets a temperature unless his environment gets a little too warm. His sore on his back is healing really nicely and I am excited about how much better it is getting. The one on his heel is healing nicely too. He is still totally vent dependant for now and we continue to pray for progress but we're not there yet. His head motion is getting better (he even nodded at me this week and although it wasn't a smooth nod, it was a nod) but his neck still cannot support it nor can he move it normal yet but we are "heading in the right direction". See how important those words are? Another milestone this month is that we only had to go the doctor twice for the whole month and I think as long as Doc stays healthy, we will see only one visit per month and then even less. Finally, one of our greatest accomplishments this month was that Doc has worked up to a full day of keeping his cuff down on his trac and talking all day long. He was excited when he finally pulled that off and we look back to how hard it was when we started with just 5-15 minutes at a time. Now, I really have to share the talk time (especially with Jaymi home on top of it!)

We continue to ask for prayers because we have faith that prayers are going to make a difference! In return, we continue to pray for each of you and ask that you feel as blessed as we feel!

Until the next update,

Your friends,

Cindy and Doc Blackmore

PS: While Doc was in Craig, he developed this imaginary monkey friend of his that he laid all the blame on for things he did to get in trouble (and yes, you can still be ornery enough to get in trouble even when you are paralyzed from the neck down!). I thought we left the monkey in Denver but we made the mistake of giving the guys a stuffed, masked monkey with bungee arms for Christmas. Now Doc tells me that his new monkey comes to life in the night time and does things! Whenever I ask Doc something, I almost always hear, "my monkey did it!" I try to hang the monkey by the back of the neck on the feeding tube pole so we can keep an eye on it all night but Doc insists he can get off (he has a cape you know so it must be a super-hero monkey!). Anyway, I think the future might hold some exciting monkey stories! The biggest problem we have had this month is that all of Doc's socks keep disappearing and he said his monkey is stashing them! Hopefully, I will find the stash soon!

July 2005

July started out with a bang (it usually does as the 4th falls in that first week). This year it was a special bang for us though. The Coal Yard crew that work with Doc at AECI gave us some awesome fireworks that lit up our 4th. Doc said they were the best backyard fireworks he has ever seen and the entire time they were going off and we were admiring them, we were both thinking of where they came from. The fireworks were great but it was the thought that meant the most to us! Thanks for lighting up our skies!

Speaking of AECI friends, we also were able to attend a fish fry at one of Doc's buddies with several of his AECI co-workers. It was a special evening for us. I haven't seen Doc eat so much food since the accident! I filled one plate up with food and thought that after Doc was done with what he wanted, I would nibble on the rest but there wasn't anything left. Not only was there nothing left, but when I asked him if he enjoyed it, he told me he would like some more. So I filled it up again and he ate & ate until most of it was gone. Then he asked for a cookie. Then he asked for some more fish a little later. They even sent a container of fish home with him which he ate the next day for lunch. He said he never had fish that tasted so good! I almost called him Porky II. But food aside, the very best part was all the laughs that were shared and just being together!

Doc had a grand adventure as he made his first trip back to the golf course. Jaymi, Joey and I played 9 holes while Doc followed along in the wheelchair cheering us on! It felt so good to be walking down the fairways talking to him again. You can do a lot of talking when you walk a round of golf. (well, actually you can do a lot of talking anytime except during church services and movies!) On top of that, it felt good to have him watching and helping my game again (I need A LOT of help!). I will have to come clean and admit that I stole his driver. I told him at first that he could earn it back when he gets out of that chair but now I am not so certain. I think I am going to have to let him buy a new one although his brother has volunteered to custom make him one so I'm not feeling too guilty! I am really having some good luck hitting the ball with his driver and he said he was fine with getting a new one (imagine that! A guy ready for a new golf club!) Anyway, it was an enjoyable afternoon and even though Doc got a little warm and a little worn, I think he is ready to try it again!

All the kids joined us on vacation in St. Louis for 3 days. The downfall with the weekend was that we picked the 3 hottest days of the year-all in excess of 100 degrees! We went to the horse races in Illinois, the zoo, a Cardinal/Cubs game, along with other stuff. Doc had a bunch of persons starring at him while we wheeled around the zoo and he told me he felt like he was one of the zoo exhibits the way everyone was starring at him! I told him it wasn't a big deal as long as they didn't keep him! (although I might have to find out how much the zoo pays for an exhibit—he might be looking at a new opportunity!) We played hard and ate well and it was a very fun weekend. As Doc likes to tell everyone, we don't let him sit around very long.

Carrissa (our youngest daughter) decided to move back home so she joined our household again and now Doc is really missing Adam. He remembers how it was when Adam graduated and went to college and he was left with 3 women in the house. In addition, he also has my mom 2 days a week now! Sometimes, I do feel sorry for him but most of the time, I think he is really lucky to have us around! You can ask any of the 4 of us! He does like male companionship though so if there are any men out there that want to talk hunting/fishing/golfing or whatever else men talk about, feel free to come around and give Doc some male bonding time! He is also always up to the challenge of a good card game!

Probably the highlight of the month was our visit to Oak Grove Baptist Church because we both feel like it is something that we are supposed to be doing. We don't write anything down or plan on what we are going to say because when it is time, the words just seem to be there for us! We also had a wonderful Friday evening at home where several persons joined us in prayer and supper and it was a special evening. We still know in our hearts that this story is not over. There is still such a glorious ending in store for us and we are always looking forward to "when" and never do we spend much time thinking about "if" it happens. We never have enough time to share all our stories with those that listen and it even amazes us when we sit down and actually think how much our lives have been touched and what has all happened to us in the past few months. We are scheduled to visit the Christian Church in Cairo on August 21st, at the 10:30 service and we are again looking forward to another opportunity to share our thanks and our story with so many more of our friends.

Speaking of friends, I know that many of you share our deep concern over another member of our community and a very dear friend of ours that has recently found out that he has cancer and that the battle is going to be very hard in the months ahead! He is a wonderful, young man that has accepted this challenge and you can see that his faith is also holding him up as he and his wife travel down their path. I know that his path is bumpy right now but I also know that his wife is right there feeling every bump with him because that is what you do when you love someone! I don't think they will care if I ask all you that know him and those that don't to take a moment and add "Mark" to your prayers. They would be appreciative of them all as we are also! The wonderful thing about faith is that you are always a winner no matter how your prayers are answered! It is the praying and the friends and the family that are the prizes and the fact that you have the opportunity to look at life in its most precious form. It really is very fragile and most of us tramp through it without having the opportunity to be glad that we are waking up and having another shot at making a difference today! So thank you if you take the time to say a little prayer for Doc & I today and if you say a little prayer for "Mark" and his wife today! You can bet it will be returned to you—just like a smile

Many of you continue to ask how I am and if I am working and how I like it. I am doing well and I have to tell you that it is wonderful to be back at work. Doc & I used to dream of the day when we wouldn't have to work every day but once we were away from it, we knew how great having a job and co-workers really were. I have been blessed to be back at it and Doc is waiting for the day when he can return too! Then, besides me working, Jaymi stayed with Doc one Saturday so I could have a girl's day out with a couple of my girlfriends. It was a wonderful break. I guess it might be like getting something special to eat during the depression because I remember my dad telling me how even an orange was a treat during that era. When you don't get it very often, everything is sweeter! I had a sweet day!

I promised you some monkey stories and I can tell you that monkey has done some stuff this month. First off, he stole some ointment that we use daily. I thought it would show up as soon as I bought a new tube but he has either hidden it really well or used it all up because it is no where to be found. Then one morning when Yvette, the wonderful person that helps get Doc up and ready in the mornings, came up to the front porch a herd of bunnies jumped from under our porch and scared her to death. Doc told her his monkey had spent all night grouping them together by the porch just so they could take a jump out at just the right moment! I find it funny that

Doc always knows the monkey did it! It is like when your kids blurted out that "I didn't do it" before you even said what had been done! In Doc's case, his eyes and his grin always give him away!!! On top of the masked super hero monkey that Doc has, he now has a new one. We found a little clinging monkey at the zoo that we put on his chair. His name is Cheeky Charlie! (we did not name him... he came with a shirt on that told us his name).

I hope that as long as I am sending out these updates that I never fail to remember to say thanks for all the help that we continue to receive. I cannot imagine how much harder this would be without all the help that we continue to get! From the persons that mowed our grass this month(especially Tha and Ed), to Dr. Furhman's office for fixing my daughters popcorn broken tooth, to those that come out every night to help me put Doc in bed, for our friend Alan and his visits & pies, for Roy & Patty and the Cardinal treasures that Doc is enjoying, the prayers that are being said, the way the people greet and visit with us when they see us out and about, the hugs I got this month when I needed them, the cards and letters that continue to come that let us know that we are being thought of, and the many, many other things that make me glad that we live where we live and that we met the people we did! I could fill an entire e-mail with just these kinds of things and I don't know about you, but I find that amazing!! I often think that we have the secret for peace because if everyone everywhere treated each other like what we have seen in the past few months, there couldn't be very much hatred left in the world! I just haven't figured out how to bottle it yet!

Now I really wanted to start the e-mail with this next paragraph but then I had two thoughts. One, maybe I should save the best for last and two, maybe I should reward those that actually read the entire e-mail! So, here is the most exciting news that we have to share! Doc made some big strides this month and we have really been excited! He is able to shake his head no (which he does when we ask him if he wants to go to Hobby Lobby again!), hold it up without the headrest (but only for a limited amt of time but it is getting stronger all the time), and he can flex his left shoulder and all the muscles in that area clear to under his armpit. All of this is stuff showed up one night and is just part of what Doc can do now. Some other improvements that we saw but that continue to fade in and out is additional feeling in areas that he hasn't felt anything before (like the arms, left elbow and right knee) and there is also a little flexibility and control of the muscles in the right shoulder/chest area but not as much as in the left. He continues to feel the "zaps" and is hoping these are good things. He is still twitching toes/fingers/hands and feet but have not made any big improvements to verbs like "moving". He still has feeling in the thighs but no control of the muscle yet. He is still vent dependent but we pray every day for a breath on his own! His health is good and his sores are almost gone so these are the things that we are most thankful for this month! The downside of sores is that a new one just popped up this morning at the base of the tailbone and it looks like it is going to be another challenge to get rid of. It seems like those sores are a constant battle! Our biggest problem this month was that the cap on the feeding tube broke and plugged the tube. I was afraid they were going to have to put in a whole new feeding tube but the nurses at Boone Hospital figured out how to save the day and they were able to unplug the tube and find a new cap for it. We are good to go again; although the way Doc is starting to eat we might not need it for food very much longer. The main purpose of it right now is just to make sure he is taking in enough fluids! I really think I can even start seeing if he can take his medicine by mouth.

Our Craig Hospital re-evaluation is scheduled for the end of next month and I cannot believe how fast those 6 months have gone since we have been home. We have had a couple of persons that have offered to help drive us out there and I cannot tell you how much it warmed my heart to have those offers. My brother, Lloyd, though, is the lucky driver that is actually going to have to spend a week with his sister! That ought to be a highlight of his life! It will be good to see all our Craig family again and to say hi. We are already signed up to join the rec dept on a fishing outing during our visit! (I know we are there for follow up testing but you have to make sure to get in the important stuff like this!) We will see just how many fish Doc can catch with that fancy pole they have for him to use! I am planning on getting Doc up in the mountains for a hike one day because we both feel at home there and it has been awhile since we have done that! Hopefully, we might spot one of those elk that started this whole adventure!

Until next month,

Your Friends,

Cindy and Doc Blackmore

August 2005

This is coming to you from Colorado again. I cannot believe that it has been 6 months since we were here and now it is time for a re-evaluation. I think after this one, we are asked to come back once a year for an evaluation. Hopefully, each time we come back, Doc will have made progress until there is a day we don't have to come back except to say hi! We wanted to especially thank several of Doc's AECI co-workers because they have been doing a payroll deduction that helped tremendously in funding our re-evaluation trip and our continued home health care needs! We have not forgotten that they continue to help us out! We just wanted them to know how much we appreciate it and what we have been doing with it!

What a fast month August was! We had some fun times in it. We hit a Cardinal game (yes, another one!) with some friends of ours. I told you that once Doc figured out how to get around in the stadium in June, we would have to go again. We have been there once each month this summer and I think we are going back in September too! Doc always has a pretzel while he is there too! Not one of those hard, in the concession stand ones but one of those fresh baked homemade kind! There are two places to buy those in Busch Stadium and I have to hit one of those stands each time we go! We also had to hit Ted Drews after the game this month for some frozen custard. It was a totally enjoyable day.

We visited the Jacksonville/Cairo Unity Church on the 21st and it was a pleasure to say thanks and share our story. We enjoyed the opportunity and if we were able to give back just a small percentage of the help they have given us, it was a success! As I have written before, it seems like the right thing to be doing. Our next scheduled visit will be to the Trinity Methodist Church in Moberly. We will be there on Sunday, September 25th at 10:15 am..

When we get back from Colorado we have 2 hectic months ahead of us. I think there is something on the calendar for every single weekend as Jaymi's wedding gets closer. The wedding showers and everything that goes with a wedding are starting to be scheduled and so now the fun begins! Just about the time that you think you remembered everything and have it all under control, something else pops up. I think most of our Hobby Lobby visits are done so at least that makes Doc happy! (Wait until he has to go to a couple of wedding showers though…I bet he will give his eye teeth to trade one of those for a Hobby Lobby trip). We aren't stressing too much about the little things because as long as we are all together and Jaymi & Joey show up, that is all that really matters! I think just the opportunity of being able to witness the sacred blessing of marriage is enough to make a wedding perfect! When it is your own child, it is even more warming to the heart though. That's what makes it so wonderful to share and why the guest list grows so long!

Speaking of sharing reminds me to say thanks to all of you that have shared with us this month! We continue to be showered with prayers, letters, e-mails, and all types of support. There have been moments (and I use the word moments because to me, it represents a very short period of time) that Doc will be sitting there a little bit down in the mouth and wondering what God's plan is for him and he usually no sooner gets it out of his mouth and the phone rings or something happens that quickly lets him in on exactly what God wants him to do next! I continue to put all these "coincidences" down in my journal and I am starting to put them into a story form to share some day. I can only tell you that after almost 12 months of coincidences, I don't believe in them anymore. There have been too many to think that they happened "just because". There has been a purpose in every one of them and I have come to believe that all of them are gifts from above! Just like so many of you comment on these e-mails and what they have meant to you. It isn't just a coincidence if something I write means something special to you and that I just happen to have you on our mailing list. I promise you that it isn't me and it isn't a coincidence. These words that have flowed together over the past year have just been typed through my hands. They are not "my" gift but instead a gift to me that I have passed on. I can only hope that in the next 12 months, we have great things to share but as Doc puts it, until God is done with his wheelchair, he will be in it. When he is done with it someday, we will move on to our next phase in life and pass the chair on to someone else that can use it.

Speaking of Doc, he continues to remain in good health! He continues to have his wonderful sense of humor and his awesome smile! Things that have gotten feeling and muscle back (like the neck and shoulder) continue to get stronger. He continues to eat a little more and little quicker with each day, although he still has a way to go to get to that steak or prime rib! His voice continues to get stronger and it always seems like he has something to talk about. He still is getting his zaps and zings so we are hopeful those are hints of healing. Our biggest joy this month was on a Wednesday night when Dana, a dear friend that helps us put Doc down on that night of the week, was working some fluid out of his left foot and he felt her hands. Several times since then, he has felt that foot so we are hopeful that is a good sign also. He was also able to tell us which finger they drew blood out of one day because he felt the prick of the needle. That was also encouraging. He has a long way to go but in retrospect, he has come a long way already.

My brother, Lloyd, helped drive us out here. I had a couple of persons volunteer to drive us and I was so appreciative of the offers because I don't think it would have been smart of me to attempt it on our own. It was too far to go and be able to handle it by myself. It has been a good week though. As a result of our re-evaluation, we made some positive changes. We eliminated all tube feeding because the dietary consultant figured Doc was getting enough calories to maintain. Even if he doesn't, he weighed in at 193 lbs so she is thinking a few less pounds for someone in a wheelchair wouldn't be all bad! He had a couple of prescriptions eliminated and every time we can take away another pill or two, I am happier! We have some new range of motion and exercises to start working some of the new stuff out and make it stronger although they told us the thing that will really strengthen them is just time. Trying to strengthen them if they aren't ready won't really help them! The main success of our re-evaluation was just seeing all our old friends and getting our hugs! It was almost like coming home (at least our home away from home!). Doc said it was good because we knew were going home at the end of the week and I think he was right! They kept us so busy and within the first hour, we were off and running again just like the "old" days and I remembered how tiring it all is! They had us scheduled for something every single minute of the day and sometimes, we even were supposed to be in 2 or 3 places at the same time. We did not figure out how to pull that off! They found out that the left side of his throat (swallow and voice area) were normal and the right side was still barely working. That explains why we are still a little slow on the swallow and a little different with the voice than we used to be. The left side is working so well, though, that he is able to function, which is good. Actually, Doc's entire left side is healing faster than the right and when we asked about that, they just said it was because his injury happened on the right side of the cord so things were starting to heal a little on the uninjured part. We were both a little disappointed that he wasn't able to take any breaths on his own yet but on the flip side, his lungs looked good and he was in overall really good health! A few highlights of the trip were a fishing trip that we took with the Rec Department. They had a bar-b-q and fishing outing that we tagged along on and that was fun. Doc finally got to do some fishing with the puff & sip pole and hopefully, I brought back enough pictures to figure out how to build our own pole! He successfully caught 2 fish but neither one was worth writing home about! Then one evening our speech therapist came over to the apartment and brought pizza with her to celebrate Doc actually eating. That was an enjoyable time! We spent one evening shopping at Gander Mtn and then I am using that as an excuse to make Lloyd and Doc join me at one of the malls that I really liked tonight. I wish there had been time to travel to Grand Junction while we were here to visit with all our friends there too but it just wasn't going to happen on this trip. It is going to take a vacation out here without a scheduled re-eval to visit there and also some of our dear friends that we met here that weren't part of Craig but that we met through the experience. There just isn't enough days in one week to fit it all in. (especially when the schedule of re-eval is so hectic!) For all of you, know that we think of you often and that we really do plan on making that visit!

They tried to talk us out of Friday so they could schedule a few more things but we both put our feet down and said that we were going to enjoy one day on our own. We want to head to the Rocky Mountains and do some hiking so that is on our agenda for tomorrow. I found 2 hiking trails that are wheelchair assessable so that is our goal! I hope the weather is nice. At the beginning of the week, it was close to 100 degrees and now it isn't getting out of the 70's so it has been a drastic change. I heard there is snow, wind and winter conditions in the Rockies so it might be a snowball fight! (I think I might be able to beat Doc but I would not put any money on it...he is pretty resourceful!) They brought their elk calls with them and are planning on trying them out. I hope it isn't illegal to call elk in the National Park because if they get arrested, I don't know if I will bail them out After the day of hiking around some of the lakes and driving across Trail Ridge Road, Doc promised me a trip to the caramel apple store so I can buy a caramel apple and I am really looking forward to that...it is my biggest weakness! Then we are heading back to the apartment and packing up Porky for a wonderful adventure back across Kansas on Saturday.

You might be disappointed but I am happy to report that I don't think the monkey has gotten into any mischief this month. Doc says it is because he is hanging from the tv by one hand and he can't pull himself up. If he were hanging by two hands, he thinks he might be causing more trouble! I am not sure if he is right or not but you can bet I am going to leave him hanging by one hand! I thought the monkey might have been at it one morning because I get a call at work that something was wrong, Doc wasn't breathing and could I come home. Carrissa was there and her Craig training paid off as she calmly bagged air into Doc's lungs until I could get there and fix the problem. Doc was calm and still telling jokes when I got home! It ended up being a bad circuit on the vent and as soon as I replaced it, we were back in business. Doc said it made for an exciting day! I asked him if the monkey had played with the circuit but he said that for a change it wasn't the monkey's fault—it was just a bad set of tubing!

Thank you for all of your continued prayers! As always, I will keep you updated and let you know any news!

Back in Denver for a week,

Your Friends,

Cindy and Doc Blackmore

September 2005

We left you last month while we were in Colorado and about to head to the mountains to do some hiking. We did venture that way and the joy of being in the mountains again was wonderful! You could see the joy on Doc's face when he got out of the van and saw that we were "at home". That was what I felt too! There is no place on earth where we feel more at peace than in the mountains. The day was beautiful but a little bit on the disappointing side because even though there isn't a place in the world that we like more than where we were, I had forgotten to take into consideration the effect of high altitudes on Doc's oxygen levels. As the day went on and we went higher, his oxygen levels started to drop and he was pretty sleepy. Even though we were disappointed that we couldn't get out and backpack like we used to and even though Doc wasn't feeling well, we made the most we could out of our visit and dream of the day that we can hike together again where we can reach that view that is always right around the next bend!

The trip home was uneventful and Porky (the ever reliable mode of transportation) did very well. The only problem we had was a rock in the windshield and then another one a little bit later. The first one only did a chip but the 2nd one, added a nice long crack! Now we have to take Porky in to get a little facelift!

We have really enjoyed this month. It has been full of places to go and people to see! It also has been a month full of parties. Doc and I both had birthdays this month and we remembered where we were last year at this time and it was so nice to actually celebrate a birthday again. It was wonderful that Doc could go out to eat with me and partake of the wonderful things that we chose. I chose Americana Grill with their wonderful grilled chicken salads and onion rings while Doc chose Olive Garden and totally enjoyed their pasta! Then, of course, we both had cake waiting for us with the kids at home! Doc wanted to go to the driving range for his birthday because I think his wish for his birthday was to be able to improve my golf swing. All I can say is that as he didn't have enough air to blow out his 46 candles, his wish probably did not come true ! We were so grateful to be able to share those moments. We also remembered the anniversary of the accident and found it hard to believe that it has been an entire year since it happened. We look back on the year and concentrate on all the wonderful things we have gained instead of what it seems like we have lost. It is true what they say about a window being opened when a door closes!

The wedding is rapidly approaching and we are getting down to crunch time. Not to say that we are in a panic or anything. I am actually worried that I am not. There has to be a ton of stuff left to do but I am sorta in the zone of it will all fall in place somehow. I don't see much panic in Jaymi either so unless we are saving it for the last few days, we are just ready for the party! We will have much to celebrate! We did have a couple of bridal showers and Doc had to attend with us but he said the showers were better than Hobby Lobby. I didn't think he would think that but he did. I think the food helped and then there were all the guys that felt sympathy for him and joined him to keep him company. That was a good thing too! Now I have to tell you that seeing a group of guys at the bridal shower all sitting at their little spot together was an amusing picture Probably what I would look like sitting in a tree stand holding a gun or something—that probably isn't going to happen BUT never say never!

This month we visited the Trinity Methodist Church in Moberly. They gave us a wonderful reception and it was truly a joy to testify there! Everywhere we go, we find such wonderful old and new friends and we always leave feeling so warmed by all the support we receive! We also were invited to share our story with a young group from our church which was a pleasure. Our next visits that are coming up are at Clifton Hill Baptist Church and Sante Fe Christian Church. I don't have exact dates yet because of the wedding plans but they should be shortly after the wedding is over. I have also agreed to be the guest speaker for a dinner scheduled on October 29th. There always seems to be an outlet for our story and so we continue to share it. As with every time, we know it is something we are supposed to be doing.

The monkey was actually very well behaved this month although Doc is telling me that it is the calm before the storm. We even had some stuff turn back up that was missing. The aide that helps get Doc up in the morning even commented on how well behave that monkey had been this month.

Doc continues to be healthy. He is eating good and going without tube feeding is not seeming to have any negative effects. We still have a sore on the heal but even that seems to be improving. I am so thankful that he is in good health. He hasn't experienced a whole lot of new stuff this month but still a few things have popped up. He feels places he hasn't felt before and what he has started to move is stronger so we remain positive that things are still going in the right direction.

We were able attend company parties of both of our places of employment and had a wonderful time at both. Orscheln's lasted into the night and I didn't think we would stay until the end but before we knew it, it was the end and we had lasted the entire evening. It was a great time of visiting and food and music. Then the AECI safety picnic fell on the same day as one of the showers so we didn't get to stay long but at least we were able to drop by and say hi to a few persons. It was a warm day but those are Doc's favorites so it wasn't a big deal to him to be out in the sun! He said the only thing bad about that day was having to leave before he got to say hi to everyone he wanted to.

As I wrote many months ago, I would never close an update without our heartfelt gratitude for all the continued support and prayers. We continue to be humbled by the outpouring of love we continue to receive. So from the bottom of our hearts, Thanks!

I think that covers most of the month of September and October is probably going to be wedding consumed so maybe you will finally get a short update next month (although I wouldn't count on it). It just seems like once my fingers start typing they just find words to write and I can't control them. Please remember to continue to keep us in your prayer as our story is far from over and we will in turn, remember all of you too!

Your Friends,
Doc & Cindy Blackmore

October 2005

I promised you a short update this month but I don't think you are going to get one. (You probably didn't really believe me anyway!). We were able to get out and enjoy the weather a little bit. We found out that we both enjoyed walking the trail at Rothwell Park so we have done that when we got a pretty day with nothing going on. Of course, it had to be in between the Cardinal baseball games (or actually, there were times that we just took a radio with us!). The team was fun to follow this month even if they fell a little short! I was going to try and get some play off tickets for Doc to go to a game but he was afraid it would be too cold and he said he would rather watch them on TV so I gave up that idea. He is pretty sensitive to the cold and now I know how serious it can be….to pass up a chance to go to a playoff game because of the temperature must make it a big deal to him. We also started to cheer on jr high basketball teams this month and next month the varsity games will start and we will be able to cheer them on too. Doc will probably like that because they will be inside and warm!

The wedding was absolutely beautiful! It was a busy 3 days but they were wonderful. So many of our family and friends spent Friday with us, helping us decorate and set up for Saturday. Then we had rehearsal and rehearsal dinner. Brenda and Joe (Joey's parents) did a great job of hosting that and it felt good to sit down and eat on Friday evening! Doc started to back off his eating about this time though and I could tell he was starting to not feel well. I prayed hard for it to hold off until after the wedding madness and it did—Just! Saturday, we were up early and going hard all day. I will never forget watching Jaymi climb onto Doc's lap and him driving her down the aisle. It was like watching a princess glide to her destination (Joey). It was a special moment! It was fun to watch them do the father/daughter dance too! Doc is getting to be a very good wheelchair dancer! I even got in a few dances myself! As Jaymi said, the best part was having all those that came helping celebrate. Each of those that came added something special to the day! After the wedding was over, I had several persons that dived in to help us clean up and even though it was close to 2 a.m. before we hit the bed, it felt good to know that we were done with it. Then on Sunday, we had a lunch and watched the kids open gifts before they headed out for Mexico (luckily it was on the Pacific Coast so we didn't have to worry about Hurricane Wilma!). We had one little problem on the day of the wedding that I am pretty sure it is our "monkey" tale for the month. After Doc wheeled Jaymi to the front of the church and got situated by me, I noticed his wedding ring was missing. I thought how do you have your ring through 25 years and then lose it on your daughter's wedding day? There were a bunch of persons looking for it but it just wasn't to be found. Then we put him to bed and it was skipping across the floor. It must have fallen off into his lap and gotten stuck in the cushion. We were both relieved to have found it and I have put it up until I can get something that will allow it to fit a little snugger. I personally think the monkey took it off and hid it for the day!

We have a schedule of church visits coming up and are looking forward to doing them. I was the guest speaker at a woman's banquet one evening, which I thoroughly enjoyed doing, this month but other than that, we didn't make any visits to tell our story. We have at least 1 visit scheduled for November (at Clifton Hill (6th). Then in December we are going to visit the First Christian Church in Moberly on the 4th. It is amazing how every time we are invited to visit, it just happens to be an open weekend. God wants us to make these visits and he opens another door to us every time we turn around. We continue to put our faith and our lives into his hands and try to remember that they really do belong to him to do what he pleases. I told Doc that I still feel like there are days that I am supposed to be floating downstream to something new and I continue to try and struggle against the current because I liked what was on the bank that I left! There are days that I just want to get back to that life and yet I know deep down that it isn't to be. I am supposed to take that curve in the stream and see what is around the bend! One of these days we will understand every step of this journey but for the current time, we are just trying to enjoy the moments as they come along and remember that each day is a gift that we should make the most of. I just have to learn that it is easier to float the current than to swim against it!

Doc had a urinary trac infection this month and it has been hard to beat. We are still trying but as long as he is on antibiotics, he doesn't feel bad at all. When he isn't, he gets a fever and his oxygen levels drop then we end up having to give him a little O2 through his vent. The Monday after the wedding was our big adventure this month. Doc had been off antibiotics for a few days and as the wedding weekend wore on, I could tell he was feeling worse. By the time Monday arrived, he had a temperature and low oxygen levels so I called the doctor and he sent us straight to the hospital for testing. They found a touch of pneumonia in one lung and the urinary trac infection still active. They put him on some IV's and then gave us a prescription and let us go home. I was pretty excited to go home because they were talking about admitting him. It is always better if we can try to fix it at home. We head home about 8 or so and are making tracks toward Moberly when I see this huge doe creeping out of the ditch and onto the highway. I tell Doc that there is a deer coming on the road and I think I am going to hit it. When you are going 70 mph you just know that you aren't going to stop if it comes out in front of you! Anyway, Doc saw it just before we hit it and all he said was "don't swerve!" So I didn't. I held onto the wheel with both hands and hit it broadside—Hard! Poor Porky! Did you ever see a pig without its nose? Well, I did! I push the engine back and lost the headlight and grillwork but at least we were not hurt. I got over on the shoulder and asked Doc what should we do now? He told me to get out and look at the damage..........WELL....I did

BUT 1) it was dark! 2) I really don't know much about body work so all I could tell was that the front part of Porky was gone and it didn't look very good to me and 3) it was pretty chilly! So I get back in the van (none the more wiser) and told him that I looked at it and it looked pretty much like it had sounded (bad!). All the warning lights were on in dash (did you know that they are different colors for different things?-anyway...) so I was trying to think how to get the van off the road and get Doc home. I can't just call a tow truck and put Doc into a car or anything AND we were way too far from Moberly to tell him to get that wheelchair moving north hehe! So Doc says that no matter what the warning lights say to keep going if the gages are reading ok. So I had to look at the temperature gage and the oil pressure gage. I made the decision that they didn't look too bad (at least they weren't in the red areas) and we pulled out on the highway and limped home! It was sorta noisy and the engine didn't sound very smooth but we made it. Then I got to worrying about whether I would be able to get the doors open and if the ramp would work to get Doc out of the van but no worries....it all worked and before you knew it we were home and eating supper! Thanks to several persons all pitching in, Porky is already in the shop getting fixed and by next week he will be good as new and we will be back on the road! We have a $500 deductible and to rent another van to use in the meantime is $600 so I figure that deer cost us about $1100. I told Doc at first I thought that was pretty expensive but then I thought about his gun, shells, camouflage, deer tag, boots, biscuit/

gravy breakfast, etc…and I am pretty sure my deer actually cost less than his in years past! He said that I might be right but at least he had some tenderloin to show for it! I guess I could have had some of that if I had wanted but I left it on the road! At least I can now brag that I have bagged a deer and I don't even have the temptation of hanging the head on the wall!

Now, I want to mention that wonderful van we are renting in the meantime! If you could only see it! It is so ugly that I can't even take it all in! It is a huge white box that sits so tall that I think I probably have to pay attention to the clearance markers on the overpasses on the highway! It is almost as long as a school bus and it has a huge blue handicap sign painted right onto the side of the van. It is old, old, old, and has 130,000 miles on it. It is rattly and dirty on the inside and smells like a stale motel room-YUCK! It is missing some hubcaps and the foam is hanging out of the seats! Even though you are probably getting the picture, I am not even doing it justice…it is U-G-L-Y! Then to top it all off, when I put it in reverse to back it up, it beeps like heavy equipment backing up! So now I get to draw attention to ourselves! Doc just sits in the back laughing but I told him they couldn't see him…..I am the one having to drive it!! He says it is like having to drive your parent's old station wagon when you were 16! To top it off, he decides we should go out on date in this thing (I call it the vanmobile). So we drive it to the movie theater and then to a restaurant! Lucky us! Just getting it backed up and out of parking lot leaves Doc & I with tears running down our faces and our guts hurting because we are laughing so hard. If anyone was watching, they probably think I had too much to drink or something! I know I should be grateful that we have wheels but there is a tiny part of me that would be glad to forego driving this thing to be stuck at home a few days. We have a whole new appreciation of Porky! We are supposed to get him back on Monday or Tuesday and I hope he is in good shape because I don't want to have to give him up again!

Other than the infections, Doc still has that sore on the heel although it continues to get better...I will be glad of the day that I can write that it is gone! It is a stubborn sore (probably nicknamed Cindy). We are continuing to improve our eating habits and even though he is still eating a fraction of what he used to, he is eating more. I can tell he has lost some weight and I worried we took him off tube feeding too soon but all I had to say was that and he started picking up the calorie intake a little bit. I don't think he wants tube feeding again! He continues to feel little things and to be able to move a little bit but nothing new substantial this month to brag big about! We continue to pray for the vent to be a thing of the past but it isn't to be yet.

We both want to say thanks to all of those that continue to let us know you are praying for us, believing with us, and supporting us! For all those that visit, do errands, send cards and love us! Our church talks every year about sharing talent, time and treasure and we are witnesses to how much of all 3 have been shared with us!

Each month our story continues to grow into an even more amazing story and I cannot wait to get to the end although I am enjoying the wonderful things and the not-so wonderful things that are happening along the way! Please remember us as we remember you! And always remember Doc's favorite saying, "Remember to laugh!"

Have a Happy Halloween,
Your Friends,
Doc & Cindy Blackmore

Jaymi and Joey Toasting

Jaymi on her Wedding Day

November 2005

I had all these plans for getting some R & R after the wedding and getting caught up with stuff around the house but none of that happened this month. Doc had me on the go all the time! He was pretty tricky about some of it. For example, while I was talking at a dinner one evening, our son, Adam calls and Doc tells him that we might be coming to Indiana to visit him the weekend of the 11th. Adam calls me the next day with all sorts of plans and is so excited that we are coming that it is hard to tell him that I am scared to try it. I managed to work it out how Doc started the ball moving in that direction but to be honest, I was really wanting to see Adam and Laura's new place and to spend a little time with them when there isn't all types of stuff going on too! I just didn't know about driving that far with just us but once I put my mind to it, it wasn't so bad. I loaded up Doc's equipment & supplies on the morning of the 10th and we were off. What scared me was that I read on the internet that Missouri wasn't even in the top 10 states for deer/auto accidents and Illinois & Indiana both were. I figured if I can hit a deer in a state not in the top 10, how was I going to drive across 2 that were? But I prayed hard for a safe trip and a safe trip we had. The weather was almost made to order and we had a blast. Even though it wasn't officially Christmas season yet, Doc let me jam to Christmas music as much as I wanted to and between that and some of our favorite 70's music, we sang our way to Indiana! It took about 7 hours with us stopping to eat lunch on the way so it wasn't too bad.

Adam and Laura surprised us by taking us to the Indianapolis 500 speedway and they had a handicap bus that we loaded onto (with big windows so Doc could get a good view) and we headed around the track for a 2.5 mile lap! Doc said it was the smoothest ride he has had since he was in his wheelchair. I think he wishes all the highways were ½ as good! We ate well all weekend and played some cards on that Saturday night. Now this is the part that Adam said that I had to write about….he did indeed win all the games we played but I am sure that we have lots of reasons to explain that oddity away!

We got up Sunday morning and went to church and then out to eat lunch and then we were homeward bound. It was a nice trip home although Doc slept most of this leg of the journey! He didn't sing his way back to Missouri so I soloed it (luckily the windows were closed!). Besides not wanting to be a deer slayer (again!) my biggest concern was how fast I was going. I started out with my cruise set on about 70 or so because I was planning on staying close to the speed limit but I had cars and trucks whipping around me like I was sitting still so I started to wonder if that deer collision that I had messed up my speedometer. As I climbed to 80 mph and then 90 mph and was still getting passed, I was pretty sure it was messed up. Then I passed a highway patrol sitting on the road with radar and I looked down to see 93 on speedometer and he didn't even give me a glance. That was when I knew for sure! I had it all worked out how was going to get out of that ticket but I didn't even need my plan!

Now that you know what didn't work on Porky, I have to tell you that we were very grateful to all of those that helped us get Porky back up and running so quickly after the deer took us out of commission. Our insurance agent/company and Moberly Motors took really good care of us. It was only a matter of days that I had Porky back and in good shape! I was so glad to return the infamous 'vanmobile" and get back into Porky! Even though he had to go back into the shop to have his speed fixed, he was in great shape! To tell you the truth, it felt kinda cool just pretending I was running 90 mph.....I know that most of you males that are reading this are thinking that you have done that more than once because I don't know of any male that hasn't tried pushing the speed up but I also don't know many females that feel the thrill in going that fast. I think most of us think that even if we knew we wouldn't get caught and get a ticket, you still are running the safety risk of losing control and having that ever-dreaded wreck! I think most males just think, "boy, this is fun" and there isn't much else running through the thought process. So all my life, I have heard stories from my brothers and my husband about their "youthful" adventures and their high speeds and now, even though it might not be "official", I can say that I had the speedometer up to between 90-100 also! AND, just in case you were wondering, I could not set the cruise control on at that speed. No matter how I tried to set it when I got up to a speed that I thought was about right, it would drop down to 85 mph and that was as high as I could run on speed control!

Besides that, we went to a couple of good movies this month and several basketball games. I think we have found our winter entertainment because I am almost positive it is not going to be shopping and/or Hobby Lobby! I had some stuff to return to Hobby Lobby after the wedding and they put it on a gift cad but I am not sure how I am ever going to get Doc to go there with me again to let me spend it! I think it is going to have to be sometime when I am on a girl's day out and he is not with me! As the temperature continues to drop and the winds pick up, I am reminded of what a Missouri winter is like. Even though you cannot know how wonderful it is to be home, I am going to miss the Denver winter we had last year. I have a feeling that based on how much complaining Doc has done so far when I take him out on days in the 40's and 50's that we aren't going to do a lot of exploring in the real bitter days that I am sure are ahead! You add any ice or snow to that, and I think the movie video store is going to be a frequent stop for me! I am also checking into audio books for Doc and as he listens to his stories of adventure and comedy, I can settle in with a good chick romance once in awhile!

We were blessed to share an evening with the Clifton Hill Baptist Church this month and we shared part of our story with them. It is amazing to experience all of the wonderful churches and their congregations that there are in our area. We haven't attended one yet that we haven't felt at home in. God continues to open doors to us where he wants us to speak and we continue to be blessed as we tell the story to date! In December we are going to visit the First

Christian Church in Moberly, 10:30 a.m., on the 4th. It is another date that we are looking forward to!

Doc still is fighting the urinary trac infection this month and he continues to battle it. They continue to test it after we go off antibiotic to see what the next step is before he feels bad again so other than staying on some medicine, it hasn't affected him at all. We start another type of antibiotic today. He is on it for 10 days and then they are going to test it again. If it isn't gone this time, they only have iv's left as a possible weapon against it so they are wanting to put him back in the hospital. I am already arguing about getting the iv's as an outpatient and not admitting him. They haven't said no but they said we would cross that bridge when we get to it. In the meantime, we pray that this new antibiotic will clear it up and we won't even have to discuss the rest of the plan! The sore on his heal continues to get better all the time! Even though we have fought that battle for a long time, I am hopeful that it will be completely gone by the next update! He has gotten consistent feeling in his left foot and now he can frequently feel the toes on his left foot so even though things are moving slowing, we continue to go forward with new things each month.

My only sad moment was really not a sad moment at all! Our daughter, who has been my right hand since May, found a job in St. Joseph, Missouri so her and her husband (Joey) moved there on the 3rd weekend of this month. I was sad to see them leave because they were not only great help to us but we had shared some good times when they just "dropped" by for supper and/or a card game! I am excited to see her finding a job though and having their own place to decorate. We will have to make a visit up there to check it out when it is complete. We did help them move but when we left, it was mostly decorated in boxes! Hehe! We still have our youngest daughter at home for the time being but she is also starting to make plans to move on with her life, which is what you always want for your kids!

Thanksgiving was a special time this year! We got Doc into my mom's house for the first time since we have been home and we had several members of the family there to share it with. Hopefully, all of the family will gather together at Christmas and it will be the greatest gift of all! Last year, Doc was really sick on Thanksgiving Day so I was especially thankful for his health this year! I am also thankful to be home and to be excited about decorating the house up for Christmas and making cookies and doing all the typical Christmas traditions that we missed out on last year! I have to admit the tree is already up, and looking beautiful I might add! Our kid's favorite tradition is midnight mass and unless the snow is so deep we can't drive through it or Doc is not well, you can bet we will be there this year to ring in Christmas day with bells and candles! My all time favorite present ever was having all my children with us last year at the hospital and I think it will remain my all-time favorite one but we are going to be blessed once again with all of them being home for Christmas this year. They are going to be with us Christmas Eve and then they are going to break away early Christmas morning to share Christmas with new families that love them. In the meantime, we are thankful that we have them with us for a day along with 2 new members this year! Our family grew this year and it has been wonderful!

If I could pray for a Christmas miracle, it would be that Doc would breathe without the vent but thinking back to last year at this time, he could not talk or eat. He was still in a halo and not able to feel or move anything so we have come a long way in the past 12 months and maybe 2006 will hold even more treasures for us! Doc shared a dream with me and even though it was just a dream it was wonderful to savor so I am going to share it with you. It is like when you go into a candy store and either you are too young to have the money that you need to get what you want or you are my age and you don't want the hips that go with the buying of what you want. You still can look and savor the wonderful view. That was what Doc's dream was like-a wonderful view. He dreamt that he just got up out of his chair and didn't need it anymore but we were scheduled to make a church visit that weekend and he thought the wheelchair spoke volumes. So he decided that we would still make the visit but we would bring the chair with us. We walked into the church and Doc pushed the chair down the aisle to the front of the church where he shared his story of how he was put in it, how he used it and how he got out of it! Isn't that a spectacular view? Whenever I have a bad moment now, I savor that view and think "it can happen!". That is what faith and belief is all about!

We realize that many of you and many churches have had us on their prayer lists for well over a year now and we both just want to say thanks to all of those that continue to pray for us. We continue to believe in the power of prayer and no matter how or when our prayers are answered, we appreciate those that have stuck this out with us and continue to do so! In this month of Thanksgiving, we continue to give thanks for each of you and for all those special things that people continue to do that enrich our lives and make each day a day worth living! We also pray that we are able to return the favor once in a while and help someone else to feel that their day is a little brighter for something that we might have done! I also wanted to say a special thanks to all of those that helped take care of Doc during a day of shopping for me. I joined Dana and Lori (2 very dear friends of mine) for a day of Christmas shopping in KC the Monday after Thanksgiving. I had several persons lined up to help with Doc during the day and people sorta came and went in shifts. I even had help to put him to bed so that when I got home everyone was asleep and all I had to do was to put myself to bed. You cannot imagine how great that felt! It was the first time since February that all I had to do was put on some pj's and crawl under the covers! Thanks to all of those that gave me such a special day!

As this coming month is filled with food (oh-oh-see what I listed first), family, friends, parties, and other wonderful bustling activities, we pray that each of you remember the real reason for the season and find time to celebrate that part of it!

Hoping each of you had a thankful Thanksgiving and that you have a very blessed Christmas,

Your Friends,

Doc & Cindy Blackmore

December 2005

HO-HO-HO..Doc started Christmas out early by trying to give me a vacation away from home but instead of that warm sand or mountain peaks, we settled for a hospital room. It was an expensive vacation but not one that I want to repeat any time soon. It started with a trip to the emergency room that resulted in an 8 day stay in the hospital. Doc ended up having blood clots in the lungs, a touch of pneumonia, a staff infection in the lungs, and a staff infection in the urinary trac. I told Doc that if he was going to have to pay to be in the hospital, he must have figured to get his money worth. It took about 2 days (on good drugs as Doc puts it) to start feeling better and by the end of 8 days, we were both ready to sleep in our own house. Not to say that I didn't appreciate the chair in Doc's room because it was better than the floor but it wasn't a bed!!! I was a little nervous about how Doc would be handled in the hospital but they put him in intensive care and pretty much just turned over his care to me with the exception of the drugs. I got him up in the morning and put him down at night and took care of him during the day. I felt better knowing that things were being done right but I actually had to work a lot harder in the hospital than at home because I have home health that helps me out some at home and I missed that morning help! They were going to keep us another weekend but Doc had his company Christmas Party that Saturday night and he told the doctor he had parties to attend. The doctor said that if he felt like going, he wasn't going to hold him back so they taught me how to administer

IV's, sent the equipment and Doc home with me and away we went! The IV's weren't hard to learn but I also had to learn to give shots. YUCKY! I have always hated needles so the thought of sticking Doc in the stomach every single morning (which is what I have to do now because of the blood clots) wasn't a pleasant thought. My boss told me that he wouldn't want to give his spouse shots either but he would rather give them than get them. I guess that is true.... so even though I hate to give them to him, I am happy that I am not getting them! Poor Doc! ☹ He can't feel them right now though so they aren't so bad. However, I hope there will be a day that they hurt him because that will be progress.....

The worse part about being in the hospital is that we missed our visit to First Christian Church in Moberly. We are planning on rescheduling and hope to fit it in soon! We were really looking forward to visiting with them. We also have a couple of other visits in the planning stages. I think the holidays and Doc's hospital visit has set us back from scheduling anything but I plan to get back to it this week and set up some dates. If any of you had planned on being there and would like to know the make-up date, please let me know and I will keep you posted. It just might be that we fit it in before the next update.

We had an absolute blast at Doc's work party (AECI). I think both of us felt like we were home and in the midst of a bunch of persons that loved us and it was a wonderful feeling. We weren't planning on shutting down the party but by the time Doc finished visiting with everyone, we were almost the last to leave. Now this is

where my fingers are itching to type….this is such a great story….
They were giving out door prizes and one of the persons that Doc
worked with had his named called. It was a first come, first serve on
the gift certificates they were handing out and you could have your
pick of the remaining ones. He comes back to our table and tells me
that he picked out one that he wanted to give to me. I look at it and
it is a $50 gift certificate for…are you ready???….HOBBY LOBBY!
It was so funny. I showed Doc and he said, "oh no!" Everyone was
laughing so hard and it was such a generous gesture! He apologized
to Doc and said that he hadn't thought about Doc maybe having to
tag along but Doc told him it was ok because it was so great that it
would be worth the trip there. I hope he remembers that when he
actually has to go! Hehe! There was also another fellow employee/
friend that brought him his certificate to Home Depot so I am sure
the trip to Columbia will balance out with a trip there too! It was a
great evening of food and companionship and it is at times like that
when you can feel the true meaning of Christmas and how important caring and sharing really are! To every single one of you that
stopped to say a kind word to us, we say thanks!

Speaking of food, you should see what Doc is eating now. I was
a little worried for a little bit because even though Doc was eating
decent, he was still losing weight and I think he was down to where
he didn't have much more to lose to be underweight. Now though,
he is eating better every day and putting a little bit of his weight back
on. It looks good on him and I am happy about it. When we go out to

eat now, he orders off the regular menu and manages to eat a good size portion. I know he isn't up to where he was before the accident but that was probably too much anyway! He is starting to enjoy his coffee again and that is nice to see too! He went a long time without that and even though he doesn't quite finish off an entire cup, he is getting close to drinking more of it than leaving it. He says the taste buds get stronger all the time and the flavor is getting back to normal and that the swallowing seems to becoming easier too.

He is still feeling his left foot and that feeling has gotten to be so consistent that it is rare that he doesn't feel it. He can feel his big toe on his left foot and that also is more often than not now. So even though we haven't gone forward in leaps and bounds, he is still going forward. His sore on his heal is still improving but not gone yet, he has a new sore on his back but it currently isn't very big and I hope to get rid of it before it gets worse, and then we have a nasty one on the behind area. That one worries me a little bit but it isn't on a pressure point so I am hoping I can get ahold of it and conquer it. It happened in the hospital when his gown got stuck under his cheeks one day and didn't get pulled out in time. That seam just dug in there and made a skin spot which expanded into the sore area we have today! It is so amazing at how much you have to pay attention to and how quickly things can happen when you miss something! The most exciting thing that happened this month was a cough. I was bending over him and he coughed in my face and my first reaction was, "well, thank you coughing in my face Doc!"-not in such a nice tone, I am ashamed to add...BUT then I thought....HE COUGHED....I was so excited because he hasn't done that since Sept of 04. Then a little bit later, he coughed again and this time he said he was paying attention. He said he felt the tickle and then he could just do it. We haven't done it again since but I am glad it happened twice or we might have wondered if he really did it. Now we wait until it happens again and hopefully, that might mean we are getting a little more back!

In the season of Christmas, I have hunted everywhere for Frosty's hat. I was singing the song about how there was magic in the hat and when they put it on Frosty's head, he began to dance around. I have tried all types of hats on Doc this month but so far, none of them have made him dance around so I am still searching for the magic one! Hehe.

Our kids all made it home for Christmas Eve Day so it was a good holiday. We all were spoiled as we always are! Christmas is such a fun time for me because it involves eating, shopping and visiting. I think those are my 3 favorite things! Plus I got to be home for the holidays and I decorated the house and had fun unpacking my treasures that I haven't seen for 2 years. I am in no hurry to put them away because I am having so much fun looking at them. On top of that, I missed out on 8 days of them while we were in the hospital so I have those days to make up too! We especially enjoyed going to church this Christmas and really feeling the reason for the season. It is amazing at how a person's faith grows in times of trouble and how very blessed you can be when you are being challenged to carry on. So even though things might not be exactly how we would want them to be in some aspects, there are other areas that they are better than ever! And as many of you know, the best presents in the world are those that cannot be wrapped! They are love, friendship, faith, hope, family (although I can just picture me wrapping up my brothers in gold foil paper and putting a big red bow on their heads…hehe…just had to throw that thought in!), laughter (Doc's favorite) and good health. As they say on that commercial…those things are priceless!

We continue to feel warmed by all the things that continue to come our way. We remember our friends when we stand under our shower and warm water comes out. We remember the friend that helped install that and he is no longer with us. We remember those that helped install the generator so that when the power flickers, the house stays warm and we continue to have electric to keep Doc's equipment going. We love the company that comes to visit during the week and pass time with Doc. What blessings friends are! We appreciated the help when the snow fell and we had someone blade our drive and sweep our walks. To those that still come faithfully every evening to help put Doc down and how we look forward to each visit! I have to write here that our Wednesday helpers (Mark and Dana) come early enough to get in some cards and for 5 weeks straight now, Mark and Doc have been victorious. Dana and I were on a roll before that but I am sure their victories are about to come to an end. What do they say about luck being better than skill? We will see! We also appreciated the help in hooking up some of our appliances this month. I had to retire our fridge and dishwasher as the parts to fix them were going to be more than new appliances so the help in getting them in working order was great…especially as it happened during the week we were in the hospital and I wasn't even around to help! I have been keeping my fingers crossed because they say things happen in 3s and I am pretty sure I do not want to replace another appliance. I think I will add Doc &my Christmas gift to each other as #3 and count it complete! We were not able to burn wood in our fireplace anymore because of the soot & Doc's ventilator so we gave each other a gas fireplace to replace the wood stove. It has kept our house warm and cozy. I told Doc that after I put him to bed each night I sit in front of the fire and enjoy it. It has the potential to be a romantic fire so I keep reminding him of that too! He always says "maybe tomorrow." As long as there is a tomorrow, there is that hope!

Tomorrows leads me to the fact that later this week we will be entering a new year. Our prayer for all of you is that you have a special 2006 full of good health and wonderful memories! I can promise you that we will not see the clock strike midnight or at least I am sure that Doc will not see it! You never know about me, I might just be sitting in front of that fireplace enjoying a moment of peace and quiet.

Your Friends,
Doc & Cindy Blackmore

January 2006

Since Christmas, we have had several adventures and plenty of monkey trouble too! There was an afternoon during the week after Christmas several of Doc's buddies came over to steal his money... or was it to play cards? Probably both....Their stakes aren't high so he only really lost what amounted to a soda or two! The worse part is that he has to redeem his card playing skills (because he didn't win a single game) so he is waiting until they can gather again for another afternoon of fun. I suspect that he might have done that on purpose....well, maybe not! He has always told me he knows how to play cards and I can't say too much because he has been beating me more often than not! Although I have to tell you that the mighty men finally fell on the Wednesday night competition that I wrote about in the last update.

Doc also lost cards on New Year's Eve as we played girls against guys in pitch and the girls walked away victorious! We had some friends that came over to eat supper with us and play some cards on New Year's Eve for awhile and then helped me put Doc to bed before they moved on to bring in the New Year Missouri time. Doc managed to bring it in New York time but that was as far as he got. I stayed up to bring it all the way in but I didn't wait for the Colorado time! I was thinking of our Colorado buddies though! I was also thinking of last New Year's Eve in Colorado and was glad that we have gotten home and back into our world. Although we think of all our Colorado friends every day! Those from Craig and also from

St. Mary's…and to all of those fellow patients/families that we met along the way….hello to all of you!

We had made plans to have an all day outing with some friends on the first Saturday of the month but we had to make a detour in them. Doc's belly decided to spit out the tube feeding tube (or it could have been me not being careful enough when I rolled him in getting him up) and even though we aren't using it for tube feeding anymore, we do need it for water intake and medicines. Doc told me he thought he saw the monkey jump over into the bed and give it a tug but that is still up for debate! So we started our outing in Columbia in the ER trying to get a new tube installed. We were done by noon and ready to go so even though it wasn't in the plans to have that happen, it didn't hold us up too much! The day was a blast and it was more like a spring day than a winter day! We shopped…first at Bass Pro and then at Penny's! It was a good trade off. Then we went to the movies and out to eat at Olive Garden. We are saving our outing to Hobby Lobby and Home Depot until spring because we both agreed that we would like to do some spring projects. The thing is that that our roles have reversed because I used to come up with the projects and Doc did them. Now he thinks of things that would look good in the yard or on the porch and I do them. I used to supervise and now he does! It is sorta like being demoted! Hehe! I tease him though that all this stuff is being documented and there will be a day for him to pay his debts!

Doc had his first dentist visit since his accident. He has some teeth that had lost a couple of fillings and several of them had some chips on them that was bothering his gums so we thought it was time to fix them up. We got him into a place that allowed him to stay in his chair and they were able to fix everything with no problems. I was getting ready to watch him try to drive his chair with his mouth frozen. I wondered how his lips would control his sip and puff if he couldn't feel them. I thought I would have a funny story to tell (and you can bet I would have made it colorful!) but they were able to fix it all without freezing his mouth so nothing exciting happened!. Instead, we were able to actually go out and have a nice supper before we came home.

We attended the Cairo Homecoming this month and it really felt like "home"coming. Last year we were still in the hospital and missed it so it felt even better this year to be there to visit with friends and cheer our teams on to victory. They played a couple of fun games to watch. It felt weird to be so old that our children were even all alumni! I can bet that there will be a day around the corner that it will be our grandchildren (although we are still waiting on those)....time seems to fly by fast without waiting on anyone!

Jaymi was able to come home for a weekend visit and that was a nice time. It is always an adventure when Jaymi comes home because you never know what to expect from her. I would say that she gets that from Doc but to be honest, she probably gets it from me. We just don't expect life to be boring and I guess we figure we should make sure! As usual, we had quite the adventure there too. Again, I suspected the monkey might have been busy but I can never quite catch him in the deed! We had been having problems with the batteries on the chair running down really quick and then one of them quit taking a charge. We had someone out to work on them on Friday Jaymi came home. On Saturday, we took Jaymi to Columbia and messed around in the mall for a little bit and then headed to the movies and then to Cracker Barrel for supper. (Doc has developed an urge to eat biscuits and gravy with 2 eggs over easy and coffee on a regular basis.) As we were unloading, the left rear wheel on the wheelchair locked up. This meant Doc couldn't drive it anywhere so Jaymi and I had to push him up the ramp and into the house. It was quite the chore but we "got r done". Then the next morning we pushed him to church and back up the ramp when we got home again. By that time, I told him that he wasn't getting to go on anymore outings until his chaired worked again. It is not easy to push 650 lbs around... especially going uphill on a ramp! (lesson of the day). Anyway, by the next Tuesday night, we had the wheelchair running again and we were back to planning outings. I was just thankful that Jaymi was home during this weekend because Carrissa had to work and I am not sure what I would have done if I had gotten stuck at the bottom of the ramp by ourselves...probably call for reinforcements that are never far away! The wheel is still not working correctly but at this point, it is just working enough that they can't find the reason it is not. Sorta like when your car is making sounds but it doesn't do it when the mechanic is listening.

Once we were able to be on the go again, we took in a couple of movies, had a couple of meals out and attended a college basketball game. We are always able to find something to do break the boredom for Doc from being home every day. And as always, the company that visits and the cards that are played are always welcomed diversions from television.

Besides those adventures though, things have ran pretty smooth this month. Doc continues to feel good and his health is good. The sore on his heel is down to just a pinpoint of trouble and I am about to even quit dressing it. He has a couple of newer sores (one on his back and one on the buttocks) that are getting pretty serious. But as always, I try not to worry too much about them because it really doesn't help! Instead I am getting him into the wound clinic to let the experts take care of them. I have a feeling it is going to take being in bed on his sides for a few days and he is not going to like that! He is eating better all the time and is at an almost normal sized portion 3 times a day. He still isn't drinking as much as he needs to but I am hopeful that might be our goal in the next few months. He can take some medicine by mouth if he has too, although he never likes it very much....but then again; I don't even like swallowing pills! It is good to know that he can though in have to situations. He has a little new sensation in his armpits and as always, it isn't much but it continues to be something new. He has coughed another time

or two but a time or two over the course of an entire month is probably not news stopping although it is something more than nothing.
We continue to be hopeful that 2006 will hold some great things!

We have a couple of new dates set up for sharing our story. We
are going to talk at St. Pius church on the weekend of 2/4 after the
Saturday evening mass and after the Sunday 8 a.m. mass. Then we
are going to talk to the sophomore group at St. Pius on the evening
of 2/12. We are finally making our visit to the First Christian Church
in Moberly on 2/19 at 10:30 a.m.. Then on March 18th, I am talking
to a group from North Park Baptist Church. As always, we really
look forward to these opportunities to share. We both feel like God
opens the doors to those that need to hear it and we are simply the
tools that he is using. I know it feels like there is a purpose in it as
we unfold the part of the story that we know so far.

We continue to be so thankful for friends and family and even
those that we haven't met that continue to remember us and pray for
us. There isn't a month that goes by that I don't have some amazing
things to add to my journal that give us such hope and faith. I am
sure we are given these things to reinforce our faith. I know that
sometimes you can look around our world and actually, within our
country, and see so much to despair about and just have to wonder
where are all the acts of kindness and love and righteousness. I can
tell you that they are all around you. You just have to open your eyes
to them and they are everywhere! They aren't hard to find and wonderful persons are around every corner! I know that we are remem-

bered across the country and on many churches and families prayer lists, but so far, what really is standing out throughout our ongoing ordeal is our own community and I think that someday, it is a vital part to our story.

St Valentine's Day is traditionally thought of as a holiday for romance and sweethearts but I think it really is a holiday that recognizes love. As there are all kinds of love in our lives, I just wanted to take a moment to thank you all for yours and to wish you a happy red and pink day! I think that must be why candy became such a traditional gift on this day. Love is one of the sweetest gifts I know!

Doc wanted me to end this update with something that we read this week. "Those who leave everything in God's hands will soon see God's hands in everything."

Your Friends,
Doc & Cindy Blackmore

February 2006

It seems like we are sending this out to so many people and yet half the fun of sending out an e-mail each month is when I go to my address book and start clicking on names remembering our special memories with each one of you! It is hard to believe that we are blessed with so many friends and family but as I go down the list each of you are so special to us! I am glad my list is so long and that I seem to add another name or two to it each month! That means that we are making new friends too! This was a busy month with lots of ups and downs so as usual, it is a lengthy update....(I know you would be shocked to get anything less)!

Last month, I should have waited one more day to send out the update. Starting the very next day (1/31) we were on a brand new adventure again. We had doctor check ups that day but it turned out to be more. Our plan was that we would get our doctor visits over and then have a little free time to fit in a visit to Bass Pro and a dinner out. Instead, they handed us an envelope and told us to head to the hospital because they wanted to admit us. It seems like Doc's sore on his back went all the way to the spinal column and had exposed bone and it had also "tunneled" (which I found out was extra spaces of missing tissue that I couldn't even see because it was under the skin. There were 2 tunnels and after they ran some cultures on them, they turned to have some nasty infections in them. So they admitted Doc and then a surgeon came to see him and the next thing we knew he was slated for some surgery on Thursday.

The surgeon thought he could remove the expose bone and cover it with muscle and pull the tissue areas back together and fix it. That left us with a whole Wednesday of just waiting. So we talked our doctors and the ICU into letting us go on a field trip on Wednesday. We had a great time! We went to Sears Craftsman Days! (almost as good as Hobby Lobby-NOT), and then to Bass Pro (almost as good at Hobby Lobby-REALLY-Well maybe not!) and then we met our daughter Carrissa for lunch. Then we found Steven's Park and took a hike around Steven's Lake. It wasn't a very long walk but the weather was so beautiful that we took advantage of it. It was hard to believe how beautiful the weather was for the first part of February! Anyway, it was a nice little escape and we were back in ICU by 3 o'clock. Doc said it felt like being on a pass at Craig Hospital! I thought it felt like I was playing hooky because I wasn't at work and it was right in the middle of the week. The hospital had asked us to stay close though, so we had to obey the rules! When we met Carrissa for lunch, she brought us some things we needed including my laptop so after we got back into our room, I was able to do some work that afternoon so I didn't feel like I wasted the whole day on fun (although fun is good!). The surgery went well and we are hopeful that we don't have to go through it again but they warned us that it is very possible that we will have to do it again. Already the sores are back and I am battling them constantly. They are working on a new material for the back of Doc's wheelchair to help alleviate the cause of the problem. The worse part was that Doc developed 2 new sores on the base of his feet the first night because his bed was too short and his feet were pressing into the footboard all night. There was an air pad down there but it wasn't enough. Now we are fighting those 2 sores too but I am trying hard to keep them free of any pressure so we can heal them as soon as possible. The good news to report was that Doc could feel his feet pressing into the footboard all night long and he could feel the pressure in his knees as they buckled all night. He didn't think it was very exciting to have that sensation because he said it was just uncomfortable. So he pouted about it and I smiled about it. We did make things better the next night. The bed was the only air bed they had so we had to make due with putting a 6'2" guy in a 6' bed. We sorta had his legs doing the splits as we cushioned his ankles and let them hang off each side. (My husband…the cheerleader) – that thought puts a smile on my face. Sometimes things happen and you wonder why. Doc and I have never wondered why this accident happened because we both feel strongly it was meant to be. I can say though that I have wondered why some things happen that make it seem harder than it should be. This was one of those times. But then we met a couple of persons that touched our lives that we would have never met if this hadn't happened and once again it made sense. I guess it is a good thing we aren't in charge because if we could see only part way down the path, it wouldn't look so good and I wouldn't choose it. I would never know that just because the path looks rocky at the start it might smooth out and be a good one.

Anyway, Doc bounced back fast and even though we were still "officially" in ICU, they once again let us slip out on Saturday evening and again on Sunday morning to fulfill our commitment to talk at St. Pius Church. It was a wonderful chance to share our story and once again give and receive. It was definitely worth playing hooky from ICU! Thanks to all the nurses there that helped us by working our schedule into theirs.

We were able to come home on the 10th but we had to bring our IV's with us and all the wound care and medicine. It is almost an Olympic event to try and keep track of all of it but so far so good. We have to stay on it until 3/16 and then we are hopeful that we can head in a more healthy direction. We had a follow up visit on the 22nd and even though there are new sores on the backbone, the surgeon was encouraged at how the wound looked when he removed the stitches. He told us just to come home and try what we thought might work and if it doesn't, call him and he will give it another go. We were glad to come home but there are times that I am overwhelmed with it all being in my court. I made an appointment with the wound clinic for later this week so hopefully, they will have some ideas on things that I can try! During all of this though, Doc has never felt better. He gets stronger and looks better all the time. He is eating a much better diet and they increased his protein intake which has really filled him back out. He was getting a little boney so this extra diet is looking good on him. He said that he actually is hungry now and that he looks forward to eating! They have him on a 2000+ calorie intake high in protein which is almost opposite of what I am trying to do for me so it is a battle to cook one thing for him and then I eat something much healthier and lower in calories! Life is not fair but then I had a teacher that told me that once a long time ago and she was right!

Then on the 12th, we spoke to a group of sophomores at church and what a pleasure that was! Young persons have always been and always will be very dear to our hearts. It is wonderful to be invited in to share a little part of a young person's day. It keeps you young to be part of it! The following weekend was finally spent visiting First Christian Church and I hope their patience was rewarded as much as we were. It was another wonderful place to visit and there has not been a church home yet that we have visited that hasn't felt just like being home! We are hopeful to be able to go back and say hi and just share their worship time!

We had a fun month of attending movies, basketball games, and eating out. That is about all that winter is good for. We also really enjoyed following the Olympics this year too! I think it was something that Doc was able to watch during the day that he really enjoyed! He has decided that he might be ready to try out for the 2010 Olympics if they decide to add co-ed curling on their list of games! I am just glad he didn't say ice-dancing or 2 person luge or something....that could be an experience! I think I can handle throwing one of those "rocks" (as long as I can get down that low and stretch my leg out behind me! I am hoping the ice might help me!) Other than that, Doc is really excited that baseball season is here!

We have some big plans for March. I have another chance to share our story scheduled for the 17th at a women's luncheon at North Park Baptist Church. Then later in the month, we are taking a long weekend to Branson with some friends to take in a show or two and do a little sight seeing. One can only wonder what the monkey might do if it would escape in Branson! We have been known to create a funny story or two with or without the monkey in tow!

Jaymi and Joey came home for a weekend and we were able to get out and do some fun stuff together. We also managed to fit in some serious games of cards! I might add that the female team tore up the male team! (I am not bragging or anything but I know that Doc would have told me to put it in here if it were the other way around so fair is fair!).

We are excited about some stuff that has been happening lately. First off, Doc doesn't feel so cold anymore. Until this past month, his body always felt cold but lately, he tells me that his temperature is more like it used to feel. He is even asking for short sleeve shirts again. Then, starting last Saturday, Doc says that he can feel his legs. Not to touch but just that he can feel they are there. He said they just feel numb. He can't move them or like I said, feel them to touch (except in the thigh area and then it isn't much), but just to feel like they are there is exciting to him. He said he can feel them from the toes to the hips and that it gets stronger each day. He is getting much more feeling in the back area too and even though it is uncomfortable, he is thankful he has those feelings. It is causing him to do many more weight shifts in the wheelchair just because he can't get comfortable but if it is the beginning of something better, he is ready to work through it! We aren't sure if it means anything but it is change and it seems to us to be positive change.

We continue to be thankful for the wonderful blessings in our lives. I know that so many of you continue to pray for us both and that this month, during our hospital stay, they only increased. We thank each of you for each prayer said and each card that was sent! As I have written many times, so many of you are part of this on-going story and we find comfort in that we have so many friends that share it with us! What amazes us is how many pray for us or send us a card and we haven't even met! It seems to come straight from heaven to have that kind of support! We continue to take it day by day and please know that every single night we remember all our friends that are out there thinking of us! We know that all of us have different hurdles to get over so it means a lot to us that you take time to remember ours when you have your own problems!

I hope each of you have a wonderful March as we get ready to welcome spring into 2006!

Your Friends,
Cindy and Doc

PS: Doc wanted me to add a note that if anyone is catching crappie in Thomas Hill Lake to let him know. We are working on a puff and sip fishing pole for him so he is probably already counting down the days until he can try it out! I just hope we are good enough to get it in working order before the fishing season arrives! If so, you can anticipate some really good fishing stories because he has always had a talent for telling them!

March 2006

Our adventures were many this month so you might be reading for awhile but that usually is the case when I mail this out! With this being the season of lent, we spent a lot of the month doing things we probably should be trying to do all year! I love the Lenten season because it is a time that things that you do make your faith stronger!

I think we both have of a touch of spring fever though so it is soon going to be time to walk (or roll) around the golf course, do a little fishing and probably a little bar-b-q'ing. Speaking of fishing, Doc's fishing pole is starting to take shape. We (me being the person that buys the parts....not the person that is actually building it! Hehe) are making progress and hopefully, by the end of the month, Doc will be practicing and we will soon be on the water catching fish!

We finally finished all the IV's and antibiotics that were part of our hospital adventure in February. I actually had my cousin come up and we had a day after the IV's were over party! My mom stayed with Doc and I took a day of vacation and had a girls' day out! That was a blast! We did a little pampering in the am and shopping in the pm. Remember that Hobby Lobby gift certificate that Doc's co-worker gave me at Christmas? Well, Doc thought the time had come for me to spend it (as he wasn't going to have to go!) so he made sure to tell me that while Tammy (my cousin) and I were out and about, we should really make some time for Hobby Lobby and that I should spend my gift certificate...All of it! Now, the week before this we had gone to Home Depot to spend the gift certificate that another co-worker had given him at Christmas. This is where it gets a little ironic! We actually went to Home Depot to buy stuff to remodel my kitchen because I wanted to do that for a long, long time! It was sorta my project so we actually spent the Home Depot certificate on stuff that I wanted! Then, I go to Hobby Lobby to spend my certificate and they have a picture that Doc has always loved with elk and the mountains and as is the case on many of the things in Hobby Lobby, it was on sale! So I spent my certificate on a picture that now hangs over Doc's bed! See how things happen in life when you think you have a plan? It always falls into place but never exactly how you thought it would!

We used to get together with about 8-10 other couples during the winter months and have pitch parties. Last winter we missed out on the card parties because we were in the hospital and this year no one had gotten around to hosting any plus we weren't sure about how to get Doc in and out of houses that weren't handicap assessable with that kind of crowd. Then one of our brilliant friends gets the idea of using the church activity center so there would be plenty of room for everyone and it would be easy for Doc to move around in. So it was scheduled and we had a blast! It was a late night but every minute was worth it! I can't think of anything more precious in life than friends and family! We shared some good food and a great many laughs! It was a great memory and one that we won't forget and that we hope to repeat.

Then, because of the improvements that I wrote about in the last e-mail (Doc's temperature control and his feeling his legs), I decided that maybe it was time to look into a spinal cord specialist. Ever since Doc was injured, a Dr. Acuff was repeatedly mentioned to us. I wasn't sure what another doctor would do for us so I really didn't pursue it. Then his name came up a few more times in the past few weeks and with the changes, I thought maybe I would take a hint and schedule an appointment. I am glad I did. Doc and I were both impressed with him and he had several ideas of things that might help with the changes that Doc is experiencing to maximize anything that might be trying to work. He shares our philosophy of living life to its fullest and that there are "miracles". He started Doc on testosterone shots in order to strengthen the muscles. He said that there might be an outside chance that Doc has more muscle or diaphragm muscle than we think but they are just too weak to register. He said there aren't any negative side effects and that they will really make a difference in how much more healthy he will feel in just a few months. That was exciting to us and we are hopeful that they work as well as he is predicting. Just feeling stronger would be good. He also has ideas to prevent bladder infections instead of treating them. Doc said that it just feels good to be trying something instead of sitting around and waiting for something to change. We will be going back to him once a month for awhile. He works at the rehab facility in Columbia, MO but he is not recommending that we change doctors or that we use this facility instead of Craig in

Denver. He actually was very straight forward in that he wanted us to continue to pursue treatments from Craig and that he thought our doctors that we have now are doing a great job. I think we just added another one and are excited about some of his ideas! I have to tell you Doc is now splitting the blame for things that happen between the monkey and the testosterone shots! I just have to laugh at him when he gets that silly grin on his face and he tries to blame one of these 2 things for something that has happened.

Speaking of the monkey, he really created a late night for me. Remember when I said that I wanted to remodel the kitchen? Well, like any project, it was bigger than I thought it would be and I ended up spending many, many hours on it. I even talked my cousin that went shopping with me to spend the night and help me with it while she was here. We made a lot of headway that day and then after she left, I worked until it was time to put Doc down for the night. After I had him to bed I thought I would close up the paint and work on it some more the next day because I had some very short nights leading up to that one. Anyway, I went to close up the paint can and that stupid monkey (it had to be the monkey because no one else was there) had pushed the can of paint off the ladder and upside down on my kitchen carpeting! There was almost a full can of white paint on a blue carpeted floor. I was thankful that it was water based but it still took until 3 am scrubbing and cleaning to get all the paint out but I finally made it!

We had several talking engagements this month and I just wanted to mention them because they meant so much to us and each one was so different. First, we did an assembly at the St Pius School for the kids and we really, really enjoyed that. Kids are so wonderful because they take everything at face value and don't try to analyze things like adults tend to do. At first Doc and I were thinking of how to tell the story in a way that the kids would understand and then I realized that kids were such a critical part of our story and that I didn't think we needed to change a thing....they are smarter than you think. They were attentive and good listeners and I am really glad that we had a chance to tell them thanks for all the cards and prayers that they have sent our way! Secondly, we attended the North Park Baptist Church Retreat to tell our story. That was a wonderful morning for me and I was so glad that they had invited us! We met so many wonderful persons that morning! Finally, last but not least, we attended the Redeemer Lutheran Church in Springfield, MO. We made so many more new friends during our visit and were able to visit with some old friends too. Many of those that Doc used to work with here that have transferred to Springfield were there and I cannot put into words how much it meant to him to visit with them and that they were all there! His face was literally beaming as he spied old friend after old friend! Just know that all of you mean a lot to us and we were so happy that you took the time to share part of your day with us! We think of you often! It means a lot to us to share the story and see the inspiration that comes from it. We are grateful for all the doors that have opened up to us and that continue to open up to us. I wrote an e-mail in response to the pastor of the Redeemer Lutheran Church that the only downside of staying so busy sharing the story is that we aren't able to return to these churches just to share their worship time with them because we would like to be able to do that some day. All of these places and persons have come to mean so much to us and we would like to say thanks for all the inspirational e-mails and cards we receive!

Probably the funniest picture of the month was me crawling across the roof of our house in the moonlight with a flashlight, 3 screws, and a wind turbine. During the storms that went through one weekend, we lost a wind turbine. We were grateful that was all we lost because we know that there were many tornados that were not far from our house and that many of our friends lost some things with a couple of them losing almost everything! Our hearts go out to each of you and know our prayers are with you! Doc just wishes that he was able to get right in there and help with the clean up! Our little episode was minor but entertaining! First off, Doc didn't really want me to climb up on the roof but I had made some calls and this time, I was coming up empty because everyone seemed to not be home and as there was some snow predicted (I know…from tornados to snow in a matter of a couple of days…but that is what they say about Missouri weather!), he was worried about moisture getting into our ceiling so I finally talked him into letting me try my hand at putting on a new wind turbine. By this time it was after dark which made it even more challenging! Needless to say, it took a couple of trips to Westlakes to get the correct turbine with the help of my mom who made the Westlake runs and then who sat with Doc so he wouldn't be alone while I was on the roof. I managed to secure it with 1 screw but the other 2 screw holes were not aligned up correctly so I will need a drill to finish the project and it has been too chilly and windy for me to attempt it again. Plus, I have already had a volunteer to finish the job so maybe my days of crawling across our roof are over! I kinda hope so because I really didn't find a lot of enjoyment in it! It was one of those things that wasn't as scary as you thought it might be but it wasn't something you do for fun!

We are in the process of scheduling additional church visits but with most of our Sundays in April already booked and with May having Mother's Day and graduations, I am not too sure of when our next visit will squeeze in. We are scheduled to be guest speakers at a couple of other events during the month of April. As always, there is something on the calendar.

Our visit to the Redeemer Lutheran Church was actually part of our get-away to Branson with some friends (Howard and Ellen Smothers). We had so much fun on those 3 days and it was great to attend some shows, play some cards, do a little shopping, and eat some great food! As always, we were blessed with some fun times and a ton of laughs! We attended the Shoji Show and several persons told us to make sure we checked out the bathrooms. I felt like a Jeff Foxworthy redneck when I thought about how part of our vacation plans included checking out the bathrooms. Needless to say, we had a great time doing that and they were something to see! I took many digital pictures of it and then I talked Howard and Doc into going into the men's and taking some pictures so we could see both of them. They were accommodating and I sat laughing thinking what another man might think if the 2 of them asked someone to take a picture of them together while they were in there but they didn't do that. I had a few of Doc in the bathroom (beside a pool table-1st bathroom I have seen with a pool table in it!) but none of Howard. We just seem to always be running into adventures that to some would be catastrophes but to us are stories that we have accumulated over the years that we sit and laugh at now. We kept waiting for that big thing to happen on this trip and we thought we were going to escape with just a tale of making some wrong turns. Not so! When we had finished speaking at the Lutheran Church and our good byes were said, we loaded up into Porky to start home. Instead, Porky was making some really weird (and loud) noises and so we had to find someone in Springfield to look at him before we could head out of town. He ended up with some bad brakes and we had to spend about 3 hours in the lobby of a Firestone shop while Porky had some out-patient surgery. I was sure glad that it happened while Howard was with me because if it had started with just me and Doc in the van, I would have been much more scared! As it was, it was almost com-ical and not unexpected. As always, it worked out and the funding to pay for it was in hand through some more of our earthly angels!

We had some fun games of pitch in the Firestone Lobby while we waited for Porky to get his shoes back on his feet! The funny part of this story is that Porky didn't even make a sound as we headed for church that morning and we were able to arrive on time without any problems but as we left, we immediately had a problem and we were just all glad that it was after church instead of before! It will make for another lasting memory! I think this one might go down in the books as the monkey's fault too!

We did have one other encounter while we were in Branson that is pretty neat to share. We were heading to a lunch one day and the place we were going to go to didn't work out so we just grabbed the next thing we passed and it ended up being an experience of hope. Our waitress ended up being a former quad that was in a wheelchair for 2 ½ years before she started to improve and she was an inspiration to us. It wasn't busy so she eventually just pulled up a chair and sat and visited with us for about ½ hour. I know that some would consider it just another coincidence but as I have stated before... there are just too many of them for me to think they are just coincidences! Her story was amazing and she just was trying so hard to let Doc know that he should hang in there....I guess she didn't know that he already is focused on hanging in there!

As far as Doc goes, this has been a great month! He has felt good and has had very little things to worry about. His wounds are not gone but with the continued support of a seating company in getting Doc's chair to fit him well, we are finally making some big strides in healing those wounds. I can't say that they are gone but they are well on their way! It is amazing at what 3 or 4 days can do if you have eliminated the culprit of what is causing them. I am so excited that maybe in the next few weeks we won't have hardly any skin issues to worry about! He continues to experience new things and the most exciting this month was some sensation in the left fingers. He even had one night when he woke me up to take the sheet off him because he said it felt like the sheet weighed a ton and he had tingling sensations in his legs & both his arms from the finger tips to the elbow. This is a come and go type of sensation for now but we are hopeful it is a good sign. His sensation of feeling his legs comes more frequently and we are both excited about that feeling too. Last Friday he was able to blow his nose for the 1st time. It is weird how we forget to try things to see if they work again. For a year and a half, Doc has not been able to blow his nose. So when it runs, we wipe it the best we can but then last Friday night, I held a tissue up there and teasingly said "blow". He did! In amazement I said "blow again!". The 2nd time was even stronger than the first. Now we know he can blow his nose again! Again, we are not sure if that means anything but it is something new. Other than that, it is just staying ahead of the skin issues and taking it all one day at a time. We are getting better at that all the time!

April is busy with Easter and Cardinal games. I gave Doc a packet of 4 Cardinal games for Christmas and two of the games fall in April. We are taking our son and his wife to one of them and our daughter and her husband to the other one. Our youngest daughter chose the game scheduled for June. Doc is already counting down the days until he gets into that new stadium!

I have moved our computer down to the bedroom and we are hopeful to test some voice activated software in the near future. If Doc can operate the software, he will be able to send and receive his own e-mails, surf the internet, and play on the computer. We are both hopeful that he will be able to do that. It will give him something else to do during the day beside watch tv and listen to audio books.

As always, we continue to receive cards, calls, visits, assistance in putting Doc to bed, and with all types of other chores! We also found out that our generator works when the electric went off during the storms and we were so thankful to have that in place! We are eternally grateful for all of it and please know that even after a year and a half, we are amazed at how much continued support we receive and how grateful we are for all of it! We continue to thank you for your prayers and know that we remember you in ours each evening too! Our story continues to grow longer and longer with more and more characters becoming part of it but that is what makes a story great! We still don't know how far we are from the last chapter but until it gets here, we will continue to follow our path and do what we can! We wish each of you a joyous Easter holiday!

Your Friends,

Cindy and Doc

April 2006

I am knocking on wood as I write this, but it has been a healthy month for us. Doc has had several weeks of feeling really good and we have taken advantage of the good days by fitting in a bunch of fun stuff. I know there are ups and downs to spinal cord injuries but it has been nice to have a series of ups for a few weeks!

We did get out to the golf course twice this month and Doc tried to give me what help he could. I do have to tell you though that on one outing we met up with 3 other couples and they were playing men against the women and invited us to tag along. So I joined up with the women and that was the end of my support! Once Doc considered himself part of the "guys" team, his assistance to me went flying out the window! If I plan on getting any help in the future I am going to have to make sure it is just him and I on the round.

I think the fishing pole is getting close to being ready for a tryout. The last time I saw it, it was almost done and there were only one or two loose ends to tie up. Doc is excited about being close to catching fish again. I think he is having a hard time to decide what fish to fish for first! We also were working on a plan to get out for some turkey hunting but as I really don't think it is worth getting up at 3 a.m. to be the right spot at the right time, I am not sure how many turkeys we are going to see. I am willing to do give a lot but I am drawing the line at a 3 a.m. wake up call and dressing in camouflage!

We have made it to 2 Cardinal baseball games and we are 50/50. We watched a bad loss and a good win! We did have a good time checking out the new stadium. We both were surprised at how much we liked it because we thought we would really miss the old stadium but this one was so good that we decided we wanted to keep it! We missed some of the foods that we used to look forward to because the choices we liked were no longer available. On the other hand, it was a much nicer handicap seating and it was possible for all of us to sit together! Then of course there was the new "Build a Bear/ Fredbird Factory". I have to admit that I stood in line with the rest of the little kids to wait my turn to make mine! I had a blast and even though I was probably the oldest "kid" there, I would do it again in a heartbeat! My Fredbird is sitting on my bed as I am typing this! Our next Cardinal game that we have tickets for is scheduled in June.

We had two talking engagements this month and I cannot tell you how much it means to us to use our experience to make a difference to someone else. We continue to see our life enriched by this experience and our faith steadfastly only grows stronger. We have just been so thankful for the good health! We continue to live life one day at a time and enjoy all the special things that each day brings!

Doc continues to feel his legs/arms/hands etc....(actually there was a couple of times that he felt everything). The feelings are frequent but they still aren't a constant sensation and he has yet to have had much movement with any of it. He continues on the testosterone shots and we are hopeful that in a few months, we will see even more improvement.

I have had a couple of experiences that I am going to share. I told Doc that as I learn more and more carpenter skills, I am going to change my name to Cindy Villa Blackmore. I did successfully put together a new computer desk for our room so I could move the computer downstairs so Doc can use it (I will write more about that in a minute) and I installed a new smoke detector that seems to be working. BUT I could not quite handle the difficult job of a new doorbell. It seemed to go fairly easy and everything looks good but I must have done something wrong because the doorbell goes off all the time and there is hardly ever anyone actually ringing it. All night long, you can hear the ding dong go off and I have gotten to where I don't even crawl out of bed anymore so if anyone comes by after midnight ringing the doorbell, I am going to be ignoring you! I think it possibly might be the monkey running out there and ringing it and then hiding but I haven't caught him yet! On the positive side, it does work when you actually push it too!

Our only downer this month was that the infectious disease dr called me because he said he finally got around to looking at Doc's chart from when he was in the hospital and there was something that showed up in the culture that somehow slipped through the cracks and it is a nasty type of infection that doesn't have any known antibiotic to fight it. Luckily, it seems to be ok for now but he is wanting to keep a close eye on Doc because he has it. It is one of those that never goes away but can lay dormant without causing any problems so hopefully, it will stay in that invisible mode!

We had 2 battles this month. The first battle we had this month was with the wounds but everything seems to be getting a little better. The two sores on the back are completely gone and I don't even have to dress them or put any medication on them. The sores on his heals are getting a little better but they still look pretty nasty. If it is like the rest of his sores, they always look ugly as they are healing. Then he still has a small one on his bottom but that isn't getting any worse and he has a new cushion ordered that I hope makes big strides in clearing it up too! They have also ordered a custom designed back cushion for his wheelchair to help with pressure on his back. The second battle we had was that the home health care agency we had the insurance would cover one morning a week decided to drop all patients outside a certain distance from them and we fell in that range. So we had to find another home health agency and get them trained. Luckily, we found one and we are in the process of training them and I think it is going to be a good thing. It is still early but the new nurse that we have assigned to us seems to be a very wonderful person that I think will do a great job!

One of the main highlights this month was the addition of voice activated software. That is why I moved the computer downstairs to our bedroom. Bonnie and Richard Brockman heard us talking at Springfield and they represent Dragon software and thought Doc's voice was strong enough and that they could help Doc get it installed. So a few days ago, they stopped by and installed it and Doc has a new independent activity. He can surf the web, read and write e-mails, work in Word and Excel, and play games. I think the more he uses it, the more he will find that he can do with it! It was a great day to have that in place and we just wanted to say thanks to them for giving Doc the gift of the world through the computer! He now has a couple of options to keep him busy while I am at work and as soon as he gets comfortable with the software, I have a long list of computer projects for him to work on!

May is going to be full of graduations, anniversaries, and weddings. It seems like every weekend is booked with something going on. As Doc tells everyone, we didn't sit around much before the accident and we don't sit around now either. Things have changed as to what we are able to do but we still seem to be pretty busy! We are also scheduled to speak at a dinner at the Cairo/Jacksonville Unity Christian Church in Cairo on May 20th and as always, we are looking forward to that opportunity to share!

As spring rolls into summer our grass is starting to grow again and I started to look into hiring someone to take care of it but I didn't get very far with that idea because there were the volunteers that insisted that was their way of helping out. I cannot express what it means to have so many special friends and such a wonderful family! Thanks to all that continue to stop by to pass an hour, say a prayer, send a card or assist in putting Doc to bed and the many, many other ways that so many of you have stepped into our lifes and hearts!

Your Friends,
Cindy and Doc

May 2006

I love summer! It is my favorite season of the year. Doc likes fall so his season has yet to arrive. I get to enjoy mine first! I think it has to do with vacations and kids being out of school (although my kids have been out of school for awhile!). I always looked forward to them being home and not having to do homework every night. It made me feel like summer was family time! Plus I love all summer activities!

One thing that I have never tried until this month was turkey hunting. Of course this is more of a spring thing and has always been one of Doc's favorite activities. I went with him a couple of times in the fall to bow hunt deer (well, I brought my camera and made too much noise!) (did you know that you aren't allowed to clean out the leaves from the deer stand? You just have to sit in them! Hehe) but I have never been turkey hunting. There wasn't a lot of difference. I still brought my camera and had fun with it and you still have to sit real still and not talk. You have to wear ugly clothes with no color other than greens and grays with leaf and bark patterns. Uptown! Plus a hat and screen mask to match no less! Luckily for me my brothers had gotten Doc a handicap blind to sit in so I brought a chair and sat in there with him and didn't have to dress up quite so much. I was able to read a book and enjoy the sounds of nature. I do love being in the woods but I could do it without hunting. Anyway, two of my brothers load Doc up on a trailer hooked behind a 4-wheeler and then pull us out to the woods.

Then Doc unloads and is able to take off down a path to a good spot. (and he did take off…my brothers were gathering equipment, guns and stuff and we turn around and Doc is about 100 yards down the path without us! I guess he was ready!). So we get to our spot and we put up our decoys (those are things that look like fake turkeys but the turkeys are supposedly dumb enough to think they are alive!) Then they put Doc and me in the blind by the decoys and they go away to start calling turkeys. I sit there listening to one brother make a call and the other brother answer him and I look at Doc and ask him if my brothers are playing. He says, "Well, they are having fun and we probably aren't going to see any turkeys." I just sat there and laughed. I don't think he cared because he just loved being out in the middle of woods listening to the sounds. Even if most of them were being created by my brothers! Needless to say we didn't get a turkey that day or even see one that was real while we were hunting. Now after we get loaded in the van and start heading home, a huge turkey flies across the road right in fun of van and then starts running for all it is worth and right behind it a fox runs in front the van giving chase to the turkey and it was fun to watch. I am not sure who won that race but it was nature at a highlight! At least I saw a turkey that day!

We had a great day on our anniversary. It seems like just yesterday I was writing about our 25th and now we have already celebrated #26. I took a day of vacation and Doc & I squeezed all kinds of fun stuff into it and it will go down as one of our favorite memories. We want to wish Happy Anniversary to all of you that celebrated one last month or are celebrating one this month. They should always be a special day (I pray as special as the "wedding" day was itself!). Speaking of weddings, we also had a wonderful time attending a wedding of some dear friends of our family! It was a special evening where many, many of our friends were gathered together and we totally enjoyed the evening of shared laughs, dancing, and hugs! We wish Julie and Curt a wonderful life together!

I also want to wish a belated Mother's Day to all you mothers! I hope all your kids told you that you were the best mother anyone could want because the highlight to my Mother's Day was that all mine did! I had to laugh though because I wonder how many mothers hear that and how can we all be the very best? I guess the very best for our kids…that is why we were matched up in the first place! I also had to laugh because there were many, many times in the years that they were growing up and following our rules, that they probably weren't thinking that I was the best! Hehe! It is all part of being the mom I guess.

Doc had to spend about a week of this month in bed because he has a nasty sore on his bottom and it is just not getting any better. They thought that if we took the pressure off of it for a few days that it might help but it was actually getting worse so I decided it was time to get up and go again. He was getting so worn out and bored just staying in the bedroom! So we got him up again and back on the move. It is actually a little bit better since then but it still has a long, long way to go to heal. We have a new wheelchair seat coming that has been "mapped" for his requirements so we are hopeful that will help. The good news is that all his other sores are either completely healed or almost there! The rest of him is looking good!

He continues to feel things and he told me that so much so that he can't really distinguish between when he can feel and when he cannot. It happens so often anymore that it is not out of the ordinary. We still don't have any movement with it though and we are still waiting for the diaphragm to kick in someday so we can try to do without the vent. We are hopeful that signs like his continued increase in sense of smell and being able to blow his nose are good signs but only the future will hold the answer to that. Those are things that are not in our hands. Instead we have faith that if they do come to pass, it will because they are meant to. In the meantime, we take it one day at a time. We concentrate on all the good things that are evolving as a result of it and there are many!

We went to watch our local high school baseball team win districts and sectionals! That was fun! Congrats Bearcats!

We spoke at a banquet at the Cairo/Jacksonville Unity Church on the subject of angels. We were able to share many of our stories about our experiences. Some of them were human angels and probably many of you that are reading this were the topic of discussion so I hope your ears weren't burning. Then we also spoke about those things that happened that seemed to be of a more spiritual nature and aren't so easily explained. Many others shared special music and messages and it was a wonderful experience. We were glad to be part of it.

Now on my favorite subject...the fishing pole! Yes, it is done and it is working GREAT! It allows Doc to cast out, catch fish, and reel them in completely by himself using a puff & sip concept! It has been tried out and has passed with flying colors. We took it fishing on the Monday of Memorial weekend and Doc caught 10 catfish. Now we have to try it out for bass and trout (and probably everything else with the exception of maybe a whale...I don't think it has the power to pull in one of those! Hehe). After we know it can catch all those fish, we will give it an A+! Doc said we might keep a catfish or two to eat but that I would have to clean them and that is when it became a catch and release day! Hehe! I do know how to clean a trout because he made me learn. It was just a few days before his accident and we had been fishing and he said that he thought that I should know how to do it. So I cleaned them all that day and now I know how. So when we go trout fishing, we can keep a few but I still have to learn how to clean a catfish (and I can't say I am in any hurry!). At the end of day, Doc said that it was one of the best days of his life! He really, really enjoyed it and I want to give a special thanks to EVERYONE that had a part in developing it! Those I work with, the Moberly Vo-tech, and especially my brother Lloyd. We also wanted to say thanks to Howard for sharing his pond (and dog) with us and for helping with our demo run of trying it out! When I made reference to the dog, his name is George and he is a fishing dog. He loves to fish! He sat right by Doc's chair and watched the bobber. When it would go down, he would bark and get excited and then when Doc got the fish reeled in close to the shore, George would wade out, pick it up in his teeth and gently drop it in front of Doc's chair. It was great fun to watch and I have attached a few pictures for all to enjoy! Doc was disappointed that I didn't have a picture of him casting the pole out so I will take one of those next time! The only down side to this endeavor is that whenever Doc is outside in the heat for very long, his temperature spikes up to 103 or 104 degrees in no time and then we are left with the challenge of getting it to go back down. It is worth the challenge though! He is ready to go again and we actually have plans to try it again this weekend.

Now the greatest part of this story is that through the development of this fishing pole, the company that I work for (Orscheln Products) has made a commitment to support a team to develop/improve the design and help manufacture these for others that want one. They have never been on the market to purchase so the only persons that were able to enjoy the freedom of fishing without the use of their body were those that had someone to design and create them for themselves. Because of the leadership of Orscheln Products and those that volunteer to participate in this program, we will, hopefully, in the near future, see many persons having this activity available to them! It is an answer to prayer and I know there are going to be many persons that get a little more pleasure out of life because of it! I know how much it meant to Doc and I know that others will gain the same satisfaction of being able to have a sense of independence in doing something that comes so simple to those of us that have never had it taken away! Thanks to all that had any part in making this come about and to those that end up participating in it!

As time rolls by and we continue to work through each day one by one you can never (and I mean never) know how much it means to have the continued support of love and faith that we continue to be overwhelmed with. A prayer or card or an act of kindness can mean the difference between a day that is hard to get through and a day that awesome! So thanks to each of you that make almost every day for us awesome!

We hope you have a great June and know that we are planning on squeezing a little golf and fishing into ours! We also have a Cardinal game planned for Father's Day and it our youngest daughters turn to go with us and we are ready! Doc rarely misses a Cardinal game and it is always a special day when we can cheer them on in person! We will continue down our path and we so thankful for each of you that continue to cheer us on!

Your Friends,
Cindy and Doc

Doc and George Fishing

Doc and George Still Fishing

George Retrieving a Fish for Doc

June 2006

I wrote in the last e-mail how much I love summer and all the things that you can do summertime but I didn't include hospital visits. Unfortunately, that is where it looks like we will be spending most of our summertime. It wasn't what we thought we were going to do and it is another bump in the road but as with the other bumps, we will get past it and move on. We have already been here for almost today weeks and then today, (Thursday, June 29th, he had surgery and will be in intensive care for 3-5 more weeks, depending on which doctor you listen to. Of course, we want to listen to the 3 week doctor! Hehe!

Doc's wound on his bottom progressed to the point that it required surgery and due to the location of it, it required some special after surgery treatment. He is in a special bed and has to stay in it 3-4 weeks past surgery, flat on his back. This is something that is not very popular or easy to do for him as it makes breathing on the vent and swallowing hard. There wasn't any other option available and we really want this surgery to be successful so we are following the rules. We have to wait one week and then they can tell us if they think the surgery was successful. If so, they will wait 3 weeks and if it looks like it is healing, they might let us go home but Doc will still be in bed for most of the day with little to no incline to the bed. We will be able to get him up in 15 minute increments 3 times a day until we finally reach a 2 hour mark. If the wound still looks healthy after 2 hours, (3 times a day), we can work back into our full day in the wheelchair at that point. If all goes well, we should be back to our normal routine after the first week in August.

We did have a little fun to our month before all of this started to go downhill. We went fishing again and this time we were fishing for bass. I think Doc caught around 7 bass and had a blast. I attached a picture of a couple of his catches. One of them is with a decent bass (again, we were only in a catch and release mode). It wasn't just because I was going to have to clean them though because we were fishing at Gregg and Kathy Jacques's place and Gregg did volunteer to clean them if we wanted them. Doc was just fishing for fun though and not because he had to put meat on the table..hehe! Then one of the pictures is of snail because Doc caught that too. Did you ever catch a snail on a fishing hook? I think it is the smallest thing that he ever hooked! It was fun watching him struggle to bring that monster in.....hehe! Then finally, the other two pictures are of something we caught when we went fishing but without the fishing pole. Gregg and Kathy had this cute little black lab puppy that they were trying to find a home for. I think Doc thinks he can get George to train it and someday he will have his own "fishing" dog. So low and behold, a few days later we had adopted a new member to our family and named him Shannon (after Mike Shannon). I am not sure how much of a compliment it is to Mike Shannon (former St. Louis Cardinal and now an announcer for anyone unfamiliar with him) but Doc really likes him and the name stuck. We were disappointed that we had to leave him so soon after getting him but I am sure that

Shannon will not have any permanent mental anguish over it. In the meantime, he is staying with George and getting to know him. Maybe by the time we get home, Shannon will have caught on to all of George's fishing tricks!

Then we headed to St. Louis on Father's Day for a wonderful day of baseball at Busch Stadium. That was a nice time and the Cardinals actually won one that day!

We were disappointed at the things that we had to cancel in July but in the scheme of things, nothing was that major. We were going to share our story with another church but hopefully, we can still look forward to that in August or September. We were going to go trout fishing but again, I think there might be a trout or two left when we are up and going again. We had to give up our tickets to a Cardinal game but at least we made it to 3 other ones already this year and I am sure we will have another one to go to someday. I'd bet on it! We also had Muny tickets but again, they are letting us reschedule those to a date in August. AECI was having a 40th anniversary celebration and even though we were hopeful to join in that celebration (mainly just to see all of Doc's buddies) I am sure we will have another day to visit!

I have been sitting and looking out of the hospital windows at nights and seeing a sky already full of fireworks so I am pretty sure that I will see a nice show of fireworks from right where I sit on the 4th of July. We wish all of you a safe and fun 4th! It always seems to be a great day of picnics, family and fireworks. My favorite part was always the watermelon and watching the kids run with the sparklers. (well, actually to be honest, it was running with sparklers myself too! It is so fun writing in the air with those things!)

As always, the experience at the hospital is not without rewards. We have met some new friends and revisited with some old ones (not really old, just prior)...I don't want to get into trouble! We wanted to say thanks to all the doctors and nurses that try so hard to make our stay as easy as possible. There usually is nothing easy about all the things that need to be done each day. I am still going back and forth to work and doing some there and some from the hospital. In the meantime, I have others that come and stay with Doc during the day so that I can do that. Thanks to all those that come and visit that allows me to break away. It isn't that I don't have faith with the hospital but with Doc being on the vent, it just seems safer to have someone that is in the room with him to monitor if there are any problems so help is quicker if it is needed. It also helps to have someone familiar with Doc's care to be on hand to assist those that are here to care for him. Although they are getting better all the time...they keep telling me that they don't want to get really good at it because that will mean that we have been here too long!. The best part about having someone here though is just so Doc has company. I think the long days are about to begin as he is stuck in bed and not at an incline that will be comfortable. One our doctors told Doc to hang in there because he is just in a tunnel right now. He said there are all kinds of tunnels in our lifes and that there is always light at the end of them. He said the light is only a few weeks away so even though it is never fun in the tunnel, we will soon be through it. I told Doc we would just put on our "happy faces" and make it through it!

We continue to work on the fishing poles. A team has been formed and they are actively pursuing the design and acquisition of the parts that we need to build them. Our goal is to have some poles ready to share as soon as possible. There are some real brains behind the construction of them but mine is not one of them. I can always tell when the wheels start to turn and I don't always understand where the wheels are going but I have faith in them! I tell them I am the cheerleader and continue to pursue the leads that I get for places/persons that would be interested in them. In the meantime, I am planning on video taping Doc fishing as soon as I can get him behind the pole again! Another one of my assignments! Doc can't wait to be in the movies if that means he is back behind his fishing pole!

That is about all that there is to report. Doc says that he feels physically better than he has for awhile so I think they are cleaning his system of any little infections that might have been brewing due to the open wounds. He continues to feel increased and consistent feeling in his limbs but still only that they are there. He can't feel them to the touch (at least not much) or move them. About the only new feeling he had this month was that he has started to feel his right foot to the touch. I get excited about all the baby steps though because little steps and new things are still heading forward. His smile is as bright as ever and even though the next 3 or 5 weeks might be boring, he knows as I do, that they will come to pass!

Thanks to all that stopped by to brighten our days! Thanks to those that are dogsitting Shannon. Thanks to those that are keeping our yard looking so nice! Thanks for the e-mails, cards and prayers. We still believe in those prayers and no matter what our days hold, we always cling to our faith and it always seems to leave us feeling very lucky and very blessed to be surrounded by so many persons that care! Faith is a powerful tool and one that we have in abundance!

Your Friends,
Cindy and Doc

Doc with a Snail he Caught

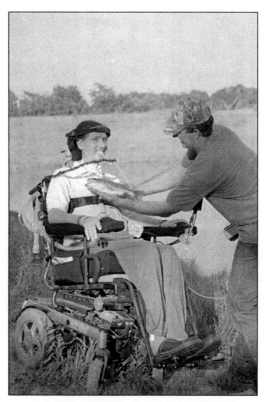

Doc and Gregg with Bass

Shannon as a pup

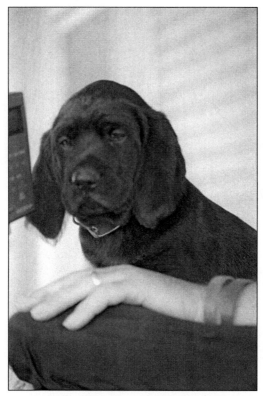

Shannon Sitting on Doc's Lap

July 2006

I have spent a bunch of this month just driving back and forth between home, the hospital and work. As I drove the highway, I got to thinking about how much of our life is like driving on roads. A lot of us spend most of our time on the 4 lane highways, making good time but always in a hurry to get to a particular exit. There is usually a lot of traffic on this road but not a lot of scenery. Yet even with the traffic, if you were broke down on the side of the road, everyone would assume that you would get help from somewhere else and few would stop. And so we travel along like this for a long time. Then one day there is a detour at our exit and we can't get off where we want to. Instead we have to take a long way around. This usually means that you have to get off the beaten track and follow some lesser traveled roads to make it to where you think you want to go. These roads are a little bumpy because they aren't maintained like the more popular roads are. Because of the bumps, you tend to travel a little slower which isn't a bad thing because it is usually a more scenic route and you can sit back and enjoy the views. There isn't as much traffic and yet if you broke down along one of these roads, just about every person that passed you would see that you needed help and stop to offer some. No one ever really plans a trip around possible detours but the experiences that happen on them can make lasting memories. That is where I feel like we are right now. We were on that highway and knew exactly what exit we wanted to get off on and instead we got detoured to this scenic route. We can't go very fast because of all the bumps but there have been some fantastic views. We have been broke down several times but there has always been someone that has stopped to help us out! I am still not sure how much longer we will be on this detour or what else we are going to see during our journey but we can only sit back and take it one day at a time. If you ask me if I want to get back to the highway, I would have to say I don't know. Sometimes I would like to be able to plan my trip again and at least pretend like I know where I am going. Right now we are on unfamiliar roads completely dependent on following the signs that say detour so we don't get lost. That being said, our detour has changed our life so that even if we make it back to the highway, we will never be the same again. Hopefully, we are better persons for being on this detour and that we have blessed those that have stopped to help us as much as they have blessed us. This month our bumpy road turned into gravel with lots of dust and rocks and potholes but it eventually turned back into a slightly better road and it looks like it is going to get better in just a few more miles!

Doc continued to spend most of this month getting over the surgery and letting the wounds have time to heal. We followed all the rules and were rewarded with being able to get back into the wheelchair. We were happy to start out with 15 minutes and have now worked up to a little more than 2 hours. We will continue to add to that until we are back to our full day. We finally were able to come home this past Thursday and it was nice to be there. (Doc said it was good because he thinks the tv is too small in those hospital rooms & they don't have the outdoor channel! hehe). Doc said that all in all, it wasn't too bad because we made so many new friends and we are appreciative at how hard the Boone Hospital staff worked to make our stay bearable. Now we are making some plans to enjoy what is left of the summer. We have some stuff to make up from July. We will hopefully squeeze some of into August. We missed a trout fishing trip that we had scheduled so we are trying to work out at time in Sept or Oct to squeeze it in. After the high temperatures of July, it might be a good thing we were forced to delay it.

We came home with no wounds except for the incision and it feels good to have a handle on them for a little bit and hopefully, a long time. That being said, Doc had a little accident the first afternoon we were home. He tried to go down the hall into the bedroom and cut the corner to close and ended up catching his forearm between the corner of the wall and the wheelchair. Needless to say, his arm came out the loser and so he gave up a little flesh so now I have another sore to watch. It looks clean though and I think it will heal ok as there isn't any pressure on it. I am not worried about infection because he is on so many antibiotics right now, that I think he would have to work at catching something and even then, I don't know if he could. He is telling me the monkey jumped in his path and he had to swerve but I am not buying it. I asked him why he didn't stop when his wheelchair started to do a wheely and he just said he couldn't feel anything. I guess he thinks he is such a hotrod that it is normal to cruise down our hall on his back 2 wheels!

This weekend we were able to get out for a couple of hours and attend a wedding for a couple that is very dear to us and it was a beautiful ceremony (congrats to Brooke and Brad!). It was nice to see so many friends and to catch up after being away for so many weeks. We have a trip planned to St. Louis later this month with some friends to go to an opera (we had it planned in July but had to reschedule because of the hospital stay. That trip included a Cardinal game with the opera and Doc seemed excited about it. Now that the Cardinal game is not part of the plan because we were not able to exchange those tickets, he isn't near as excited…..Things that make you go mmmmmmmmmm!)

We are also rescheduling the visit to the Seventh Day Adventists Church in Moberly to one weekend this month and are really looking forward to it. It is also so heartening to know we are on so many prayer lists and then to have the opportunity to share our experiences and say thank you is a special reward.

Doc is especially looking forward to Shannon coming home. He has been well taken care of in our absence and obviously been fed well because they called us from the vet today where they were updating Shannon on his shots before returning him to us and he has gained over 12 lbs since we have last seen him. All day today, Doc just keeps repeating "12 lbs!". He will be home tomorrow! I don't know if he will be so glad because he loves water and there is a pond where he was. When he gets home, he just gets a dry yard! Doc did ask me tonight though if I would drive the truck to work on Monday and stop and get him a plastic pool so I guess that is the next thing on my to-do list!

We were supposed to being scheduling a re-eval at Craig this month but I have to be honest and say that we are completely burnt out on hospitals and tests. We need to take some time to live again and do some fun things. Plus it just feels good to be back home and in our own beds! I think we are going to put off our re-eval until we have some time to recoup from this last experience. Hopefully, we will regroup and get it scheduled at a later date. We do want to visit with all our Colorado friends. We just aren't ready for the battery of tests and the busy schedule that we know await us there.

After all the months of writing these e-mails and sharing all the wonderful things that so many of you do, you would think we would not be so overwhelmed at how it continues and yet we are. This month has been long and Doc has almost counted each day down by the minute. Yet, so many of you through visits, calls, cards and prayers have helped to pass the time and make it more bearable (I wanted to say a special thanks to Dana, Roy, Brandon, and Mom, along with several other family and friends, as they went an extra mile during our hospital stay!). I am sure that all of you have been in the hospital or have had loved ones in the hospital will understand but those of you that haven't had that experience, all these things mean so much! And even though I was able to be closer to home than when we were in Colorado, I wasn't able to spend much time there. Mostly it was a stopping off point to shower, do laundry, pick up the mail and head back. So thanks to all those that kept the home-front ready for our return. Before we left the hospital, several of the nurses and therapists got together and told me that they are planning a 24 hour shift between them to come to our house and stay with Doc day and night so I can have a whole day/night off. I was speech-less and you know that is unusual for me! I am having as much fun just thinking about my day off as I probably will be having it! I think Doc is planning on having his own little party here with all his new friends! What a wonderful gesture! We were watching CMT this morning on tv and they said there is an old saying that says "Money can make you wealthy but friends can make you rich." I am not sure how old it is but I hadn't heard it before and I thought I would share because we are sooooo RICH!

Your Friends,
Cindy and Doc

August and September 2006

Maybe it was because I was a little later in the month sending out the last e-mail but it sure seems like I just did this! However, I know that many of you look forward to the updates so I will see what we had going on. Most of the time I don't even know what I am going to put into it until my fingers start working.

It seems like we squeezed a lot of fun into September and maybe that is one of the reasons that I feel tired. Actually, probably the real reason we are tired is from the only real down side to this month and that was that Doc hasn't been sleeping much. He has so many secretions that he has to be suctioned out about every 30 or 40 minutes so our nights aren't very restful for either of us. The doctors have targeted some infections in the lungs and Doc started some antibiotics this week but in the meantime we struggle with the sleeping and with staying off oxygen for any significant time. The silver lining in that though is that I get to see Doc's face about 12 or more times a night that I ordinarily won't be gazing on it and each time I do, I thank God that I have such a beautiful view!

We made a road trip to St. Joe one day to visit with our daughter and her husband and we explored the Pony Express Museum. That was a lot of fun and it was nice to spend some time with them. Any time with any of our kids is a special time!

We had a couple of birthdays this month so we ate wayyyy too much cake but it was good! We actually went out to eat 3 times to celebrate Doc's b-day and each time I had the waitresses sing to him so he had an entire weekend of celebrating his birthday. We traveled to Odessa to celebrate his day and went antiquing and Doc acquired this "beautiful" (I use this word loosely) bobbing head dog that is holding a "welcome" sign in his mouth. He sat on Doc's lap for 3 hours bobbing his head until Doc finally made his mind up that we were buying him and taking him home. Now he welcomes our guest by the front door and he is for sure a conversation piece.

I put a cd player in the van for his birthday (which we are both really enjoying!) and I conveniently scheduled the installation to happen on my birthday. The reason I did that was because the installation was at Best Buy which just happens to be connected to Hobby Lobby. As it was going to take an hour to install, we might as well do something fun and as it was my birthday, Doc didn't say a single word about an hour in Hobby Lobby. He actually found a couple of things that he thought I would like and had someone put them in his lap so by the time I caught up with him (he travels through the store at a much faster pace than me), he had some stuff for the cart. Then we went out to eat and he made sure I had my share of waitresses singing to me too! Hehe!

We went down in history this month with about 40,000+ other persons because Doc finally talked me into buying some Cardinal tickets to replace the game that he didn't get to go to because he got stuck in the Hospital and it just happened to be the first rainout in the new stadium. We arrived in what looked like a decent day but it soon turned into a downpour and all they were able to fit in was the

National Anthem. I think Doc just enjoyed being in the stadium for a few hours though and now we get to go back because we can trade our tickets in for another game in 2007. Speaking of the Cardinals, they have given Doc a few grey hairs but they finally made it to the play offs so GO CARDS! Doc is having a blast watching baseball!

One weekend we had a great day in Cairo. It was the annual Pioneer Day in which many in the community gather together for a day of fellowship and fun. It is always nice to gather together and celebrate friendship. It was even more special because Doc won the under 60 Lions/Lioness citizenship award for the year. Doc said the award was special to him but much, much more special were the words that were written in his nomination that ensured him that even in his situation; he contributes to the community since his accident!

Doc got in several more days of fishing this month. Probably not as many as he would have liked but he was determined to catch a fish big enough to give his new fishing pole a run for the money. He finally did! He caught a couple of catfish that had me standing on the fishing pole stand to keep it upright! I had a volunteer that cleaned one of them for us and we took it home and had an old fashioned fish fry for 2. Doc joined me in the kitchen and together we had a blast cooking up our feast of fish, cornbread, hushpuppies, fried potatoes, cole slaw and baked beans. Just thinking about is making my mouth water again! Yum!

I almost forgot to tell you that one of Doc's birthday gifts was another monkey (the ugliest one that you have ever seen) that hangs on his wheelchair and when you squeeze him, he can make the most awful noise! Of course, Doc is always asking someone to give him monkey a squeeze!

We don't have a ton of plans for October so I think we will spend it trying to get and stay healthy because we have some big plans for November. Doc and I have been talking for a long time now about how we used to take at least a week every year to take a nice vacation and we haven't done that since the accident. We finally decided that we needed that break from everything except a little fun for a week so we booked a week in Branson and we will be gone for 9 days. Doc really wanted to catch some of the Christmas stuff in Branson and we wanted to try and beat the winter weather. Christmas things kick off on 11/3 in Branson so we are hoping that if we travel that way early in the month, the weather might not be too cold. We are already exploring all the things that we want to do and trying to fit it all in. I am hoping that we are sleeping a little better by that time so we will be rested enough to enjoy it all! If not, we might just enjoy sleeping late and starting our day a little later than usual!

As far as what is going on in the medical world with Doc other than the increased secretions, we are battling a sore again but so far, keeping my finger crossed and my prayers flowing, we aren't losing any ground. It isn't going away but it isn't turning into one of those monster things either so I remain hopeful that it heals before it gets worse. As always, you do what you can, take it one day at a time and turn the worry over to the one that is really in control! I have a great resource that I found through Doc's last operation that I can turn to if it gets any worse. That, in itself, feels good to know! Some new things continue to pop up each month and even though they continue to be small things, we remain focused on the fact that improvements seem to happen each month!

Shannon (Doc's to-be fishing dog) continues to grow and is rapidly approaching pony size! He is all puppy and there are times that I think "why did we do this?" but most of the time we have a ton of fun watching him. He has a ton of personality and is a very smart dog. He loves to play Frisbee and ball but so far, he isn't looking like much of a fishing dog! We keep trying though. Right now all he does is jump into the water and swim around until he is completely tangled up in the fishing line and then I have a mess that is worse than a bunch of necklaces all tangled up! He loves to go though!

Missouri University sponsored an annual photo workshop and Moberly was selected as featured community this year. So 30 photographers came to Moberly and each selected a topic to cover for a week and then displayed some of their photos at an open house. A young woman from Vermont, named Jessica, found her way into our home & our story and captured a week of our life. She did an excellent job and became a new friend that we think a lot of. We attended the open house and found so many of the stories that were displayed to be outstanding. Our congrats to each of them for their hard work. If any of you would like to see our story and/or some of the others, they are displayed on the web at http://www.mophotoworkshop.org/58/. We are on team D and the title of our story is "Ever Changing Love". It is worth checking several of them out.

We are visiting South Gate Baptist Church in Springfield while we are in the Branson area. We are scheduled to speak at their services on 11/5 and are looking forward to it.

We continue to have help mowing our grass, putting Doc down in the evening and many, many more acts of kindness and we continue to feel blessed and to be thankful for each and every thing that each of you do. For each prayer for us, we give thanks each night! I hope all of you have a great Halloween season. That used to be one of Doc's favorite holidays. He really got into trying to come up with some creative way to scare our trick or treaters each year! Sometimes, he did a pretty good job at it!

PS: I always share this with Doc for his input before I send it out and I have to be honest and tell you that he was disappointed that I hadn't given you an update on the card games. All I will say on that subject is that we aren't talking about it. Doc says that is good enough! We actually are taking a break from our nightly card games for the next couple of weeks and replacing it with an evening at MU watching women's volleyball. That is turning out to be really entertaining for us! We do have an upcoming card party though that I will have to tone my skills for!

Your Friends,

Cindy and Doc

October 2006

I am sure that all of you that know us very well, know the highlight of our month! GO CARDINALS! I know Doc really wished he could have been jumping around the room and pumping his fists as his Cardinals won the World Series but his face showed all the pent up excitement! I had printed some heads of the Cardinal players and put them on sticks so I stuck the one of Jeff Weaver (the pitcher) in Doc's headrest and every time he got a strike out or did something neat, Doc was shaking his head so that Jeff was bobbing all around! (I was going to say weaving as a pun but I changed my mind..hehe) It was a great month of baseball and we loved every game! We actually managed to get ahold of some tickets (after I patiently called about 12 times because they told me to keep calling because tickets were always opening up) to one of the playoff games with San Diego and that was a blast. The atmosphere there was unexplainable and it was a memory that we will both treasure for a long, long time! They gave us a rally towel when we entered the gates and Doc had me frame his so it is hanging in our room to always remind us of that magical night!

The antibiotics that the doctor put Doc on for the infections in his lungs worked and it wasn't long that we were sleeping a little better and off oxygen and ready to go again. Unfortunately, as soon as we were done with them and they wore off, we were back in the same boat. So they renewed the prescription and he is now feeling great again. He still gets up about 5 or 6 times a night but that is much better than 20! He was scheduled to be finished with this round of drugs today but I called the doctor and explained that we were heading out on vacation for 9 days next week and it was our first real vacation for any extended length and we would really love for Doc to continue to feel good so he agreed to extend the antibiotics until vacation is over and then we will see if they worked. The bad side is that I feel like the problems are due to Doc not swallowing correctly and some of his food intake is going to the lungs. I took him off all food and put him back on tube feeding and I know he is anxious to get back to eating but he just isn't swallowing well right now. I tried again last night but it didn't go well. We are confused as to why it went so well for a year and now it seems so weak again but it just another one of those bumps in the road and we will take the steps to battle back again. We are starting today with our throat exercises and ice chips again to see if he can build the strength back. I know he is dying to eat while we are on vacation as we have 2 dinner shows scheduled! I hope and pray that he can eat because I know how badly he wants to but if not, you can bet we still have fun!

Now speaking of vacation…you cannot believe how excited we are about that! Doc has been wanting to go to Branson, MO during the Christmas season for a long time and they start all their Christmas shows on 11/3 so I decided to go as close to that as possible to hopefully still have some tolerable temperatures to enjoy it all! We have a full schedule every day and as always, there won't be any grass growing under our feet but that is how we like to do it. It will be a week full of fun all day long! We always say that we might take a vacation for just relaxing with no sets plans but when it comes down to it, we can't do it…we would both be BORED! We are much more active than that!

We had a card party at the activity center so their would be plenty of room to move around and we had a great turnout for that and it was another special night to make memories with our many, many friends! We are so blessed with those and I can't think of anything that is more precious than that! We took a group picture and it is sitting in my living room and I think it is one of my favorite pictures! Although I would probably say that my house has more pictures than almost all others! Every square inch is covered with a picture of some sort but I always find a spot to squeeze another one in!

My mom stayed with Doc one Friday while I took a day of vacation and met up with my cousin Tammy to have a girls day of fun. We started at Cracker Barrel for breakfast and they just happened to running this awesome porch sale that day (which we had a blast at!). Then we rented bikes and rode the Katy Trail at Rochport and I took my camera to catch the fall foliage and it was great! After that we had a late lunch with a glass of wine while we over looked the river off a bluff! I don't have to tell you that was good! Then we took advantage of it being "girls only" to make a trip to Hobby Lobby. After that we did a little damage at the mall and then headed back to my house to put Doc down and visit with another cousin that was visiting from Colorado. It had been a long, long time since we had been together and it was blast to see each other.

The next day we took my mom to St. Louis to go to an anniversary dinner (by the way, congrats on 50 years to my Aunt Rose and Uncle Don!). My cousin Tammy and her husband Greg had taken the time to put up a ramp so we were able to get in to have supper with them and several others joined us and we had a mini party (while we were watching a Cardinal playoff game) and it was a great time! They also have a trail in the woods behind their house so we ventured down that too. Doc got stuck a couple of times on the way back up it but with the help of a couple of strong females (hehe), we made it back to the yard! He has talked about that hike a lot since then. He said he was scouting for deer and turkey signs! I am sure we will have to do that again! It was a wonderful visit!

Halloween was fun and we had several spooky trick or treaters! Doc used to love to sit outside and scare the you know what out of the kids but now we have to be content on just treating! It is still a fun night. I had 3 of the cutest little girls come over and help me carve a pumpkin so it was glowing on the front porch as a welcome on Halloween night. We actually were taking pictures last year with a pumpkin in the background and it fell and broke. I thought I threw it away but some seeds must have taken root and I had the most awesome involuntary pumpkin plant that grew over the summer and we ended up with 19 huge pumpkins and a few smaller ones! I could never have done that if I was trying to because I do not have a green thumb. It was fun to share them and I actually still have 4 or 5 out there because they didn't turn orange quick enough to give them away!

We are excited about speaking at South Gate Baptist Church in Springfield, MO this Sunday. They have a couple of services so we are going to talk at both. Their pastor told us he would be in trouble if he didn't ask us to do both! We don't mind and it is something that we know we are supposed to be doing. On top of that, we are scheduled to talk at the Presbyterian Church in Moberly, MO the first Sunday in December and then at the FBLA at Macon High School in January. We always look forward to sharing our story and some of the miraculous things that have happened to us during the past 2+ years.

The weather was a little cool and damp this month for fishing but Doc still made me drag him out into the yard just to practice with his pole. We put a different switch on it and it seems to be working a little better for playing fish. He can regulate the start and stop of reeling a little better so he said it will make for better bass fishing. Now I think he is ready for spring....more fishing and more baseball! In the old days, he would have been happy with this time of year with bow hunting and deer season but it is a little cold for him to do those things yet. My brother is hoping to get him out there but I am not sure Doc thinks it is worth the effort because he feels so cold and doesn't last very long. I tease him that he has become a fair weather hunter only!

We have found a new pastime that we really enjoy though (like we needed another one!). We have been going to watch the women's volleyball team at MU and it is a blast to watch those girls. Volleyball is sure a sport that you have to pay attention too so there isn't much talking if you want to see the game…bad for me but I manage to pay pretty close attention. Mark and Dana have been our partners in that new adventure and we have enjoyed the evenings that we have done that!

Oh yeah! I almost forgot my greatest achievement this month! I hardwired a new chandelier for my kitchen. I have never had any electrical experience at all but I have wanted a new light for my kitchen for a long, long time and Penny's had one for sale that I really liked but it said "hardwiring required". Doc said to order it and he was sure someone would help me. So I talked to a friend of ours (thanks Mark C!) that works in the electrical field and he said would help me if I needed it but he was pretty sure I could handle it myself. So he gave me a couple of hints and then when it arrived last week, Doc patiently sat in the kitchen with me and taught me how to strip wires, splice them together and how to ground wires, ect…then he had to talk me through drilling a hole in my ceiling and inserting an ceiling anchor so I could hang it. All in all, it went fairly smoothly and now I can step back and look at my new light and know that I wired it! I was excited! I am glad Doc kept the monkey in the other room on that project! Hehe! I also called someone to repair the shower stall that got a hole poked into it when we had that water leak a few months ago but he also said that he could come up and do it but it would cost me quite a bit and to be honest, he thought I could do it myself. So he talked me through what I would need and how to do it and I followed his instructions, and once again, job completed. Now I do have to get some guys to help me set the shower back in place though because it is not a one woman job. Hehe…I just re-read that, maybe it is a 2 woman job….maybe I don't need to find any guys..hehe…although I probably will…heck, we all need a break once in awhile—even women!

Doc's sore isn't going away and I have to be honest with myself and say that it is worse! Sometimes I want it to be better so bad that I look at it and try to rationalize it but it isn't getting better. I know it is going to need some attention but I am putting it off until after vacation. I have babied it so hard but it just isn't helping. It isn't horrible yet but has the potential to get that way very quickly. There is also another small spot that is just starting on the other side and I am attempting to put a hold on that one but sometimes there just doesn't seem to be anything that I can do to stop them. So we might be battling a couple of things after vacation if the infection in the lungs flares up after we get off the antibiotics and the sores stay in their current shape. I have already warned Doc though that I have spent the last 2 Christmas seasons in the hospital and this year, I want to be home! I am not sure he has any control over heeding my warnings but I tried!

Our puppy is now a 59 lb puppy of boundless energy but we are still enjoying him. I know there will be a day that he will be great company for us! I am not looking forward to challenging the winter weather to feed and water him but I am sure we will make it through it.

Our ramp started to sink in the mud so it was getting harder for Doc to get up on the porch without a little push and as my hands were usually full of stuff that was always a challenge and the porch had a soft spot in it that Doc's chair was threatening to fall through so I was grateful when Howard, a super friend, came out and fixed both for me! Those 2 things have made my month great! Isn't it funny how much little things can change your life? We also got an e-mail from one of Doc's co-workers that said his wife was experienced in Doc's care needs and wanted to know if she could relieve me some on his restless nights. I haven't taken them up on the offer yet because I am just trying to get organized for vacation and stuff but if Doc is still restless when we return home, I probably will once in awhile. Just the offer overwhelmed me! I also want to say a continued thanks to Steve for taking my trash down to the corner every Monday and for all those that come by and visit with Doc or come in the evening to help me put him down. The list is never ending and I cannot tell you how much ALL of it means. The cards and prayers that we continue to get are at the top of the list too. Prayer is a powerful thing and there is not a day that goes by that we both don't know how much those are helping us!

I have mentioned in the past how Thanksgiving is a time to especially remember all that we have to be thankful for and our list is a long, long, long list! Every single one of you (whether we know you are not) are on that list and we remember each of you every night by asking for a blessing for each of you just for reading these e-mails, keeping up with our adventures and remembering us in prayer. We will be spending Thanksgiving at my mom's with the whole turkey experience. I just hope Doc can help eat it by that time. It will all work out no matter what though…it always does! So a special Thanksgiving blessing to each of you and if you are traveling, we pray for a safe journey!

Your Friends,
Cindy and Doc

November 2006

We have passed Thanksgiving and are well into the season of Christmas but still the excitement of the Cardinals winning the World Series hasn't worn off. Doc still smiles every time he thinks of it. While we were on vacation in Branson, we found a Cardinal Clubhouse store that had every possible Cardinal thing you could ever wish for and Doc had a good time in there! He mostly was window shopping but he did find a few things that he took home with him for his Wall of Cardinal Fame! Plus he had to have a Championship hat for his head! I took a picture of him in the store and have attached it!

Speaking of vacation, it was wonderful! We stayed busy and by the time we got home, Doc said he was in the mood for a boring day! We did a lot of Christmas shopping and a little (maybe a little more than a little) for ourselves! We went to see the Christmas lights and shows at Silver Dollar City two days. One day it was in the 80's and the next time we went, it was in the 30's so we experienced it in two different extremes. I can't say which one was the best because I enjoyed the warmth of the 80's but the 30's gave the whole Christmas theme a much more realistic feel. Plus, I enjoyed the hot chocolate and hot cider in the cold temperatures! On top of that, we hit 6 other shows and the Titanic Museum. The hotel we stayed at was a little upscale but they were of great help to me in unloading the van and setting stuff up in the room and making sure we had plenty of room so I am glad we decided to stay there!

It was much easier and on top of that, the experience of staying in a place like that was really neat! It is easy to take much of Doc's stuff in laundry baskets (like his batteries to charge his equipment and his larger supplies) so I felt a little like a redneck (most of the other guests were arriving in Cadillac's with fancy luggage). I pull up in Porky with clothes baskets! Hehe! I did have suitcases for our clothes though and not Piggly Wiggly bags like Jeff Foxworthy talks about! Anyway, the persons that work there treated us like royalty and after 9 days there, we had made several new friends!

I think Doc would agree with me that the highlight of our trip though was probably the visit to South Gate Baptist Church to share our story with them. As a result of that, God worked through us and performed many wonderful things. We continued to run into folks the entire week that had been there and told us how our story changed their lifes and each story was a fantastic testimony to how God is using us to do positive things. As the week went on and we added stories to stories, we continued to be amazed at the magnitude of how powerful our story is. You would think that I would be used to it by now but it still leaves me in wonder at some of the stuff that happens. I continue to document it and someday, I will put it all together in a book and there will be persons that will think it is a fiction novel but it is all true! We were so grateful for the opportunity to share and as their pastor put it, "we have a whole church worth of new friends!" Now our story is part of their story and as I have said since the very beginning, this story belongs to every one of us!

Our next church visit was scheduled at the Presbyterian Church in Moberly on December 3rd but we ran into some difficulties on how to get into the building so we are going to come up with an alternative plan for speaking to their congregation. We still are looking forward to sharing our story with them as we always are. We trust in God's plan and goes where he sends us so we are sure there is a reason for this ripple too! Other than that, we are schedule to talk at Macon High School in January as long as Doc is not in the hospital yet. (as you will read below, we are going to have another visit there in the near future.)

Our daughter and her husband bought a new house and they invited us to help them furniture shop and move into it so that was an exciting thing for us to participate in. We met them in Kansas City to furniture shop with them and although Doc tried very, very hard to get them to buy all their furniture from Cabela's, it didn't happen. Jaymi just did not go for that outdoor cabin look! I am not sure why because her husband shot a nice buck during deer season so she is going to have a perfect compliment to the furniture hanging on her wall! I had to laugh at her face when she figured out he wanted to mount it. It was the same look that would have been on my face! Luckily for me, Doc never managed to bag the one he wanted for our wall and I never had to deal with it! (yet!)

Then they moved in the Saturday after Thanksgiving and we were able to help a little with that too! Doc isn't able to get into the entire house, but he can get into a couple of the rooms in the downstairs area (which is probably where the deer head is going to be so it will work out nicely! Doc said to add that it is also where Joey wants to put the big screen tv so that is another big bonus point to being in that room!).

Doc continues to feel good and even though we are still struggling with sleeping at night with all the suctioning that needs to be done, his temperature and oxygen levels remain positive. We did have a bump this month came when I took him to the clinic to check on a wound that he had that was looking a little scary. It was the small area that they tried to doctor up while he was in surgery with the big one last summer and it just didn't take. It finally started breaking down and I was hoping that there would be a way to treat it but the surgeon is saying that it is going to take a flap (much like the surgery he had during the summer) and that he will be back in the hospital for another 4-5 week stay. We asked if we could do it after Christmas and they were agreeable to that so I think we are looking at 4 hospital walls for the month of January BUT if you have to be in the hospital for an extended time, January would probably be my pick. Other than that, Doc and I both have had the flu bug but that is going around and I guess we all take our turns at getting it!

One of the reasons we are so excited about waiting until January for surgery is that our December is so full of fun things to do with all our family and friends. We have a never ending list of activities on the calendar and we both are looking forward to every last one of them! I have to admit though that the best one is having all the kids home at Christmas! I am really, really looking forward to that!

I hope all of you had a wonderful Thanksgiving and are also looking forward to Christmas. As we started off the Christmas season the first week in November at Branson with all the Christmas activities they had going on, we feel like we have an extended Christmas season! We are totally enjoying it though and are just glad to be home during it. We pray that each of you are having a wonderful, blessed Christmas season and that all the gifts that are the most precious and that cannot be bought are wrapped up for each of you. Many of them are the type that keep on giving and the more you share them, the more you have of them. It is like magic!

We continue to offer thanks for each of you that help us, pray for us, or support us in anyway. All of it makes such a difference and I hope you truly know how much we treasure each effort! There are many emotions that run through our heads each week and sometimes we catch ourselves hoping for tomorrow or yearning for the yesterdays but then I think that if we waste our time doing that, we are likely missing today! Sometimes "today" might not be the perfect day but it is the day that God gave us so it is ours to treasure or to toss. The choice is ours but I can tell you that no matter how bad the day might be, if we look close enough, there is ALWAYS something to treasure in it! At this time of year, all we have to do is look at our fireplace hearth and see the nativity set sitting on it to remember what is the most valuable part of every day for all of us!

Merry Christmas from Your Friends,

Cindy and Doc

Doc in the Cardinal
Store at Branson

December 2006

Can you believe that another year has gone by? Each one seems to go faster and faster! I hope all of you had a joyous and Blessed Christmas and Happy New Year! Our Christmas was joyous because our kids were all home and New Year's Eve was special as we celebrated it with some friends! Doc rarely makes it past 10 in the evening but he made it until around 11 and by the time we got him home and put him to bed, we got to see 2007 come in! I don't think he really cared though…whether he was awake for it or not! It is like birthdays, sunsets and sunrises….they will come and go whether we want them to or not!

We had a huge snow this month (not as much as our friends in Denver though!) and ordinarily, we would have been buried for awhile but so many persons thought of us and were there bright in early in the morning to clean walks, ramps, driveways, and even the county road all the way to the highway! We had several phone calls all concerned about us & offering to help and I was just amazed at how quickly we came to the minds of so many! We are thankful to all of those that helped us and/or thought of us!

Every month is full of ups and downs (for all of us, I am sure). This month was no exception! Doc still isn't sleeping very well, which consequently means that I am not either. I would guess that in the course of a single night we average getting up to take care of one thing or another at least 10 times each night. Sometimes, well over 20 times a night. If I weren't doing it, I wouldn't believe it because it is hard to understand how anyone could get up every 15-20 minutes night after night after night and yet still function. You do though. I don't know if it a survival instinct or the grace of God or both but as bad as it sounds, it doesn't ever feel so bad. Well, sometimes in the middle of night when I am struggling to exit a dream that I have just drifted into and I look at the clock and see that it has only been 15 minutes since my last wake up call, I am not very nice. Doc says that I am downright mean but it could be worse. I never cuss or hit him or anything really mean. I just let him know my frustrations by griping a little bit-(ok, maybe at times, a lot!). I know he can't control it though and he is as tired as I am but that isn't what comes to mind in the middle of the night! I am trying to train myself to have more patience with him and hopefully, I am teaching myself to be nicer! We had the nicest offer from someone that is familiar with Doc's situation volunteer to help me out through the nights occasionally and every night I think, "I will call her tomorrow" but then tomorrow comes and I think that maybe tonight will be a better night and I hate to bother someone to do what I know is so hard. I have had it on my reminder to call her for over a month and I keep moving it to remind me in a day. I know she is getting ready to go back to school so if I am going to take advantage of her offer, I will have to call her in the next day or two. Even one night would be a good break but to tell you the truth, Doc had a night over the weekend that he actually slept 3 hours in a row and that was nice! We finally found a doctor that had some ideas that helped a little. He prescribed a decongestant that seems to have decreased the secretions a little bit and he recommended that we don't inflate the cuff on Doc's trac anymore but leave it down instead so we can keep the higher tidal volumes on all night. That has helped in two ways. Instead of 3 times a hour, we are only getting up about once an hour and when Doc does need help, he can call out my name, wake me up and verbally tell me what he needs instead of just clicking which was getting harder to wake up to. The bad side effect to this is that Doc talks all night. I can never remember Doc talking in his sleep but he does now! I guess going so long without being able to talk, he is making up for lost time. It is funny to listen to him jabber all night. Most of the time I can understand what he is saying but it doesn't make any sense! He said he even wakes himself up when he talks too loud! Hehe!

One of our highs was to actually be home through the entire holiday season. It was the first time in a long time. I decorated, listened to Christmas music, baked cookies, watched Christmas movies and read Christmas stories until I had my fill of it! (almost) I think Doc had his fill much faster than I had my fill but as he is at the mercy of me, he had to endure my limit too! (and I have a VERY high limit! I love all those things!) To have our kids home during it was at the top of the things that were most precious to me. Actually, I didn't even get around to taking down the decorations until today and even then, Doc said that he really wasn't ready for me to do it. He said he wasn't tired of the snowmen yet. I have to agree but it is time to move into January and get the house back to normal. It always feels so good to have it all packed away again but I miss all the lights and glitter!

We would also have to put our many Christmas gatherings at the top of the highs. To attend Doc's AECI Christmas party and visit with so many of his friends was a nice highlight to our season. I sat back and listened to full grown men telling Doc how much they love him and I think 'would they tell him that if he wasn't in his chair?' Probably not but I know that they have always loved him. Sometimes we go through life and forget to tell people we love them. It just is something that isn't always comfortable to say. I had someone (someone we have never met) write us a letter this month to tell us how God changed his life through our testimony and even though the message in it was something that was out of this world, one of the best parts of the letter were the last three words…"I love you"…and I felt in my soul he meant them. So as we gathered with Doc's friends and they shared their love with both of us, we were so thankful to be able to be there! And while I am at this point, "We love you too!"

Then there was that annual party with our friends that we have done for more years than I want to count where we exchanged our many special hillbilly gifts. It was so fun and we enjoyed our evening of food, presents, and games until tears streamed down our cheeks! Doesn't it feel good to laugh? I mean really laugh? To have friends to laugh with has to be one of the greatest gifts of all! Speaking of gifts…Ladies…I don't think that any of you could have gotten some of the gifts that Doc thought of for me…did any of you get a Ford Truck Calendar? Did any of you get Charlie's Cheese Catfish bait? He did make up for these with some really nice ones though! Hehe! I got the most beautiful diamond earrings and he also gave me a couple of gift cards so we could go shopping and they were to places that I would actually try clothes on. He didn't go so far as to do a Hobby Lobby gift card but they say things happen in baby steps!

Then there was the family Christmas time. The time when those that are so dear to you all gather together to share those special memories and hugs! When you remember those that are missing and feel a little sorrow for that but at the same time, you are making new memories with those that are there! Sometimes it takes a long time to grow past the presents being the best part of Christmas because as a kid, that was the best part for me but now (even though they are still fun) other things have climbed to the top of the ladder!

A low was that the sore on Doc's bottom was worse and he actually started to battle a 2nd one. That concerned the surgeon. He said the condition of the sore told him that something was still putting pressure on it and it was a major problem. He said that until we fixed the problem, it would be senseless to do the surgery. So we spent some of the month going from appointment to appointment hoping to find someone that could help us find the culprit of the pressure points. They have made a couple of adjustments to the wheelchair seat and the positioning of the leg brackets and using their computer "map" process, it looked like great strides were made. We were wrong though and within a week, even though the 2 problem areas looked slightly better, we saw 4 other sores starting to form. I quickly undid all the changes because I didn't want to battle 4 new ones. I think we caught them in time and even though the red marks are still there, I think we saved the skin from breaking down completely. I have been teasing Doc that he has 'sissy' skin! Like the princess in the pea story! The two initial sores are getting worse by the day and they are fairly certain it is a problem with the wheelchair seat so now they are trying to get approval to make a molded seat for him that will keep him elevated off the bottom and actually keep all the pressure off the bottom and keep it dry. Once he gets approval, Doc will have to make a mold and then it takes 10 days to make it. After that, we will have to try it out and make sure it works. The downside to this seat is that he will have to be positioned in it perfectly or he will be fighting other sores! After all that is done, they will talk about the surgery. In the meantime, I try to dress them each day, keep them clean, and hope they don't get infected. Something I have not been fretting over too much though because it is sorta out of our hands anyway. I have learned to turn over most of our scariest things to the Lord because he can carry it so much easier than we can. Plus as Doc says, we take it one day at a time and whatever happens, it will work out! Our path is already laid out and we are simply following it!

Doc had one of his days brightened when some fellow friends that he worked with showed up for an entire afternoon of cards! I was able to work on some laundry and watch a chick flick movie so I enjoyed it too! I heard much laughing come from the kitchen and I think they were having a good time! I know Doc did! Doc even managed to win a couple of bucks so he has now offered to take me out for supper one night this week! As many of us do, I have gained more pounds than I wanted to over the holidays so I am eating smart for awhile so our date won't cost him too much! Hehe! Appetizers and desserts are only a dream for now!

As many of us do, when something comes to an end you look back over it and remember. So as this year ends, I think back over the hospital stays in February and the extended stay over the summer as the major bumps in our road. I remember a few friends that left this world and I miss them. I also remember all the great things that happened. I remember taking an extended weekend trip with some friends and having a great time. I remember getting brave enough to take Doc on our first 'real' vacation since the accident by myself and how much fun we had. I remember all the churches that we visited and the new friends we made. I remember all the things that our families have done for us! Our brothers/sisters/mom/cousins/ aunts and uncles! Thanks to each of you for making 2006 better by the things each of you did for us! But most of all, there are 3 things that stand out. The first is that even after 2 years, we still have so much assistance in everything we do. We have so many friends that continue to assist me in Doc's care, whatever I might need. We still have those that volunteer to come over every evening to make putting him to bed so much easier. We continue to get cards, notes, prayers and messages of encouragement that keep us going. Someone mowed our yard all summer. Someone helps me take the trash down every Monday. There are those that come faithfully to visit with Doc each week and pass the time of day with him. My mom and my daughter continue to help with Doc's care and that allows me to continue to work. When it snows, persons are there to help us get out of our drive. I am sure that I am leaving something or someone out but the message is that we have a whole flock of angels taking care of us and we just wanted to say thanks! 2nd, we remember all the mystical and magical things that have happened to others as God works through us and our situation to touch so many. We remember each and every church we visited and how special each visit was! Each time we hear of another story, we sit back in amazement at how we are being used. It is the most important thing that keeps us going. But what is the most amazing about the stories are the miracles of unexplained things that happen. I have a journal that I keep and when I read back over these events, it is almost unbelievable! Almost! I do believe! The 3rd thing that stands out is how many of those that were inspired through us, inspire us! I know I try to keep these updates upbeat because that is how we try to live our lifes but I would be lying if I didn't say that there are days that you wonder why anyone would have to live paralyzed from the neck down, letting a machine do your breathing. We know why though and we have a stack of cards and letters telling us why Doc is still here and why we are living our life the way we do. As we have said in the past, if we had a choice in whether Doc stayed in this chair or got out of it, he would be out in a split second BUT knowing what good has come out of Doc being in the chair makes us never wish it had never happened!

Well, I will close in hoping that all of you have a healthy new year and that we make it through January (my least favorite month of the year). It is usually just long and cold. We have an appointment to see the surgeon again on Wednesday of this week and unless there is a change in his viewpoint, we are probably pushing the surgery out until at least February. Doc said he just wants to get it done and be recovered before the Cardinals baseball and fishing seasons start! We do have a couple of plans though that will make January fun. We have a couple of outings that we are planning on taking with some friends. We have a visit to Macon High School to address the FBLA that we are really looking forward to. January is also special when someone has a birthday in it because birthdays are always special, no matter where they fall (and we have a several persons that are very dear to us that are celebrating birthdays this month)! So stay warm and safe until I send our next hello and we truly wish for 2007 to be full of more good memories than bad for each of you!

Your Friends, Doc and Cindy

January 2007

For someone that wrote that January was a cold, boring month I sure have a lot to say about it! I was so frustrated at the beginning of it and if screaming or pulling my hair out would have helped, I might have tried that! Even though we have been working with a seating and mobility place out of Columbia since November trying to figure out what was causing Doc's pressure sores and how to relieve them so we could get the necessary surgery done before any bone was exposed in the open wound area, nothing seemed to be moving! I called our insurance case worker because I thought that might be the hold up but they told me they have never gotten a request to make any improvements to Doc's chair. So I called the seating place back and was informed that they hadn't filed any paperwork yet because they had been busy and everything has to follow a procedure. I should just sit back and be patient. I know that I am not the most patient person around and especially when it comes to Doc's health but I think 5 or 6 weeks is a fair amount of time to identify a problem and have a solution in place if that is truly what you do for a living. So, I hung up the phone, frustrated that I didn't know where to turn to next. We had gone to Rusk Re-hab for a follow up on the issue and I asked them who they would recommend and low & behold, they recommended the place we were working with and the particular persons we were working with. All I can say is if that is the best Columbia has to offer, it wasn't good enough for us! So now what? Not knowing where to turn next, it was a welcome call when my phone rang 2 days later and it was a neighbor friend who had been to a seminar and a name popped up of someone that works out of Jefferson City that is well known for his ability of resolving skin issue problems and preventing future skin sores. She didn't know of my recent dilemma but she had just called in case I would ever need a resource in that area. Now sometimes I can be dense but I don't need a brick to fall from heaven and knock me in the head on this one! I call the number and he volunteers to drive from Jefferson City to meet with us and see what he can do to help the very next day! He shows up and immediately knows what the problem is, heads back to his office and within 3 days, he has everything researched and submitted to insurance and is already talking to them about when he can order it. On top of that, he is going to work with us every step of the way and be there when Doc starts using the new solutions to make sure they are working. It is a good feeling that someone is not just turning it over to me to judge if it is going to work or not. He is actually going to let me be the wife and he is going to be the expert....isn't that nice? I can only say that is a wonderful feeling after 2 years of trying to figure it all out on my own! As far as the wheelchair goes, they are changing the seat, the bottom part of the back cushion, the arm rests, the leg rests, head rest, puff and sip straw design, and creating tilt options for the legs and the back along with the entire body tilt that he currently does. Doc says they are "tricking out his wheelchair!"

We didn't take too many field trips this month and one or two of them that we did take, we maybe shouldn't have! The ice and snow was plentiful, not to mention the cold temperatures and cutting winds! However, we decided on a day or two to take a chance and go anyway! Doc was getting cabin fever and after awhile that can wear on a person. You need a little spice in your life to keep you bubbly! I figured what is the worse thing that can happen? Slide off in a ditch? Have a wreck? Have Doc stuck in the van on his side and not be able to get the van door open to get him out? Get stuck somewhere without the necessary equipment that I would need? All those things are thoughts BUT they were thoughts that were running through my head on the drive home…not before I left! Hehe! Before I left, I was only thinking Doc is bored and I can do this! So there was a time or two (like every time the vehicle in front of me slid off one side of the road or the other!) that I was pretty nervous but Porky and a little help from above kept us safe. I did have to refresh my memory at how to jump a vehicle because after Porky sat for almost 2 weeks without moving or starting, he wasn't much in the mood for it on the day that I decided to explore.

On one outing, we saw a great movie. Doc literally slid into the show on that one! The handicap part of the sidewalk going into our theater is on the downside of the building so all the ice piled up in that area and it looked like a huge ice rink. As Doc could not hop a sidewalk, we had no choice but to try to ride up the ice and the wheelchair needed some chains on the wheels. It was sliding all over the place and more gas Doc gave it, the more it veered around! He came close to smashing into the brick wall but I managed to pull him back from that and between a little push and shove, we managed to finally make it to the concrete part. It was after we finally made it up to the top that we gave thought that after the movie we would have to go down it! I secretly think Doc was enjoying it…he always did think sliding around on the roads was some special type of fun! I was never that keen about it to tell you the truth. I sorta like going in a straight line and staying on my side of the road! When we came out of the movie though, my sister and her husband were waiting to pick up my niece and they helped us to the van and then had to give me one more jump because we didn't live far enough away from the movie theater to give my battery a good charge. Then they followed us home and made sure we made it up our driveway. That was a good thing because I almost made it to the top when we starting sliding backwards. Before I knew it we were sliding down our east to west drive with the van going north and south and Doc was just sitting in his wheelchair behind me saying, "now you're done, now you're done"-No confidence at all! Mark and Pat helped straighten me out though and I backed up and got another run at it and this time, I made it to the top! So with their help, we were soon back in the house and talking about the movie!

Our second adventure that I probably should have more sense than to attempt was to go to Kansas City to explore a big antique mall that we like there and then to eat out at one of our favorite restaurants even though there were winter storm watches out for the weekend for the entire area. I discussed it with Doc and he was already wheeling toward the door before I had a chance to explain that things might get bad. We knew a watch was only that it could happen and a warning is when it actually is going to happen so if it is just a watch, go ahead and take a chance! That works until you are stuck in KC and the watch is upgraded to a warning right in the middle of your day! I don't think this storm knew how to tell time either because it wasn't supposed to hit the KC area until 6 p.m., when I would be on my way home. Instead it hit at 3 p.m. and by 4 p.m., the storm was raging. Needless to say, we didn't get to eat at our favorite restaurant which was disappointing. I will say that Doc and I had discussed it and decided that we were just going to stop anyway…BUT I did call home and got ahold of someone that told me not to stop and to come straight home. I listened to him and by the time I finally made it home 5 hours later, I was glad I listened this time! Lucky I didn't get ahold of my mom…I can be stubborn and I never did listen to her very well…sorry mom! So I owe Doc a fried chicken dinner now………I think Doc was trying to reassure me on the way home because he said that if something were to happen and if we did have a wreck and it ended up being our last day on earth, "he sure had a good time today." Like that made me feel any better! hehe!

We went to see the surgeon towards the end of the month thinking that now that we had a seating solution, they would want to schedule the surgery but we were wrong. Doc's wounds were actually looking better and they thought there was some natural healing going on so they want to let nature take its course and try to heal as much of it on its own that it can which would make the flaps that they have to do much smaller. The smaller, the better chance we have at it healing correctly and quickly! The surgeon was also concern because Doc did have some lung problems this month and has been on 2 antibiotics. He wants to make sure Doc is in peak health when he has the surgery because he said with there being 2 sores to work on, the surgery will be a lengthy one and Doc needs to have a good blood count and healthy lungs. So we are also working on getting Doc in tip top physical health at the same time as trying to improve his seating options. So, they made us an appointment to come back in 4 weeks and we can discuss it then. I think they are even looking a month or two past that and Doc & I are both afraid that we are going to end up in the hospital in the middle of fishing and cardinal baseball again!

Doc did have a poker party one Sunday afternoon and some unexpected events kept some of his male poker friends from showing up so three of us female joined in and I have to say that maybe the guys have something here. That was a lot of fun and if you think males can't figure out how the female mind works, you are right. They could never tell if it was a bluff or a good hand or if we were smart enough to tell the difference. I guess that is why the men don't usually invite the females to join in! Now their secret is out! I think Doc has plans to try it again though…he still has a case of beer…which I guess is a poker staple but we didn't partake! Hehe!

We did get to share our story at a couple of places this month and as always, God used it the way he wanted to. We just tell the story and watch him work! It is always good to remember that whatever we go through a daily basis is serving a purpose. This month, we are next scheduled to talk at St. Pius Church on the 1st Friday of lent (2/23). We continued to get all kinds of support, assistance, cards, letters and prayers this month and we thank each of you for all of it-it all means so much more than you can imagine! Valentine's Day is coming up soon and while I know it is mostly directed to the love between sweethearts, it is about all love too! So for those of you that have that sweetheart, remember to give them a big hug that day (I have discovered that is something you cannot buy and I now treasure a hug above most other things!) and for those of you that don't have that special sweetheart, you are still loved and Doc & I wish you a special "heart" day!

Your friends,
Doc and Cindy

PS: This month is ending on a sad note for us. Many of you know our dear friend Mark but for those that don't, I have asked in past e-mails for prayers for him as he battles cancer. This morning Mark made his final journey. I could write that he lost his battle to cancer but Doc tells me all the time that you can't lose to anything on this earth. In the end, all that are Christians are winners so no matter how hard the cancer battled, in the end, Mark was a great winner. It has left a huge hole in our hearts though and we will miss Mark terribly. He was there almost every single Thursday night to team with Doc and battle us gals in a game of cards before we put Doc to bed. He was even a trouper this past Thursday and showed up for our final game around our table even though you could tell he wasn't feeling very well. It is just like him to leave on a winning note without giving us gals a chance to redeem ourselves! (I guess you can tell who won!) I am glad that I was able to add a smiley face to this PS because that is the way Mark would have wanted it! As the days ahead will be a challenge for all of us, they will be especially for his wife, children, parents & family, so I would ask the favor of each of you to ask for special blessings upon them during this time. Thank you.

February 2007

As I ended my e-mail last month with our losing a dear friend, his funeral was the beginning of this month. I do have to say though that his funeral was one of the most uplifting and wonderful funerals I have attended. There were so many good memories and so many smiles at the many stories that will live on forever that there was a constant combination of tears and laughter. Doc and I both just said that if our friends have as many wonderful memories of us to share at our funeral, we would be happy! It really is true that the most important things in life are the memories you leave behind and the faith you die with.

Just a few days after Mark's funeral, we were once again bomb-strucked with more bad news. Another family that is close to our hearts was faced with a son, only 21 years old, having to battle cancer. They are very hopeful though that they have caught it early and there is a good chance of complete recovery! He is going to have a hard time in the next few weeks though as he goes through his chemo treatments so we will remember to pray for Michael and his family!

On the same day that we found out about Michael, another family close to ours lost their father/grandfather. There was a sense of peace when I attended his visitation though. As it should be! Then, just a few days after that, another friend made her journey to heaven after a battle with cancer also. So we remember Donna this month and pray for her family.

Valentine's day started out pretty rough. We got up and I could not get any medicine or water to go into Doc's feeding tube. I tried all the tricks that the many nurses have taught me over the years but nothing would work to unblock it. I finally decided to take him to the GI lab at the hospital and let someone professional deal with it. Then while I was loading him up in the van, the rearview mirror fell off the window. It was not turning out to be a very good Valentine's Day! ☐ In the end, we found out his feeding tube was bad and they replaced it with a new one and we met a couple of really sweet gals in the GI area and it is always nice to meet new friends. They told us that we should remember that we need to replace the feeding tube at least on a yearly basis. Doc said that would be easy because we could just remember that on Valentine's Day we do that! Can you imagine that? And here I thought I had finally put a little romance into him after all these years! I quickly told him that a person does NOT take their wife to the GI lab for Valentine's Day and that he could remember to do it on the 13th or 15th but NOT on the 14th! I think he got the picture! The day ended well though because as we were heading home, it was lunch time and I happened to see the frozen custard flavor of the day at Culvers was chocolate covered strawberries so I treated myself to a small one (I should have made it a large) of those and it made the whole morning better! Then when we got back home, I started working on some stuff for work and we had a friend show up to visit with Doc and in the end even volunteered to fix my rearview mirror so I didn't even have to try to figure that one out! Doc actually gave me a wonderful Valentine's present too because he actually slept from 3:15 to 6:30 and it was wonderful to have 3 hours in one stretch!

If you haven't caught on up to this point, we have spent a lot of this month in hospitals and funeral homes. Not places that you really want to spend your time but all of us will go through it because that is what life is all about. Being born, fighting times of illnesses & accidents, and dying. It is what is in between all those times that make up living! But in those times of need, it draws all your loved ones together and focuses them on what is really important in life! I think in the end, it increases the value of the living part!

We did have a great outing in between all of that and spent an entire Saturday just having fun! A couple of friends joined us for some Bass Pro time, dinner at Cracker Barrel, some mall time, supper at Macaroni Grill and finally a movie! Now Doc will say it was all fun except the mall but if he were honest, I think he did enjoy that part too. He and his buddy went off and did some tool buying at Sears, picked out a new CD to listen to in the van, and spent some time picking out the perfect Valentine Cards for their sweeties. What he probably will complain about is that we probably spent a little too much time in the mall and not enough in Bass Pro. As a matter of fact, we found the 2 men sitting in the middle of the mall, right in front of the store that we were going to try and slip into for one last stop! We thought maybe we would get stopped in our tracks but as we were making the turn into the doorway of the store, we glanced back to see if they saw us but Doc was sleeping and his buddy wasn't far from it! What enthusiasm they were displaying! Hehe! Anyway, we finished our round in that store and talked them into loading up in the van and then driving around to meet us at Sears because we hadn't had a chance to explore their sales either. That ended up being a good stop for us as we found a couple of bargains that we might have missed! Hehe! The guys were sure happy about that! The day was awesome though and if we were going to complain about anything, it would have to be the movie that we let the guys pick. We thought it was going to be a thriller but it ended up being a horrible bloody, fouled mouth movie that didn't even have a decent plot. The movie theaters should have a refund policy that would allow a person to leave a movie before it was half over and get half credit to go to a different one. This one was so horrible, I was ready to leave it after a few minutes and it never got any better. I spent most of the time with my head under a blanket so I didn't see all the shooting scenes. They were way too graphic! By the end of the movie, we were almost laughing just because it was so horrible that it was funny! I think we made a memory and we will always remember the night we went to see that movie!

On the Friday, the 23rd, we were invited to share our story at St. Pius Church at a lenton supper. As always, it feels good to share our adventure to date. As Doc usually reminds everyone, our adventure is not over though and we continue to add to it. Our next engagement to tell our story is coming up this Sunday. We are going to talk at the Madison Community Center at 6:30 in the evening on March 4th in Madison, MO.

Doc's wheelchair got tricked out but to tell you the truth, it didn't go so smoothly. About ½ the parts were missing when they came out so they had to rig up the chair to make do until the rest of it comes in and it made life much more difficult. I know part of it goes back to training old dogs new tricks but some of it I just do not like! The leg rests are neat because they go up and down but only the left one works right now. So when Doc uses that feature he is sticking out one leg and that looks sorta funny! Like a ski accident or something! Then there was a toggle switch on the back of the chair that allowed us to manually lean Doc's chair forward or backward which was really handy when getting him up or putting him to bed or loading him in the van. They removed the toggle switch and instead put in a flat module that has arrows on it to press but unless you are able to look directly at it, you don't know which arrows you are hitting because you can't feel them. AND there isn't a front and back arrow. Instead there is just a tilt arrow and when you hit it, you have to wait and see if it is going forward or backward and if you want it to go the other way, you have to remove your finger, wait a minute and press it again. That doesn't work so well when Doc's head is stuck in the doorway of the van and you need to tilt him back a little bit more and instead it takes him forward-Ouch! They also slowed it down so the whole thing goes so slow that it takes forever to tilt it anyway. On a cold, blustery day when you want to get that ramp up and get in the van quickly, you better know you cannot do that! Then they attached everything to the cover on the batteries which I remove when I need to work on the batteries and I also use it as a storage area when we are out and about. They quickly figured out I wanted my storage area back and I wanted all those boxes and wires to be put elsewhere. Somewhere out of my sight! The arm rests didn't make it in but the framing for them did but that was another problem because the 2 pockets that Doc stored his personal stuff could no longer hang from them. Then they removed my handles on the back of the chair and I have no way to pull or push the chair anymore. They are currently trying to figure out how to get all these things back onto the chair because to us, it is important. The seat does seem to be helping the bottom area though and that was a main objective. The headrest is still to come in and they are getting an additional control box which should make it easier for Doc to know if he is going forward or backward, tilt or recline, or moving his leg rests. Right now, it is sorta like Russian roulette, he puffs or sips and never knows for sure what he is going to get! They have promised to get it all right in the end and I just need to have patience and I am trying but some days are really hard when I am trying to get around in the outside world with something that isn't working just right.

Besides all of this traumatic stuff happening, I also had a flooded basement because ground water was coming in a hole that REA made to install our heat pump years ago. They were very nice about coming out and helping me rig something up to stop the gush and giving me an assignment list of things to do to try and address the problem (but that is going to have to wait until spring). It was coming in at 5 gallons every 3 minutes and that was not cool! Then a few days later, the basement was almost dry and I went downstairs to do laundry and it ended up that a tube behind the toilet upstairs had sprung a leak, was leaking through 2 floors and the floor was all wet again. This time, Brandon Bailey, one of our "adopted" children (so to speak), was there to save the day and he had it fixed in no time! The check engine light came on in the van so it had to go to the doctor where it was discovered to have 2 wires that had been chewed on. Either Doc's monkey was out of control or some mice had found a warm place to stay! At least it wasn't anything major! My daughter said, "darn those country mice!" but this time I think it was city mice because I didn't have any problems until I parked by a bunch of low cedar bushes by the Columbia mall. If it did happen there, Doc might be right that I did spend too much time in there! All I know for sure is that when I came out and started the van, the light came on!

Then Doc went through a nasty health spell this month and we had a few rocky days. Even after I hooked him up to oxygen, he wasn't improving. We had to get him on some antibiotics and run some tests for what type of infection it was this time. Just going to the hospital for x-rays and lab work was an adventure because we had to take Porky (with the engine light on) and the wheelchair that is possessed! Doc was struggling to stay awake and I had to keep waking him up because he would put the chair in gear and then take a nap while the chair was heading for something solid…like a doorframe, or a wall, or a person-oops! Then he passed out once because his blood pressure dropped and I couldn't get the stupid chair to go into tilt mode and lay him back so he could come to! That was about the time that I wanted to take a baseball bat to it and smash it! I finally did get him laid back and he became alert fairly quickly but it was a battle of wills between me and the orange machine! I don't cuss and I don't drink but I was close to both of them that day! I still am blaming the monkeys because now there are 3 of them hanging from his chair. He had his original "Charlie" and now he has one from Dana and one from his brother. They must all be male because my grandma used to tell me that one boy was a boy, two boys made ½ boy and 3 just made 1/3. I believe those monkeys work in the same way! Anyway, I am not sure if we have a handle on what is wrong yet or not but we are certainly working on it. I contacted our resources in Craig hospital and they had some thoughts for us to ponder on and I was so glad I thought to do that! They really are our extended family and I was sure glad to hear from someone who understood what was going on. I think one of our options is to make another trip back out there and let them fix Doc up but I am not sure if we have decided to do that or not. We are also talking about checking out a SCI unit in St. Louis to maybe find some good resources closer to home. I am torn because I know Craig can help us but it would be nice to have something closer and we won't ever find it if we don't seek it out and try it.

Our final adventure of the month was just a couple of days ago. We went to Columbia to get a pic line put in and some tests run so we could get Doc on to the correct antibiotics to fix his problems and some reason they admitted us to the hospital. Doc and I tried hard to make them understand that we wanted to do everything as an out-patient but as our dr wrote the order to be admitted, admitted we were. We were hoping to make it just a few hours but it rolled into an all-nighter. We ended up being in there for about 24 hours and were glad to make it back home, although the silver lining in it was that we got to see some dear friends that work in the MICU unit at Boone Hospital. We know we have to go back for surgery but we are not sure the exact date yet. If this round of drugs work, I think we are looking at before the end of the month but in the world of medicine, nothing is ever for certain!

In the meantime, for everything that went wrong, there was someone right beside me to offer an ear for me to vent or a hand to help fix something or a word or prayer of encouragement to hang in there! I can sit and write this and still smile, even over the bad stuff so I guess it is still all ok! I just have to remember that today will soon be a yesterday and even though I don't want to wish my life away, there are some days that I would just as soon skip! Even on the day that things were all going wrong and we were heading to the hospital because Doc was really out of it, I looked in my rearview mirror (now that it was fixed) and Doc was looking back at me with the biggest smile on his face! That's when I remember that his motto is to Always Remember to Laugh! If I could always keep that foremost in my mind, I would be ok!

I pray that each of you have a great St. Patricks day (don't forget to wear green!) and remember that the first day of spring is less than a month away! As always, we remember to say thanks for everything to all of you! I especially wanted to say thanks to a new friend, Melissa! She has volunteered to help out a couple of nights a week with Doc so I can sleep. She comes fully experienced and I am once again amazed at the angels that God puts in our lives! We tried it one night this week and even though I didn't go to sleep until midnight, I woke up at 5:15 completely refreshed! We realize that almost all of us could actually sit down and write a book so we appreciate all you remembering us even though you have your share of troubles too! Life is funny that way.....a HUGE list of problems and yet one little smile or one good day can make everything seem a little brighter!

Your Friends,
Cindy and Doc

March 2007

I must be getting older because here it is April Fool's Day and I haven't played single joke on anyone! I couldn't even come up with a good one for Doc. Maybe it has something to do with it falling on Palm Sunday! I know something is up because Doc hasn't pulled anything on me either! (at least not yet.... ☺)

We started out the first weekend in March by sharing our story with several persons in Madison, MO. They had a great turnout and the evening was full of blessings for everyone that came, including us! There was a great group of musicians that provided some inspirational music and everyone that attended seemed to be tapping their toes! It was great to be able to share our thanks for the prayers that have been directed towards us and to be able to share some of the experiences that we have had in the past 2 and ½ years! As far as we know, our next scheduled speaking engagement is for June 24th at First Baptist Church of Huntsville. We never know for sure where God is going to lead us next but at this time, it looks like that will be our next location and we are looking forward to it.

Just about the time that I was convinced it was going to take a miracle to find out why Doc wasn't sleeping and wasn't feeling well, we finally might have found an answer! They found some infection in his lungs and put him on some antibiotics but the infectious disease doctor really wasn't too concerned about it and didn't think it was our major problem. Instead, what seems to be the real culprit was fluid. Doc was building up more and more fluid in his system and with his body not moving much, all of it was sitting in the legs and feet all day. Then when we put him to bed and the fluid leveled out it was building up around his heart and the lungs were absorbing it, causing us to be suctioning all night long. They put him on some medication to limit the fluid buildup and it seems to have made a huge difference. He only has about 10% of the secretions that he was having and we are only getting up 3 or 4 times a night vs. 12-20 and that is MUCH better! Now his biggest problem is that he spasms during the night and that keeps him awake some but it is not bad enough to want to add yet another prescription to our every growing list. Even though the spasms are a hassle, it does create muscle tone and so far, it has been bearable for him.

Doc still is struggling with a good strong swallow but we are working hard at building those muscles again because he would really like to get off of tube feeding. He said even though he is getting a lot of calories through tube feeding, he feels hungry and likes to eat. We are watching the intake of food through the mouth though trying to make sure we are taking it to the stomach and not the lungs! If I suspicion things might not be just right, we limit our intake and go back to a few more exercises and try it again later. Eating is one thing that Doc just does not want to give up on!

It was a good thing that Doc was feeling better than he has for awhile because we have been on the go! Our local high school's girl's basketball team made it to the final 4 in state and that was exciting following them through their adventure. Lucky for us, sectionals were in Kirksville, MO and the finals in Columbia, MO and both were less than an hour from home. Not only did our Bearcats make it to the final 4 but a couple of other schools in our community made it also and we were able to cheer for them too! We followed LaPlata and Huntsville too and enjoyed all of it! Our congrats to the coaches and players that were all part of the fun!

Other than that, we saw a few movies, played some cards and even attended a 50th birthday party. I won't say who turned 50 but Doc says to tell Lori Hayden happy birthday again! ☺ I think Doc had 2 or 3 nights this month that bedtime was past midnight which is very late for him so that is a good indication of the fun he was having!

They finally came back and made some more changes to the wheelchair and it is on its way to being more user friendly. They still have about 6 things left on their list and maybe those will be in place soon. The best parts are that the cushion seems to have relieved the pressure and the batteries are back to giving us 12 hours of good battery power. We were down to less than 5 hours of battery power and that made our active life style a little harder to manage.

We are excited that the lenton season is almost over and the celebration of Easter is only a week away! I have always enjoyed lent and how it focuses you on what Easter is all about and how special it makes Easter seem! When you make some lenton sacrifices, it is like Easter Sunday is an oasis in the desert! Easter has always been my favorite holiday! I think as a Christian it is one of the most significant celebrations of the many we remember. To be honest though, I also love the pastel colors and the chocolate rabbits! AND especially the chocolate covered coconut eggs....yummmm....I hope that each of you remember all the joys that Easter really stands for and that is as special for you as it is for us!

The monkey has been up to his usual mischief....at least that is what Doc likes to blame it on! We took Shannon, our puppy, to the park to walk one night this week and he LOVED it! He was so well behaved too! I was impressed! Most of the time, he wasn't even trying to jerk my shoulder out of socket! It was good exercise for me too! Doc gets his wheelchair going at a fairly good speed and sometimes, it is a challenge to keep up with him and keep ahold of Shannon all at the same time! We were walking along with Shannon behind me and all of sudden dad said, "you lost him!". I turned around and the collar had come off of Shannon and he was running free and I was just pulling an empty leash. I bet that looked funny if anyone was driving by...Doc in his wheelchair and me walking in front of him pulling an empty leash! I was scared that Shannon wouldn't come to me when I called and that he would think it was a game of tag but he came right to me and I got the collar back on without any problems! ☺ We went shopping yesterday because Doc wanted to get some things from a western store. All of a sudden, I saw this huge red stain on his shirt sleeve and I get worried that his new arm rests are causing more skin sores. When I pull the sleeve up, it is really ugly! Doc doesn't come clean right at first but he finally came clean and said that maybe it happened when he accidently ran into a shelf earlier! I said that maybe that had something to do with it. Then I see that the arm rest is almost cut in two so I think he caught it and did a real number on it! I don't know what the shelf looks like but I am thinking it isn't the same as it was before Doc tore into it! All I know was that Doc had all 3 of his monkeys with him so I am not sure who we will blame this one on! Then we come home, later than usual, and the lift wasn't working. I couldn't figure out what the problem was and I decided that we would just use the manual lift but that didn't work either. It was the first time that I had used that at home and the bed frame was too low to the floor for the lift to slide under the bed. Luckily for us, we have a dear friend that was there (even if it was after midnight) to help me transfer Doc to bed without the use of a lift! Then he came back this morning so we could make it to church on Palm Sunday. (Thank you Brandon! ☺) Even after all of that though, yesterday was a GREAT day and we both had a really good time! Then after church, a friend that I work with came out and checked things out on the lift and it didn't take long and he had it working again so we are back in business. (Thanks Jim! ☺)

Besides the upcoming Easter weekend, we also have a couple of Cardinal games that we have tickets for and Doc is counting down the days until they get here! He is actually counting down the hours until the opening day game starts (it is on ESPN tonight for those that don't know!) We also have plans to do a lot of fishing this month if the weather gives us a few sunny days! April holds too many plans to fit in surgery so we have pushed it out until May. We are hoping to schedule it sometime during the week of May 7th because that seems to be the best time to block out 4 or 5 weeks of not being mobile. We haven't secured a definite date but they are supposed to be calling us with a scheduled time.

Our new friend Melissa has come out twice a week all month to give me some good nights sleep and after a week or two, I made the decision to move up into our old bedroom and sleep on my own bed. That was a special night and I will never, never forget how wonderful that night was! I had forgotten how comfortable our bed was and after 2 ½ years of sleeping on a twin bed and the sofa, it was really, really wonderful. The nights that I have been able to do it since are still wonderful and I will never take these types of moments for granted again but that first night I was able to do it will forever be etched on my mind! As comfortable as the bed was, it was also nice to revisit the room and remember the pictures and memories that surrounded me! Melissa gave me a gift that I can never truly give enough thanks for.

That being said, we have so much to be thankful for and so many to thank! Our daughter gave up one of her spring break days so I could have a girl's day out with a couple of girlfriends which was an awesome day. We had so many persons that sent cards or notes, came to visit with Doc to pass part of the day with him or to play cards with him, came to help with his care, plus the many, many that continue to remember us in their prayers…all of these are things that we say thank you for every single night when we say our prayers together! We truly feel blessed! As I close for this month, I just want to again wish each of you a very blessed Easter and a safe & happy month until I write again.

Your Friends,

Cindy and Doc

April 2007

If April showers bring May flowers, we ought to have a plethora of color next month because we have had our share of rain! Although I heard that our Colorado friends are still getting snow and I am not sure what that brings in May?

Doc anxiously awaited a day good enough to go fishing with the ground hard enough support his wheelchair being near the ponds! We finally got it this past weekend but I didn't have the batteries charged correctly so now I owe him another outing! I think he enjoyed just sitting by the pond and being outdoors but it might have been a little better if he could have fished. Although, I will have to say that the fish weren't very interested in jumping on any of our hooks! Our new fishing pole design that we are working on will make it much easier to keep the battery charged so hopefully, we soon won't have to worry about all those 6V batteries! We did get one evening that was nice enough to get out on the golf course and I think Doc really enjoyed that too. Part of the time I was golfing and part of the time I was holding my breath as Doc thought he was in an all-terrain vehicle and was going in all sort of places that had his chair leaning one way or another. We were joined by a couple of friends that saw that we were out there so I was glad that they were there just in case. Doc's chair stayed upright though and with the exception of a push or two, he managed the entire course on his own.

Easter weekend was a great weekend for us and our daughter and son-in-law were able to come home for a long weekend which made it super special. We played some cards and watched some movies and just had a good visit! Then we joined some of my family at my mom's and we played a game called Apples to Apples that our son and his wife gave Doc for Christmas. That is a really fun party game that always leaves you laughing!

Doc continued to improve all month with needing less suctioning but the spasms increased to the point that they were keeping him awake all night. The more I thought about it, the more I realized that the spasms didn't start until the suctioning decreased so that took me to the prescriptions that they put him on for the fluid that he was retaining. The pharmacist had warned me that one of the prescriptions was pretty potent but as the doctor prescribed it, I just sorta stored that in the back of my mind. When the spasms were at their worse though, I remembered the conversation and made the decision to take him off that and just see if that was causing it. That was about a week ago and every night since then it has gotten better although it is still an issue so I feel like we are going to have to discuss this with the doctor.

We only made it to one of our local highschool baseball games so far due to the unsettled weather and it was still a little cool and breezy! But we did have an absolute beautiful day for our first Cardinal game. We had gotten a letter that said they had oversold the wheelchair seating and had moved our tickets for our 5 game packet down to the first level so we had excellent seats…almost scary because it is very likely that we could see a foul ball and I have to pay more attention to the game and less to talking in order to make sure Doc doesn't try to catch a foul ball with his head! That is difficult for me! Now, he has 4 more games in the same area and is looking forward to every one of them. Our next game is the 1st Sunday in May so it is coming up quickly. The game we were at was the first home game that they won this year and I was joking that I hoped they didn't wait until we come back to win another one but it was looking like that for a long time!

We have been taking Shannon for walks in the park and that is entertaining. So far, he has kept his collar and leash on and I haven't lost him anymore! On our last walk, we met 3 very young girls that came up to ask us what happened to Doc and to meet him. They were 3 of most polite little girls that I can remember meeting and they had a bunch of questions for him. They asked him if he was going to get out of his chair. Doc told them he would like to but he didn't know for sure. The little gal named Melissa told him that she was going to pray to Jesus for it. It is amazing at the repeated displays of faith that we see in children. It was special blessing to meet those young girls!

I think the wheelchair modifications are getting close to being completed and so far, they seem to be helping some of our problem areas. We usually have to work through some initial problems or get used to changes but in the end, we are pretty satisfied. They have a couple of things left to do and with a little patience from us, I am sure they will get done. They seem to have the knowledge on what is needed but they are so busy that you have to wait for your turn.

Melissa was the name of the little girl that we met in the park that is praying to Jesus for Doc and also the name of the angel that was sent to me to allow me a couple of nights of sleep each week. It is hard to put into words when someone does something for you that is so profound that you can't describe it and that is where I am when I am trying to type this. Melissa's husband (a former co-worker of Doc's) is moving on to another employment opportunity which will allow them to be closer to Melissa's father, whom also requires care giving. I am happy that they have the opportunity to move on to a new adventure and it has been a privilege to be their friends. I can only say thanks for hours of care that they gave to us and wish them luck. I am sure we will stay in touch!

Mom stayed with Doc one day while I took a day of vacation and met my cousin, Tammy, in Columbia just to go to stores that Doc would just as soon skip! You know the ones! Hehe! Anyway, it was blast as it always is when we get together. She is as goofy as I am (oops…she may not have known that but she does now!) and time always flies when we are together! Actually, I have fun with all my cousins and most of them are goofy because it just runs in the family! I suspect that is one of the reasons that Doc asked me to marry him!

We still have our Wednesday night card games and Dana has recruited Doris Mutter to be Doc's card partner and I am not sure how that is going to work out. So far, they have made it hard for Dana and me to win! I think we get a victory in every now and then but if I am honest, I would have to admit they win more than us! Doris recently went to Hawaii for a vacation and came back with an arm full of cards as she bought Doc a deck of playing cards at every tourist attraction she visited! So far, Dana and I haven't won while playing with any of them!

May is a series of busy stuff. Our calendar looks crazy until the point that we put the brakes on with an upcoming surgery. For the first few days of the month, we are going to be in Indiana to visit with our son and his wife and attend his graduation of his Masters. We were in Colorado when he graduated with his Bachelors degree so it will be a great pleasure to attend this graduation. One the way home from that is the Cardinal game that I was wrote about earlier. Then the next week is our anniversary and I took a day of vacation for us to spend the day together and do something special. I am not sure exactly what we are doing yet but just spending it together will make it perfect. Finally, our final weekend of busyness might find us hooking up with our daughter to celebrate her birthday and then we are going to see one of our nieces graduate from high school. That is where we have to slow down because Doc is scheduled to be admitted to Boone Hospital on the 14th, with surgery scheduled for his two wounds on the 17th. Once again he will be confined to the sand bed, flat on his back for 3 weeks. They warned us that this surgery would be a little riskier because of the length of it and I asked

Doc if he was scared and he said, "What do I have to be scared of?" Obviously not as much as me, because I will be glad when he is back in his room and the surgery is over! After the three weeks, he will eventually move back into the sitting position in his wheelchair little bit by little bit until he is back up and going again. During that time, we have a daughter graduating with an Associates Degree and a niece graduating from 8th grade so I might have to eat a piece of cake for me and Doc both as we celebrate those special occasions! We also have 4 upcoming weddings that we might be missing because of the hospital stay but if there is a way for me to attend them, I will be there. All of them are very important persons to us! Hopefully, we will be up and going again on schedule because we have tickets to a Cardinal game on June 23rd and we are scheduled to share our story with the Huntsville Baptist Church on June 24th, which we both are both excited about.

As any of you that don't live on cement know, the grass is growing and once again we have had several volunteer to help us keep our yard in shape. A dear friend of ours, Keith, is also helping us get our riding mower in working condition so I can do a little of it myself. Doc and I have worked out a way that we can communicate while I am mowing! We wanted to say thanks to everyone that helps with the yard and especially to my sister for putting a rotation together. I also have someone that has volunteered to help me fix a wind turbine on top our roof (after I forgot that I even needed to fix it!) and I wanted to say thanks for that too! I also don't think I mention enough how precious our employers and co-workers are to us! Along with all of this, we continue to be so thankful for the prayers, words of encouragement, those that come to help me with Doc's care, and all the other support that we receive each month. All of these things make life so much easier for us and we will NEVER take it for granted! Have a great May and by the next time I update you, we will be ½ done with our hospital stay! Yippee!

Your Friends,
Cindy and Doc

May 2007

I hate spending holidays in the hospital! It is hardest to be separated from "real" life on the days that you know you would normally be really enjoying! So far, Doc has spent at least one of every holiday in the hospital except for Easter and Labor Day. This month fell into line just like I predicted although I didn't have to a physic to be right on this guess! The first part of the month flew by in a series of fun and activity and then we got to the scheduled hospital stay and most of the fun stopped-especially for Doc! They say life can't be all about having fun but I don't understand why not! I think that is a good plan! We aren't alone in ICU though because I have 2 two persons that I work with that have loved ones in here and a neighbor from the Cairo area also was admitted a few days ago but he is doing better and was moved into a different room this morning. While it feels good to run into persons that you know, you don't want to do it because they have loved ones in ICU!

We spent the first few days of May in Indiana with our son, Adam. That was a real treat for us! We got to see his new house, play some golf with him, get a tour of where he works, and watched him graduate with his master's degree. All of that was pretty special to us! I have to admit that while we were playing golf, I was wishing Doc could have been playing with us instead of just trying to help our games but as Doc often says, "maybe one of these days!". We ended up having a really nice sized room in the motel and Adam came over to help me put him down each night so it was a relatively easy travel trip. The worse part is always the extra planning that it takes to make sure I have everything loaded up that I will need because the days of the past vacations aren't the same. Doc used to laugh at my planning and would tell me that if I forgot something, he was sure there was a Wal Mart somewhere to get it but most of what I need to pack now, Wal Mart doesn't carry and so much of it is critical to have that it makes me a little nervous to make sure I don't forget anything! Plus I have to navigate my trip out to know exactly where I am going because Doc used to be the driver and I was the navigator but now I have to drive and I can't sit there and read the map at the same time! Well, at least I had better not be driving like that! We did get into a traffic jam on the way to Indiana as we crossed the state line because there was a nasty accident on I-70 that held us in one spot for almost 3 hours. I was glad that I had just stopped to go the bathroom and fill the van up at the exit before we got stuck! I was also glad that we had electric installed in the van so I could keep Doc plugged in while we were traveling. If we hadn't had that, we might have been looking at some serious battery problems by that time of day! If I can't look at a map and drive at the same time, I know I can't be bagging air into Doc and driving at the same time! As is the case most of the time though, things worked out and in a matter of time, we were back in motion and no worse for wear!

Then we made it home, I worked a couple of days and than squeezed in another vacation day to celebrate our anniversary! We had a road trip to a western store that Doc likes to visit in order for him to get me a pair of red cowboy boots. I had seen them there on a previous visit but couldn't justify buying them because I wasn't sure how practical red boots would be but when I asked Doc what he wanted to do on that day, he had it all planned out that we were going back there to get those boots. So now I even like them more than I did because of the thought he put into them plus, I have found they match more than I thought they would. Doc's gift from me was a replica of the Cardinals World Series trophy that I found in a charm and put on a chain for him. I think he has enjoyed that too! All in all, it was a wonderful anniversary and I had several responses from others that were celebrating anniversaries this month and I pray that all of them were just as special!

Speaking the Cardinals, I think the only good thing that we can say is that they won the game that we went to see them play! Doc still cheers them on though and never (and I mean never) misses a game! He gets frustrated with them but he still LOVES to watch them play! Now I know how Cub fans feel! Hehe! We have tickets for June 23rd so I hope we are out of the hospital and in traveling mode again because I know Doc would hate to miss that! He even bought a new pair of shorts for it because when we went this month his temperature shot up to over 105 degrees and it wasn't that hot! We have really good seats but the price you pay for sitting by the field is that you are in the sun! He said that I just needed to find some shorts for him and keep him wet because he was going to be there in June, July and August...one way or another!

So off we go to get shorts. Now that is a typical, funny, male story....take a guy shopping for clothes! We had gone to visit our daughter (Jaymi) and her husband (Joey) in St. Joe to celebrate her birthday the last weekend before we went into the hospital. After we ate lunch, she wanted to run by Old Navy and Doc thought that was a good idea because he could buy his shorts. I found a nice mesh pair that I thought would work fairly well but he had spotted this sweat pants style that looked like just cut-offs...no hem and sorta..hmmm...I think ugly is the word I am looking for. I asked him, "Are you sure?" He said, well we will let Jaymi choose. So he wheels around until he finds her and asks her which pair she likes the best. She says, "The mesh ones." He says, "Well, I think I will see which ones Joey likes best." So he finds Joey and asks him. Joey says, "The cut off ones." So that was that, we had to get the cut offs! Not only that, but here comes Joey to front of the store carrying a pair for himself. Then Doc shows Brandon (one of our dear friends that helps put Doc down at night) and he shows up on a visit to the hospital wearing a pair. After seeing Doc's he decided that he liked them too and he made a trip to Old Navy to get some. And so now I know that guys do NOT dress to please a woman...they dress simply for comfort!

We also squeezed in a couple of movies before the hospital doors closed on us. One of the outings included the Larry the Cable Guy movie that is out with our other daughter and her boyfriend so it was a good month for spending some bonding time with all our kids and that was really special!

The last thing we slipped in was graduation! We got to see our niece graduate from high school and go to her reception and that was cool. We usually miss the stuff like that so it was good to finally be able to share in some family celebration time! We wish her and all the graduates the best of luck! We missed the 8th grade graduation of our niece but we celebrated in our room one night when she came to visit us at the hospital!

Speaking of the graduates being special to us, I almost forgot to write that Doc was invited to be their guest speaker at Baccalaureate. That was really an honor for Doc! I asked him on the way to the church what he was going to say and he said, "I am not sure yet, it will come to me." I had to laugh because he was going to be talking to them in less than 20 minutes. But as usual, God supplied the perfect words and it was a treat to be at the receiving end of them! I think that was the highlight of my month....listening to Doc speak! Then he ended up being on the front page of our local newspaper and in color, no less! Hehe! It was even a good picture! Seriously though, his message was about what he considers to be the 3 most important things in life: Faith, Family, and Friends. Every word he said was so exactly right! There is nothing more important than these 3 things!

So then that is where the fun stopped for Doc. He was admitted into the hospital and I was reminded what it is like to sleep in the beautiful green chairs (although they aren't as bad as you would suspect). If you could keep them from folding up in the middle of a sleep, they are actually not bad at all. It is when they pop you straight up and you have to try and recline them back again while keeping your pillow and blanket all in tack at the same time. They aren't very easy to get in and out of when Doc needs something either but to be honest, Doc has been sleeping better. I think they have worn him out and with them coming in all night long to turn him and take care of him, he sleeps well when the room is quiet! The surgery looks like it was a big success. The wound areas are healing nicely and he has remained healthy! From today, (Monday), he has to remain flat in the sand bed for 10 more days and then he will be slowly moving back into the wheelchair. If his new wheelchair seat works like we hope it does, we will be heading home a week or so after that! They are also going to start some e-stem therapy on Doc's throat starting tomorrow. That is what was so successful in helping him eat the last time he was able to. They did an evaluation on him last week and said that everything looks good except that his swallow seems a little slow. They are optimistic that this new treatment will allow him to return to eating so we are praying that this works. They will give him a treatment each day that he has left in the hospital. In the meantime, the doctors & nurses have been great and have been providing Doc with top notch love and care!

They finally made some of the finishes touches to Doc's wheelchair but a few days before we went into the hospital, both of his elbows broke down so I know the new armrests are not positioned properly. Then the new headrest that they put on it is much better as far as allowing air around his head but it only has a small headband that holds his head in it and it is constantly sliding off his forehead and then his head falls forward. I cannot even count how many times that happened while we were on a trip to Indiana and how many times I had to pull over to adjust that. I have tried to adjust it and play with it until both of us have some not so very nice words to describe it. I called them and they said that if we call them on the day that we are dismissed to go home, they will follow us and make sure they get everything adjust correctly before they leave.

Our youngest daughter is out of school and has a couple days off work a week so she is relieving me so I can go into work a couple of days of week. I work the rest of the week off-site and it seems to be working out ok. I appreciate the help that she is giving us because without her it would be so much harder. She even spent a Friday night and most of a Saturday with Doc so I could play in my company's annual golf tournament. That was a real treat for me! I didn't contribute much to our threesome but we did have a blast!

My Friday evening at home did not go quite to plan though. I thought if I hurried home and got the chores done, I might have a couple of hours to eat supper with a chick flick...uninterrupted... which never happens! Again, plans changed. I thought I would start with the laundry but upon going down to the basement to start it, I found a snake stretched out right in front of our washing machine. I thought about it awhile and finally got the courage up to grab a cardboard box and throw it on top of it. Then I went upstairs and slowed my heartbeat down and thought that I could surely get up the courage to go back down there and somehow dispose of it but after a couple attempts of going up and down the steps, I figured out I was too chicken for that! I might as well break down and call someone for help, AGAIN! Seems like I do that almost every day for some reason or another...anyway, I called our neighbor, Tha, and he bravely came to my aid even though he doesn't really like them anymore than I do! He grabbed the tail of it and wrapped it around his arm until we got to the head and then keeping a firm grip on that, we take it outside. Before he flings it over the fence I tell him I want to look at the eyes because I thought a poisonous snake has slanted eyes. I observe that this one has round eyes and so I feel a little better. I told Tha what a was looking at and he just laughed at me. He said, "Cindy, I am squeezing this snakes head so hard right now, his eyes can't do anything else but bulge out into little round circles!" hehe! Anyway, he walked it over to the cow pasture and gave it fling so it will live to see another day...hopefully, never another one in my basement!

We have 4 upcoming weddings that we might miss because of our hospital stay. Weddings are so special to us! We have always known that marriage is for better or worse and I can only say that when it is at its' worse is when you actually need each other the most! I pray that each of these couples are blessed in a special love that will last forever! We will be there in spirit if we don't make it in body! I also have a couple days of vacation left at work that I need to use up before the middle of June and one of the nurses here that has become a good friend to us has offered her lake home to me. She asked me if I could take a couple of days of vacation while Doc is stuck in the hospital. She said that if the girls could get vacation and join me, we could use her house on the lake and have some mother/daughter time. She said that she would arrange for some of the crew here to remain in the room with Doc so his care would be covered and then we could have some time away. I asked the girls and they were able to get off work so I think we are going to do that a couple of days next week. I am looking forward to a little swimming and some mini-golf! She has also offered Doc and I the chance to use it after his hospital stay and she thinks it will work for Doc to get in and about the house & lake and maybe fit in a little fishing. This will give me the opportunity to make sure it would work for him but if it does, we will probably take her up on her offer and give Doc a treat too! (Thank you Marilyn!)

Probably the thing that we are both looking forward to the most though is the upcoming visit with the Huntsville Baptist Church on June 24th to share our story! The most amazing things have happened to us since the accident and it always seems so surreal to share parts of it because the only way to understand how many blessings have been rained down on us is to know that "all things are possible with God". It is in believing this and seeing how he works in our lifes that makes it easier to carry on! We had a new doctor that visited us while we were in the hospital and he said he read Doc's chart before coming into our room and he thought to himself that it was going to be a sad visit but then he came and met Doc and said that he didn't feel sad at all. He asked him what the keys were in staying in such a wonderful frame of mind and Doc told him it took faith, attitude, and a good support group and that he all 3!

We are so grateful for all the special prayers that were coming our way during the surgery. I know that there were many, many prayers being said for Doc during that time! I also know that so many of you pray for us every day and some of those that pray for us, we haven't even met! I can only say that we remember to say thanks for each of those unknown prayers every night! While we are stuck in this hospital limbo, it is also helpful to know that our yard is being kept up and that there is always someone just waiting to help in whatever it is that we need-even snake retrievers! Thanks for the visits to the hospitals, the cards and all the things that go into making each day a little brighter! It is also comforting to know that by the time I send out another update, we should be back home and into a routine again with so many of you ready to jump back into your roles of providing help to us each evening with the bedtime rituals or the weekly trash takeout or the visits and card games... and the list goes on.....thanks to each and every one of you! Our lifes' are so much richer because of these things! We hope that you are having a great summer experience and Doc said that he hopes someone is enjoying a brat for him! I think he is craving a brat...he has talked about eating one a couple of times this week!

Your Friends,
Cindy and Doc

June 2007

Have you ever watched a kid play with one of those cars that you put on the ground, pull it backwards to wind the wheels and then release it….to watch it speed across the floor? That is how Doc has been since they let him out of the hospital. The wheels on his chair hardly stop rolling except when he is sleeping! He told someone this month that "Craig Hospital taught us how to keep living, even if he never gets better, and that is exactly what we do". He is right! That IS what we do! We start each morning giving a prayer of thanks that we opened our eyes, that we have each other, and then we start planning what we are going to do before it is time to go to bed again! Always with enthusiasm and appreciation that we are able to do these things! Doc says he has a month to make up for and I can tell you that he is giving it a good shot!

While we were in the hospital, I got an overnight getaway! There has only been two nights since we have come home from Colorado that Doc & I have not been in the same place. One of them was last month when Carrissa (our daughter) spent the night with him in the hospital so I could play in our company golf tournament. The other one was this month when one of the nurses, Marilyn, who I might add, is a dear friend to us, offered to spend the night with Doc on her time so the girls and I could have some fun. She had a place on the Lake of the Ozarks that she let us use and it was right up there in my 10 best days ever list! The last time that I had time with both our daughters at the same time, they were still "girls" but this time, they were young women and we had a blast! As always, we fit in a bunch in a short time. It is fun when your kids grow up and you can be friends instead of always playing the "mom" role! We went swimming in the lake, soaked up some sun and had a picnic (that my daughters planned and surprised me with!). Then we went outlet mall shopping and enjoyed a good Mexican supper and even shared a pitcher of margaritas…even though I knew both of them were over 21 now, it was the first time that it really sunk in!. Then we played some miniature golf and headed back to the cabin for some cards and laughs. The next day we shopped a little more, had some lunch and was back at the hospital around 1 so the girls could visit their dad before heading home. Marilyn had wanted me to check out the house to see if I thought Doc could get into it and out onto the deck to fish because she wanted us to use it sometime if we could. I think he can so we are looking forward to spending a night or two there sometime! (Although the dock is just a flat, standard dock and Doc's monkey's will not be allowed out on the deck. I am sure that I will keep Doc far from the edges too because it makes me nervous just to envision him driving off the edge of it! I do know though, that I will not be able to keep him of the dock because while we were there, there were several fish that jumped out of the water as to say, "Here we are-try to catch us!")

It was also exciting because when we did get back to the hospital, they were already moving him out of his sand bed and into his regular air bed—ahead of schedule! That continued to be the trend and we were released on the 14th to head home! Doc's surgery was very successful and everything is healing well. It is the same as his last flap surgery though and they have warned us to follow the rules and make sure we take good care of it because it will actually takes months to heal it completely. Everything is good so far though and the new wheelchair seat seems to be working very well. Doc is also swallowing much, much better. He is eating with no trace of aspiration to the lungs and we are very excited about that! He is truly enjoying the food! He is up to enough calories for me to reduce his tube feeding by one can and hopefully, another one soon! He is also sleeping better and is only waking up about once or twice a night instead of the old once or twice an hour! I am truly enjoying that!

Speaking of the wheelchair, we are taking slow steps at finally getting it to where it needs to be. It has been a long "trick my wheelchair" experience though. I think they "trick those trucks" faster than they are doing this wheelchair! They have finally made some head rest improvements and the strap is holding Doc's head more securely, which is a blessing! When I brought him home from the hospital, I had to stop 3 times in our 40 minute drive just to put his head back in place! They have one more part to switch out on that but then I think they will have everything completed!

Now let's see…what have we been up to….the first Saturday we were home, we went to a wedding reception and had a great time. Doc danced a couple of dances with his new butt, as he calls it, and broke it in! They also had shot glasses that they were giving away as a memento and Doc had someone go fill his up at the keg. Then he drank it and told everyone that he had his first full glass of beer since his accident. They just don't know it was a tiny shot glass. That was probably more than he should have had anyway as he is on some medication that doesn't mix well with alcohol but it wasn't much and he was tickled to have a swallow. He came away no worse for wear so I guess no harm done and it will probably be another year or two before he tries it again!

Then on Sunday we went fishing! Again, I thought I had the batteries all charged up but they ended up corroding on us so Doc had to watch a bobber and wait for another day to go fishing with his pole. We (when I say we, I mean a friend (Tim)-I only bought the battery) changed the design on it this week to use a 12V battery though instead of the 24V so that will make it easier to keep in working condition. We can just use a common battery that you can buy about anywhere and keep it charged with a simple charger that even I can operate! So the plan was to go out today and give it another shot! (Or cast as the case may be!). We haven't decided for sure yet, but the rains that we have had in the past 3 days might have soaked the pastures a little too much for us to make it out. We might have to wait until next weekend or one night this week!

Then after that, we spent the rest of the week either going to a movie, to the park to watch nieces/nephews play ball, or playing cards with friends. There was no such thing as idle time. At least for me! Doc has idle time all day while I am at work and he spends it planning on what to do when I get home! I told him it would help if he would do some of my laundry and housework for me while I am at work and he always smiles and says that he thinks about it but never gets around to it! Hehe! (I know he would if he could!)

We made it to a Cardinal game on the 23rd and our record is still in tack. Every game that we have gone to, they have won! Now we are going to test them on July 8th because that is the next game we are going to attend! While we were there this month, we won 3 more tickets so I am sure that will mean another trip to St. Louis. I think Doc even has a game picked out already! It was also Christian Day at the ballpark and they had a Christian concert after the game and several of the players introduced their families and talked about their faith and what role it plays in their lives. It is always special to hear those types of messages!

On the 24th we shared our story with the Huntsville Baptist Church and it was such a wonderful evening of good food and fellowship. As always, we made new friends and visited with old friends!

Doc's monkey got into a little trouble and I haven't quite figured out what happened but I hope it doesn't happen again. I noticed that our lift on the van was acting up a little bit but it got scary last Sunday morning when I was letting Doc out of the van for church. Even though his clutches are up, his wheelchair still seems to slide/ roll occasionally on inclines. The ramp inclines a little bit but there is a plate in the front of the ramp that catches the chair and doesn't release until it hits the ground. On this particular day though, I think one of the monkey's must have jumped from the front of Doc's chair and released something because the plate dropped down and Doc's chair slid off a good 8-10" from the ground so he did a nose dive and about scared me to death. I tried to hold on to the chair and keep it on the ramp but there is no way that I was strong enough to do it! Anyway, Doc took a good bounce but just put it in gear and took off like that is always how I dump him out of the van! Nothing ever seems to shake him up. He did look at it with me when we got home and he noticed the release plate was a little rusted and sticking so he had me put some WD-40 on it and run it up and down a few times. Since then, it is working better and the problem seems to be fixed! I hope so!

This past week, we have hit the golf course for some green time and caught 2 more movies. We have fit in our weekly Wednesday night card game (and I might add that Doc is really struggling because he would make sure you knew it was me if it was…but it isn't…hehe!).

July is shaping up to be an equally busy month! I don't think we have any special 4th of July plans but we have been tossing several ideas of things we could do! I think we have almost planned out a day adventure! There is also a friend that we have that I work with and we have ordered a Disney movie that dates back to the early 70's that we have been looking for and finally found on the internet and he ordered it so now we are having 'stupid movie night' at our house with a bar-b-q! I haven't seen it but he has and although he assures me that it is entertaining and a "have to see" movie, it is stupid humor! It is titled Scandalous John if any of you are wondering and if I remember, next month, we will give you a movie review. Our son thinks Doc should do that for a living as he attends so many of them now! I am sure it will include the upcoming Cardinal game, much more fishing and sometime in the near future, probably a visit to the Lake of the Ozarks to check out Marilyn's house on the lake! We are also going to check out a campground that one of Doc's nurses owns a spot at to see if it might be something that would interest us. On top of that, I think Doc's working buddies are planning another card party at our house too! Doc ALWAYS has fun at those!

Speaking of Doc's work, we don't want to neglect saying thanks to his AECI co-workers for giving us a lawn mower this month. We had one but after much sweat and even a little blood, a dear friend that had taken it upon himself to fix it, had to give up (thanks Keith!). When AECI heard that we needed one, they all pitched in and delivered us a nice new lawn mower! As always, it left us speechless because there isn't a whole lot you can say to acts of kindness like that except thanks but you do hold it close to your heart and in your memory. It is something that you never let go of except to somehow pass that generosity on in some way! Even though we have so many persons that help us keep our yard in nice condition, it is nice to be able to offer the use of our mower to them without them having to haul their own over and it gives us the opportunity to help some too.

We may not be able to do the whole yard but Doc and I have worked out a system that I can do the smaller front and back yards while he sits on the porch and jiggles his chair with each lap that I make so I know all is well. If he doesn't jiggle his chair, I know to stop and see what he needs. I think we both feel a little better helping out our cause a little on our own.

Besides that, we continue to be blessed by so many special friends in all the things you do....whether it is in assistance to something we need or a prayer said in our behalf! We wanted to say a special thanks to the Boone Hospital doctors and nurses that are so much more than that to us! Thanks to all of you for always being there and being so special to us! Have a safe and wonderful 4th of July!

Your Friends,
Cindy and Doc

July 2007

Summer has always been my favorite time of year because we have always made it time of family vacations and activities. July was a month of go, go, go…at least until this week! Starting tomorrow, Doc is going to be confined to bed for a few days to see if I can get a handle on some new sores that popped up yesterday and one that has been growing for about 2 weeks. Unfortunately, I found 5 staples and 3 stitches that were missed after his surgery and when I pulled them out, a sore resulted that has consistently grown over the past 2 weeks. So yesterday, I thought I would add a little more air in the cushion to see if that would help and evidently, it was the wrong decision because last night when we put Doc down to bed, he had 2 additional spots that had broken down and the initial spot was worse….I let the air out of the cushion and I will see what happened to these areas today but the past history of me and healing sores is almost as bad as the Cardinals record this year…for sure less than 500! Doc had the idea of a week in bed and see what happens so we will give it a shot. As with all sores, it will take a long time and a lot of luck to heal. We have so many things that we are looking forward to in the next 2 months that we are hopeful that this downtime will work!

Back to this month first though….We started out celebrating the 4th of July (actually on the 3rd though!) with a bar-b-q and fireworks. It was a great time with family! I remember as a kid getting together with family on a regular basis but it seems like everyone (including us) is involved in so many things that it is really difficult to find a time that we can all gather together and catch up! We finally found a day though and at the end of it, we wondered why we don't do it more often! On the actual 4th we invited my mom out for a day of fun and to take advantage of a buffet coupon that I had. Doc said he might not have eaten much at the buffet but just getting to eat anything off of it was worth every penny!

Then, as I wrote in the last update, rain put us off of fishing the last part of June so we planned to try out a friend's pond the day after the 4th. However, some places in our area got over 3" of rain on the 4th! Nothing would put Doc off this time though so off we go in Porky for some fishing! The ponds were overflowing with water but we managed to brave our way into the pasture and get close enough for Doc to cast his line into the water. Probably because they had all the food they wanted, the fish weren't much interested in what we were throwing at them! Doc's pole was working great though and that was the most important thing. He was sitting there fishing and listening to the Cardinals on the radio and telling me that life doesn't get any better than that! We stayed almost until dark and then I ran into a little problem. Luckily (I think) our friend had gotten done with his chores and had come to throw his line in with us for awhile so when I got ready to leave, he was helping me back up and my tire gave a slight spin and I think he thought I was being a little tentative so he asked if could drive the van out of the pasture....needless to say, I sorta liked that idea! So he gets in and gives it all its worth and all it does is dig down deep! So he gets out and tells me I already had it stuck…mmmm…the things that make me go mmmmm…I am pretty sure I was the sucker on that one…BUT as he was the one that was going to get me out of my mess, I wasn't in a position to argue! So he gets out and hooks a chain up to Porky and his truck. Between him pulling me and Doc sitting behind me, telling me how to drive when a chain is pulling me with only 3' between me and the bumper of the thing in front of me, we manage to get out of the hole and back onto the road! Porky was a mess! He had mud everywhere but then someone said it serves us right…naming our van after a pig! OR maybe we can blame this on Doc's monkey as there has been relatively a small amount to blame on him this month! (do you notice that I always refer to Doc's monkey as a he? I wonder why?)

The next Saturday we head to another friend's house for some cards, supper, and more fishing. This time the catfish were in the mood to bite so while the guys fished, the gals took a walk and it felt really good to finally get some exercise in! It also felt good to have someone else loading that stinky catfish bait on Doc's pole. Somehow that stuff seems to stick to everything! When I first met Doc, his dad had this old, ugly, blue van that was their fishing mobile and it always had a smell about it. Now I know what that smell was…catfish bait! So even though Doc fished to almost after dark this night, and by the time we got home Porky & Doc both stunk like stinky bait, it was another great day!

Then we went to our Cardinal game this month and our record stayed in tact! 4 games, 4 wins! Doc is excited about that! They might not be playing well on the whole but they have played well every time we have gone to watch them! On top of that, Doc managed to eat almost an entire bratwurst at the game. He has really wanted a brat for a long, long time and now he had one. He would chew a little bit and then say, "ooh, this is good!" I am not sure that he won't order the same thing the next time we are at a game and that is going to be soon as we have tickets for the 12th! Our daughter and her husband are going to join us at that game.

On our way to the Cardinal game, we had some excitement. As usual, I cannot get all the way from home to the stadium without having to stop at one of the rest areas for a break. I hurried in and out and was just pulling out of the parking lot when I heard Doc say, "that stupid car!"....that was a mega second before I heard crunch! Somehow, this car pulled out of her parking spot and drove right into the side of the van as we were driving toward the highway. I was scared at first because it was the side of the van that has the doors that open up and let the lift down. My first thought was what if Doc is trapped, or even worse, what if he misses the Cardinal game ? But it ended up that most of the damage was to the running board and it had buckled into the front tire. With a little pulling and prodding though, I managed to get it bent back into a more normal shape and it pulled back from the tire. There was a nice gentleman that stopped and had me turn the tires and he made sure I had clearance!

She gave me her insurance information but I figured a little wave in the running board wasn't going to hurt anything....after all I put Porky through, he isn't exactly worried about his looks anyway! She told me she was heading to North Carolina to meet her husband so I am hoping it was true love and she just was in a hurry to get to him! Plus, it was something that I could have done myself! As they say, all's well that ends well!

We spent one Saturday with a good friend and took a field trip to St. Louis. We traded Doc some hours in the mall trying on clothes for some time at Cabela's! (more than fair) I think we might have held out for a little more but I didn't push it and to tell you the truth, Dana and I actually found some neat stuff to look at in Cabela's! On top of all of this excitement, we also got to eat at Texas Roadhouse, one of Doc's favorite places to eat but we hadn't tried it since the accident so that was a real treat! There were several things that we fit into the day and we didn't arrive home until around 2 a.m. but it didn't seem late...it was a special day!

We finally fit in some trout fishing too! One Saturday a couple of our friends joined us and we made a trip to Bennett Spring to try Doc's pole out on some trout. Unfortunately, Doc couldn't entice them to jump onto his line but I am sure we will be trying it again. I already have some ideas that might help. I was able to catch my limit and we grilled them tonight and they were quite tasty! The heat got Doc's temperature up so he ended up spending some of our fishing time sitting in the shade trying to regroup while I cleaned my fish. (Doc made me learn how to do this just 2 weeks before his accident so I was prepared for this. I do not know how to filet bass or skin catfish but I do know how to clean a trout!) We combined our outing with a picnic and then a nice meal on the way home and it was an enjoyable day!

On top of the sores that are popping up on Doc's bottom, there is still a couple on his elbows and one on his foot. They have finally come out and adjusted the arms on the wheelchair though so maybe we can fix those. The problem is that the one on the right elbow has already tunneled and that one is a little scary to me. The color and size of it worries me some. Just this morning, I was really stressed about all of these issues and I found out that Doc still has a shoulder to cry on...literally! With Doc's help though and the fact that it was Sunday and somehow it is always easy to leave your crosses at the door of the church, not to mention the love and caring that you find in the inside, I regrouped and remembered that stressing wasn't going to help the sores and we have only made it through this whole ordeal by taking things one day at a time so I went back to that philosophy. Now I am back to doing what I need to do the best that I can and leave the rest up to a higher power!

Speaking of a higher power, one of the movies that Doc and I went to see this month had a couple of lines in it that has stuck with us and has given us reason for serious thought. The lines were, "When you pray for patience, does God give you patience or provide the opportunity to be patient? When you pray for strength, does

God provide you strength or the opportunity to be strong?" I think this stuck with us because we do pray for these things nightly and we are given every opportunity each day!

August is going to be a fun month. We have 2 Cardinal games planned and we are tentatively planning a trip to Branson sometime this month if it works out. I am hoping to take vacation time to fish, relax, shop, and catch a few shows. The last time we visited Branson, it was the Christmas show season so we will get to see a whole new variety! We are finding many things that we want to do and it takes a lot of effort on our behalf to sit around and do that "relaxing" stuff! We have never been very good at it! We are even thinking about wheeling around a golf course if we can find one that allows us to that. So between packing Porky with all Doc's equipment, I have to find room for the fishing gear and the golf clubs (And leave room for the shopping treasures!!:)

We are still waiting on a couple of wheelchair adjustments and parts and they assure me they are ordered and are checking on them. For some reason, though, they just aren't coming in! Anything involved in the medical field takes one thing....patience!

This week has been a wild week with one of my brothers having some tests ran that we are waiting on results for and he has been in our prayers, my mom had a spell and had to be taken to the ER but seems to be recovering with some of those "good drugs" (as Doc calls them!), my uncle had a heart attack, my sister-in-law's father had open heart surgery, and a couple of our other dear friends are struggling with health issues. I expected that when we got older we would see more of these things happening around us but I really didn't think there would be this much of it before we even hit 50! Some nights it is hard to stay awake long enough to list them all by name in prayer but we give it a shot every night!

Our next challenge is going to be finding someone that wants to make a little extra money by spending a day or two a week with Doc and feeding him lunch and operating the television. Our daughter has been doing that for past couple of years but she has finished her Associates Degree and has been accepted into a nursing program so she is pursuing her dream of becoming a nurse. I am very happy for her but we are certainly going to miss her help! She took good care of her dad while I was at work! My mom will continue to help us out too but I don't want her to have to do it every day so I am sure situation will resolve itself in good time. Everything has continued to fall in place and I am sure it will continue to! Every saga ALWAYS has an ending! It may be different than we expect or different than we want, but it always ends!

Overall, if we could just throw out the wound issues, Doc is feeling and doing great! He is eating better and better, sleeping better than he has in a long time, and pretty much just planning on where he can go or what he can do next! His stats and temperature are better than I have seen in a long time too! There is a lot to be thankful for! So most of this month has been full of fun and good memories and it has been nice to be able to say many more prayers of thanks than of needs. Prayer still is the foundation of our every day! Much of our fun could never be available to us if it weren't for all the wonderful things our family and friends do for us! So with every smile and memory we make, we remember each of you and all you do to make our "foundation" so strong! We know that all of us have many things to face each day and know that each of you are in our prayers and we ask to stay in yours! Stay safe and make a few good memories of your own until we write again!

Your Friends, Cindy and Doc

August 2007

We had a month opposite of last month. Last month we started out on the go, go, go and then ended up in bed trying to heal some wounds on the bottom. This month, we were still trying to baby those wounds into healing the first part of the month but then Doc said enough was enough! He was tired of lying there when he physically felt so well! When you don't have many days that you feel really good, it is hard to give them up to lie in bed waiting on a sore to heal. Doc put himself into bed rest and I told him he was able to take himself out of it. I had several helpful hints on what has worked for others on pressure sores and I tried them all! Unfortunately, none of them worked completely and even after 2 full weeks of being in bed, the wounds were still there. Slightly better, but still there. Doc finally came to the conclusion that he could lay there for 2 or 3 months and they might still be there and by that time, he might be dealing with other issues so he decided he wanted to get up and go again and take his chances on them getting worse. So we did! It is hard to tell another person how to live so I leave those kinds of decisions to him! No matter what the future holds for him, his philosophy is that the quality of life is more important than the quantity. And I have to add that I have never met anyone that can add more quality to life than Doc!

Before we made the decision to just keep going with the sores, we did make an appointment with yet another wound clinic to see if they could give us another opinion. Unfortunately, their opinion was the same as the rest. No one seems to have any answers except that we are doing all the right things and this is just a high risk that is associated with Doc's condition. To fix one thing, you have to risk the chance of something else popping up. After all the options were laid out on the table, Doc proceeded to choose the one that he had initially established for himself. Put the prescribed medication on the wounds, try to stay off of them when there isn't anything planned but get up and go if we have something on the calendar. We continue to pray for the wounds to heal and we are aware that prayer is probably the only thing that is going to heal them. The only medical solution that we were given that was the best shot at healing them was for Doc to lay on his stomach for 3 or 4 months and even then, they weren't sure it would work. I cannot imagine how horrifying that would be! Just putting Doc in bed that long would be bad enough for him but to add the face down part would be impossible! The wound doctors told us that some people can live for a long time just taking care of open wounds that never heal. So we do what we can and pray that if they do worsen, that they at least wait until the middle of October before they need immediate attention because until then, we don't have any down time to take care of wounds! We have a lot planned for the upcoming weeks and we don't want to give up any of it! Especially if he continues to feel as healthy has he does right now!

He stayed put in bed until my mom celebrated her birthday and then he decided it was time to get up and go out to eat! During all of this, Doc's swallow muscles continue to improve and he eats 2 fairly normal meals a day. He still isn't able to consume all his calories by mouth but more and more of them each month! That is a step in the right direction. One that he is thoroughly enjoying! So needless to say, my mom's special day was just the opportunity he needed to get up and out and eat! Once he was back in the chair, he tried to stay there. He wanted to catch up with the recently released movies that he had been seeing advertised on television and he wanted to hit some restaurants for some specials that he had seen advertised on television. All in all, the advertising market paid off for some because Doc succumbed to many of them!

The heat kept us from the fishing world for most of the month! Our August reminds me a lot of our July from last year. We just moved from one hot day to another with very little rain!

The heat also kept us away from an annual fish fry that we usually enjoy attending at one of the churches that we shared our story with. We missed visiting with many of our friends from there and catching up...not to mention their wonderful fish! But there is always next summer and the hope of a little cooler weather! Maybe we can "catch" it next year!

The heat did not keep us from the Cardinal games though! I think there is very little that could keep Doc from a game that he has tickets for! He told me to pack lots of ice in the cooler and several towels. I was supposed to wet him down and keep him that way! So that is what we did....I was thankful that our daughter, Jaymi, and husband, Joey, were with us this time though because I wouldn't want to fight the dangers that heat can bring on by myself! Plus it was just nice to spend some time with them! We went again on August 22nd and this time we took my mom. It was still hot but at least this game was in the evening and it was a little better than high-noon! Our record is now 6 games and 6 wins! We have 2 more to go (unless we would happen to make it the playoffs and then you never know...we might squeeze another game in!)

Our highlight of the month though had to be our vacation! We spent a few days in Branson and were hopeful to visit a couple of the churches in the area that we had already visited but the way our time was scheduled, it didn't work out. Doc's brother had shared some of his timeshare with us and we had a nice condo to stay at that was close to a lake so we did some fishing and found a handicap trail that wound around Table Rock Lake that was awesome. We added a few shows, a lot of wonderful food and a little shopping to round it off to a great vacation! We also added an AAA minor league baseball game which is part of the St. Louis Cardinals program. We were able to meet with our nephew that is going to school in Springfield and spend the evening with him. They won that game also so Doc is claiming his new "Cardinal" record is now 7-0! I am actually sending this update out from Branson! We are heading out though before the weekend gets here which is why we were unable to make Sunday plans! Next we head to St. Louis to spend some time there with family. We are spending Saturday at the zoo with my cousin.

If we get out of there without them keeping us, we are spending Sunday afternoon at a family reunion with Doc's family. After that, we head home to start the unloading of the van after vacation… yuck…but it has to be done so we can go again! We still have plenty to look forward to though so it isn't like we are heading home with nothing on the calendar!

The monkey has caused me a few gray hairs this month and most of it while on vacation! First, we somehow got a hole in Doc's air cushion that he sits on and that was pretty major. It was big enough for me to stick my little finger in so we weren't talking about a pinhole or anything. I finally figured out how to patch it and luckily the patch held until we were able to make it to our resource in Jefferson City and they gave me a back up cushion to use, just in case, while we were on vacation. Then we get here and we are trying to squeeze in as much as we can so we have to end up using Doc's backup battery most every day and it just sits on the back of the wheelchair as we are rolling around. As "flat" isn't in the Branson vocabulary and everywhere you go seems to be uphill, the battery started sliding off the back of the chair and hitting pavement. Although I tried several things to get it to stay put, nothing worked and before I could figure out a good solution, it fell off one too many times and the case broke open and pulled the wiring out of the plastic covering on the fuses. It split the plastic covering so I wasn't able to put it back together. I spent a half a day trying to find someone in Branson or Springfield that had a battery box but I might as well have been on Mars! No one seemed to understand what I needed and no one had any experience with ventilators or quads and just the thought of that scared them to death....I kept trying to explain that I had a battery problem and not a ventilator problem but the brick wall was already built and they couldn't hear around it! So, I finally tried 2 other things and they both worked. I called Jefferson City and they knew exactly what I needed and agreed to try and locate one and overnight it. I also thought to try the O Reilly's store down the road and see if they could help me re-wire it. The manager there was very helpful and in about ½ hour, he had me rewired and ready to go again. Of course the battery box was being held together with Duct Tape but we are in hillbilly country and no one seems to notice anything out of the ordinary! Other than that, I want to mention that although I have totally enjoyed having time together on vacation, it has been a huge chore to get Doc up and put him to bed every morning and night on my own! I appreciate more than ever all the help that I ordinarily have at home! No one is more appreciative of my efforts than Doc though and I know he and I both think it is worth it to have this time alone! He is also very, very patient with me because it doesn't always go smoothly! And I am not going to share any of those stories because I heard that what happens in Branson, stays in Branson!

We are committed to share our story in September in Atlanta, MO at the Methodist Church. The time is 11 a.m. on 9th and we are excited about it. They asked us a couple of months ago and we finally got it scheduled and we are looking forward to it.

Even though sharing our story is probably the highlight of our upcoming month, September holds several scheduled pleasures for us! We have tickets to 2 more Cardinal games, my company's fall festival to see Sara Evans perform, some more trout fishing, and an upcoming visit from our son that we haven't gotten to visit with since May! Seeing your kids is always a good thing! We have a ton of birthdays to celebrate, including Doc's, mine, Doc's brother, our son, and many friends! September seems to be a popular month for birthdays! Happy Birthday to all that have a birthday this coming month!

I find it hard to believe that the 11th of this coming month marks the 3rd anniversary of the accident! Time has flown by so quickly and things have changed so much that there are times that I can hardly remember life being any other way! What amazes us both the most though, is the continued prayers and support from all of our friends and family! They still help us out and are there with the slightest call of help! Most of the time, they are there before I even know I need help! How blessed we are!

God answered many of our prayers again this month in the most unusual ways. So many times things and/or persons show up or call at just the right moment with answers for the exact problem of the day and as we have written many, many times, we do not believe in coincidences. We had help with wound issues and cushion advice just when we were wondering what to do next and even though these issues are probably the most serious we have faced since the accident, we have found comfort in having these resources. We continue to believe in taking it one day at a time and doing what we can and turning the rest over to God! We have found an angel that is going to fill in for Carrissa while she starts nursing school. We are going to call her right after Labor Day and set up a time for her to start training so she feels comfortable before she is on her own. We are so thankful for her! Over and over we have seen someone guiding our lives and taking care of us! And I have to admit that I still spend time trying to think I am in control and I am the one that needs to find answers to our problems. It usually results in a lot of wasted worrying because it always falls into place and it usually has nothing to do with anything that I have done! It is a gift from someone that maybe we have never met before or haven't heard from in a long time or even just a friend that lives right down the road! You would think that I would eventually catch on.....I have caught on enough that recognize it and to pray for it but not enough to let go completely! Doc and I have discussed it before though and we agree that between us, we make a pretty good couple...I keep praying for all our needs & doing all the worrying and he just prays for me!

We are going to close by remembering to say thanks once again because we can never, never say that enough! Please know that as we added each one of you to the address on this e-mail, we remembered you individually and remembered what a wonderful place you hold in our hearts! Thanks for your continued prayers! I hate it that this is the last e-mail that I get to send out that is officially part of the summer season! I love summer and I am going to miss it…heat and all! Time stands still for no one though and to discover what lies ahead in our lives, we must move forward! So until we write again, please stay safe and know that we have you in our prayers too!

Your Friends,
Cindy and Doc

September 2007

Talk about squeezing in as much fun as possible into one month! We did it! We have always enjoyed life and have always seemed to play a lot, even before the accident. It seemed like there were things that had to be done that we managed to hurry through and then other things that we could work on but set aside for another day while we played. I am not sorry that we did that! We made a lot of memories that we are enjoying now. We still are following that life style though. There is more that we have to do now as far as things that have to happen but then again, there is more that we choose to save for another day too! Our priorities are still the same but we savor some of them more!

As we sent out the last e-mail, we were in the middle of vacation so that is where I will start this e-mail. We had a great time in Branson and then from there we moved north across the state of Missouri and found a Bluegrass Festival to chill at for a day. That was a relaxing and entertaining way to spend an afternoon. We left that and headed to St. Louis where we had some more fun and shared some time with family. We started off with a day at the zoo and some time with my cousins. The next day we had a family reunion with Doc's dad's side of the family and then we squeezed some time in with a nice visit with my uncle and my grandma. We headed home the next day, but not until after we managed a visit to the new Cabela's store. I know I could say that was a "Doc" treat but actually, if I am honest, I enjoyed that store too! They have a lot to enjoy in it! We purchased a fire ring there and have fixed a spot in the backyard that we have had some nice campfires at on some of the cooler evenings that we have both truly enjoyed! One of the things we miss doing is camping and having our fires brings back some good times! We roast a hot dog and make a s'more and all is well! The best part is that Doc can smell it! He isn't able to smell very often but somehow the campfire smell always gets through to him and he savors that aroma!

The weekend we got home from our vacation, we had my company fall's festival and they had such a nice party for all of us. They had some good food along with some fun entertainment. We started the night off with a comedian, added a couple of talented young men from Nashville called the Lo Cash Cowboys, an opening band called Sierra, and then the main feature was Sara Evans. She put on a great show and we had a great view. Doc managed to carve a spot out close to the stage and at one point she knelt down in front of him and sang part of a song just to him! She winked and pointed at him as she moved on and his night was made! He had a birthday coming up and he really wanted a puppy for it but he told me that he might change his mind and take her home with him so she could sing to him but I reminded him that she would come with 2, 4, and an 8 year old and he said he thought he would stick with his puppy! They ended the night with an awesome firework display and even though it was the next day before we headed home as it was well after midnight, we both had a great time!

The worse part about getting home so late was that we had to get up early the next morning because we had a commitment to share our story with the Methodist church in Atlanta, MO. Somehow it wasn't very hard to get up for it and we were even on time! As usual, our visit there has to be the highlight of the month because when you experience the feeling that surrounds us as we share our story, there is nothing that compares to it. To watch how God works through us is always a blessing to us and to the ones that he touches! We were grateful to be there and it was a pleasure meeting some new friends!

The next weekend we headed to Columbia, MO to attend the Heritage Festival. That was so much fun too! The weather was perfect for that type of outing and as we browsed through the different camps that they had set up with persons in period dress and telling stories and displaying their craftsmanship and selling their wares, we were totally enjoying ourselves. They had different entertainment on 3 different stages and it was almost like you didn't know what to watch! We spent a good part of our time at the fiddle contest and it was a super time. Some of the contest was little kids and it was amazing at what songs they were playing. There weren't hardly any twangs that you would expect and we were impressed! Then the adults that competed were all good and I am glad I wasn't a judge! We enjoyed the sun, the food, and the many talents that were displayed and performed! It was a two day festival and we really wanted to go back for the 2nd day but we had Cardinal/Cub tickets and we couldn't miss that!

Now this is where this e-mail gets sad! Doc's 7-0 Cardinal victories for the games he attended this year was shattered when we attended the game against the Cubs. It was a close game and it was a good game but it had a bad ending for us! ☐ We did have a fantastic day though and the weather was actually even a little cool. I had a jacket on the whole day and I had brought a blanket for Doc but he never asked for it so I never offered it to him....(I was using it and it felt really good!) It was hard to believe that less than a month before it was over 100 degrees and I was throwing ice-water on him every 15 or 20 minutes! Our daughter and her boyfriend attended that game with us! Then the next Sunday we attended the last home game of the year with my sister and her husband as they played Houston. What a special closer it was! Doc is a huge Mike Shannon fan and it was a tribute to Mike Shannon's 50 years with the Cardinals so it couldn't have been better for him! Then we had a come from behind victory in the bottom of the 9th so with the exception of one silly Cubs game, we had a great record of 8-1 for the games we attended this year.

In between all this fun, we squeezed in a couple of birthdays! I had a very special day with all my friends and family remembering me! That is the best part....to see how many people care and to feel so special! The only downside to it was that one of our best friend's dad had passed away and I attended the funeral that morning. I told Doc that 3 years ago, I was sitting in intensive care trying to take our new situation in and this year it was a funeral....I think I am working on a top 10 list for how not to spend your birthday! When Doc's birthday rolled around, we went fishing! Surprise, huh? Then after we fished for awhile, we stopped and got his new puppy. (I can't remember if I wrote that we lost Shannon or not but we did and Doc has really missed him. We both have but I think Doc even more than me!) So now we have this new little bundle that we have to start training all over again! Maybe this one will be a better fishing dog…Shannon was only interested in swimming and was not very good about wanting to sit and watch! Doc named his new puppy Buck. At first he wanted to name it Hee Haw just to listen to me go out on the front porch and yell "Hee Haw"…he thought it would be funny! (he is probably right but it would only had been humorous to him!) So then he thought about the Hee Haw show and thought of Buck Owens and then that led to Jack Buck and Joe Buck with the Cardinals and Buck seemed like the perfect name! I liked that name much better! Buck doesn't know his name yet though! We are still working on that! He is getting better at responding to it each day but we have only had him for one week and I am sure he will be a quick learner!

Our best birthday treat was that our kids all made time to come home the last weekend of the month and we got to spend some quality time with them. It always seems like when you get together after your kids are grown it is because there is something going on and there are usually many others around. I enjoy those time but the times that you have with just your kids are very rare (at least for us!). So having them together for awhile for some games and some fishing was a real treat! We made some memories that we will all treasure! We ended the weekend by golfing with our son but I am not sure if Doc's monkey didn't jump off the chair and into the mechanics of it because about ½ through our golf round, the chair started acting funny and when I put Doc down tonight, it still wasn't acting correctly. I have a hunch that getting caught in the rain didn't help it or possibly it is the mud that he accumulated on the tires and packed in around the wheels! Hmmm! I tried very hard to keep the rain off him and the wheels cleaned but it was impossible to prevent it totally! So it is just easier to blame it on the monkey! I am praying that in the morning, the problems will have disappeared and all will be well. If not, we will have to have someone come out and check it out because we are on the road again this weekend and we sure don't want to think about pushing the chair around! That was what we were concerned about on the golf course because it started acting up at the hole that happens to be the furthest from the club house and the next hole was straight up, neither my son or I thought it would be fun to push the wheelchair to the van from that point! So we babied it slowly in that direction and we made it home...now we just have to fix things to go again!

I thought I was going to have another "monkey/Doc" story to share this month for sure because while we were on vacation, there was one meal that we had at a dinner/show that had steak on the menu. Doc wanted to try and chew on it and even if he couldn't swallow it, he wanted to "suck the juice out of it" as he put it! So he was chomping away on this piece of steak and broke a tooth! I had to make him a dentist appointment to put his tooth back together and I didn't know how he was going to puff and sip on the wheelchair if his mouth was frozen! I could just see the problems I was going to run into if he couldn't control it and I didn't see how he was going to control it because I can't even control getting a milk shake up a straw after a trip to the dentist! His straw is so much more sensitive and technical (hehe-imagine that! I would hope his chair would be more technical than a milkshake...sorry, blonde moment!). I couldn't see myself being able to push 650 lbs around where I wanted it to go so I was almost ready to sit it out and wait for the numbness to work its way out! But there was nothing to worry about because the dentist was able to fix everything back in tip top shape without numbing Doc's mouth so in no time, he was wheeling back down the hall with a huge smile on his face saying he was ready to go out for some supper...we had to make it soup because he couldn't chew on it for 24 hours but it was just a relief to me that he was able to drive that chair! Doc says he would go through it again if he had to because that steak was worth it! AND believe it or not, he said he was actually looking forward to going to the dentist because it meant getting out of the house! Like he never gets to do that!

I have had a long list of to-do things since we got back from vacation and I am slowly working my way down the list but it is too overwhelming to take it anything except one day at a time. We had some wonderful hints on some new therapies for Doc's wounds if I cannot get them to heal. We are still working on getting his cushion fixed. I have someone helping me to put a real porch on the front of the house instead of the plywood that we have been working with because is getting in bad shape. I have someone giving me an estimate on some foundation and basement water problems that we have been having. And Doc finally talked me into trading his truck and my car in for one vehicle. I have wanted to hold on to Doc's truck because I know how proud he was of that and it was so new when his accident happened. But he is right, it doesn't make sense to try to upkeep 2 vehicles and pay taxes and insurance on them both when I probably don't drive 20 miles a week in either one of them. Most of our time is spent in the van! So he wanted me to find a 4 wheel drive vehicle that still had some hauling capacity & would work well in winter on our gravel road but was more like a car's ride because he knew I like driving cars better than trucks. After trying out a few, I chose a Dodge Nitro and I really like it! Doc and I picked out an orange one and it is a neat vehicle. It was hard parting from my car and his truck but I am glad that I found a vehicle that I like well enough to make the switch easier! I found the vehicle and then I took Doc in to negotiate the trade! He has always loved to go through all that car buying negotiations (he actually said that is a blowing smoke process....they blow some and then you blow some back and so on....I can't figure out why I don't enjoy it!) He had a great time and after an hour or two of them going back and forth, a compromise was made on both sides and I had a vehicle to drive to work! Doc said the only downside was that he would really like to be able to ride in it so that is my next goal…find a way to get him in it and take him for a ride! They say where there is a will, there is a way so I am sure I will figure it out!

We are getting ready to head out this coming weekend for a trip to South Dakota. We have a couple of friends that are going to be making the trek with us. Doc and Brandon are both avid Terry Redlin fans and he has an art museum in Watertown, SD, that they have wanted to visit for a long time. So plans were made to just go and see it! I have to say they are being very fair though because they are promising Amanda and me some "girl" time too! It will be a short but fun 3 day roadtrip!

The good news that I have to report is that I have very little bad news to talk about. I had someone call that wanted to tell us that she had been thinking about offering some healing oils that go back to biblical times for Doc's wounds if I would be interested in trying them and I figured nothing else had worked so we gave it a shot. It was exciting to see it working! It will take a long time for them to heal completely but the nurse that comes out once a week has been amazed at how healthy tissue seems to be growing back so rapidly. We will continue to use it and maybe in a few months, we can report that they are indeed healed! Wouldn't that be great? At least I can write this month that they are not worse and they are very healthy looking! On top of that, Doc has felt great all month and it has been so wonderful to have had a nice long stretch of good health! I can tell that he is feeling good because he always has something to talk about and his sense of humor is sharper than ever! On top of that, his appetite continues to grow and even though we still have to subsidize it with tube feeding, he enjoys what he can consume!

We have a new person hired to sit with Doc during the day while I am at work and we are both coming to care for her a lot. I think it will be a good fit! Our daughter still helps out on Fridays and my mom continues to also be a valuable resource! I continued to be blessed with some good morning help in getting Doc up and some fantastic friends that continue to help me put him back down in the evenings! Once again, we want to say thank you for the prayers, the many things so many of you do to make our life easier, the cards, and the visits! I thank God that we are blessed with so many good friends! Someone sent me an e-mail this month and there was a line it that has stuck in my head that is so true if you have faith...."I am too blessed to be stressed and too anointed to be disappointed!"—I hope this applies to every one of you!

Your Friends,

Cindy and Doc

October 2007

Well, Doc can mark another thing that he wanted to do in his lifetime off his list. We started this month off with a road trip to South Dakota to visit the Terry Redlin Art Center. Brandon and Amanda Bailey went with us and it was worth the trip just to watch Brandon and Doc (both are huge Terry Redlin art fans!) slobber over the paintings. Amanda and I had to admit though that the museum was better than our expectations and we truly enjoyed it ourselves! We spent a couple of hours in it, left to eat lunch, and then headed back to enjoy it some more. They had 3 gift shops in it and Doc had his birthday money so we had to spend some time in them trying to decide what to bring home with us! He ended up happy with his new treasures (I attached a copy of him with one of the linen prints he bought!) but is already planning a return trip sometime!

I was a little nervous with Doc's wheelchair in the gift shops because one of them was pretty tight and it was full of plates, ornaments, and other breakables but Doc is a good driver and the monkeys were behaving themselves! Besides the art center, we were able to fit in a few other activities and it just ended up being a really nice 3 day weekend! It does make a nice weekend roadtrip!

I have to come clean though and tell you that there is a series of plates that Terry Redlin painted dedicated to the song "Oh Beautiful for Spacious Skies"…Doc worked for a long time collecting all 8 of the series. We have had them sitting in a pile for a long time while we decided how to hang them. We were planning on buying a neat plate rack while we were at the museum but they didn't have what we needed. My brother had torn down an old barn that had lots of sentimental value to us kids and he ended up bringing me some of the wood out of it and I had been looking for a way to display it too. So I had this idea to make a plate holder out of it for Doc's plates. It came out even better than I thought it would and I was so excited but while I was hanging the plates on it, I dropped one of them (or the monkey pulled it out of my hand...I like that excuse better) and it shattered. I glued it back together even though it was in over 20 pcs and to tell you the truth, you really couldn't tell....I thought that would cover me until I could find a new one and Doc would never be the wiser. However, I just got that mess covered up when I knocked over a table that had some more of his Redlin artwork on it and broke another piece...Doc has collected this for over 10 years and has never broken a piece and I break 2 in less than 24 hours! So I fessed up to all of it (although Doc just smiled at me like he always does at my mess ups—God knew what he was doing when he gave me a patient man!) and was lucky enough to find the 2nd broken piece on e-bay at a very reasonable cost....the plate in the series was a little more of a challenge though. I finally asked my cousin in St. Louis to run by Cabela's before she made a trip up to see us one weekend and they had it so his set is once more complete. It is hanging on the wall that he looks at most of the day and I think he really is enjoying it!

After that, things slowed down a little bit again and we are back to just an occasional movie or some cards with friends or whatever Doc could think of while he was waiting on me to get home from work. We did have a good time following the Cairo softball team to the Missouri State Finals and finally to the State Championship! That was so much FUN! Congratulations to the Lady Bearcats! We were very proud of them!

Then there was the World Series and even though the Cardinals weren't in it, we cheered on the Rockies instead! Once the Cardinals were out of the picture, I told Doc that if the Rockies won the World Series that I would take him to Denver next summer to watch a game and he became a big cheerleader! That was before the Rockies were even in the playoffs so it was funny to watch it all fall into place...like destiny! Unfortunately, the ending wasn't so great but ride there was!

Doc had a couple adventures without me this month and I think he enjoyed them. I was a little nervous but all went well and I was glad he had some time to feel more independent. He talked our daughter into giving him a ride one day while I was out and about and they were able to catch a softball game. She really did well at loading him and driving Porky by herself. I think they had a good outing. He even talked her into getting him some supper on the way home! Then one evening, Brandon came and picked him up to go scouting for deer. He had it all set up and when they got back home they were excited to report that they had seen a nice buck. Of course,

Doc thinks it is because he had me put his camouflage shoes and hat on! My cousin was up visiting us and while he was on that outing, we were able to waterproof the back deck and steps. Chores like that always go faster when you can talk through it. AND we can talk our way through almost anything! Talking is one thing we are both really good at!

Buck (our new puppy) is growing like a weed and Doc wanted me to attach a copy of him so that is the picture you will see if you were able to pull up the attachment! He loves to give Doc smooches every night and Doc seems to like it too! (As long as he keeps his tongue off my face!) All I have to do is ask him if he wants to give Doc smooches and he runs into the bedroom and sits by the bed until I pick him up to tell Doc goodnight! (He is rapidly outgrowing that pick him up stuff though..he is getting BIG!) He knows his name now and he knows "NO"…he just doesn't always listen to it! He is much more trouble than Shannon was! This puppy is all puppy and all that goes with it but Doc is totally entertained by him and always has several stories to share with me by the time I make it home! He has a way of getting in trouble and then looking at you with those eyes and melting your heart! He is timeout A LOT!

I got tickled at Doc because someone came to help us put on a new front porch with something more durable and attractive than plywood and he warned Doc that he wouldn't be able to get out for a day or two while he had it torn up but Doc quickly told him not to worry about it because he had a backdoor and ramp! I don't think

Doc had any intention of getting "stuck" at home! It took about a week because the weather kept throwing us some curves but we finally finished the porch and it is like a lot of things that when you are done with it, you wonder why you didn't do it sooner! It has put a torch under me though and I have created a whole list of things to do and I am marking them off one by one! For the past 3 years, it has been like we have been in limbo and the house was the least of my concerns but it is need of some attention & some updating. With Doc feeling so good for the past few months, I have been able to redirect a little of my attention to the house. Doc has been a great resource on how to fix things and I actually have been enjoying some of it! I have always liked building things and using the table saw…when I was in high school, I loved taking shop over home-ec (it isn't called that anymore…now it is consumer sciences! Hehe)… although I enjoyed the cooking and sewing too, it was the tool thing that I found interesting! Now I am finding they are both coming in handy!

The sores aren't improving at the same rate as they were but they aren't getting any worse either so I guess I will look on the sunny side of it and be glad that they are holding their own! The nurse that visits us on Tuesday continues to tell me that she has never seen the flesh grow back like it appears to be doing so she continues to be optimistic. She tells me that the wound has to heal from the inside out so it staying open is a good thing! Plus they are bleeding which tells us there is good circulation there! Doc continues to feel great and is eating a decent lunch and supper each day. What a great blessing good health is!

We appear to have lost our wheelchair/seating support as we have gotten a letter that they closed their doors...suddenly...the letter stated that they were trying to start again but you have to wonder why they closed the doors so suddenly and to tell you the truth, we have noticed that their support had seriously slipped in the past 2 months so we had an inkling that something wasn't right. Now we are back to square one on who to turn to with wheelchair/cushion/battery issues! I am not fretting about it as I know that our path will lead us to someone!

As November is the month of Thanksgiving, it doesn't seem right to close without giving thanks for all our blessings and that would be you! Thanks to each of you and your cards/prayers/support/helping hands and visits! Doc and I always are amazed at no matter how bad our day might be, when we say our nightly prayers, our list of things to be thankful for is always much greater than our list of needs! One of our Sundays at church this month highlighted the fact that you can never pray too much for any need. So we continue to pray and be thankful for your prayers as our life continues along! I am not sure if it is our situation or our age or maybe both, but as the seasons change each year and yet another year is quickly getting close to being over, I reflect often that it is not so important at how long we are on this earth but rather, what we do while we are here and how quickly it can be over...whether you die young or live to be old…it still is over in a blink of an eye! I think the best we can do is look back and say, "I like the way my life turned out!"….For now, neither Doc nor I know our future but even with the challenges that we currently face, we both like the way our life is turning out—mostly because we have had each other & so many persons that love us! Our prayer is that each of you are too!

Your Friends,
Cindy and Doc

Buck as a Pup

Doc with his Terry Redlin Print

November 2007

I am later getting this out this month because I took a couple of days off to go Christmas shopping and that has put me behind! I thought November was going to be a slow down month because we really didn't have many pre-planned activities but as the month went along, I had absolutely no down time! We started it off with some community time with our friends from our local Christian church. They had a fund raiser the first weekend of the month and it was nice to join in their evening! They had a fantastic dinner and then an auction and it was nice to be a part of something so good for the community.

After that we jumped right into attending a few JH basketball games and cheering the kids along! Somehow it was more nerve-racking when our kids were playing in it than it is watching it just as a fan! The game changes a lot when you are no longer a parent of one of the players (or the coach). Even though I really miss our kids and watching them compete in sports, I actually do enjoy just being a fan! It is fun cheering for the kids and visiting with our friends! Now that the junior high season has ended, we have already started cheering for the high school teams!

Then deer season started and we had our nieces, nephews, friends and family keeping us busy sharing their stories and pictures! We had several that were in town that came by to visit and say hi and we thank all of them that took the time to fit us in their hunting trip time!

Doc is ALWAYS ready for a good deer hunting story not to mention just the visiting part!

We spent some of our time revisiting some of the churches that we have shared our story with because it has been a goal of ours to always get back with each of them and simply share a worship service with them. Every single one of them was so welcoming to us and mean so much to us and we are having a good time re-visiting them! If you belong to one of them that we have not revisited, you can know that we are coming! I am not sure if that is a promise or a warning...hehe! Doc has had his onery shoes on this month so I am not promising that we will both be on our best behavior but at least one of us will be! Hehe! Seriously, it is nice to be able to come back to each of those places and simply share our faith! Doc said it may take us a few months to get around to all of them (especially as winter has rapidly appeared!) but we are trying!

Besides that, we also found a bluegrass festival in Hannibal that we ventured out for and not only did some friends of ours join us but they brought their 2 grandsons with them. One of them was 2 and the other is close to celebrating his first birthday but those two boys were totally enthralled with the music! They sat there and watched everything for hours! They blew that theory that small children have short attention spans out of the window. We decided that we should have taken our kids to listen to bluegrass because I can't ever remember ours behaving that well for that length of time! We had a good time that day! We must have worn them out because before the van was out of the parking lot both those 2 young ones and Doc were sound asleep!

Thanksgiving was a great four days off and gathering together and remembering all the things that we have to be thankful for made it for a very special holiday! I was not trying to rush through that holiday to get to another but I have to be honest and admit that I used those days off to decorate our house for Christmas. There is not much that I enjoy more than our house at Christmas! It takes a lot of work but when I am done and I sit back with the music and lights and smells…there is nothing like it!

Speaking of Christmas….I know that the real reason for the season is the gift that God gave all of us but all of the symbolism and fun that goes with it reminds us of the special things attached with that gift.

- The wonder of gifts and sharing goes back to the first gifts of the wisemen and while I am shopping for our gifts to share, I remember those gifts too! I can't think of many joys greater than giving and sharing!
- Every time I see a candle burning I think of that song about this little light of mine and I rejoice at our situation and the ways that it has allowed us to pass that light on!
- The nativity scene and what it symbolizes speaks for itself!
- The stockings that are hung waiting for treasures to be added are special because they have the names of our children on

them and I wait in anticipation of knowing they will be home for the holiday! (And yes, our full-grown children still want their stockings! They told us once that if they had to choose between the stocking and a present, they would rather have the stocking....I have to admit there is something to be said about digging down deep in a stocking and not knowing what you are going to pull out!) Although, our daughter said the family being together is the best part of Christmas and I tend to agree!

- Probably what is most abundant in our house (Doc would say there is no probably about it, but he helped build this collection) is the snowmen! We have added plenty of snowmen over the years and a look at each one of them brings a smile to our faces. I can't help but think how much we like each of them even though they are so different! Some are made of wood, cloth, paper or plastic. Some have arms or boots and some don't. None of them are dressed alike and yet each one of them is special! Just like each of us! And I truly think that was one of Jesus' messages....there cannot be one favorite or one that is better than another....we are all different and yet loved so much!

- I am not sure what purpose all of Doc's quirky gifts play in all of this but they certainly bring joy into my life! We have a day already set aside this month to go shopping with our friends for our annual "special" gifts....I will keep you posted on what they end up being next month! It is the one day that Doc truly does love to shop!

So how can one not get excited about Christmas? No matter how much commercialism or hustle/bustle results during the next few weeks, all of it can be tied back to the beginning of the holiday and everything that resulted on that one special blessed night so long ago…no matter what the actual date may be…

Buck is still growing and the vet is telling us that in another month, he will probably exceed 50 lbs! We are trying hard to teach him some manners and how to mind but he is just like a kid…he will pull some stunt and know it was wrong and then run and hide behind the coffee table and just peek around it! We have to laugh while we are disciplining him (although there have been a couple of times, it wasn't very funny!!). I know that some day he is going to make a great dog. I was impressed one day because Doc was watching television in the bedroom while I was cleaning the living room area and his vent started to beep because of low power and Buck was down the hall in a flash, sitting at the door and barking for me to come and check it out. As soon as I rounded the corner, he shut right up and just waited until I had changed the battery cord around and then he followed me back to the living room perfectly content! Not bad for only 3 months old!

Doc continues to feel good and his sores are still holding their own. Sometimes we measure his health on whether his temperature is low enough to earn a sheet at bedtime! I am happy to report that he has been so healthy that not only has he earned a sheet, but we have been adding a blanket on top of it! He is thrilled to have the extra covering as he stays chilled feeling much of the time. As his body cannot regulate its own temperature, I have to be careful not to overheat it but at the same time, I try to give him as much warmth as possible for comfort reasons!

Now I am going to write something that came to my heart while I was praying one day and I had an overwhelming need to share it. I thought about how when two are joined in marriage and per the promise of Christ, they are made one body. Included in that promise is that whatever joys or sorrows belong to one, they belong to the other. In our situation, Doc and I are carrying the same cross-just different ends of it! I could say we are each carrying our own cross in that we are definitely facing different challenges each day but they stem from the same issue so doesn't it make more sense to share the carrying of one cross instead of bearing the weights of two separate crosses? How much easier it is when the weight is shared! On top of that, so many of you help bear the weight as Simon stepped up to do so many years ago. I am not sure why this thought was laid on my heart this month because at the season of Christmas you would think I would have thoughts of little Jesus' birth instead of the cross he carried at the end but here it is now; so it goes down on paper and maybe some of you will think to throw off your separate crosses and pick up the other end of the cross that your other is half is carrying, or to be that Simon that helps someone else carry on, and that will be our Christmas gift to you because it will enlighten your world immensely!

Have a wonderful, blessed Christmas Season,
Cindy and Doc

December 2007

This has been such a whirlwind of a month that I hardly know where to start. I suppose that even though you are just on the first line, you already know there is much more to come!

I can't even start recapping the month without mentioning the weather. Usually weather is a fill-in for conversation when you really don't know what else to talk about but this month it dominated our lives! It didn't slow us down or stop us from doing very much but it should have and it sure challenged our guardian angels! I don't even know how many winter weather advisories were posted in the past month but I would have to think it was more than the norm. Plus, they all seemed to happen on the weekends! The first one hit while we were in St. Louis celebrating my grandma's visitation and funeral. I use the word celebration because that is what it should be! Death is the ultimate reward for each of us if you put some thought in it! Doc and I spend a lot of time discussing that and how wonderful it is going to be! There was a peace about her funeral that I hope all of us can feel that when our loved ones pass away. I was honored to be able to do the eulogy and I think my family was a little afraid that I might have more to say than time allowed but (and I know this is hard to believe) I kept it at a respectable length...Doc said it was like Goldilocks...just right...not too long and not too short! Hehe! Well, maybe she said not too hot and not too cold OR not too hard and not too soft...something like that anyway! All in all, it was a great opportunity to catch up with my family, especially my cousins and see how their children had grown up. Family is a wonderful thing but I think what makes is so wonderful is the love that you feel when we are surrounded by them! That is what I remember about my grandma the most too...how much she enjoyed that! While we were at the visitation, Doc shared part of his story with our family that had not heard it and when he was done, one of my cousins said that it was the first time they heard Doc talk more than Cindy...then my other cousin said that now they had witnessed a miracle! Hehe! The weather hit hard during our stay in St. Louis though and poor Porky had to brave some slick stuff! Not to mention the ice that accumulated on the van while we were in the funeral home. I am not sure how many guys stopped to help me chip away at it when we went outside though but I was able to hop in and keep warm while an army of ice scrapers made quick work of the ice! That was a treat for me! Then my uncle ended up following us to the motel to make sure we made it safe. Doc told me he thought someone was following us (although I think it was just a lucky guess!). How could he know that when we were on a 6 lane highway and he can't see out of the windows? Anyway, we were well taken care of and during the stay, Doc even managed to wiggle visits to Starbucks, Cabelas, Bass Pro, and Cracker Barrel...4 of his favorite places!

Doc managed to talk our daughter into loading him up in Porky one day and taking him to Columbia to go Christmas shopping. I think they had a blast until on the way home Porky had a blowout. That was scary to me but by the time I knew what was going on,

AAA had already been called and were on the way. I was very proud of how competent our daughter was and to be honest, I was glad that I wasn't driving the van when it had the blowout! It would have scared me! Needless to say, the next morning I got up and drove it into town to get the tire replaced and once again it was in a freezing rain so I spent ½ the trip to the highway going sideways in Porky. I wasn't very scared though because I wasn't going fast and I didn't have Doc with me. I had left him at home with our daughter. By the time I headed home, it had warmed up to make it just rain and it was much easier to drive in. I think the monkey might have had something to do with this incident!

The next storm hit the next weekend on a day that we were going Christmas shopping with some friends but Doc said he wanted to go and our friend was going to drive Porky and he thought we'd be ok so I just sat in the back and went along for the ride. I can't even tell you how many semi's, busses, and vehicles we witnessed in the ditches but Porky stayed on track for the mall. It took about twice as long as usual but we made it. We decided that we should cut back on some of our plans and head home before it got too late so the guys were supposed to call us when they finished up. Over 7 hours later, we were still waiting on their call! (and they say men don't like the mall!) Then by that time, we figured we might as well eat some supper before we headed north. I thought there was a chance that things might have improved while we were shopping but they didn't. We drove home in the same mess we started the day with. In the end, our driveway and Doc's ramp ended up being our biggest challenges but we overcame both of them. I knew that they had found some special Christmas presents because about from that point on, Doc became as excited as a little kid about the upcoming Christmas! I think it was the most he has looked forward to Christmas in his life! I know that since the accident, it was the most healthy he has been and that played a big part of it!

The next weekend was Doc's work Christmas party and he really wanted to make it to that, but once again a major winter storm his the scene. He had a friend that he worked with that called & offered to come out and drive Porky to the party so we took him up on the offer and once again, I was along for the ride. I just loaded up Doc, said a prayer and off we went. We made it and although we had to shovel some snow to make Doc a path to get into the party, we were early enough to be able to find a good parking spot and clear the way for him. He absolutely had a blast and there wasn't much time that he wasn't visiting with someone. At one point, there was a small pinch of time that he was just sitting there and I leaned over to ask him if he was having a good time and he just looked at me and said, "there are a lot of good memories in this room." You actually spend just as much time with the folks you work with as you do with those that you live with and in the end, they become like an extended part of your family! Sharing that Christmas dinner with them and rehashing so many fun times was a present that has no dollar value but is worth more than anything you could buy! I was so thankful to be able to be part of that and to make sure Doc was there! I was also thankful that Steve Wood came out to drive the van! Thanks Steve!

I wasn't so lucky the next weekend. We went over to our friends, Howard & Ellen's, house to celebrate our annual Christmas get-together with them and exchange those wonderful gifts that we went shopping for a couple of weeks earlier when another winter storm hit hard. We spent the first part of the evening exchanging our special gifts…speaking of which, a couple of examples of what we received was a magic worm and Rudolph that when place in water, grows 100 times it's size! I even got some elephants wearing a santa hat earrings! We also were spoiled with some 'real' things too! They received a toy craftsman set of tools, with a tool belt, I might add…unfortunately, the tool belt was only 18" or so long so they had to hook it to their legs but it would work! Hehe! We had many, many fun gifts like that but we also got them tickets to the Martina McBride concert in February. Doc said that he thought he was going to have to wait for Cardinal baseball to have something else to look forward to but he backed up the calendar to February and is already counting the days down to that concert now! Anyway, after the gifts we shared a wonderful meal and some cards. Sometime during the 2ⁿᵈ game of cards, our daughter calls us and wants to know if we are home yet. I told her not yet because it was still early in the evening. Needless to say, she had us look outside and sure enough, we were in the middle of a sleet storm! Isn't it amazing at how when the kids grow up, they start checking on you? Hehe! So we decided we had better start working our way home. That was the worse of all of them and I am not sure if it was because it really was the worse or if it was because it was after dark and we were way out in the country on back roads or if it was because I had to drive and we were on our own. Probably a little bit of all of it! The first half of the trip home was all sleet and I had to keep shaking the wipers to be able to see out the window and hope that I was on my side of the road because you couldn't hardly see it. Then the 2nd half of the trip was spent trying to drive through a blinding snow...I thought the sleet was bad but the snow was harder to see the road. I was really wanting to just cry or figure out a way to get the knot out of my stomach but I knew that wouldn't help the vision problem at all and Doc was sitting behind me encouraging me and talking to me about anything and everything and told me that even if I was only driving 5 mph as long as I kept it on the road, we would get to where we wanted to be eventually! He was right! It took a long time to get home but we made it! I have given thanks for that trip many times since then!

By the next day though the sun was shining and it was beautiful! We managed to make it to church and I could hardly believe how bad it had been the night before. Then by the time we got home, our most special present was waiting for us...our kids! It was WONDERFUL to have them all gathered with us and we had a great time sharing some games, some food, and some visiting! It was a very special Christmas! We decided that for my Christmas gift, Doc would add an anniversary band to my wedding ring set. The wedding ring set that he picked out for me though is really unique and so I had to find a jeweler to custom design it. I found a guy in Chillicothe, MO, that undertook it and on the Friday before Christmas we made a trip up there to pick it up! It was even more amazing and beautiful than I thought it would be and I have totally enjoyed having it back on my finger and looking more beautiful than ever! I think Doc was as excited as I was to do it and get it back and he was pleased with it too. How fitting to have the engagement ring, the wedding ring, and the anniversary ring all together in one setting! 29 years ago we started with just the engagement ring and now it is even more beautiful…as is our blessed marriage too! It is hard to explain how special our rings are to us and what they mean but I can tell you it isn't the dollar value that they are worth that make them special..it is what they stand for!

Doc's special gift from me was an autographed Terry Redlin print that I had purchased for him in October while we were in South Dakota. I don't think I could have kept it a secret much longer because I was bursting at the seams in excitement of him seeing it! I even got some trac lighting from Lowe's and figured out how to hook it up so I hung it on the wall after he went to bed and had it all lit up in the morning! It was fun to see his reaction when he saw it hanging there! That will always be a special memory to me!

The kids were able to stay through Christmas Eve before they headed out to the in-laws and their extended holiday plans. It was sure fun while it lasted though and we enjoyed every second of it!

For you that read this that already have children that have grown and gone, you understand how we sit and marvel at where the years went and how did they go so fast. Those that read this that have little kids or will one day, I can only tell you to enjoy every single minute of every single day because it does all come to pass, and very quickly!

Doc continues to feel good and to be healthy and we are thankful for every single morning that he wakes up and feels like this! It has been over 6 months since he has had any type of medical problem that has made him feel bad. Our only medical issues right now are the 3 wounds that he has that we are struggling to heal. We have taken him to another doctor to get yet another opinion on them and have just started trying something new on them. We are still using the oils that we were using because she thought we were on the right track…she has just added something more to it. On top of that, we found a seat that has alternating pressure in it that operates much like the bed Doc sleeps in and they have sent us that seat and we have been using it for a week today. They actually have taken the air out of the pockets in the areas that his wounds would be to relieve all pressure there and so far, it appears that it might be helping some. Time will tell but at least we are finding things to try. That is much better than what some of the doctors had told us to do. Some of them were willing to give up and send us home with very little hope. Not to say that we ever paid too much attention to them because we have a ton of hope! We truly do believe that with God all things are possible and only he knows which way our path will wind. In the meantime, we continue to have faith and be thankful for each day we spend together!

Buck continues to be a challenge and a wonderful friend all at the same time! He continues to grow and is rapidly approaching the 50 lb mark and yet he still thinks he is this little puppy that can curl up on your lap! We continue to house break him so he can spend his time entertaining Doc and he is getting better all the time. He is so big that we have to remind ourselves that he is only 4 months old. He has moved up to sleeping on a rug in our bathroom and spending the night inside and is actually doing very well with that. He wakes me up about once a night to go outside for a little bit but other than that, he hasn't had one accident in the house and he sleeps all night. Doc laughs because he was sleeping at the end of my bed one night and Doc couldn't sleep so he asked me to turn the tv on. When I turned the tv on, Buck gave him that look and whined and slowly got up and went into the bathroom to curl up on the rug. I don't think he appreciated the television noise very much. Hehe! Doc laughs at that one all the time!

January holds very little in the line of planned activities. There are a couple of things we are looking forward to but we both agree that there is nothing on the calendar right now that would make us take a chance on any more driving in bad weather. For right now anyway, we feel like we have pushed our luck as far as we want to and are ready to stay indoors during any future winter storms. We both have enough new books, games, music, and movies to keep us busy for the rest of winter. On top of that, Doc is looking forward to watching the MU Tigers play football in the New Year's bowl game! That is probably the time that I will start packing up my Christmas treasure and putting them away for another year! Doc is anxiously awaiting some Cardinal baseball moves and is so far very disappointed in the lack of anything productive. He has tickets to go to at least 5 games though and will wear his Cardinal read to all of them.

We have a lot of plans for the upcoming holiday weekend but nothing that is going to keep us up very late on New Year's Eve. I think after I put Doc to bed, I might try to stay up and bring in the New Year but I will have to stay busy because if I sit down to just read or watch tv, I am asleep before I know it! Our days of partying and bringing in the New Year with noise makers and kisses are behind us for now. There might be a day again but I do not expect it to be this year! I pray for safe travels for all of you that are going to be out and about! As this year comes to a close, Doc & I both just wanted to say thank you to so many of you that pray for us, send us cards and let us know you are thinking of us, come to help us in anyway, or just come by the house to say hi! Whatever you have done for us this past year…whether we know for sure who it was or not….we just wanted to say thank you very much! All of you literally are the wind beneath our wings! I also got a couple of things that for Christmas that said some things that meant a lot to us. The first one was a sign that someone made us that said BELIEVE. I am not just assuming that means Santa but I think it refers to faith…for that reason, I plan on leaving that up year round. Secondly, my daughter gave me a picture that states "Faith is believing in something when common sense tells you not to."….then she put a picture of Doc and I beside it. I thought it was special but then the very next day I was watching the old version of Miracle on 34th St and that line was spoken in there but I had never paid attention to it before. That was pretty neat! On a rare day when Doc was struggling with his purpose in life, another friend brought by a plaque he had made for Doc that said "Faith, Family, Friends"…all the things important to us both. On the same day, our sister in law sent Doc a sign that says "This too shall pass" which is dear to our hearts and goes back to a story at St. Mary's Hospital in Grand Junction shortly after Doc's accident. I don't know if I had ever shared it in the e-mails but there was this little boy that came over to me while I was standing outside of intensive care and put a note in my hand that said, "Trust in the Lord and this too shall come to pass." I didn't know the boy and all he said was that I could keep the note because he had written it for me. It as the beginning of many more unexplained events that continue to this very day! And finally, another friend gave me a plaque that read "God answers knee mail" and I know he does! All of those are now hanging on our walls (I can't "believe" that I found wall space but I did)

Have a very blessed and wonderful New Year full of good memories and good health,
We love each of you,
Cindy and Doc

January 2008

We started this year out with Doc watching football, football and more football! I guess it is just that time of year! If Chuck is reading this, I know he will be proud! While he did that on New Year's Day, I started putting away all the Christmas treasures for another year. (I have to admit that I left out a few of the snowmen because I wasn't really ready to take down everything!). I worked really hard all day planning on giving myself the pleasure of a bubble bath at the end of the day as a reward (something that I hardly ever have time to do!). During the holidays, I really loved those 4 day weekends!

Things went as planned and by late afternoon, I had marked all the "have to have done" items off my to-do list. So now I was able to really sink down into a warm bubble bath while Doc was watching his umpteenth football game of the day! Now I will tell you that in the old days, I could shut the bathroom door and turn on some relaxing music and really enjoy it but now, I have to leave the door open and forego the music in order to be able to hear Doc's ventilator in case there is a problem. I thought the only downside to that was that it allowed a cool breeze to penetrate the bathroom which took away from the warmth of the water....I was wrong...I was sitting there enjoying the bubbles (which I might add was a Christmas gift from Doc) and reading an article in a magazine when all of sudden the image of Buck is flying through the open doorway and the next thing I know the bubbles are flying through the air and my magazine is dripping wet! His tail is flinging the bubbles everywhere! Then he realizes that he might have made a mistake so as fast as he came in, he is jumping out! By this time, I am catching up with what has gone on so I am jumping out of the tub to slam the bathroom door in order to contain the mess to one room! Buck was one dripping mess of bubbles and dog hair! He was looking up at me with the most puzzled dog face you have ever seen and I am pretty sure he did not gain the same pleasure from the bubble bath as I was (well at least before I had to share it with a wild puppy!). hehe! So that ended my peace and tranquility for as long as it lasted! I did get two more things marked off my to-do list though...I figured as long as he started it, I might as well finish Buck's bath for the week and then by the time I cleaned up the mess in the bathroom, I had a sparkling, well-mopped bathroom floor! Doc swears he did not tell Buck to "go find Cindy" but I am still not positive about that!

As much as we enjoyed all the holidays, though, it did feel good to have them behind us and have a fairly opened calendar staring at us for the month of January! I decided that maybe it was time to incorporate a routine into our lives that included the YMCA. I had a trial one month membership that I had gotten in a fund raiser for the United Way so I signed us up for January and gave that a shot. I figured Doc could listen to books on tape while I worked out IF someone wasn't visiting with him because we rarely go anywhere that he doesn't end up visiting! Before Doc's accident we both were regulars at the Y and spent several hours a week working out but I hadn't seem to find any time to devote to that since then. I have really enjoyed the exercise again and our new YMCA facility is really a nice place that our community can be proud of. I have not been able to devote the same time that I used to but I am giving it a shot anyway. There are some days that it feels like a workout just getting there! It does feel good to be getting in shape although I think taking care of Doc is conditioning me each day more than I thought! Anyway, at least twice a week, I try to hurry home from work, load up Doc, head in to workout and then make it home in time to feed Doc some supper and have a little time to visit before our bedtime help shows up to help me put Doc down! Doc said that he enjoys all the people he runs into that he visits with and he is glad that he is getting to listen to his books on tape. When he tries to listen to them at home, he falls asleep but he said something is different at the gym and he stays awake!

Doc's wounds do appear to be slowly improving with the new cushion! Not at a rapid pace but I can see and measure improvements. I think it is going to be a long healing process but I am excited to see some healing! His elbow was probably the wound that was worrying me the most this month but I had a couple of suggestions from a couple of persons and we have been trying them and that wound too, is slowly starting to improve. We are still waiting on wheelchair parts and it is amazing to me how many times I have called and how many times that I have been promised that they will be out in the next day or two and yet we are still waiting! To say it is frustrating would be putting it mildly! It feels sorta like what I would imagine it would feel like if your house caught on fire and you had called the fire department and they said they were on their way but they just keep making wrong turns while your house continues to burn and the whole time you are standing there with a small drinking glass trying to throw what little water you can on it but knowing you really aren't making a difference! That is how I feel. I keep trying to improve the things with creative ideas of my own but in the end, I know it is going to take the expertise of someone other than me in addition to equipment that Medicare and/or insurance has to agree to pay for. Speaking of Medicare is a whole other frustrating issue! The place that Doc gets his supplies from called me today to tell me that they are only going to send the amount that Medicare will allow and everything else I will have to find a supplier and buy on my own—starting the 1st of the month-that is tomorrow! Some of it is fairly expensive and some of it is very critical to keeping him breathing so I started a battle this morning. I told them that I didn't think giving me one days notice was very fair so they backed down and agreed to start it in March. That gives me a month to get my ducks in a row! It is going to take a lot of political stuff and there is no guarantee it will work but I have put the wheels in motion to try and fight it! I have also contacted Doc's insurance case worker and have gotten a letter from our doctor stating why Doc needs these items faxed to her and she is also trying from their side to get approval to pay for what Medicare denies. They told me in the hospital that they hadn't met anyone in Doc's condition that wasn't on Medicaid and I am beginning to understand! They just try to drain you until you have no will to fight and no resources left! I still believe in the will of God though and we still plug along knowing that everything that happens, happens for a reason! There are moments that I let it consume me and then I think how blessed I am to still have Doc and whatever it takes, it will be worth it! Doc told me once that there are only 2 reasons that he was still here…one was that God wasn't ready for him yet and the other was that I won't let him go! I will continue to be an advocate for Doc and will continue the phone calls and hopefully, there will be a day that it all comes together! What we continue to give thanks for daily is Doc's continued good health! He feels good and that makes everything so much easier to deal with!

Even though we didn't officially have plans on the calendar, I would work through the week, try to get out Doc an evening or two, and Doc would come up with plans for the weekend. Mainly Saturday because on Sundays we would go to church and then I had chores to do at home and he had football to watch! So Saturdays would roll around and we would take off somewhere. One Saturday Doc wanted to see the new movie "The Bucket List"…that was an awesome movie that had everyone in the theater crying, laughing and cheering at various parts! If you are unfamiliar with it, it is about 2 guys that meet in a hospital room and find out they both are dying and don't have much time left and they develop a "bucket list" (a list of things you want to do before you kick the bucket!). It makes you think about the things that you would want to put on your list. Doc said that we might not have written them down but we have been marking things off our mental bucket list since his accident (and actually even before that because that is how we have always tried to live our lives). We try not to waste any of our precious time and we don't put off until tomorrow things that we really want to do! Of course, it goes without saying that our list was totally different before the accident and if Doc would ever walk again, it would change once more because there are some things that just are not feasible for us in his condition. Besides the activities that we do for fun though, there are the most important things on the list....like being kinder, helping someone when you can, spreading some of what we have experienced to make life better for someone else, in short, just making life better for others and in return, for ourselves! It is funny how that works....no matter how much goodness you give away, it always seems like it comes back tenfold! You have to stop and think that the things that really count are having people that love you. People that are going to care that you are gone! People that will remember you with a smile and a laugh and think what a special person you were!

Speaking of people that have gone that we remember with a smile...today is the year anniversary since we lost a friend and earlier this week another great friend was buried. It is nice to be able to remember both of them with a smile!

One of the highlights this month for Doc was being invited to share some of our experiences with the health related classes at the

Moberly Vo-Tech facility. It is amazing at how many good and bad stories we have regarding healthcare. It was good to share some of the situations so that if any of these young people pursue something in the field of health care, it might make a difference! They in turn, sent thank you cards expressing what they gained through the experience and I cannot tell you how precious each of those cards were to Doc & me!

We took a Saturday to visit our daughter in St. Joe, MO, and while she stayed with her dad, I got my hair fixed (Doc didn't plan that Saturday). It always feels good to have the gray gone! Then we played some cards and the guys started out hot but in the end, that gals were victorious! Doc has really been struggling at cards lately but I do have to say that a friend, Lori, came for a visit and between Doc & Lori, they managed to come out on top during our card playing that night! Before he will let me send this out, he will probably insist that I recognize there were one or two other times too! All I will say is that if his old card playing buddies want to come and win some money off him, now might be a good time!

Beside these activities, we fit in a little shopping, a lot of basketball, and spent a lot of our time just reading and visiting with some quiet nights at home in front of the fire. It was so cold and there were nights that neither of us wanted to be anywhere else!

February looks to be a little busier than our January was. We start off the 1st weekend with Doc watching the Superbowl. I have to say that if there were a team in it from closer to home, it might excite me a little more but I don't even have to be a football fan to know we had nothing to cheer about. From either side of our state! What is worth celebrating is that it will be the last football game of the season! Yippee! We have several basketball games scheduled on the calendar, some upcoming birthdays to celebrate with family and friends, a Martina McBride concert, and whatever else Doc can come up with! Also, Doc is talking to the youth group at our church on the 10th and I think if you asked him, he would probably rank that above all else. We always feel like it is the right thing to do when we are sharing our story. Like that is our purpose! Everyone should have a purpose and pursue it! That is why we were created!

Our only other decision this month might involve Porky! He currently has over 61,000 miles on him and although he plugs along and does a good job for us, I worry about the miles. I keep thinking that he is probably going to have troubles while I am driving him and I cringe at the thought of being out with Doc along the highway and having to figure out what to do. That being said though, he belongs to us and seems to be in decent shape. However, we have a chance to pick up another van that is already decked out to our needs and only has 1,000 miles. It is still 5 years old but with those low miles, I think I would have several years to drive it! I think we are going to get to look at it in the near future and then we have to make a decision on whether to make that investment. I think we are leaning toward doing it because we are always on the road and this opportunity doesn't pop up very often! Again, some things are just placed in your lap and you feel they happened for a reason. One wonders at what name Doc will come up with for this van if we get it!

As always, I end this update with a special thanks to everyone that helped in any way to make our January a little better! For all the prayers that were said for us and for all the kind deeds that so many of you did! As I have written in past February updates, Valentine's Day is a day of expressing all kinds of love and we love each of you! May all of you have a very blessed February until we write again!

Your Friends,
Cindy and Doc

February 2008

I have to warn you right up front that we had a lot going on this month! We spent a bunch of it with some friends on some outings and then some of the outings we just went solo, made a few memories and enjoyed each other! We fit in some card games, a movie, and a few basketball games. We also battled a bunch of problems.

Lenten season started early this year so it hardly seemed like I had put away our Christmas stuff until we were already looking at Easter around the corner. In the middle of all of that was Valentine's Day! I like to try and decorate the house for the season but somehow, this year, I had snowmen, pink bears, green shamrock stuff, and rabbits all out at the same time! It was interesting to say that least! We both really enjoy lent though. It is a season of reflecting on our lives and doing something about improving it! It seems like no matter how hard you work at your faith life, you will always be able to find ways to improve it. Doc and I have spent the first part of lent making some sacrifices so that as we struggle through them, it reminds us of the sacrifice that Jesus made for us! We also have tried hard to attend the Friday night Lenten suppers at our church which features a guest speaker sharing the faith in their lives. We also found a book that we both thought would be inspirational to read and we read a chapter each night out of that and we should be done around Easter. All of the things that we are doing during the season of Lent will only make the arrival of Easter more special. It is wonderful to have that time of reflection each year!

I had a bunch written here about our wheelchair experiences this month but Doc said it sounded like I was on my soapbox. I know that I can get on those but if anyone ever deserved it, this company does but I decided that Doc was right and not everyone needed to know all the exasperating details. So I will shorten this by saying after prodding for a year, they finally did come back to help fix some things that they had not done correctly in February of last year. Then in the process of fixing those, they broke some other things. Some of them were in the control box and it caused Doc not to be able to do his own weight shifts and caused some hiccups in the driving controls. They are trying to tell us that it is just a coincidence that some things quit working while they were working on it but as many of you know, we don't believe in coincidences! Those functions are fairly critical to us and I am hoping that they come back soon and address those issues but I have already been calling for 2 weeks and I am still waiting on a follow up date. While they were here, they also suggested that we make several new changes. After our last experience though, I am jumping right in the middle of it and giving a yeah or nay on everything! It would be nice to think that you could call someone and just turn over your problems to them in a particular area and know that they are taken care of but it doesn't work that way and we found that out the hard way. But you know what they say, once, shame on you, twice, shame on me!

We had to deal with some home health care issues this month. Insurance pays for one 4 hour nursing visit a week and that is the only time during the week that I can actually leave for work as soon as Doc is in the shower. Well, the nurse that we have had for awhile quit and now they are searching to find us another one and when they do, we have to go through the whole training cycle again. BUT they say when a door closes, a window opens somewhere so in the end, we have the opportunity to meet another caregiver and probably another friend!

Our ups and downs this month continued with our supply situation and Medicare. The downs were that it seemed like they were calling me regularly to let me know that Medicare had added another supply to their limited or denial list. We continue to battle that by having doctor's letters of appeal submitted and we continue to try to visit specialists to prove that we are doing all we can to limit the needs of the supplies! In the meantime, the good news was that Doc's insurance, which originally denied the supplies when Medicare took over, have changed their minds and are going to cover them. At least until December, when will lose Doc's insurance and have to become acquainted with a new insurance provider. BUT no sense crossing any bridges before we have to! I will save that for another day! I am just glad that we have a few months to fight Medicare and possibly get them to give in a little! Actually, a case worker associated with Senator Bond's office called me and offered me some help and some advice so I am in the process of following up on that. Doc just smiles to think how our situation and our problems get around and who is next going to call and offer a helping hand just when we need it!

But seriously, we are thankful to Jana and to Chloe who are trying to help us....(well, to Senator Bond too but you know what they say about women working behind the man!) hehe....

It is strange at how a light bulb went off in our heads this month! A few months ago, when we saw the writing on the wall as far as what the future held financially and medically for our situation, we were referred to a social worker to see what our options were for some home health care and other types of support that Medicare doesn't cover. What we were told was that we could leave Doc homebound or put him in a nursing home and he would qualify for more aid. That wasn't an option because homebound means a doctor visit and one trip to church a week. No fishing, no hiking, no dancing, no shopping, no movies...everything that makes up the pleasures in life were to be denied him! So on to option 2: Lie about being homebound and hope you aren't caught. Hmmmm, NO! Option 3? Cheat...move all our assets into someone else's name and pretend we are broke. Hmmmmm, NO! Option 4? Believe it or not, this is the most commonly accepted option from what we under-stand and that is that I should divorce Doc and take him for what he is worth and leave him desolate. Again, hmmmmmmmmm, NO! A resounding no actually! They went on to tell us that we could still live together and in our hearts we would still be married but the legal system would recognize the separation and there would be more aid available to Doc and I would be safeguarded from losing everything that I had too! Let's just say no more on that and move on to our final option. Option 5? Continue on as we are knowing that when insurance runs out and our savings run out, we would be required to relinquish every thing we have of value (even our household items, artwork and unused Cardinal tickets-if you can even imagine Doc giving those up!)...although they are gracious enough to allow us to keep the house and a vehicle....and then when we are completely worth zero, Medicaid will kick in and start paying for home health (around the clock even if needed!) and almost all our other needs! That isn't even an option to choose but one that will simply befall us if we don't choose one of the other. At first, it was devastating to think how low we would go before this was all over but since then I have had a change of heart! Even though it might be hard (well, probably no might about it!), it is better to be able to hold our heads up and know that we did not choose the options that were immoral to us and that we did everything that was in our power to pay our way and do what was right. The social worker told us that if it meant anything to us at all, he admired us and the fact that we weren't taking any of the options that he proposed and that we were actually the first persons that he had met in our condition that had survived for 3 years without already succumbing to the Medicaid system or one of the options listed above. I have to credit that to Doc's employment mostly! Mine a little too in that I am able to make a paycheck every month still, my employer continues to be patient with me and allows me flexibility to do what I have to do and to those that we have found that sit with Doc each day so I can go to work. BUT, most of the credit goes to the excellent benefit plan that AECI has and to the extended insurance coverage that has lasted us these 3 years, with one more to go! AND to the fellow employees at AECI that make payroll deductions each pay period that covers all of the home health costs associated with getting him out of bed and ready for each day! For all of this we give God thanks every night!

Now, the light bulb part! We were asked to share our story with the youth group in our church one Sunday evening and instead of just the youth group staying after services to listen to us, the entire congregation stayed after. As always, God gives us the words to stand up there and say what is on our hearts and it is never difficult to see his message. This particular night, during services we read the story of how the devil tempted Jesus in so many different ways and how Jesus refused to give in to that temptation. As we began to share our story that night, it became clear to us that we had been down a similar road. As we shared about how we came to be in our situation and then where we were with it now, we saw that we had been tempted. It didn't seem like temptations at the time because the choices were never anything that we would have considered! But all of those options would have made life easier for us IF we could have done them. So without knowing it, we had been tempted and by the grace of God and in thanksgiving to our parents for raising us in such a way to know these things were wrong, we were able to dismiss them as unfeasible options. Amazing, isn't it? So now that we know we made it past that milestone, it is easy to put our needs into the lap of God and say take them away! I know that no matter what the future holds, it will be ok! Man is not going to be the one that ever has the answers to anything, while there is one that has the answers to everything! I actually wrote this update and then I am inserting this next part. I was sitting in church and thinking about all the battles that I have been fighting and asking for some words of wisdom. So I closed my bible, shut my eyes, opened it at random, pointed to a spot on the page, and opened my eyes....don't tell me the grace of God wasn't listening to me because I was pointing to Jeremiah, Chapter 17, verses 5-11. (now that I wrote that, I will see how many of you look it up! If you do, you will smile!) They say your faith grows in baby steps and you learn what you can comprehend little by little! Again, we have learnt a great lesson this month! One that caused me tears when I was worrying about it and now brings a smile to my face to know that I have nothing to worry about!

We laugh sometimes when our kids are dating and they have their "one month" anniversary and then their "two month" anniversary and so on.....I do have to admit though that Doc and I have always thought the anniversary of our engagement is as important as the anniversary of our marriage. (Actually, I think Doc has always been better at remembering that date than any other!) I think it is because we both made the commitment to spend the rest of our lives together on the day he asked me and I accepted. Or maybe he just remembers it because he was so nervous. I laugh to remember how he used to ask me, "IF I were to ask you to marry me now, would you say yes? Not that I'm asking for real..." and I would usually say no because I really wasn't sure yet. So time went by and then I think he finally mustered up the courage to ask for real and this time, I was sure. The ceremony made it official and our lives together started on that date but when we said yes to each other and he put that first ring on my finger, our future together started right then! So this month, we celebrated 29 years since that day! It was a great day!

We were able to make a weekend trip to Springfield and revisited the Redeemer Lutheran Church that we once share our story with. That was a special weekend for us and we truly felt we were where God wanted us to be that day! It was like gathering with old friends and they made us feel so welcomed! We also squeezed in some special time with Matthew, our nephew, who is a senior at a college down there! He works at Bass Pro so we got to go shopping with him, which Doc especially loved! Then he joined us for some supper and gave me a helping hand in putting Doc to bed. Our challenge was getting in and out of the van in a drenching rainstorm. I was just glad it wasn't ice or snow! We still have another church to visit in Springfield and several more in our area to revisit but we will get to all of them before we are done.

I do have a monkey story this month. It happened on our way to Springfield. There is an antique mall about ½ way to Springfield that Doc & I enjoy looking around in as it is a good stop to break up the trip. I unloaded Doc and was entering the shop when I saw this really neat pink and black display of boxes/bags & stuffed animals sitting in front the cashier area. I made a comment about how creative it was. I turn around and see Doc heading straight for it. I am thinking, "wow, he is going to check that out…I didn't think anything like that would interest him….maybe he is just trying to make these ladies that run this shop feel good…" but he isn't stopping! He gets closer and closer and right before we crash, I hear him say, "Cindy, I can't stop." Luckily, he hit the cashier counter at a very slow pace and didn't do any damage and managed to miss all of the display, if only by inches! There is a red beam that is supposed to stop his chair when the plain is broken but once again, I think it all goes back to the problem we are having with the controls but that did not work. I threw the clutches off and that stopped the chair but the control box was still grinding like it was in forward motion so I shut the box off and rebooted it up. That seemed to work and I am not sure what happened but that was the only time we had that experience. I can only imagine how those ladies were cringing to think we were going to walk around their shop of numerous antiques and glassware! Hehe! Actually, I was the one cringing because we would pay the price if that chair acted up again! But it didn't…the monkey must have jumped back into his position and stayed put! I am glad that it hasn't happened since but I have to tell you that I am a little concerned about that too. I made sure the wheelchair support person heard about it because I kept thinking what if that had happened as we were heading out on a dock to fish, or off the ramp of the van, or crossing a busy city street….what a horrible thought!

Buck has been relatively well behaved this month! Not perfect, mind you, but better! He did his share of "puppy" no-no's but all in all, he wasn't a bad puppy this month! He is just a like a kid...if it is too quiet for too long, you know there is trouble. If you find him hiding under the kitchen table with an innocent look on his face, you know there is trouble. The scary part is when you go to look for it and you don't know what it is that you are going to find! I always find it though!

It also looks like Porky is going to stay in the family for awhile longer. We checked out the other van and it was very nice but a little out of our price range. While we were asking around on its value though we found out that they give Porky at least 175,000 miles of reliable mileage so at only 61,000 he has a ton left in him! That was good to know because I was afraid we were only a year or two away from having to put Porky out to pasture but that was not the case. So unless we find something better than Porky and it is a bargain, we will stick it out with what we have for awhile!

Our highlight for entertainment this month would have to be the Martina McBride outing, as we called it! Ellen and I gave Howard and Doc a day out as a Christmas gift. So we started the day with a movie, made a short stop in the mall (Gals checked out Penny's and the guys bought some tools at Sears-although the tool Doc bought was a sander that I wanted), went out to eat some Italian food and then to the Martina McBride concert. What a wonderful time we had but then when you are with special friends, you can have a wonderful time no matter what you are doing!

I always save the best for last! And that is each of you! Thanks for the continued prayers, cards, support, e-mails, visits, ect....every little thing means so much to us and some of the things that many of you do aren't so "little". We had a couple of amazing things happen this month that went down in my journal and will one day go into a book because that is what our life is right now....one amazing story after another. As Easter is fast approaching, we pray that each of you is blessed with a time of reflection too and that you are able to celebrate the feast of Easter with all that it stands for!

Your Friends,
Cindy and Doc

March 2008

I thought about making up some elaborate story and leave you all with your mouths hanging open and then end it with April Fools but I didn't do it! I think I just couldn't decide on which story to use! Hehe! I had several creative ideas! Plus it wouldn't work if some of you don't read this on April 1st! So I will just start with the highlight of this month and for us it had to be Easter! We had some special services with some special music at church and it was just a special holiday season for Doc & I both. Our faith is the most important thing to each of us and having such a special opportunity to celebrate it is very heart warming.

Now just so you know how special Easter was to us, the second most exciting thing this month was watching our local high school girl's basketball team make the final four in state playoff. That is a pretty spectacular thing to come in 2nd! They won their semi-final game in a double overtime and played the next day for the championship. The semi-final game was played on a Thursday morning and I did not feel like I could take 2 days of vacation for the playoffs so I told Doc we could listen to it on the radio but unknown to me, he had made arrangements with our daughter that happened to be off that day to load him in Porky and drive him Our congratulations still go down to the games. He was pretty sneaky about it but it worked! Then I was off on Friday and we got to go down and cheer them on to first place. It was so exciting and they are such a fine group of young women and we have special feelings for many of them. Two of them are our nieces and we had a special right to be especially proud of them! They also made history because it is the first time in history that a school has managed to claim the state title in softball and basketball in the same year! So Doc bought a picture of the team while we were at the playoffs and then when they had an assembly to recognize the team, he managed to get all their signatures on the mat and it is framed in our living room! Our congratulations still go out to each of them!

We shared several nights this month with various friends, playing cards, sharing a meal and/or watching movies and it is always so much fun to make memories. It also makes us feel extremely blessed to have so many wonderful friends to make those memories with! There is no way to express how much these friendships mean to us but every single one of them mean the world to us!

Doc had the opportunity to share part of his experience with a group that were being baptized over the Easter weekend and I think that would rank up there in what was important to us also. Doc has said many times that it feels so right when we are sharing some of the wonderful things that have happened to us in the past 3 and a half years. So it was also a blessing to us to be invited to fill in on a Sunday afternoon at Ravenwood Assistant Living residence also and share our story once again. Doc & I wondered how we would share anything with those that have lived much longer than us but in the end, we all learned something from each other and it was being in the place where we knew we were supposed to be. I had to laugh though because several of the older women came up to me to tell me that it was a shame that something like this would happen to someone so handsome…I guess it might have been better if Darwin was ugly? Hehe! We both got a chuckle out of that and I was glad to get out of there with him still belonging to me! It looks like there might be a couple of future opportunities that haven't quite been set up yet but when the dates are established, I haven't forgotten that some of you have asked me to contact you to let me know when we are next sharing our story. I will be letting you know if/when something comes up.

We were also able to revisit one of the churches that we had visited just to say hi and listen to their message. It is always so good to gather again with those that shared our story with simply to share their worship. We are trying to do that at least once a month. I think this month we are planning on heading back to Springfield and revisiting the South Gate Baptist Church just to say hi and share their services. So if we visited your church and haven't come back yet, we plan to.

We had a new nurse start this month and hopefully, she will work out. It isn't easy on her because insurance only covers 4 hours of care a week so she comes once a week and it is hard to train someone to be comfortable to do everything that Doc needs done when you only have them once a week and for only 4 hours. I have to remember to be patient because I have been doing it for a long time and I can forget how much there is to remember.

The wheelchair didn't act up anymore so I don't have anymore monkey stories to share this month, thank goodness! He is still riding in the orange chariot and even though they said they would be contacting us to discuss replacing it with a Cardinal red chair, it hasn't happened yet. As long as the orange machine continues to work like it is though, it is almost hard to want to take a chance on a newer machine working as well.

Even Buck and Porky have both been well behaved this month. There just aren't any exciting stories to share about either one. Porky is getting us to and from where we need to go and Buck continues to improve with age even though he has a way to go to be a "good" dog! He continues to give Doc's face several wet slurpies every morning when he wakes up and again right before he goes to sleep. It has become a habit with Buck and it is funny at how he doesn't start his day or end it without getting those wet licks in! You can tell he loves Doc!

We also were able to attend the National Wild Turkey Federation banquet and auction this month. We have been trying to get to one of those since Doc has returned home and this is the first year that it has worked out for us to be able to do that. It was also exciting because Doc is a huge fan of Terry Redlin and he has officially retired and is not able to sign prints anymore. He had always been commissioned to paint a picture and sign a limited edition of them for this cause. After they were printed and signed the plate was broken and the particular print for that year would not be available anymore. Because of the retirement this was the last available opportunity for Doc to bid on one. It so happened that he won the bid and he brought home his new print. Even though our living room wall seems to be full of Doc's many treasures, he found a place to hang his newest addition to his collection. It was a fun evening and we look forward to attending the next one.

Doc is excited about this coming month because he has several big plans! First, he has 2 Cardinal games coming up. This is opening day you know! He has the first game coming up this Sunday and we have our son and another young man that we consider to be like a son, joining us and I cannot wait! For the game or the time with them! Then the last Saturday of the month, we have tickets and our son and his wife are going to join us and that will be a great day too! Whenever we have an opportunity to share time with our kids, it is a good day. We never took any of those days when they were growing up and we would have them around the house all the time for granted because we knew they would spread their wings someday and be independent. That was our goal for them... to be able to survive without us....but we miss them as much as we thought we would! The years you are raising your kids and you are a "family" have to be the best years of a persons' life and they just seem to go by so quickly! The second thing that he is looking forward to is the "F" word...FISHING! The fishing pole is about to be worked out again. As soon as the weather and the ground around the ponds allow it, we will be out and catching fish. He has already been talking to some friends that have ponds they share with him about what the fishing is going to be like this year!

Doc continues to be healthy and we give thanks each night that we have avoided the flu that seems to be hitting everyone hard around this area! It is so much easier to deal with Doc's needs when he feels good. When he sits in the chair all day and cannot do anything on top of not feeling good, it can weigh on both of us but when he sits in the chair but feels good, we don't let life slow us down at all. He can keep me busy just trying to keep him busy!

I usually have a verse or a saying that comes to me when I am going through the month to refer to but this month I don't. We have just enjoyed each day and have celebrated that we were able to greet each morning with an opportunity to make something special out of each one. We continue to give thanks for every blessing that we have, and we have many! We want to tell each of you that remembered us in prayer, sent a card or an e-mail message to say hi, stopped by for a visit, or did any type of favor for us this month thank you! A big thank you!

This coming month looks like it is going to be a good one and I cannot wait for each weekend to get here to enjoy those moments with Doc! And you know the highlight of it all has to be that the Cardinals are back on the field!

Your Friends,
Cindy and Doc

PS: after I read this to Doc he wanted me to add one thing…GO MEMPHIS… that was his pick in the NCAA men's basketball bracket!

April 2008

This was almost like a month of mini-vacations. Each weekend was full of fun and exciting stuff to do. I filled the weeks up with work, housework, mowing (yes, this year I am going to attempt to keep our own yard up with the help of our daughter and the new mower that Doc's co-workers got for him) & laundry and tried to free up the weekends to enjoy the spring weather & my time with Doc!

Our first weekend started with a Bluegrass concert that was held in Moberly that featured Doc's favorite bluegrass band. I have to admit that I really like them too. Doc would probably tell you that bluegrass is his favorite music (which scares his kids to death!) but he is wearing me down to the point that I appreciate it also. It is still not my favorite form of music but I find it entertaining and I really find it entertaining to watch him enjoying it! Doc often jokes "that if you aren't tapping your feet to that kind of music, you must be paralyzed!"

The next day we were out on the town to do some shopping (and yes, he traded some Bass Pro time for some of my type of shopping), went to see the new movie Leatherheads (which we both found entertaining), and then we spent some time in church and finally finished it off with supper. I didn't realize Starbucks had sandwiches but Doc must have been thinking about how to get his cappuccino because by the time we got out of church he had it all planned out. We headed over to Barnes and Noble where they have a Starbucks in the back of the store, ordered a sandwich and drinks and proceeded to have a nice quiet supper. Doc has to really chew and concentrate on eating so just taking 5 bites can take him up to an hour to eat. I absolutely love to read but haven't had much opportunity for that habit for a long time. So this was a treat. I bought a book and sat back to enjoy it while Doc ate and we both had a wonderful hour of peace. I am pretty sure that experience will be on our "repeat again" list!

Then we ended up the weekend with a trip to our first 2008 Cardinal game. Last year I think we were 8 for 9 in wins so I was afraid that the law of averages might leave us at the losing games this year but the first one was a success! It was picture perfect sunny day in the 70 degree range! It felt good to be part of the sea of red and have a hot dog while we cheered the Cardinals on to victory! Gas was much higher than last year but at least the parking stayed the same. I have seen Doc & I change some of our habits with the gas prices going up but the only concession with regards to the Cardinal games was to back off a couple of them that we had planned to go to. We will still hit the remaining games that were part of the package that we got and I rolled the free tickets we won at the Wild Turkey Federation banquet into a weekend plan with one of those games we already had in the package so we would only have one trip back to St. Louis. So where we would have usually picked out a couple of the promotion games we wanted, we decided not to. So now we can start tracking 2008…we started out 1 for 1! By the way, Doc got to meet one of his favorite Cardinal characters in our first visit this year and I have attached that picture plus another one of Doc at the game!

The second weekend had us journeying to Jefferson City for a church activity, celebrating a friends 50th birthday (which is almost right around the corner for Doc and I—although he is 11 months and 21 days older than me so he will hit that mark first! We had a great time celebrating that 50 mark with Doris oops, did I write her name?! Her husband surprised her with dinner in town with her friends and then a barn dance back at their place. They have a heated barn with a concrete floor so we had plenty of room to move. The band played a few songs and then Doc must have had his wheels tapping because soon he was heading in my direction asking for a dance. We did the first dance solo as no one else was dancing yet but soon there was a large group out there on the floor! Doc told one of the co-conspirators in getting the dancing started that "now we have a party!" Before we knew it the clock was pushing midnight and we decided to leave but the party was still going strong! It was a little difficult to roll out of bed to get to church on time the next morning but we made it..barely…but we did! Then we finished the weekend with some dear friends coming over to play some cards and share supper.

The third weekend found us back in the Springfield area to revisit a church family that we had spoken with to share some time with them. Of course, that meant more visiting and another enjoyable outing! Plus we took our nephews to Lamberts while we were down there and that is a GREAT place to eat if you haven't ever tried it. It is known as the home of thrown rolls because that is how you get your rolls…they toss them across the room in a game of catch… and they are worth catching! For those of you that have eaten there, I know your mouths are watering just to think of it! Doc ate more there than I have seen him eat in awhile but then everyone that eats there does that!

We finally finished the month off like we started it. We were back in St. Louis at another Cardinal game on another picture per-fect day. This time Adam and Laura (our son and daughter in law) joined us and it was another sunny but cool day. Doc actually does better in cool weather though so I am enjoying it before we get to those scorchers! Our streak stayed in-tact so now our record is 2 for 2! Our only blemish this day was that Porky started to act up and then the check engine light came on…just as we were in the middle of downtown St. Louis. After Doc tried to blame the monkey, he said not to worry about it because it was only a warning light. We would just need to get it fixed when we got home. So I didn't worry (but I did pray because I had no idea what I would have done with a broken van in downtown St. Louis or beside I-70!) and he was right. We made it home safe and sound. I actually took Porky in today to get him all fixed up and they said he just needed a good tune up and some minor things…(I can't say that I understood it all but they didn't say any words like transmission or anything so I was happy).

I am just glad he is ready to go again because May is full of travel too!

All in all, it seemed like we were too busy enjoying life to spend much time worrying about it! We still had wheelchair issues, home health issues, prescription issues, and the medicare supply issues are still not resolved. All of that being said though, we just set those problems on the back burner and worked through what we had to and decided that we would tackle the rest of them some other day.

Oh yeah, speaking of tackle…..well probably not the same tackle but that is the beauty of the English language…one word can lead you to a totally different thought….you put that vocabulary and my brain together and you usually can end up anywhere! But this time we end up by the edge of a pond because fishing weather is upon us! So this time I am talking about the tackle in tackle boxes! Doc is savoring every cast! I think this summer is going to be a good one because for the past 2 summers, Doc has had to spend about 1/3 of the summer in the hospital and this year, (knock on my head), with a little luck, he will be able to enjoy the entire season! We only managed to fit in one fishing outing but the weather has severely limited us. I am sure that will change shortly!

Buck is as fun as he ever was and even though May is hardly here yet, I have almost given up thinking about having any flowers and/or yard decorations. (although Doc is already telling me he is making a trip to town before Mother's Day to buy me a hanging basket for the front porch because he likes the way it attracts his hummingbirds…hmmmm…how does that work?—sorta kills two birds with one stone, he buys flowers for his wife and gets what he wants all at the same time! He is a smart man!) Anyway, back to Buck…he is really good about leaving the stuff in our house alone that he knows he isn't supposed to touch but for some reason he thinks he has free reign in the outdoors! All my sidewalk lights, pots of flowers and rock garden beauties have fallen into Buck's mouth! I continue to try and make him understand that those things are no-no's but he hasn't quite comprehended that yet! The more I yell at him, the faster his tail wags! Now that spring has arrived, he loves it outdoors! You can tell by our yard too! I don't know where he even finds everything he drags into it but I think the neighbors are thinking if they have some trash, they can set it out in their yards and Doc's dog will come by and drag it to the Blackmore house! We have everything from cans & bottles to skeletons & bones! I even found him playing with a dead box turtle the other day! Every once in awhile he will want back in the house for a nap so he just jumps up on the front door and looks through the window on the top of the door and barks. He just stays like that until you open the door. It is funny to walk around the corner of the hall and see a dog staring at you through the front door window! You can imagine with all the rain that we have had what our front door looks like. I really do clean the front door and the yard frequently but if you visit us, you won't believe that! Buck continues to tuck Doc in every bedtime and wake him up every morning and I managed to snap some pictures of that ritual which I thought you would enjoy too. It isn't anything that I would enjoy at all but for some strange reason, Doc actually likes it (in small doses!).

It seems like May is always a crazy month with the calendar full of events and this May is no exception. We have some special kids graduating that we are pretty proud of and plan on helping them celebrate. We have our daughter's birthday and our anniversary this month so those are both worth celebrating too. We are also going to share some of our "blessings" with a local church that has a congregation that are very dear to us so we are really looking forward to that! I am also excited because there are about 4 outings that I get every year just for me and one of them is our company golf tournament and that is coming up this month. Finally, we decided that instead of taking one long vacation, we were going to break it up into several long weekends. As Silver Dollar City, in Branson, MO, is having their annual bluegrass/bbq festival in May, we decided that might be worth a trip down there. So we bought season tickets and are making a 5 day weekend out of Memorial Day. I think Doc will be there for the music and I will be there for the BBQ! Although I am sure that we will both enjoy a little of both! I can guarantee you that even if the toes aren't moving, his spirit will be! With the purchase of season tickets, we can take in some of their other festivals throughout the year and make some relatively inexpensive outings as the season tickets were almost the same price as a day pass.

Doc feels better than he has in a long time and thanks to our Dr Ripley from Colorado and our family doctor here, we finally resolved some of his night spasm issues and have actually started sleeping more and we are both feeling better for that! He still does have some sores that I continue to have to fight but even those are slowly (and I mean slowly!) going in the right direction. It is good to see them closing up instead of getting larger! As I have written before, Doc really believes in quality of life over quantity and for the past few months, he is living it. His sense of humor is evident in almost every conversation that I have with him. His smile and his faith continue to inspire and amaze me! Maybe that is why we have those storms in our lifes....to make the flowers that grow as a result of them so beautiful!

As always, in conclusion, we give thanks to every one of you once more for the prayers, cards, visits and special things that so many of you do! I read something this month that stuck with me so I am going to share it. "Life isn't about waiting for the storms to pass. It's about learning to dance in the rain." I hope that all of the April showers bring out the May flowers for each of you and that they are blooming with extra special color this year and that if you are having a "storm" in your life right now, that you can figure out how to dance in the rain!

Your Friends,
Cindy and Doc

PS: A special prayer goes out to all mothers and mothers-to-be from us as this is the month to remember those that are so dear to us!!!

Doc with Fredbird

Doc Concentrating on Cardinal Game

Buck Putting Doc to Bed

Buck Giving Doc Smooches

Buck

Buck Again

May 2008

Last month was similar to mini-vacations but this month it actually was. It seemed like I was loading and unloading Porky all month long!

We were constantly fighting the wet weather but it always seemed to work out when it came time to load and unload so it wasn't a major hurdle as far as Doc was concerned. I was just very tired of driving in the rain …I have enough practice at that! We had lots of time to visit with friends and family and make some memories because a big part of the month consisted of graduations. Some were high school and some were college but they were all equally important. Some were close enough to fit in more than one in a day and others were out of town and we had to make an over-nighter out it.

We actually spent our anniversary celebrating graduations and then speaking at a banquet at a local church. It was a good way to spend our anniversary because both those activities were very important to us. We did manage to squeeze in an anniversary breakfast at Cracker Barrel and I think it was the first time we celebrated with a breakfast so it ended up being something special! Anytime Doc gets coffee with his meal, he thinks it is a special event! I ended up breaking down and ordering some Cardinal tickets for Doc for our anniversary so he ended up getting to go to another game in May after all. Something he didn't mind at all! Hehe!

Then we spent a couple of days in Springfield attending our nephew's college graduation. That was a fun family time and we had a beautiful day to share a picnic at the park. I was glad that my brother happened to notice that my back tires had metal shavings showing. I had noticed that they were looking a little bald when they were on the front so I took the van to the tire shop and they told me that if I moved them to the back they thought they would be ok but they weren't. A week later, I have metal showing and they actually had broken belts. So I had to stop and get 2 new tires before we headed home but with a trip to St. Louis and Branson rapidly approaching, I was glad to know my tires were good!

So off we were to St. Louis for another game. This time Porky behaved, the weather was beautiful, and the Cardinals won again so now our streak is 3 for 3 in wins this year! I think one of us must be a lucky charm for them because in the past 2 years, our win record is 12 for 13. Our next scheduled game is going to be July 5th. I am pretty sure I will be battling the heat in that one! These spring games have been nice because I haven't had to worry much about Doc's temperature getting away from me.

We had some problems with the headrest but the seating and mobility service was very helpful in getting the problems resolved before Doc had to take any long trips in the van with his head bopping around. If I didn't know how horrible it is, it is almost funny to look in the review mirror and see my bobblehead Doc sitting behind me! I am glad that we were able to resolve that problem.

Then we had to start over again with our home health services (AGAIN!). We have a nurse that comes through the home health agency in Columbia, MO and she has been with us for a month now and she is working out well. She only comes one day a week but already she arrives ready to just start the day while I head to work. Our wrinkle happened in the health care that we get from our local home health agency for the rest of the week and unfortunately our "angel" there had to take an indefinite leave of absence so we were back to square one in getting someone trained to take over for her. She was one of those perfect persons for the job though so it is hard to replace her. We spent a couple of weeks training a new gal but then she quit so now we are waiting for another candidate. I am often tempted in just setting my alarm earlier and taking care of getting Doc up myself because it is much harder to deal with the problems of training and retraining than it is to just do it (as the Nike slogan goes!). Unfortunately, if I am the only one doing it though, I don't have a backup plan if I get sick or need a break so I keep plugging away at trying to make sure that someone else knows how to care for Doc if I cannot.

When we finally finished with all the graduations and scheduled activities, we decided to take a break from all our supply, equipment, and homecare issues and head off to Branson for a 5 day get-away. The weather forecast wasn't good but other than once again driving through some torrential rain, the weekend worked out well weather wise! We took in a few shows, did some shopping on the landing (mostly Bass-Pro, I might add-because it is fishing weather you know!), ate some awesome food, and enjoyed a couple of days at Silver Dollar City listening to some of our countries best Bluegrass music! One devastating storm passed through Silver Dollar City while we were there but we happened to be in an indoor theater where 3 hours of a youth bluegrass music concert was going on. By the time that was over, the crowds were gone, the sun was shining and it was a picture perfect evening so we went to the out-door country show that they had in an amphitheater. One of the best parts about our trip was meeting so many wonderful persons while we were out and about. We met a couple from Kansas that invited us to sit at their table for lunch one day and ended up visiting with them for 2 hours. Then the last day we were in Silver Dollar City we met a pastor from Arkansas and spent a good part of the day continually being seated by her in various shows so we became well acquainted by the end of the day. As we don't see anything as coincidental any-more, it wasn't strange to us that in a place with thousands of per-sons we would be constantly sitting by the same person show after show. Once again, we felt like even though we were on vacation, we were being used to inspire others as we were being inspired by their stories also!

We had a few wrinkles that I would blame on the monkey if I could figure out how. Porky's check engine light came on before we reached Branson and stayed on the entire trip but he ran well so I ignored it. Our cot in our room was not much better than a camping cot, at best, so it was challenging trying to turn Doc and dress him when the whole bed turned with him-especially when it was so low to the floor. I was afraid I was going to drop him on the floor but it was only a 5" drop so even if I had, I probably wouldn't have done damage...he told me not to worry about it because as long as it wasn't his head, he couldn't feel it anyway! Then on the last day, his compressor went out in his seat so the alarm starting sounding that the air wasn't circulating and no matter what I tried, I couldn't fix it. Of course, I didn't know it was the compressor at the time or I would have given up a lot faster than I did. I ended up taking Doc in and out of the chair several times and taking the cushion apart and trying to breathe just right when I would turn it back on but nothing worked....so Doc had to sit on a fairly flat cushion all the way home (which did not help his wounds) and I had to listen to the stupid beep, beep alarm! Then when I checked out, they told me I owed them extra money for the fridge that I had requested. I told them that I did not request a fridge and we had not had one in our room. It took a lot of convincing to convince her that we did not have one but I finally did it. Gracefully too, I might add...after my morning, I was really trying hard to stay nice because I didn't want to take my frustrating morning out on her but she was pushing me in that direction. Lucky for both of us, she finally gave in before I gave into the temptation to let it "blow". Next we get out on the highway and we go a few miles and the next thing I know, I am being pulled over by the highway patrol. He tells me that I was driving 82 mph and was too long in the left lane and had expired plates and that they weren't registered to Porky. Instead, they belonged to a BMW… now I would never want to hurt Porky's feelings BUT he is not a BMW! I had my cruise set on 73 so my running 82 really was a surprise to me. He told me that he saw I had new tires on the van and he thought they might have played into my speed (sorta like new tennis shoes on a two year old…they can make them run faster you know!). So after he checked my registration out and saw that I really had gotten my inspection and license plates done on time and that the plates did match my registration, he told me that he would check my driving record. If it was clear, he would let me go on a warning and ask me to go the license bureau and get things straightened out and set my cruise down a little. And it was so we were off once more! This time though for the first time all weekend, Porky's check engine light didn't come on…Doc said it was because he thought he was a BMW now! Hehe!

When we finally arrived home amidst all the beeping, I unloaded the van and got things squared away. I called the seat company and made arrangements to send the compressor back to them for service. Doc had to stay in bed today because the cushion dilemma but I made arrangements for them to overnight us a loaner that we can rent until Doc's is fixed and ready to go again. I will get that in the morning and be ready to go again. We talked about blessings at a church this month and so when Doc's seat was beeping all the way home from Branson, I just kept thinking that it was a blessing that it happened on the last day of vacation instead of the first. I just keep thinking that we all have good days and bad days and you have to make the most of whatever type of day you are having.

Getting Doc back into his chair before this weekend is going to be perfect timing because we finally have the new fishing pole designed, working and ready for tryout. (so for our friends at Craig Hospital, we finally do have a design done and ready to start manufacturing….yippee! It is so much improved; all the parts are available to purchase, the guts of it all is in a nicely enclosed unit and it is able to run off a standard battery without having to run a bunch of wires to different ones because it is all one standard votage!) Doc is going to put it to the test in the next few weekends and work out any kinks and then we will be ready to start manufacturing them and get them into the lifes of those that want to fish but don't have those hands and arms to do it! I can promise you that you can catch fish using your mouth! I have seen Doc do it many times!

I am attaching a few of pictures again this month. Those of you that can pull them up seemed to enjoy them. I think I am going to choose the one of Doc's smile as we won the Cardinal game we went to this month in the bottom of the ninth and then the one of Doc meeting the mom and dad of the family bluegrass band called Cherryholmes, which is probably the best bluegrass band we have ever heard. I also am including the trail that we tried to walk in Branson and as you can see, it is well under water. Then there is also a great picture of the sun stretching it's fingers from heaven to earth.

And finally, I thought you would get a kick out of Doc with the saloon gal! I can't leave him alone for a minute and he is making up with someone! I left him for about 10 minutes to run and get a back up battery from the van and by the time I got back he was on first name basis with an elderly lady named Joan who thought he was "gorgeous, beautiful, wonderful!" I think those straps on his chair are necessary for me to hold on to this man!

June looks a little slower than May although we all know that there will not be anything slow about it. I am sure that it is going to include a ton of fishing (maybe I will have some fishing pictures on the next e-mail) and he is working hard to get a date with one of our dear friends to go the horse races one Saturday night in Illinois. We have some friends celebrating their 50th wedding anniversary and we are looking forward to that! Finally our daughter has invited us their way for a bar-b-q one weekend so that will be fun to look forward to also! Of course she made sure to let me know what she would like us to bring and they just happen to be her favorite dishes.

In closing, we want to make sure say thanks for the continued prayers and deeds that so many of you do for us. It was easy to talk about blessings because you only have to look at the number of persons who want to be on the e-mailing list each month to see how very blessed we are! Stay safe during the summer activities and if you are traveling, safe travels!

Your Friends,

Cindy and Doc

PS: just for the record, we are still playing cards every week and Doc & his partners have had the crying towel (which is the prize for losing) for several weeks now. So much in fact, that it is almost worn out! I am sure I will pay the price of losing just for writing this but it is ok...it is worth it!

PSS: I have been tempted many times to stop boring everyone with our adventures but so many of you continue to ask for updates so I continue to put together these updates but if there is anyone that is totally tired of getting them, please just tell me and I will take your name off our distribution list!

Doc with Cardinal Victory

Doc with Cherryholmes

Branson Flood

Branson Sunset

Doc with Saloon Gal at Silver Dollar Cityv

June 2008

We are sooooo glad that summer is here! We always have so many things that we try to fit into the season while it lasts but it always goes too fast! It seems like you barely get the yard the way you want it to look before you are putting the yard furniture back in storage for winter! My daughter and I are keeping up with the yard (with just a little help from my neighbor because I am chicken to the do the banks by the road) and we are so thankful for the reliable mower that we have to help us! I also had some help in changing the oil and getting the mower ready for the season so I am thankful for that also (Keith)!

As I wrote last month, the new design of sip and puff fishing pole is done so you can guess what most of our month was spent doing....FISHING! Not that I mind....I like fishing myself so when I take Doc, I always take my pole too. What is funny is that I can have the same bait on my line as Doc has and yet he will be pulling in fish twice as fast as me....The good news is that the pole had a couple of small things that we are tweaking but all in all, it works excellent! We are now working on an option that allows a person with limited arm movement to use it with a joystick. That should not be a very long process and then they will be distributed to be used in the field! It is a beautiful design and is able to run off an ordinary battery that can be purchased about anywhere. The cart that was designed to support the assembly has wheels and a pocket for the battery so that transporting and storing it is very easy. It has a plate with a push pin that allows a very easy transition on the angle of the pole which is a great feature when changing your casting distance. I have attached a couple of fishing pictures....one of them is of us catching some catfish (the fish in the picture was caught by Doc) and the other one was Doc and our friend Howard giving a good attempt at trout fishing (however, none of us were successful that day)...trout is turning out to be challenge and Doc is now wanting to go back and actually spend a couple of nights so he can fish later in the evening. Of course, every good fisherman has an excuse on why they didn't catch anything and Doc's excuse was that we were trying to fish at the wrong time of day! As you can tell from the picture, the water was really high so that was my excuse! It was a picture perfect day though, we had a super picnic, and the temperature was great so even though we didn't catch any fish, I don't think any of us thought the day was wasted!

I hope all of you dads had a special Father's Day! Doc wanted to go fishing but it turned out to be a little stormy that day so we headed to Bass Pro to shop for fishing supplies instead. While we were there I had to play the hunting game for Doc. He loves to watch me go hunting on a video game that they have in the back. This time he wanted me to go moose hunting and lo and behold, I made him proud! By the time I was done, I was the new top hunter and my initials went on the machine as top hunter in several hunting sites. That was pretty exciting for me....now you have to know that the only hunting that I have ever done is with a plastic gun pointing at a make believe animal and that is all that I ever want to do! After we finished that adventure, we headed to Cracker Barrel because a new favorite of Doc's is their apple dumpling and cup of coffee. Plus, as a bonus, the Cardinals won that day!

We traveled north to Macon, MO, one evening with my mom to attend a country music show that they have up there on Saturday nights and we enjoyed the evening with her. They had a nice crowd and it was a pleasure to visit with the performers and to spend some fun time with my mom.

We spent one weekend traveling to St. Joe, MO, to visit with our daughter and son-in-law. They had a bar-b-q and we brought some fixings to go with it. It was another beautiful day and was perfect for a road trip. Luckily it was last weekend and not this weekend because now that highway is flooded and we would not have made it through! Some friends of ours, Howard and Ellen, rode along and we spent the day playing cards and yard golf. And we had some good food as Joey is a great chef at the grill!

We are still wrestling with our supply issues and it seems like we just make one step forward and then we are taking 2 steps back. I don't stress about stuff like that anymore because somehow it always works out....you just have to stay in the fight and not give up. Sometimes I feel like waving the white flag and giving in but then somehow, I find the fight to continue. It only takes one look at Doc's face when we are doing what we consider "real" living to wonder why anyone associated with our medical world would want to squash that. We are so fortunate that our doctor supports our activities and has stood behind us in all the issues. He is a special person and we have a great respect for him!

Speaking of the medical world, you cannot even imagine what our home health services were like this month. It was a crazy thing! Once again, we just got another aid almost trained and on the day that she was to be signed off to actually do the work, she quit. So they had a back up training with her and they called and said that she would be coming instead. So I got up and got ready for work and when it got to be later than normal for her to arrive, I gave them a call and they told me they had made a mistake in telling me she was coming. They actually sent her somewhere else and they had no one else to send me to even train so until they hire someone, they were sorry but they couldn't support us. So I had to take off my good clothes and put on some scrubs so I could get Doc ready for the day. About 10 minutes after I got him in the shower, our phone rang and it was the 2nd health agency that we use out of Columbia, MO that insurance had been helping with. They had been sending out a nurse on Thursday mornings for 4 hours. They were calling to tell me that our insurance had contacted them to tell them that they had been paying in error and while they weren't going to ask for anything back, they weren't going to continue to pay and that they actually were denying the open claims from October, 2007 on....so that meant they were suspending our care and asking how we were going to pay that balance. Then about 5 minutes later, the phone rang again, and once again it was our local health agency and the nurse that comes out once a month to change the catheter was sick and would not be available. So within 15 or 20 minutes, before 8:30 in the morning, we had lost all our morning support! How crazy is that? I felt like it was pick on Cindy day and I hadn't made it out of the bedroom yet! So now I am talking to our case worker with insurance trying to determine what happened because I only employed the group out of Columbia because I had pre-approved the services with insurance. She is working hard trying to figure it out for us. I told her I would like to continue to receive this service but even more importantly, I didn't think it was right to discontinue something as of 9 months ago....Hopefully, she will be able to help. She is great case worker and we are blessed to have her. Doc is back to only having me as a morning option and once again, my employer is patiently working with me. I pray that they will be able to hire someone that will stick it out and we will be able to hire assistance again soon. It isn't the work of doing it every morning that scares me but the fact that in an emergency, no one else would be trained to help Doc. I want the security of a back up plan so Doc is not stranded if something would happen to me or if I needed a morning off.

Our license bureau was very helpful in straightening out our Porky/BMW mess! It took them a little while because I think it was a nice little puzzle for them but they assure me that if the highway patrolman runs my plate now, it will indeed belong to Porky! The funny thing was that they told me that the highway patrolman had to be running it wrong in order to see it registered to a BMW but even at that, when they ran it correctly, it belonged to a motorcycle so it was still wrong. So I had to go home and tell Doc that instead of riding in a BMW, he had been on a motorcycle! He got a big kick out of that! Poor Porky—he is going to be a psychiatric mess in knowing his real identity!

Speaking of Porky, we had a bump in our road yesterday with him (or at least part of him)....we went to Columbia to go to a couple of movies and then we were going out to eat and then for a walk in Stephen's Lake Park. Instead, we made it to the movies and then when I loaded Doc, I turned around to step out on the lift and it was on the ground. It had fallen down and even though the motor was working, the hydraulics were not! So there I was sitting with the ramp on the ground, Doc in the van and no way to get him out and no way to drive him home. I have to be honest and tell you that even though I wrote earlier that in certain instances, I don't stress any-more, I was stressing at this! I was thinking between all the issues that I have had on my plate in the past week, my cross was feeling pretty heavy-Doc said his side felt heavier too. Needless to say, AAA could not help me, I tried to call the ramp installation places in Columbia and of course they only work M-F and have no emer-gency # to call on their answering service, and I was feeling really out of options. Then I found out that my brother and brother-in-law were on their way home from St. Louis and were only ½ away! They stopped and even though it took a little bit, it was determined that either a seal or a pump went out and Porky has to go to the ramp shop! So they had to manually figure out a way to lift and fold the ramp up and hold it in place until we got home. They followed me home and a friend met us with some portable ramps we have at church and between everyone, Doc finally was able to get out of the van after about 3 hours. Now tomorrow, I have another to-do on my list because you can bet we are going to do everything we can to get this fixed ASAP...4th of July is coming up and we have all kinds of weekend plans. By the time we went to bed, we were laughing again so the moment of pure stress was behind us and we were just glad that our family was so close and that the lift didn't collapse with Doc ½ on and ½ off the ramp...that would have put him on his face and I would guess that we didn't miss it by more than a minute or two! Maybe those monkeys on his chair actually helped this time...I can't imagine they wanted to fall either!

On a Cindy note, I have been having some fun on Wednesday evenings because my mom or my daughter have been volunteering to sit with Doc while I go to the golf course to play "women's night". That has been a wonderful outing and some physical exercise that I have totally enjoyed. On top of that, as a fringe benefit, I can see that my golf game is getting a little better too. I guess it does hold true that the more you do something, the better you get at it! I really appreciate them volunteering to allow me to do that! Although that leads me another issue....this week has been a challenge for my mom....she has had some issues catching her breath which has led to some tests that exposed a need for surgery so she is heading to see a surgeon next week. She told Doc that she would be back to spend time with him again soon but "The old gray mare wasn't what she used to be". If any of you want to add her to your prayer list in the meantime, I am sure she would appreciate the prayers (as we would too!)—She just happens to mean a lot to us! The worse part is that whatever help I can give her, it has to work around what I have to do for Doc because whenever I needed to do something without him she was my backup. Now, anything involving early morning or late evening is not an option for me. Especially now that I don't have any home health to rely on. My brother and sister & their families have really been taking good care of her though!

I am going to share something that I can't get out of my mind. I was having a discussion with someone this month and they were sharing with me their idea of how to handle terrorism. It was an extreme plan that actually was a form of terrorism in itself. The person did reference how the bible says to turn the other cheek but how that wouldn't work and anyway, "we aren't Jesus, are we?" I just told him that I doubt any of us could measure up to Jesus but that was to be our goal. To try our best to follow the commandments and to love each other-even our enemies! It made me think of all the times that when I was passionate about something, that I forgot to turn the other cheek. I am glad that I had that conversation and I pray that maybe the thought of us striving to be what Jesus would want us to be, might change the way this person was viewing that particular situation. I know just in talking to him, it has changed how I see things too. When someone says something like that, it is eye opening—especially when you know that you probably have said or thought similar thoughts! So that has been my focus this month. When I don't understand something, I go back to the WWJD (What Would Jesus Do?)…it helps!

I am excited to report that we do indeed have a Cardinal game to attend in July after having a whole month off! We will be there to cheer for them as they play the Cubs on July, 5th, in the heat of the day. I am hoping for an unusual mild July afternoon but preparing for the heat! At those types of games I spend more time watching Doc and piling ice on him than I do watching the game. His temperature can spike really fast in those situations but he thinks it is all worth it to be there!

Besides that, the only other thing that I have on the calendar for next month is to take Doc to a doctor's visit at the re-hab hospital in Columbia. The doctor that he has there proposed a plan to us a year or so ago about trying an experimental process to artificially activate the diaphragm but it meant a trip to Atlanta, GA without even knowing for sure if Doc would be a candidate. It has now been officially released as an approved FDA procedure and from what I can understand, it works sorta like the pacemaker works a heart only this set of electrodes is activating the diaphragm. It is has gone from a 3 hour surgery to a 30 minute outpatient procedure and I think it is just a matter of training and time in order to work your way off the ventilator. Doc would start at 15 minutes/day without the vent and eventually move up to hours (hopefully all 24!) but it would be a gradual process. It does not "fix" the diaphragm but it does allow it to operate. We would still have to travel because only Houston, Atlanta, and Cleveland do this procedure at this time. I checked it out and Atlanta is the closest facility for us. Now I just have to make sure Doc would be a candidate, make sure we understand it completely, find out if our insurance would cover it, and how long they would need us to stay after the procedure was done to start the "weining off the vent process" and to train me.

I know this is long this month but I am sure that Doc will want me to add that he finally won an evening of cards and relinquished his crying towel to me and my partner (sorry Dana!) for one week but we came right back and returned it the next week so he didn't miss it for long!

And finally, I wanted to say thanks for all of the kind replies from last month letting me know that so many of you faithfully continue to pray for us. Also, thanks for the visits, the card games, the help in putting Doc to bed, the cards & notes, and the list could go on for a long time....all of it means so much to both of us! I hope July is full of beautiful fireworks for all of you with a family picnic tucked in there somewhere!

Your Friends,
Cindy and Doc

PS: Doc wanted me to add that he was having a dream this week about being at work at AECI. He was on his break and heading to the breakroom to help Sue Brown fix the handle bar on her bicycle but someone had waxed the floor and he had to find another place to work on the bike. He was wondering why he could walk at work and not even be able to use the restroom for himself at home. Sometimes you have to wonder at the thoughts that run through you head in your sleep! I do know that he misses his friends at work though so maybe this is a good time to say hi to all of you from him!

Cindy and Doc Catfishing

Howard and Doc Trout Fishing

July 2008

I have to say that I had an experience this month that would make me think I was celebrating Halloween instead of the 4th of July! I arrived home from a golf night and my daughter is yelling at me to hurry up. I run into the living room thinking something bad has happened and there she is sitting on the couch and Doc has this funny smile on his face! Then they proceed to tell me that he had a "HUGE" spider crawling on his lap but by the time Carrissa went to get something to kill it, it had crawled over the knee and out of Doc's sight. So now they knew the spider was somewhere on his chair but couldn't tell me where. All I was thinking was how much I hate "HUGE" spiders! So I have Doc move his chair and at first I don't see anything but then I spot it on the outside of the bag that hangs from his chair. They were right….it was "HUGE"…so I grab the bag and throw it off the chair so that at least I don't lose it inside the chair or up Doc's pants (which was where I was afraid it had gone!)….I throw a washrag over it to stop it from crawling away because that was all I had in grasping distance and then I start hitting the rag hoping that I am squashing it…Buck comes along and starts using his paws on the rag too…I think he thought we were playing this great new game but there we were in the hallway pouncing on this washrag until I was fairly confident that I could lift the rag without anything crawling from under it! We had indeed taken care of it so all I had left to do was dispose of it but that wasn't much fun either…I found out that I really don't like dead spiders any better than crawling ones…well, maybe a little better!

Our Independence weekend was sure a lot of fun. We spent one evening with some friends and shared their grandkids, supper and some cards. Then we spent most of the 4th with my sister and her family as we caught a few sales (I think Doc would probably say this wasn't the best part of his weekend because it was mostly women's clothing and although he and my brother-in-law were patient, we stretched it almost as far as it would go) and then went to see a movie in the afternoon. After that we headed to my brother's place for a bar-b-q and fireworks. I think it is always special to spend time with your family and friends. Probably the highlight of the weekend though was our trip to St. Louis on the 5th to watch the Cardinals. It was a little warm but not horrible for July! Doc lasted until the 5th inning and then he got a little hot so we moved out to the breezeway but the ushers were really nice and found us a place to watch it on a tv screen and provided me with a chair to sit by Doc. So we stayed there until the 8th inning and then Doc couldn't take it anymore and we headed back to our seats to cheer them on! They were down by 2 and came back in the bottom of the 9th to beat those Cubbies! I think Doc doubted them because he was even practicing his "pouty" face so I could take a picture for our update but he ended up being all smiles! Now our streak is 4 for 4 in wins this year! For the past 2 years, our win record is 13 for 14. Not bad!

It was either too hot or too wet this month to do a lot of fishing, although we managed to fit in some. We were just picky about doing it in the evening when the temps were a little cooler. As you might notice, we do not have any pictures to attach this month of the "big" fish—that is because we never caught anything worth bragging about! We also fit in quite of bit of indoor, air-conditioned stuff! I think we watched 6 or 7 new movies and we took several trips to the park with Buck late in the evening when the temps dropped a little bit. Buck LOVES to go the park and he really is getting to be a very good park dog except when he meets another dog that he thinks would like to play with him…then he gets a little hard to hold onto! He is always ready to go! As soon as we head to the van and let the ramp down, he is jumping on board and winding his way to the front passenger seat and will just sit there, looking out the window, waiting for us to load Doc and get in so we can go. Most of the time we aren't going anywhere that he can go with us and I have to end up unloading him to put him in his kennel but that doesn't stop him from trying almost every time! One day we took him fishing with us because we were just going to a pasture with a pond in it and we didn't think he could get into much trouble. There were a couple of horses in it though and at first I was afraid that we might have made a mistake but it was GREAT! Buck would chase the horses and then they would turn around and chase him. If either of them quit, the other one would sneak up and start it all over again! I never saw animals playing tag before but there was no doubt that all 3 of these were having a grand time! By the time we were ready to go, Buck collapsed in the front seat until we got home, drug himself into the house and plopped on the floor and almost didn't move for 24 hours! He was exhausted!

We celebrated our 30th class reunion this month and it was such a good time to see all our "old" friends! Doc actually was part of our senior class for about a month before he transferred to college to play basketball so although he didn't officially graduate with us, I guess we can say that he was part of the class! So that is why I say "our" class reunion. It is hard to believe how fast 30 years can go by! Although some of us hadn't seen each other since graduation, it was like it was just yesterday. When you are part of a small class, they always seem like your "family". We laughed, hugged, and relived good memories! (and some that we probably should have left buried)hehe…but it was fun! When I was younger, I wasn't much into reunions but it must be another sign of age because now they are important. As a matter of fact, we all decided not to wait another 30 before we have another one! Hehe!

I do have a monkey story that happened at our class reunion. We knew someone that was in the restaurant that had their little 3 year old grandson with them and they wanted him to meet Doc. So he went and got him and when he came in the room, the little boy said, "look at the monkey" and he was pointing at Doc. Someone in our class group thought the little boy was calling Doc a monkey but I knew right off he was pointing to one of the monkeys that were hanging on the wheelchair. It ended up being a funny moment and in thinking about it, maybe Doc has a little monkey in him! Hehe!

The solution to our supply issues continues to be a work in progress. I do have a Medicare social worker now that is assigned to us and has been trying to help us. It feels good to have someone else to share the burden with although we still don't have answers. We also finally have a new person that is in training for some of our mornings again. Now if I can just train her and actually use her for awhile before she quits, we will be happy! She tells us she is going to be around for awhile so hopefully, that comes to pass! We finally resolved our wheelchair seat power box issue and received it back, running again. For some reason, however, it came back in with noisy motor. It was much louder than the original motor and that bothered Doc so I called them and they agreed that they might have done something wrong. They recalled it and sent it back in good working condition and much quieter so we assumed they had done something wrong but at least they owned up to it and fixed it! The ramp on the van is working again and we weren't down for very long. I actually have to write that I did very little to address this issue. A good friend of ours (Roy) came and picked it up on the Monday morning after it broke, drove it to Columbia for me and took care of everything. I didn't have to plan it or make any decisions or anything! In the morning, it wasn't working but when I got home it was! That was a wonderful treat and it meant A LOT! It was nice to have an issue that I didn't have to do anything to fix! So all in all, things in the "headache" part of our world still remain but I pick and choose which issue I want to tackle each month so I am not overwhelmed by all of them at the same time. I accept the ones I can't change and work on those that I think I have a shot at! It is much easier that way!

My mom had surgery during the first week of this month and our prayers were answered with a successful surgery along with a fairly rapid recovery. She came home the day after the surgery and Doc said that he knows for sure she is ok because her problem was that she couldn't catch her breath because most of her stomach had been pushed up into her chest cavity by an hernia; but now every time you call her house, you get the busy signal so she has enough air to do her fair share of talking! We made her take a couple of weeks off from watching Doc and our daughter has been filling in some and between us all, we have managed to try to get her to take it easy for awhile but this week she is back to sitting with Doc for a day or two a week and we are so grateful to her for her help!

We have struggled with water, water and more water…anyone living in Missouri probably can relate…especially if they drive on any back roads or live anywhere near a stream or river. Things are flooded all over and there was even a day that our gravel road was flooded and I had to wait a few hours for the water to go down to make it to work and even at that, you had to be careful because part of the road was missing for awhile. The road crew is good though and they always have us up and running again in no time! Rain and floods have really put a kink in our fishing pole project because we are ready to release the design but we had made one small change to it and we really want Doc to catch a fish to make sure that we want to implement the final change before we release everything. Without us being able to get Doc out to the water, we are in limbo for awhile. However, we have started on the design that would allow someone with limited arm or hand control to also have a version of it so we haven't been in "stop" mode completely.

We finally were able to meet with a doctor at Columbia's re-hab facility this week to discuss the new diaphragm procedure that might allow Doc to breathe without the necessity of a vent. It would be a 30 minute outpatient procedure and then I would be taught how to eventually take him off the vent when we get back home. It would be a slow process but we have a goal and a starting point. The physician in Columbia is going to research it for us and discuss Doc's case with the appropriate physicians in Atlanta, GA. If after that, they determine that Doc is a candidate for this, they will schedule something for this fall and we will take Porky on a road trip. They are supposed to be calling me back to discuss this after they investigate it a little further. Hopefully, I will hear something in the next week or so. I think Doc is already mapping the trip out because he asked if I thought Nashville was half way and if I thought we might squeeze in a visit to the Grand Ole Opry..hmmmm....I am sure he will come up with more than that too before he is finished. After I finish this project, I am investigating a new wound healing procedure that looks promising and I plan on pursuing that as soon as I have this diaphragm procedure taken care of. Like I said earlier, one thing at a time!

August is going to be another fun summer month. We have another Cardinal game on the 3rd and then we have a couple of other things that will take us to St Louis during the month. After that, we are planning on heading to Silver Dollar City again for the Gospel Music Festival at the end of the month. With us already having season tickets, we can enjoy that with a tank or two of gas and a couple of nights in a motel. We will be gone over Labor Day so your next update will come a little later because I don't think I will take my laptop on vacation! !

There was one thing I wanted to add this month. One of persons that visit Doc each week asked him a question. They asked him what he would do if he knew for sure he would die tomorrow. So when I got home, Doc asked me what I would do. Of course, my list was a little hectic as I tried to prioritize what I really "needed" to get done and I narrowed it down to what would fit into one day. Doc then shared his reply...it was pretty simple..."I would take a nap and then go fishing because I love both those things." To be a man! Hehe! But that did make me realize once again, something that I already knew...Doc is the one person that I know that is at peace almost every waking minute (or napping minute) of his day! I also know that his only major worry is when he worries about me but with his stabilizing sense of peace flowing over into my life, he makes every situation more tolerable! BUT, my point was...what would you do if you knew you were going to die tomorrow? After you think about it, mark off some of those things that you think you "need" to do and fit in more of those that you "want" to do and try to live your life like that for one day this month! I tried it and it was a pretty cool day! I think what you will find is that it isn't really too important what you do but who you do it with! It also allows for a lot of soul searching and peace making within yourself!

As always, we will end with heartfelt thanks for everything that everyone helps us with in order to make our life better. We thank you for the prayers, the cards and notes, the visits, for the help my brother gave me in fixing a problem in our front yard and any other things that any of you did to make this month easier for us! I also probably should include special thanks for my employer because they are always so patient with me in allowing me to do what I need to do-if they didn't, I would need a 30 hour day instead of a 24 to fit everything in. None of it ever goes unappreciated or without a return prayer for each of you! We even pray for those that pray for us when we don't know the person or church family that is doing it because we know God knows…we just say a prayer of thanks every night for them, whoever they might be, and a request that all those prayers are returned to them from us! Like a circle of friendship!

Hope everyone manages to stay cool and enjoy the last full month of summer. Oooh, that makes me sad. ☹
Your friends,
Cindy and Doc

August 2008

We thought the perfect way to start this month off was with a trip to a St. Louis Cardinal game. I was a little concerned because they moved the time from an afternoon to a night game and it was a Sunday. So that meant we would get home really late (or early, depending on how you look at it) and then I would have to get up for work the next morning. But it ended up being worth it because it was a scorching hot day and I don't think Doc would have fared well in an afternoon game. Now the bad news is that we suffered our first loss of the year. So now we have seen 4 victories and 1 loss. For the past 2 years, our win record is 13 for 15. Not bad! But Doc still had a pouty face on and since I had forgotten my camera, you will just have to imagine it! (It was pathetic though!) It was a good game and we only lost by one and we had bases loaded in both the 8th and 9th innings so we had some excitement…just not the ending we were hoping for!

My mom celebrated her birthday this month and it happened to fall on the weekend that we had her family reunion going on so we decided to make an entire weekend of it and celebrate her birthday in St. Louis on Saturday and take her do some of her favorite things and eat out somewhere special! It was especially memorable because several of family was able to join us on Saturday evening to help celebrate mom's b-day, which was a surprise for her, and then we met up again for the reunion on Sunday. It was nice to have 2 days to visit!

The weather finally cooperated so we were able to get out and do a lot of fishing. We tried out our new changes with the pole on the catfish first and it worked great! Doc caught several and he put his seal of approval on the improvements made. Then we really challenged it because we took it trout fishing! I took some vacation time and we made it 3 days of fishing! Doc caught two rainbow on the first day but just as I would go over to net them, they would break the line....then we remembered that the 2 lb test line we were using was out of our trout tackle box that was from before the accident. Doc figured it was old so we went to the park store and bought some new. Evidently that was the problem because Doc caught several more fish and his line never broke again. Now, all that being said, Doc did not catch anymore edible fish. He by far won the race on the most fish caught but I brought home the only 2 edible trout. We have many stories about the ones that got away and unfortunately, they are all true. We had a little bad luck with a few things but some fishing trips are like that! The weather was perfect though, the crowds were light, and neither of us can picture anything more peaceful than to be sitting on the side of a crystal clear river (or standing in the middle of it as was the case with me!) fishing for trout! Especially, when at least half the time, we had the river (or at least our little hole) all to ourselves! Every evening we were there, we would fish until the horn sounded then head to the park store to buy our tags for the next day and give Doc a chance to visit on his fishing adventures. He wanted really badly to catch a trout so he could post a picture of it but we will have to be happy with a picture of him with one of his catches (not a trout but some type of sucker fish!). I promised him that I would take him again and one of these days, we will get a picture of him with a trout! I also added a picture of the view from our window. Our room was huge and was great for getting Doc up and down to bed but you could tell it was a trout fishing haven. Doc said it was the closest thing to camping that he has experienced since the accident and I think he meant that in a good way for those of you that hate camping..hehe! Then finally, I also attached a copy of him fishing with the pole so you could see how we shut the day down... there was never much daylight left when the horn sounded to stop!

Based on the tryouts of the pole, it was decided to add a little tilt to the final construction and proceed with the production build. We should have the first production model ready in about 2-3 weeks and then we will start distribution soon. It has been a while in coming but we wanted to make it durable, with a build that we could duplicate for years ahead (by finding easy to purchase components), and at as low a cost that we could manage. It feels good to see the light at the end of the tunnel. I once told someone that hospitals teach you how to stay alive but recreational re-hab with activities like fishing teach you how to live. You really need them both but I can't say which is most important. It is like the egg and the chicken and which one came first. You can't "live" if you aren't alive but being alive isn't worth it if you are not living!

As I mentioned in the last update, the reason this update is a tad later than I normally send it out is because we were vacationing in Branson. We used our season passes to attend the Gospel Music Festival at Silver Dollar City. I thought going to a gospel music festival would be like recharging your spiritual batteries and it was great but what really recharged our batteries were the people that we met! We left there with several new and wonderful friends! On top of that, our local radio station had some bargains on some other Branson shows so I kept Doc hopping (or rolling)....not that he minded! He absolutely loves all the activities in Branson! (well, me too!). (I attached a copy of him on vacation and you can tell by his smile how much he loves it!) He even spent some time at the pool one evening so I could swim (which I love) for awhile. He always makes sure to remember me too! I guess that is what makes a relationship work...thinking of each other!

I have started researching some insurance changes because in about 4 months, we are going to see a change to those. Doc had to change to Medicare several months back but he has had a wonderful benefit through his employer that has continued to support us as a secondary insurance but their 4 year time frame is about to run out and so we will have to start that part of our adventure on our own. I am trying to work out what is the most cost effective vs. what is the best coverage for what Doc's needs are. It is the area that I have directed most of my efforts this month. We finally have some home health support on some of our mornings and we are keeping our fingers crossed that this person will stick it out awhile with us. I have been battling with the supplies still and have actually started to see if I can find a different supplier because am tired of banging my head on the wall with our current one. Our Medicare case worker is supposed to be doing some research in that area. As always, I have many irons in the fire and I try to only pull one or two out a day or I get burnt!

I did get some good news this morning on health care though. Our insurance case worker called us and they have finally worked out our claim. They have agreed to pay for the home health care we were getting one morning a week from Oct of '07 through the spring of this year AND they have re-instated our nursing care with a yearly dollar limit on it. So based on that, IF (and that is usually a big if) the health insurance agency that falls within our healthlink plan has someone that they can send to us, we will have some paid home health care soon. Now all I have to do is train them and hope they stay. As they discontinued it earlier this year and we have been paying for it on our own through a local provider since then, we should have a lot of nursing care left for Doc for this year. Now I just have to balance it between what we do pay for because I don't want to sacrifice their experience or availability while I am using the other.

We have not forgotten that bow season is here so Doc wanted to wish all his fellow bow-hunters luck! I think if Doc could make a list of the top 10 things he misses the most, this might be on it! Hugging me better be number one though and if it isn't, he better lie about it!

Buck celebrated his 1st birthday this month (well he didn't really celebrate- it was just another day to play for him!). We didn't make him a cake or anything! Hehe! He is learning new tricks all the time and most of the time he behaves now but he frequently has to be reminded that he is not suppose to greet our guests by jumping or them or putting their hands in his month!

I wish I had an update on the diaphragm procedure that I referenced in the July e-mail but unfortunately, like everything else in the medical world, it seems to have fallen into that black hole. I called the doctor's office last week because I hadn't heard anything. He was supposed to research it and if Doc was a good candidate for the procedure, he was going to set up the surgery for October, call me to discuss the pros & cons and then have the Atlanta hospital give us a call. I thought that a month would have been sufficient time to research it so when I called, it was as I suspected—Doc's chart had gotten filed back without anyone remembering to do anything. When I returned from Branson I had a message on my machine from the doctor. It said that he checked with Atlanta and they aren't set up to do it yet. Cleveland is our only option. However, he didn't bother to follow up on that for us or even leave me a number. Instead his message told me to check it out myself and if I need anything from him, just let him know. So it is back in my lap again and we are not sure if or when it will happen. It is putting a little damper on our

October plans because we can't make any! Hehe! I am overwhelmed this week with a long to-do list but I will start some research next week on this.

September is looking to be one of our most busy months yet this year! (I know that some of you are thinking what more can they possibly fit into a month! But we actually have quite a bit planned). Doc's brother and his family are putting together a time to visit for a few days. Then the company that I work for is having their annual Fall Festival and are featuring Phil Vassar and we know that we will have a good time there because we always do. That actually falls on my birthday so I guess it will be the biggest party I have ever had on my birthday! Hehe! (well, maybe it isn't all about my birthday but I can pretend!). The next weekend takes us to St. Louis for my cousin's wedding! Finally, we finish it off with an extended weekend in St. Louis to catch our final 3 Cardinal games of the year! It is actually the week of Doc's birthday (his b-day is the 22nd) so celebrating it with the Cardinals is probably a good idea! In between the games, Doc suggested that we do a little pre-Christmas shopping. Yes, you read that right…Doc suggested that we hit a mall or two and check out some early ideas on our Christmas list! Before the accident, we often would take a day or two in September or October to get our Christmas shopping done early and I guess Doc thought that might be a good idea again! As long as I don't drag him to Hobby Lobby, he is almost ready for anything. Of course, he suggested that Bass Pro, Cabela's and Starbucks might be some good starting points! Hehe! Maybe with us staying so busy, we might just skip right over 9/11, the 4th anniversary of the accident, and not even remember how horrifying some of those moments were. Of course, we wouldn't want to skip it completely because it causes us to stop and be thankful for the blessings of the past 4 years also! Our list of blessings since that day is long!

Speaking of blessings, we would not forget to save the best for last as we give thanks to each of you for all our blessings, whatever it might be. You cannot imagine how thankful we are for each and every thing that is done on our behalf, especially the prayers! As time passes we recognize how much stronger our faith is and how it continues to grow and that is without a doubt our greatest gain since this all started. During a particular sermon at church this month, a short line has stuck in my head and I have done much mediating over it. It has a profound meaning to me….what was said was, "the greatest and longest journey of your faith is covered in 18 inches" …from your head to your heart!" I realized that a person can know something but to feel it and experience it is the ultimate destination…especially when it comes to things of faith! I find myself making that 18" journey many times throughout each day! I pray that each of you make it too!

Your friends,
Cindy and Doc

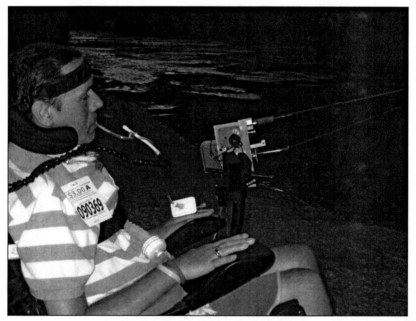

Doc Fishing for Trout at Dusk

Doc Wishing he had Caught a Trout and not a Sucker Fish

Doc in Branson

September 2008

We had so many things go wrong at the beginning of this month that I have to think the monkey was on the rampage. Things like the electric company turning off our electric because they are building a new house on our corner and our generator not kicking in like it was supposed to. Our heat pump went out and we couldn't keep the house cool enough to keep Doc's temperature down. The weather was a little cooler so as long as I could open windows and doors, it helped. The bad part was that it rained and rained though so I had to shut them. The back blower for heat and air on Porky started making some horrible noise so I had to try to keep Doc cool with just the front blowers which left me with icicles in my eyebrows and my fingers frozen to the steering wheel…well maybe it wasn't quite that bad! Hehe! I actually did have to put a jacket in the front seat though to use so I could keep Doc cool enough. If I went into all of it, it would sound like I was whining and I sure don't want to do that so I will just write that we had some challenges this month that we have worked through or are working through and they will all eventually just become "experiences".

Although I really did have some days this month that I wanted to throw everything up in the air, let it land where it will and just walk away from it all, we had more days that I would want to repeat! At the end of every day, I try to remember that it was a gift from God and I look at it to see if I treasured it as much as I should have. I think about if I could have another one just like it, how I would do it different or if it was just perfect the way it was. Most days, before we go to sleep, Doc says, "this was a good day, Cindy" and then "I love you". Those 2 short sentences usually make a good day better and a bad day, good. Just to have the opportunity to hear those words makes it a good day! On almost every day that I am struggling, just to walk into the house and hear him yelling from the living room, "Is that my wife?" (and, you can hear he is saying it with a smile! Did you know that if you listen, you can hear smiles? You can), things seem to slip off my shoulders and I just sit and talk to him about his day and he listens to mine and before you know it, nothing that seemed so overwhelming seems that way anymore. He feels the same way. He said he can be bored and the day seems a little long and then I get home and he is better too!

Rain, rain, and more rain…that is how I would describe most of this month. We didn't have any time to fish just because it was either raining or the timing would be so that the ground would still be too wet to go even if the sun was shining. We are hoping to fit some into October if the weather cooperates a little better though. We did still get in some fishing pole progress though. They built the first "production" model and I think they ran into one small snag but the part is ordered that will fix it and then we will be ready to run with it! I was actually on vacation last week when they did that so I have to get up to date on the change they are making but for the most part, I think the build went well. That part is exciting!

We had the joy of celebrating a wedding ceremony this month which is always a special time for us! My cousin got married in the St Louis area. It was a beautiful outdoor, sun-setting ceremony and the message was so perfect! The message was about how in some languages, there are more than one word for love but in the English language, there is only one word. It has to encompass all types of loves, which a marriage has to do also. It has to encompass the physical love, the love of friendship and the sacrifices that have to be made for each other through love. To share those words and the memory of watching those two joined into one through marriage was a total joy and I am so thankful we were there! To share special moments like that with family is one of those treasures that are "priceless". I have to say that Doc & I were discussing it and although you always have your immediate family, it is wonderful to have the extended branches too! We are blessed to have the most awesome cousins!!!! From all our family branches! If any of our cousins are reading this, we mean you!

I was on vacation last week for a couple of days because Doc & I had tickets to 3 consecutive Cardinal games! We were hoping when we got them that we would be in a pennant race when we got there but instead, we went knowing that our season would soon be over but hoping for our own personal record to improve. It did too! We won all three games and in big fashion. Two of them were by huge leads and the other was a smashing, exciting, ninth inning hit! So now our record in the past 2 years is 16 wins and 2 losses. When we left the stadium on Saturday night, I told Doc to take it all in because we would probably not be back downtown until next summer and his reply was, "well, probably the spring!" I know he is already counting down the days until spring training! (actually, while we were working on this update, he actually told me the date!) We sure had a great 4 day weekend! We filled it in with a movie, some mall shopping, some Cabelas and Bass Pro shopping, and some good food! My cousin took us to a weekend flea market in the area that was a blast! It is always fun to rummage through other people's junk and find something to treasure! We got home just in time to unload the van, start some laundry and then head to church where we had a guest entertainer. He was born without arms but had learned to play the guitar with his toes and he had the spirit soaring through the rafters as he sang praises to our Lord! It was for sure a group participation concert though so as we all joined in, the spirits went higher and the sounds got louder but it was a fun time! It was like a perfect ending to a special 4 day weekend! I added a picture of us at the Cardinal game and then one of the last game we were at this year and you can tell from the fireworks that we won!

I have to come clean though about our one wrinkle in our weekend! I have to use a manual lift to transport Doc out of his chair and into bed while we are at motels. It can be challenging to it by myself but if I take my time, it is usually not a problem. One night during this stay though, I was pumping the handle to take him up and his foot swung around and I squeezed his toes in the bar.

I noticed that I had some blood dripping so I looked closer and I found that I had pulled a toenail completely off one of his toes. It just made me sick to know that I had done that but Doc was like, "I can't feel it so don't worry about it!"....I still felt really bad though and now I have another wound to take care of! Doc is laughing at me because he wanted me to throw the toenail away but I put it back on and taped it in place....at least it looks better...I didn't superglue it or anything though so it is probably going to fall off anyway.... he will just have to grow another one! I can laugh about it now but I was far from laughing that night!

Our supply company finally has agreed to support me in our battle to appeal Medicare for some of our supplies. It was like banging my head on a brick wall for months and months but they finally have a resource in their office that understands that we need them to supply what is not covered, bill it, have it denied and then appeal it. Hopefully, we can keep this resource in order for us to follow this path long enough to have the paperwork to start the battle. It has been like fighting a war with no weapons for the past few months and we finally are going to get the ammunition we need to at least appeal. That is no guarantee that we will like the outcome but at least, we will be trying.

Also, our home healthcare had a couple of surprises this month! Our help that we loved so much from our local facility is back off of medical leave and is helping us out again one day a week. Then I got a call and Doc's insurance has finally agreed to give us some nursing care one day a week again (and pay for the balance that was left from when they cut it off) so we have that help back. We were able to get the same person we had before they cut our service so it is taking minimal training to bring her back up to par. Then the person that our local agency had provided in the absence of our regular help finally seems to sticking it out with homehealth and provides the additional morning care that we need. So we went from having zero help for almost the entire summer to having 3 trained persons back with us within the same month. Sometimes I think homehealth is like the weather…it is either pouring rain or you are in a drought!

Our birthdays were wonderful and we had a good time celebrating them! They were very special days and many of you helped to make them that way! Our thanks to all of you! I spent mine at an outdoor concert my company put on for their employees and even though it was a monsoon that weekend, the turnout was good, the music was fantastic, and we had a great time! Doc spent his at a MU women's volleyball game and then out for Italian food. He actually wanted a lamb chop and that is what he got! The MU volleyball game was great but it didn't have the ending we were hoping for so we will have to go back and try to watch another one to see a victory! I am sure we will be returning…especially as they gave us a season pass! Some type of senior plan….I am not sure if we looked like a senior couple or what but if we did, I am sure it was all Doc's fault! Hehe!

I wasn't getting very far on exploring the diaphragm procedure and so I just put it all back into God's hands and told him to take care of it! Then I get a phone call from the doctor in Columbia and he had a change of heart and had taken it upon himself to do a little more research. He had a phone number and a contact for me. When I called her, she was actually the nurse practitioner of the surgeon that would be doing the procedure. She has been very helpful in explaining things and helping me follow the course of action to see if we can do this for Doc. We should know something by the end of this week but I can tell you that we are excited! We had an MRI sent from Colorado to Cleveland and after they review that, they will be able to tell me if they think there is a "chance" for this to work for Doc. If there is, I will be heading to Cleveland in October to have the procedure done. We have to be at the hospital on Monday morning where they will run some tests. Then we go back on Tuesday to visit with the surgeon and go over the results. If all the results are favorable, they will do the surgery on Wednesday morning and it will take about an hour. They will keep him overnight, and then spend about 15 minutes training us on the "pacing" machine and we will be on our way home by lunch time. Doc would still be dependent on a machine to breath but it would be an independent form of living. We wouldn't have to plug in his vent or worry about battery power for it. We wouldn't have the filter issues anymore! We wouldn't have to worry about the tubing during transfers or showers and I can only imagine at how much easier travel will be! It would be safer to leave him alone for short periods of time if we needed to (he is excited because IF I would go to Hobby Lobby, he could stay in the van safely and listen to the radio). I have called some references of others that have done this and they just tell me that it has changed their lives! It has given them some independence back and has opened up avenues that weren't there before the surgery! All of this being said, we are still waiting on the call that MRI shows that Doc will be a candidate for this! To say that we would be disappointed if they tell us not to come, would probably be an understatement now that we are so pumped about it BUT it isn't like our world would come crashing down or anything! We would still go on as we are and "go" we are good at! Just say a prayer that this works for us though because it would make life so much easier!

As we are on hold for the Cleveland trip, I had to save my vacation so we might not to get to take that trout fishing trip we wanted to take this month. There is always next year for that too! Doc and I were discussing that it is too bad that the Cardinal season and trout fishing are almost the exact time frame. It makes it hard to choose when you have a perfect picture weather weekend!

Summer has officially ended and we are now in a new season of fall…or autumn…I sorta like that word better…it sounds so pretty…."autumn"…like orange pumpkins and spiced cider and wiener roasts and hayrides! (while I was writing this, Doc said autumn to him means colored leaves and tree stands!) Things to treasure and be thankful for! Things like each of you! I am leading up to my ending which always has and always will be the most important part of our updates…it is in thankfulness to each of you that we continue to write these. We are thankful for the visits, the cards, the prayers, and the continued support! Just because 4 years has gone by, what we go through each day has not diminished…it is only through our stubborn perseverance & belief that there is a reason for all things, the support that we get from family and friends, and our faith that God has us exactly where he wants us, that keeps us going! Life is a surprise each day…sometimes good surprises and sometimes bad! I pray that each of you have good surprises this month but if you get tangled up in some bad ones, our prayers are with you!

Your friends,
Cindy and Doc

Cindy and Doc at Cardinal Game

Cardinal Victory

October 2008

For all the rain that I wrote about that we had last month, this month started off as if to order! Perfect temperatures and sunny skies! We had intended on taking a long weekend to go trout fishing during the first of the month but with being on hold with our Cleveland opportunity, we found other adventures, closer to home, so that I could save my vacation time. We started the month off by attending another MU volleyball game, which they won this time. Even though I felt like a "young" senior, it was neat attending the pre-game dinner and visiting with the other persons there. I think Doc loves being a 'Golden Tiger' and getting that season pass. As usual, everyone quickly knew Doc's name and we made many new friends although most of the time I am still just "Doc's wife." We did that several times during the month but unfortunately, by the end of November, we will be done with volleyball season. The high school basketball season will be starting though, so we will still have "ball" games to go to! That should take us clear to spring training and baseball!

We spent a couple of days exploring Rocheport, MO. We had a great time hiking in the Katie Trail State Park along the Missouri River. One day we hiked south on the trail and then the next time we visited we took off north. (I added a picture of Doc trekking down the trail heading north). We ate at a restaurant and vineyard overlooking the river from on top a bluff and that was really neat. We couldn't pronounce most of the stuff on the menu but we ordered anyway and we both chose wisely. We are ready to go back and explore another choice! It is a wonderful fall excursion that is a short drive away from us.

Even though we weren't fishing for trout, we did get to go fishing for some catfish and bass in some of the local ponds in the area. Buck always loves it when we do that kind of fishing because he gets to go with us. He is actually starting to be a pretty decent fishing dog. He isn't very patient yet but he does understand what we are doing and he loves to play with the fish when you catch them! He will sit and watch the line for a little while and then he is off and running through the pasture, returning every little bit just to check in!

We finished the design on the fishing pole and gave it a last try out before we decided to put more of them in the field. We still have some durability testing to run on them for warranty purposes but in the meantime, we are building some to give away to test so we have some feedback at how they are working in the field. We know they should cast and reel in but we are not guaranteeing that they will catch fish every time! Even Doc had his "dry" days! Hehe! When we placed the orders for the first production run though, we did run into one small snag…once again, the motor that we thought would be available forever has been discontinued across the board and is no longer available. We have found another standard, off-the-shelf, motor though and have ordered it and hopefully, it will not hold up our design for long. Most of those working on it feel like it will be a small adjustment but we will still be into the assembly process in the next couple of weeks. Still a little disheartening though when we thought we had every wrinkle ironed out! I guess this is called rolling with the punches!

Now for the exciting news.....We waited on pins and needles for the Cleveland facility to let us know if Doc was a candidate for the pacing procedure and even though it ended up being much later in the month before we heard something, they finally did call with good news. They reviewed the MRI and based on that, they felt like the trip to Cleveland would be worth it to explore the diaphragm pacing system. We had less than a week to get our act together once we heard because they were ready to run the tests in just a matter of days. So once again, we were burning Porky's rubber and were out on the open road heading east! We did have a friend that volunteered to drive out there with us and although we usually go solo, we thought we would take advantage of the offer considering the distance. It was about a 12 hour drive one way with no guarantees that the nerve would respond when we got there. But you can't walk if you don't put a foot forward and we really wanted the opportunity to get Doc off the ventilator. There are so many benefits from achieving that feat!

Once we arrived at Cleveland, our first hurdle was to have a nerve in Doc's spinal cord tested and to have it respond, which was very successful. Then our second hurdle was surgery the next day and they had to stimulate that nerve again and find 4 muscles in the diaphragm that would respond to it. They had a good response from that so they attached 4 electrodes to it and implanted the pacing machine. We spent one night in the hospital and then the next morning they turned off the ventilator and turned on the pacer to see what Doc could do right off the bat. He could breathe for approx 3 minutes before he tired out so we have a lot of conditioning to do. That became our baseline and now we will start working on becoming more and more dependant on the pacer until hopefully, one day soon, we will not be dependant on the vent anymore. If a young person had the same response Doc had, they would be normally be off the ventilator in less than 30 days but they said because Doc was of an ambiguous age, (I think they meant old but they said they didn't mean that-) it would take him at least 3 months. So how it works is that we allow some time for the surgery to heal (about 4 days) and then we start taking Doc off the vent and let him breathe with the pacer for about 3 minutes once an hour, 10-12 times/day. We do that for a few days and when he feels like he can do longer, we increase it. When the times on the pacer grows longer, we back off the number of times a day we condition until he can eventually be completely off the ventilator. They did find some chronic damage in his lungs because of the length of time already on the vent. They are hopeful that once we are vent free, that will correct itself but it might not…at least we have found a way to live healthier. I think we were at first just thinking of the convenience benefits of having a pacer vs. a vent but now we know that it is much more than that. It will create quality and quantity of life! That answers a prayer on being vent free and solving our filter issue....I didn't foresee the answer of our prayer coming like this but that is the wonder of prayer....it can be answered in ways that we couldn't even fathom. This procedure should reduce secretions and the chance of pneumonia. It will free Doc up from having to be plugged in and stationary. We will not have to worry about battery power while we are out and about anymore. It will make transfers between the bed and the shower and the wheelchair so much easier without having to stay in a particular distance based on his tubing length that was attached to the ventilator. It will reduce the cost of supplies that we were purchasing to support the ventilator system. There is much to cheer about if it works and time will tell that story although they have documented a 97% success rate for those that have gone through this process. That is in our favor! The downside is that Doc has 5 tiny wires coming out of his side and hooked into a small plug that plugs into a cord that runs to a small pacer machine (about the size of a digital camera). Those wires and plugs have had a history of breaking so if the cord breaks, they can send us another cord but if the wires break, we would have to travel back to Cleveland to have those fixed. The good news was that they are getting ready to perform the first 2 surgeries of this nature at Craig in Denver in about 2 weeks. Once they have implemented the procedure there, we will have a choice of travel destinations. Both are quite a distance but I think we both would rather just load up and head to Denver and visit with our old friends! Hopefully, we won't have to cross that bridge but with our luck and the fact that we are very active, I would say we will be breaking a wire or two. At least we are prepared for that and we won't panic! (although I can't really see Doc in a panic over anything!) Our trip to Cleveland seemed to be long but we managed to squeeze in a couple of things for enjoyment. (I attached a copy of a picture of Brandywine Falls that we stopped to explore on our way home in Ohio-that was really pretty!). We took 2 days to travel both ways and it was nice having help with the driving. I got a lot of cross-stitching done while I was riding and playing navigator. We also met up with my cousin and her family on the way there when we passed through the Chicago area so that was a very special treat for all of us

We also celebrated with friends at one of their b-day parties and attended another dear friend of ours funeral this month! It was a roller coaster of emotions as we celebrated both life and death! That is the cycle of time though and how it flows.

Like last October, our local high school softball team made it past their districts as District Champs and spent part of the month on the road to state competition again. Unfortunately, they did not make it all the way but they can be very proud of their season. We tried to follow them as much as possible but with softball being an outside game, there was a time or two that we missed because the ground was too muddy for Doc's chair. I haven't gotten him stuck yet but I think I would have to call a tow truck or tractor to pull him out if I ever did....his chair can be pretty heavy! I know that for sure because we went golfing one evening this month and the motor in

Doc's wheels started acting up and then the chair lost most of its power. Luckily it was at its worse on the final hole so I only had to push and pull for a little distance. The hardest part was pulling him back on the ramp and trying to get him loaded in the van without him being able to back up. Doc and I were both dreading the big ramp at home and I was pretty sure that I was going to have to make a SOS call to a couple of healthy men to get him in the house but when we got home, there was just enough sunlight left for me to see to pull off the motor cables and re-attach them (which I did on the coarse without much success-I am not sure if that was some "monkey" business going on or what)…but this time it seemed to help a little and he was able to make it in the house on his own. The wheels are still sticking occasionally and I am still trying to keep it running by playing with the cables but we are both keeping our fingers crossed that we make it until the seating and mobility service can fix it. I don't know what the life expectancy of power wheel-chair is but we are definitely in the maintenance era. Every time I called our wheelchair support though, they sent someone out and addressed the problems so we are still in running condition! They have some new parts ordered and we are hopeful that will fix our problem.

This upcoming month is full of wonderful adventures! We are starting the month off in Branson and using our season passes to explore the Christmas festival. That means lots of Christmas music! Boy do I love that! Doc likes it too but only to a point…I could outlast him by far in listening to it! I have a couple of Christmas shopping outings planned. The first one is with our eldest daughter and the 2nd outing is with a couple of my girlfriends. Our youngest daughter also gets into the Christmas shopping spirit but she saves it for a day that she is off work and she & Doc head out on their own. I think they both look forward to having that independence! We have another outing planned to check out the new Bass Pro in Kansas City....my brother highly recommended that we make a visit there and it didn't take much to convince Doc that he needed to go there! Then we finish the month off celebrating Thanksgiving Day with family. That is the best part of Thanksgiving because with life being so busy, busy, it is nice to have the family take a moment to gather together in one spot and catch up! My daughter and her husband are coming home to celebrate it and so I am going to take advantage of some of their youth and get them to help me haul some Christmas crates down so I can dress the house for Christmas.....Doc & I both look forward to that....I think at Christmas time, our hearts will always be a "child's" heart! What a magical season!

Thanks for all the extra prayers that I know were with us as we ventured into the diaphragm pacing procedure this month. We had such a huge amount of good wishes, prayers and support as we prepared for our trip that it was successful before we even left Missouri! Thanks for anything and everything that was done on our behalf this month! This month has been a wonderful autumn experience for Doc & I and we hope that it was the same for you. We start each day giving God thanks for the blessings in our lives and this month, it was super easy to see them! We hope that each of you experiences a special Thanksgiving and that your list of things to give thanks for so long that your food gets a little cool while you are praying!

Your friends,
Cindy and Doc

Brandywine Falls (Ohio)

Doc Hiking on Katy Trail (Missouri)

November 14-2008

I am sure that most of you have questions on how Doc is doing on the pacer. We are making progress but it has been SLOW! Much slower than we anticipated! BUT, we are still heading in the right direction and the Cleveland facility is still assuring us that the results should still be the same…the race is just going to be a little harder and a little longer! Doc started out going about 40 seconds without the vent before running into breathing problems. They are pretty sure that is all connected to the chronic damage that is in his lungs. So they gave me some hints to try as additional exercises and those appeared to help some. Twice a day we use the vent on special settings to assist Doc while he uses the pacer. That started out being a 2 minute time frame. Now we up to over 8 minutes when using that setting and over 3 minutes (as of today) (that is a nice increase over the 40 seconds that we started at!) without any assistance! So we will continue to plug away and one of these updates I will be reporting how many hours we are off the vent until you get an update that says, "yippee, we are vent free!"

Now for our adventure! On the way home from Cleveland, Porky's check engine light came on. It didn't seem to running too bad though so we just drove the rest of the way home and then I took him to the "van doctor" for a check up. We were heading out to Branson for some "real" vacation time on the Thursday after we arrived home from Cleveland so I was anxious to know Porky was ok. They had trouble finding the problem and by the time it was to leave for Branson, they had pretty much determined that Porky either had a cracked intake or a cracked head....either way, it was going to run into some time and money to fix....so I asked them if Porky would be ok to drive to Branson and then fix when we got home and they were ok with that idea. Some of our friends were a little nervous about it but Doc & I were fairly confident that it would be ok. We got up early in the morning and loaded up and were on our way! About an hour from home, Porky started to climb a long hill and gave out a huge pop and coasted to the side of the interstate. Oops...the "van doctor" was wrong and our friends were right! So I had to quickly call a contact that I had in my cellphone that we rented a van from when Porky hit that deer and luckily, they had one on their lot that would work for Doc's chair and they volunteered to meet us out on the highway so we had a way to transport Doc and I back to town to sign the papers. That was nice because they were only 15 minutes away! Then I called AAA and they sent Carl's Towing with a big-hearted driver named Sam that took good care of us. He pulled Porky off the highway to a church parking lot where the rental van met us and between us, we unloaded Doc and all our vacation equipment, supplies, and luggage and reloaded them all into the rental van. Unfortunately, the van did not have a plug-in for Doc's vent so we had to pray that the batteries that I had with us would be enough to last us our journey and what we had planned for the day (which it did, barely!). Sam said that he was sure amazed that neither Doc nor I seemed to be too upset about anything but we just told him that it would all work out because it always does. There is a peace in knowing that if you live through it, it will one day just be a memory and if you don't live through it, it doesn't really matter! So, within 2 hours, we were on the road again and even though we added a $95/day fee that we hadn't figured on, it ended up being a blessing! It was a blessing that we didn't break down on our trip home from Cleveland, far from home…it was a blessing that we were still close enough to home to tow Porky back to Moberly and to know who to call in Columbia to find a rental van….it was a blessing that the rental van that we got was actually pretty nice! It was nice because Doc could see out of the windows and that was GREAT! He can't in Porky and so this was our first roadtrip that we have taken that we could discuss things that we were passing…that was neat. Then on top of that, the gas milage was much better, it handled more like a car instead of a big old van, the door and ramp were both power so I was able to sit in the warm van and open & shut the ramp/door without standing outside in the cold, and then because it did ride more like a car, Doc did much less bouncing around! When we considered how nice all this was, we have given some serious thought to trading Porky in for something a little more user friendly, safer and economical. They told us that if we made a trade before six months goes by, they would apply our rental fees to cost of the new van so if we are going to do it, we will try to do it within that time frame. Doc said he was already thinking of a new name because this style of van would not be a "Porky". It would be something much more feminine!

My first thought while we were sitting on the side of the road and I had Doc in the back of the van with cars zooming past us at 70 mph was something one of my cousins once said, "well at least the cost was worth the story!"…it wasn't then and it wasn't this time either! Hehehe! BUT at least there was a story and we can still smile about it!

During our entire Branson stay, between the batteries on the chair and the portable battery I brought, we were able to fit everything in. I did make one small boo-boo in that I forgot the portable battery in the motel room on the day we went to Silver Dollar City. As his last chair battery gave out and we headed to the van to hook him up to the portable battery, I was a little concerned when I saw that I didn't have it with me. As always though, I had his bag with me that had what I needed to keep him breathing in case of no power and I also had some backup battery time built into the ventilator. As it would happen, we didn't need either of these things….we made it back to the motel room and hooked him up to the portable battery and we were off again to get some supper and see some lights (which he could see from the warmth of the van!). The only damper was that it cut our stay at Silver Dollar City a little short but as it was already dark and we still got to enjoy the lights and as it was only 37 degrees and a little breezy, I don't think anyone minded getting into the warm van. Plus it allowed us more time to play cards. We met up with Doc's brother and his wife in Branson and I won't brag about who won at cards because Doc would accuse me of being a bad winner but I guess you can draw your own conclusions! While we were there, we did a little shopping (I have attached a copy of Doc with his brother outside of Bass Pro), attended several good shows and spent one day at Silver Dollar City. We are already making plans to be back in Branson in 2009. It is a fun place to go for a few days that doesn't take us long to get to.

The amazing thing that happened though was that we were totally dependent on Doc's batteries to get us home and keep us going without the power supply in the van. The very night we got home, Doc blew a fuse in the big battery and there is no way that we could have kept going in the van without finding some type of way to fix it. Of course, I always carry some spare fuses and my tools so I could have worked on it if I have had to but I was glad to make it home and plug him in and then take my time at fixing the battery situation.

That was because we made it home on Sunday evening and our daughter was already there. We unloaded the van and finished putting everything away so we could return the van the next morning before we headed out to do some Christmas shopping. That was fun and I totally enjoyed the day away from all the problems. Our other daughter stayed home with Doc as they have their own shopping expedition planned for next week. While we were sitting on the side of the interstate, Doc had asked me if I was still planning on going Christmas shopping (I am sure he was thinking of our streak of bad luck too) but then, before I could answer, he told me he really wanted just to tell me that he wanted to make sure I was still planning on going. He said he thought I needed to shop more than ever so if I would worry about how to pay for all the things that had popped up in the past week or two, he would take a nap and worry about how much money I would spend shopping! Hehe! He had his funny little smile pasted on his face when I looked into the review mirror to see his face! He is a wonderful husband to have and we are lucky God paired us together!

Now, that being said, I have another funny story....and ladies... it is sorta scary at how our men can keep tabs on us....I left on Monday morning and returned the van, paid the rental bill on the credit card and then set off shopping not thinking too much about it....just marking things off my list and feeling pretty proud of how much progress I was making....then about 7 p.m., I get a call from my youngest daughter because our credit card company called Doc because there was so much activity on our credit card, they were making sure it wasn't fraudulent. Imagine that! Your credit card company calling your house to tell your husband that you were spending too much money before you can even make it home to tell a good story! Hehe! Actually, they were most concerned with the rental charge and then a charge at an electronic store...I guess that is a red flag. Even though our charges were legit, I was glad to know that we have someone watching our account like that. Even if they called Doc on me! I am still laughing about that one and you can imagine how much fun Doc is having telling that story!

So, was that end of my Christmas adventures for November? I think not! I also have a big annual outing with some dear friends of mine next week which is a good thing because even though my daughter and I had carved several things off my list, I still have a few more to go. At least this time, I hope I don't get a call from the credit card company asking me if I was shopping again! Hehe! My problem might be Doc because that is the same day that he and our other daughter are going too. IF we get Porky back...we are still waiting on a verdict from that. So far, they haven't been able to find the problem. I am going to call them today though and if the are totally bamboozled I am going to ask them if they think we should tow it to somewhere else...I am thinking after 7 working days, if you can't find the problem, you might not ever find it! We are sorta lost without Porky to do our adventures in!

Then on top of the shopping, I have already been enjoying Christmas music (they even have satellite music being pumped into our bathrooms at work and starting on 11/1, it changed to Christmas music!) That was much to the dismay of many of those that I work with because we have no control over the station being pumped into the room but I have to be honest and tell you that I am enjoying every time that I took a break to the bathroom and hear another Christmas carol...even if most people thought it was too early! I hear all the time from persons that they think Christmas has become too commercialized but I think we need to make Christmas what it needs to be by looking into our own hearts. We are not here to judge each other or the world…we are here to make ourselves accountable. Giving is a wonderful thing to do and there is no other season that gives us as much opportunity to share with others….whether it is in the form of a gift, a Christmas card, a prayer, or an act of kindness. Christmas can be whatever we want to make it! I think the birth of our savior is something to be celebrated all year long anyway so instead of remembering that "Christ" is in Christmas, I would rather remember that "Christ" would like to be in each of us every day! So as Thanksgiving approaches in the next two weeks, I personally am already enjoying 2 holidays! The very best part of all the festivities is just having family and friends gather together. I hope you can enjoy them both too!

I will let you know at the end of the month how the rest of this month went and how Doc is doing on the diaphragm but there was so many of you inquiring on how he was doing, I thought I would send out a middle-of-the month update. Plus as Doc put it after just the first few days of this month…this update is going to be a long one! What a busy month we have had so far! It is probably a good thing you are getting two of them!

Your friends,
Cindy and Doc

November 2008

Usually words come easily to me as my fingers fly across the keyboard putting our adventures and my thoughts down on paper. I cannot take credit though for anything that might have been written that might have touched someone's life because Doc and I feel like these updates have been a part of God's plan to touch certain lives in particular ways and without Doc's accident, they would have never come to be. I think I have written before that I was never really talented with the English language and my English teacher probably knows that there is a distinct difference in how I normally speak and write and how it flows into these updates (and, just in case you were wondering, my high school English teacher is on our e-mail address list!). But even sitting here in front of my computer screen, praying for the right words, I am not sure I will find them for this update.

When I wrote in the last update that I was going to try and investigate a new mode of transportation, I never dreamt to see the development of the "Retire Porky Fund". Doc and I discussed our opinion of it and to tell you the truth, it is something that was hard to adapt to. Not that we aren't appreciative of all the response that we have gotten, because we are (overwhelmed might even be a better word), but rather that we always are looking around and seeing those that have so many more needs than ours. It bothers me to feel selfish on a project of this magnitude when I know that there are persons that are hungry or that can't pay their heating bills. The other side of us, however, also has enough respect for God's plans to sometimes let things fall in place. Maybe he has a special need for us to have this van. I know that he knows that we probably weren't going to get it without the outpouring of support. With each note or card that we received with such special prayers enclosed with the cause, we were humbled…many times, beyond words.

We had a friend that talked to us a few weeks ago about accepting help and how we needed to do it gracefully and to allow persons to help, then less than a month later, we are facing this dilemma…. (sometimes, I have a stubborn streak and for sure Doc and I have always been very independent!). It is so much more fun to be a giver and not the taker! So, at first we struggled with how to handle this. We had another wonderful friend though that put it into a thought that we were able to embrace. She wrote us a short note that said that we should not look at the checks as donations or dollars and cents, but rather as a tangible outpouring of love. She wrote, "who would turn away love?"…..We would never turn away from love and it is easier to accept this help thinking of it in this manner.

I have researched this and it only seems fair to us that before we cash any of your checks that we have received, that we need to know for sure that we would be applying it to the cause of obtaining the van. We also want to contribute as much as we can toward it before allowing others to bear more of our burden than they need to. So we have applied for a loan that the state of Missouri has available for handicap persons for specific needs. If we are approved, it would be for $10,000 at a very low interest rate and we could afford the payments that we would have from that. That combined with the trade-in value of Porky would put us at least 1/3 of the way to the better vehicle. So I am waiting to hear the results of that application, which should be by the end of next week. Even if we aren't approved for that one, we will investigate borrowing that amount from another source because it doesn't sound like the interest rate is going to be too high anywhere. Once we reach that point, there have been a few contacts that have offered to pursue larger fund raising opportunities and I promised them I would contact them as soon as I felt we were within reach of our target. Somehow, I think we will reach it! Maybe we will be searching for something different as early as the first part of January. There are a couple of other options that we will also pursue as we heard of a couple of persons selling handicap vans that might work for us. We do want something with low miles though and that isn't always easy to find. When you combine it with all Doc's special needs and his huge chair, it just makes it harder BUT not impossible! Nothing is impossible!

In the meantime, we do have Porky back and he appears to be running pretty smoothly! The problem ended up being a melted coil....they also had to put a new fuel injector on him. All in all, it wasn't as much as I was afraid it was going to be. It took them almost 2 entire weeks of labor to find the problem because it was hidden inside of a heat-resistant conduit that didn't appear to be damaged. I know that they didn't charge me for all the hours they spent on it, or for a tool that I know they purchased just to fix our problem, so I give a prayer of thanks for Porky being in their hands. Finding a fair mechanic is a little like finding the right hairdresser or just the right babysitter…once you have confidence in them, you never want to have to change!

We have had some problems with the lift since we have Porky back though and we are trying to work our way through those too. I think my brother is tackling that one. I think that if we do retire Porky, that will be my favorite thing about it. I know Doc will most appreciate being able to see out of the windows but I will like the fact that Doc is only inches off the ground while on the lift instead of feet. How much better it will be to have a safe, reliable and easy way to load and unload him! So thanks for the support and the prayers that might make this a reality!

So as Doc would say, "nuff said!"….now to move on to the adventures!

After I last updated you, I had another Christmas shopping day but I was mostly done so I spent part of the day just sitting and enjoying 'people watching' at the mall! It was a wonderful day to catch up with some very special friends of mine! I can't even remember how many years we have shared these shopping adventures but it has been more than I care to count. (They even came out to Denver the year Doc was in the hospital and took me out for a few hours so that Christmas was still special when our kids arrived!) While I was in KC shopping with them, Doc spent the day shopping with our youngest daughter and I think they had a good time too!

At least this time, Discover Card didn't call him to verify that I was shopping!

Thanks to all that brought their deer conquests by the house to share with Doc! He enjoyed seeing the deer and hearing the stories! I know that he missed it horribly but it helped that so many of you shared your adventures with him. Doc had a deer hunting game that he used to play on the computer so I loaded it on the downstairs computer and helped him hunt all morning. That was fun for him but I was sure not a great hunter....I shot a buck but by the time I told the computer that I wanted down out of the tree stand, I had lost my direction and was never able to find the buck! I think I had Doc torn between frustration and amusement! But that was enough to let me know that if I can't even handle a simulated hunt, I will never be able to handle one in the real world!

We are ready for varsity basketball now, as our junior high games are over and the college volleyball ended this weekend. We are always looking for some type of "ball" games to cheer for! My great accomplishment was that in the next to last volleyball game, I actually heard, "Doc and Cindy are here"...instead of "Doc and Doc's wife are here!" hehe!

I finished decorating the house and it feels good to have it ready for Christmas. I have to admit that even with the help of our daughter and her fiancé, it took me 2 days to finish and that was after I decided not to even open several of my totes. I downsized a little bit this year, although some persons wouldn't believe it because the house still looks full of snowman, nativity sets, and trees! I still have a few items to put up outside but I am hoping to have that done by the time I mail this out.

Did you notice the word, "fiancé"? We are delighted to be adding a son-in-law in 2009. Our youngest daughter is now busy planning her upcoming wedding! Doc only had 2 words to say when he saw the ring...."Hobby, Lobby"....and he didn't say it with delight in the tone! □ BUT, he too is excited and we know that the next 9 months will fly by. I think they are planning a September wedding.

Doc has made improvements with his pacer. I think he sometimes gets a little discouraged because it isn't moving faster but when we think where we started, it does seem like leaps and bounds. When he first started, he could only be off the vent for 40 seconds. Now, 3 weeks later, he is never under 3 minutes and his record is over 12 minutes....probably the average is closer to 5 minutes but that is still much better than 40 seconds. I think the problem is that last week he seemed to add another minute each day and for the past few days, he has just been maintaining....he is still working hard though and he still anticipates the day that he can be vent free! I admire the way that he works so hard to achieve that goal! This past weekend wasn't as good as the past couple of weeks because Doc seemed to be struggling with a cold or something and he just wasn't feeling very perky. Hopefully, that will pass in the next day or two and not turn into anything big. I would not look forward to another Christmas in the hospital and I know he would not either!

So, what does December hold in store for us? While we can't say for sure, we do know what we have planned. Our son and his wife are relocating and will be moving to Kansas City. He started a new position on 12/1. It will be wonderful to have them close enough to visit with just a couple of hours drive. Hopefully, they think it is as wonderful as we do! We hope to visit them next weekend while we are in Independence, MO, for a family Christmas dinner and get to see where he will be working and living. We have several Christmas activities planned as we gather with friends and family for various engagements....all of them so special to us! Along with our youngest daughter and sister-in-law, we also have several friends all celebrating birthdays this month so I am sure there will be some fun times involved with those dates. The theaters are bursting with new movies that we want to see so as long as the weather doesn't get too icy or snowy, we will be catching several of those also! All in all, if the weather stays good and Doc stays healthy, it will be a busy month!

In all the busyness of the season, we will not forget the reason for the season. Remember Mary & Joseph and what can happen when you say yes to God. Remember the miracle of the birth of Jesus and how the trinity resulted from the birth of that special child. When you get or give a gift, think of those wisemen and those first gifts that were given as they followed direction from the stars in the heavens! Remember those that struggle through the season missing a loved one or wondering where they might find a dollar to buy their children that special gift they want or those that might need a blanket, some heat, or maybe food on their table. Things we should be aware of all year long but somehow come more to the forefront during this time of year. Maybe it is because of the wonderful souls that we have that stand out in the cold weather ringing their bells by the red pots that give all of us a chance to drop some spare change that might not buy much by itself but combined with other loose change, will add up! Whatever the reasons, it can be a wonderful time of year but it can also be a sad time of year for some. So if you are blessed to know how wonderful Christmas can be, don't forget to say a prayer for those that are struggling in some way, that they might come know the reason for the season and rejoice in it! If you are reading this and fall into the group that find it a sad time, you can now know that there are a ton of prayers hoping that your season is brighter!

Thanks to all of you for being our friends and our prayer is that each of you have a wonderfully blessed Christmas…that you stay safe if you are traveling…that you have good health…and that you have friends and family to celebrate it with! I know there are little cliché sayings floating around everywhere but I read a sign today that I thought was worth repeating if you haven't heard it-"A day hemmed with prayer, is less likely to fray". From someone that likes to sew, I especially thought it was clever (and true)!

Your friends,

Cindy and Doc (Darwin)

PS: Some of you commented that you still think of him as Darwin....
me too...he just doesn't care for the name for some reason...hehe!....
he will always be Darwin (or Dar) to me too! I remember calling
him at work though and asking for Darwin and how much fun his
co-workers had at paging him using that name...he would come
home and remind me not to call up there and ask for him under that
name...hehe!...so I guess when I type Doc instead, it just means that
he finally has me trained!

Doc and his Brother, Owen

December 2008

We have so many things to update you on that and they all seem so important that I am not sure where to start this month. I think I will start with Doc's pacer progress. Although, it isn't near as fast as we want it to be, we are still making progress. There are some days that don't go so well and we have tried to figure out why some days he can go for long lengths of times and then the very next day, he doesn't do so well. All we can figure out is that maybe that diaphragm just really needs to be strengthened and if it goes well one day, we tire it out and it needs time to get itself together again! Anyway, Doc's record currently stands at almost 17 minutes with one pacing exercise and he does several a day so that was a good one! I would say that it isn't uncommon to see 7 or 8 minutes on a regular basis. When you think that when he started he did about 40 seconds, 10 times a day for a total of 6.6 minutes per day and now he is up to 7 minutes, 10 times/day for a total time exceeding an hour… it is progress…still a long way to go to be vent free but no one ever won a race without a start and finish line. We are someone in the middle of race with a long way to go but I don't think Doc is even thinking about stopping! We are full speed ahead!

Another small drawback on the pacing is that I think Doc as been fighting a bug of some sort in his lungs or possibly it is just that time of year but I know he has had a bunch of congestion. We have had to do much more suctioning and have struggled all month with trying to keep his oxygen levels up. He was too stubborn to go to the hospital to check it out because there was too much going on that he didn't want to miss. So we have muddled through the month giving him oxygen boosts while we were home and struggling through the outings with the help of toting along a breathing treatment or two. Dr Darwin has diagnosed himself as having a common cold and that he will get over it but I finally called someone with a doctor degree to check him out! I had to drag him to the hospital for an x-ray and some lab work and they called me back with the news that his lungs do not look good. So now they are setting us up with an appointment with a pulmanologist and letting him take it from there. Doc is hopeful that a few good drugs and he will be on the go again! I try hard to remember to say a prayer of thanksgiving that I have the blessing of being able to take care of him each time I feel tired or frustrated with the situations that arise because to not have him would be a bigger cross to bear. I am sure that those of you in those types of situations would agree. I was reading something Mother Teresa once said and it was something along the lines of poverty being the saddest thing in the world and that poverty was not about just finances…it also, and even more importantly, referred to the poverty of feeling unloved or being lonely….to feel alone is the worse poverty of all! I would have to say that I never looked at loneliness as poverty but really poverty is just the lack of something… and as love is the greatest of all things, it makes sense!

Speaking of love, the prayers and support that we have gotten in regards to the "retire Porky fund" continues to amaze us and humble us. We have heard from persons that we have never met, persons that we haven't heard from in a long time and those that we know well. At a time when taxes are due and Christmas is draining, making time and resources to let us know that you are thinking of us meant a lot... even if it was just knowing that you were praying for the success of the endeavor. We heard back from our loan application and they needed some additional information before they could process our loan so I gave them the info and we are in the holding pattern again. They called again yesterday and promised to let us know something by the beginning of next week. I felt encouraged by the things that they said so I have some positive feelings about it. Because we feel certain that we can obtain the $10,000 in a loan through another avenue if this one does not come through and because of the support of so many of you, we are 62% of the way there so we are going to go ahead and deposit the checks that so many of you wrote into an account to find a replacement for Porky.

I can't tell you how much that I am excited about that too! As it has been so cold this month and I have shivered while I opened doors and lowered/raised the ramp, I dreamt of being able to do that operation from inside the warmth of the van and just the thought of it maybe being a reality was warming to the heart! We might not have been able to drive around and view the Christmas lights this year but by the time our next Christmas is here, Doc might be able to share in that enjoyment! Then along with the ice and snow came the thought of how Porky's replacement would probably have front wheel drive and would handle so much better than Porky does. I thought that I might miss Porky and all the memories with him but then we took a trip to KC to see Darwin's family at their Christmas dinner and before we started home, the check engine light came on again and I wasn't very happy with Porky. If he keeps mis-behaving it will be easier to replace him! Just for the record, Porky made it home from KC all in tact and the light went back off after about 3 days. I think he is just like a kid…he knows just how many buttons he can push before he has pushed "mom" too far! Doc still swears it is the monkey's fault! In the past few days, the battery has been the problem and while I hesitate to put in a new battery when we are thinking about trading it, I think that maybe the next recipient of Porky might like it to start so I will probably break down and purchase a new one. I thought it might just be the cold weather but when it struggled to start even after a recent stretch of 50's, I suspect it is more than that. Even though I am getting to be an expert at jumping him, I would rather not have to do it every time we leave the house!

I know that when I go over this update with Doc he is going to insist that I add this following little bit of news so I am slipping it in the middle hoping that some of you start at the beginning, get bored, and then skip to the bottom. It would, however, be remiss of me not to mention that Doc and his card partner (Doris) have won every single card battle in the month of December. I and my card partner (Dana) have tried to convince them that it was part of our Christmas gift to them but I don't think they believe us. On top of that, we had these nice towels embroidered for them that had their names and "crying towels" stitched on them, which we had intended on giving them when we conquered them one evening but that opportunity never arose! So we were humbled into giving them on the pretence that "there would be a day" that they would need them again! hehe

Our adventures took us to the movies to see a couple of the new releases. One of them was Fireproof and I have to say that it was a message close to our hearts. Doc and I have strong opinions on the bond of marriage and what it stands for and this movie exemplified that message. If you have not seen it, I would recommend it. Especially if you want a reason to remember why God gave you the partner he did and why it is important to never quit loving him/her! We also had to go see Marley and Me. A dear friend had given us that book years ago on tape so we were familiar with it and then on top of that, Buck is almost a carbon copy of the dog in the film…at least in looks…Buck actually is a saintly dog (well, that might be stretching it a little bit!) compared to the one in the movie although there were times that similarities showed through!

I already made mention that we were delighted to join in Darwin's family Christmas dinner in KC. After that was over we met up with our son and did some shopping (at the New Bass Pro shop in KC-so I don't want anyone to feel sorry for Doc!) and then went out to eat supper. That was a nice visit and to know that he and his wife are now located close enough to us to see them once in awhile is heart warming.

This was a "party" month because we had all types of parties to attend. We celebrated my sister-in-law's "over the hill" birthday and then we had another party when our youngest daughter turned 23. There were several other birthdays that we enjoyed with friends too that made this a great month to give! It is so wonderful to have friends to share their special days with! A special December treat that we always look forward to is the annual AECI Christmas party. Many of Doc's former co-workers and friends are there and he always just glows while he catches up with all of them. Friendship has to rank up there at the top when it comes to the special gifts from heaven!

Christmas was especially heartwarming because all our kids were home and we had so much fun playing games and sharing memories! We went to my mom's on Christmas Eve and that was a great time too! Family can be like that song…the worse of times and the best of times….unless you come from a "perfect" family, you probably know what I mean. Family is also one of those special gifts from heaven! Doc calls the 3 most important things the "3-F's"… Faith, Family, Friends….("F" was never something that I strived for in school but now it has become a very important letter in the alphabet to me!)

We were ready to start cheering the varsity ball teams on but the weather did not cooperate very much. With every home came that arrived, so did some nasty weather which canceled the games (or at least us getting out) and so we are still waiting on our first trip up to the school to cheer the ball teams on. Hopefully, January will give us some nice days to get out!

I have to tell you the story of one particular nasty day. We had an ice storm which ended around midnight one evening and it warmed up above freezing so I decided that our roads would probably all be melted off by morning. Wrong! The hard surfaced roads were ok but the gravel roads were like ice-rinks. I never saw them so smooth and completely covered in ice! So I went outside to see if I should call Doc's caregiver and tell her not to drive out on them or if they might be more slushy than they appeared. As I stepped onto our driveway, I slipped and went down on my hands and then proceeded to slide down the drive, across the road and into the ditch on the other side. I was sliding on my hands and feet as I was trying hard to keep my seat off the ice so it wouldn't get wet (although it was solid and there was nothing slushy about it). What was funny was that Buck (our lab) thought he needed to test it with me so about the time that I went down, he went down too. So there we were…both sliding down the driveway together and I have no idea what I looked like (I was thinking that I was looking pretty smooth) but I know that Buck looked like a mass of tumbling legs! His body was rolling and sliding all the way until it landed on top of me in the ditch. His tail was almost beating me to death and I could tell he thought that was a blast! He tried to jump up and go up the hill to do it again but he would take a step or two and land right back down where he started from. It took us awhile to maneuver our way back to the top of the hill and into the house. So needless to say, I had to make a call to tell Doc's caregiver not to try it on her own. Then I called one of the guys that I work with and asked him to deliver her thinking that a 4-wheel drive would make it. By the time he made it out, he made me leave my vehicle parked (even though it is 4-wheel drive too) and gave me a ride to work and back because there were cars (and 4-wheel drive vehicles) stranded up and down my gravel road and he didn't think I would make it. On top of that, it was the weekend before Christmas and I had to do my grocery shopping before I got home because I knew I could not get Porky or Doc out so he even had to participate in that adventure. He was my angel that day! I said a special prayer of thanks for him!

I especially am hopeful that the weekend of the 17th is clear because someone gave us tickets to the Cardinal Winterfest in St. Louis. Doc will have the opportunity meet Cardinal players (present and past) and to visit with them and I think he will enjoy that. I managed to book a room in the same location that they are holding the event and it will last 3 days so we can just relax and enjoy the events as we want and not be far from our room at any time. I might even get some time to do some cross-stitching or reading done.

They are holding a fund raiser on the 30th of the upcoming month with a dance in Moberly to raise money to replace Porky and we are looking forward to that too. Hopefully, Doc will save at least one dance for me!

We promised Carrissa (our daughter) that as soon as the holidays were over that we could jump into wedding plans so that is what we are starting to do now. Doc is almost weeping that he has at least 8 months of this but he is exaggerating! I am sure we will discuss things and do things that are not connected to weddings in the next 8 months!

As always we celebrated Christmas with family and friends and one of our favorite exchanges is with some dear friends that we have shared many, many Christmases with! For those of you that have read these updates for more than this year, you already know that the guys and gals have an outing to shop for unique, "special" gifts and then we exchange them at a Christmas party. So now I bet many of you are wondering at what our annual Christmas exchange with the guys resulted in. We were given such wonderful things as a cookie from Starbucks that they purchased 3 weeks ago…Doc said it looked good when they bought it! …We received a Christmas tierra, cool white sunglasses, a huge ring (Doc says it has a bushel of carrots in it!), and many more wonderful treats. We decided to add a picture of myself with a dear friend wearing part of our Christmas treasures. That ought to put a smile on some faces! The guys were equally treated to "special" things too. Then our gift that we always share for a weekend outing happens to be to a music concert in KC in February so that is something to look forward to! I thought that maybe some of you would like to see our family in total so I have attached a family picture that we took on Christmas Eve.

We weren't planning anything special for New Year's Eve but then my sister and her husband called and we ended up double dating with dinner and a movie in Columbia. We made it home in time to see the ball drop in New York but Doc was sound asleep by the time the clock struck midnight here. The first time Doc wakes me up needing something after midnight, I will be able to wish him Happy New Year and give him his kiss! Our treat is going to be starting the year off right with a church service in the morning and then joining some very dear friends and family as we have a card party to attend on New Year's Day. After that, we will focus on getting Doc's lungs back into shape so if you see your way clear to remember that in your prayers, we would appreciate it....Hopefully, we will find a doctor that can help us in the next few days!

We have said it before and we will say it again but we are so thankful to all of you for being our friends. We are thankful to each of you for enriching our lives! We pray that each and every one of you are blessed with the very best that this year can give you! Have a Happy and Healthy New Year!!!!

Your friends,

Cindy and Doc (Darwin)

Cindy and Ellen Decorated with New Christmas Gifts

Blackmore Family, 2008

January 2009

I usually try to start our updates with the first part of the month and work my way through it but this time, I have to start with last night. There was a benefit that was sponsored for us in our area to help raise money for replacing Porky and I cannot begin to tell you what it meant to both Doc & I to see how many persons showed up and how much fun we were all having dancing to the wonderful band that volunteered their talents, the BeerNuts! Several times during the night, Doc and I let our eyes rove over the masses of persons that came and were amazed at how many persons made the effort to come and lend us support. We had new friends and old friends... several of our wonderful family...persons from Doc's work and my work...persons from our church and from our community ...from all walks of our life! In spite of the hard times that I know several are facing with economic troubles due to loss of jobs and income, there was still $4,000 raised and we were humbled by the benefit and by those that have assisted us in the past 3 months get to our goal. We are now close enough to having what we need to replace Porky, that we are going to start seriously shopping this month for something that will work for us. I found out about the loan last week and we were approved for the amount we were trying to obtain so between that and what so many of you have generously shared with us, we are on our way to having a better vehicle. I told Doc that I was giving him the honor of naming it so when I learn what the new name will be, I will let you know! If you had told me 2 months ago that this could be done, I might have not believed you but God does work in mysterious ways and here we are! Hopefully, he will be leading us somewhere soon that we can continue to share our story. Doc said to let you know that the van really belongs to all of us but you can't all borrow it on the same night! Thanks doesn't seem to be a big enough word to use but it is the only one that the English dictionary has to express gratitude (well, the most appropriate word that I know) so I will use it! Thanks to each of you!

Now, I am going to back track to the beginning of the month- 2009 came in with a mess! Doc blames it on the monkey but it was his foot that caused the damage. He was heading to bed one evening and as he swung his chair around, he caught part of an extension cord around his foot that wasn't tucked out of the way enough (probably my fault but after 29 years, Doc knows that nothing is my fault-hehe!)…..the cord was actually attached to a power strip that had a bunch of stuff plugged into it and as he pulled it tight, everything it was attached to came crashing down. Included in that mess, was a large candle warmer with a large candle completely melted. So onto my cream carpet came a huge amount of burgundy colored wax! It also covered some furniture, some decorative things, and the walls! It took me awhile to untangle him to even access the damage but it was not pretty-you cannot imagine how much wax there is in one of those jars! I threw away most of the decorative pieces covered in wax because although I gave it a valiant attempt, I could just not figure out a way to remove all the wax. Someone helped me find a tip on how to get it out of the carpet with an iron and paper towels and it was almost like a miracle at how good that worked! That was amazing and as I ironed the scented wax onto the towels, it even made the house smell good! Then someone else gave me the tip of using WD-40 on the walls and the glass portions of our furniture and that was amazing too! So with the help of a couple of persons, I was able to clean most of it up and you can't even tell I had that mess… plus I learnt something too! (something besides tucking my cords back along the wall a little tighter!)

We made it to a couple of movies, a few basketball games and then we had a couple of adventurous weekends but all in all, we were stuck a little closer to home because Doc has been struggling if he gets off the oxygen for very long. We have been fighting all month to figure out what was wrong. We had tests run, CT scans & x-rays taken, and been to a few doctors trying to figure it all out. They ruled out pneumonia, infections, and any other type of bug…. finally they found a sack of what appeared to be fluid or puss in the bottom of his lung. So they put him on his side and went through his back and ribs to the lungs to drain it out. They were surprised to find it was a pool of old blood but they managed to remove it all. Almost immediately, he was feeling better and sleeping better too! We went from getting up a couple of times an hour all night long to maybe getting up once! His oxygen levels have been better also so hopefully, that was our biggest problem. They have several other ideas of the root causes that they are in the process of addressing so hopefully, he will be back to full health soon! In the meantime, we are trying to justify a portable oxygen concentrator that we can travel with that would allow Doc more freedom when he does have these types of problems.

If you have to be stuck close to home, there were a few frigid days this month that made it easy to do. It was just too cold to want to go anywhere. Now I write that but on the very coldest day of the month, it didn't matter that it was in single digits or that we didn't have portable oxygen to take with us yet because Doc was heading to the Cardinal Winterfest in downtown St. Louis for 3 days and nothing could stop us! Someone had given Doc a pair of tickets to that for Christmas. That was a full 3 days and although we popped up to the room occasionally, where we did have some oxygen available, we spent most of the day gathering autographs and visiting with players. I have attached some pictures of a couple of them. We met a couple of new friends that had been there several times that helped us make the most of the 3 days! (thanks Ryan and Tyler) With their help and advice, we were able to have an almost surreal experience that I am not sure we will ever be able to duplicate. As Doc said, "If you are a Cardinal fan, this place is almost like heaven!" It was nice to be able to spend 3 days with thousands of other persons that share a passion with you and to have the opportunity to be one on one with persons that make up (or have been part of the past) Cardinal teams! Besides the fact that Doc is without a doubt, one of Fredbird's favorite persons, we spent the whole 3 days meeting players, getting autographs, and talking baseball. We were surrounded with booth after booth of Cardinal clothing and collectables that were simply amazing to see gathered in one spot! I am still not sure exactly how it happened but somehow I ended up running into Tony LaRusso (the Cardinal manager), and one discussion led to another and to make a long story short, we ended up being invited to a benefit concert that he was sponsoring as his guests. Tony was a super nice guy and the concert was full of entertainment... Lady Antabella, REO Speedwagon, a couple of comedians, Vince Gill & Amy Grant, and Huey Lewis and the News were all performing and although Tony told me he thought it would last around 3 hours, it was more like 5 hours but I don't think anyone was really too upset about getting 2 extra hours of that kind of entertainment! On another evening, Doc and I went up to the top floor of our hotel where they had a 360 degree revolving restaurant and we were able to take St. Louis in with all its glory as we ate. We overlooked Busch Stadium and then rotated around to the Arch and the river until we made it a full circle! Doc & I both agree that it was probably the most romantic dinner we have ever had...Doc called it a "chick flick restaurant" but I know he enjoyed it too! I can't say that I can remember a weekend that we enjoyed more but Doc was ready to come home....they said the crowds were down from years past but I wouldn't want to be there in any bigger crowds. Even the way it was, it wasn't easy getting Doc's chair through some of the areas. They were really great though about not making Doc weave through the lines…they actually took him to the front and we were in and out in minutes with the players that we had tickets for to get autographs. They had a very good system in place for order and crowd control too so although it was crowded, it was still manageable! All the money they made off the autograph sales went to a good charity too so it was all a win/win situation.

I wanted to give you a pacer update…Doc broke several personal records this month for single times off the vent with the current record standing at 22 minutes and 14 seconds….amazing! It isn't the norm yet though so although we are making progress….we have a ways to go. The Cleveland facility called me this month and gave me some more ideas to try so we will start implementing them and see if those help us at a little faster rate of improvement! I think they are thinking about incorporating some oxygen in on the pacing exercising too to see if he can get increased times.

We did get to spend a day in the KC area meeting up with our son/daughter-in-law/daughter/son-in-law for some quality time. It was a real treat to know they are all living within driving range now and we can do this occasionally! Doc was having a good day that day and he was still in tip top shape when I put him to bed at 11:30. It was great to see him having such a good day!

Since I bragged about Doc and Doris winning at cards on Wednesday night, they hadn't won another game until this past week so we finally were able to give them their crying towels for real and I have a wonderful picture of that night attached! As sad as Doc's face is in the picture, it has to make you smile!

There is not a ton of stuff going on in February. I think we will probably dive into some wedding preparations whether Doc is ready for that or not! And then there is a day that is set aside for several of Doc's work buddies to come out and play some pitch with him. And then, finally, we also are heading to KC for a night because of the tickets that Doc got for Christmas to the Trace Adkins concert. That will be a nice adventure! Especially if we are driving a new vehicle by that time!

I have to admit that this was a harder month than most for me because not only was Doc not feeling really peppy, but there were also several of my friends that were being laid off work. I know the economy is hard right now and so many are worried about the future. One thing that I can say that I have learnt over the past 4 years though is not to look too far into the future or spend much time worrying about it either. Worry will not change it and you just might miss something special that is happening today. Taking life one day at a time and trying to find the silver linings in it (and there are ALWAYS silver linings in every day!) will bring you so much more peace! So even though I KNOW it is hard, try to resist the temptation to give into despair and worry and instead concentrate on the fact that we know there are things that no-one can ever take away from us...the most important thing in life is ours for keeps! That is the love of Jesus....knowing that, all other things can work themselves out! It doesn't hurt to add a little prayer for that peace though and Doc & I pray every night for the needs, whatever they might be, for each of you that read these updates…we might not know everyone that reads them or have any idea how many do…but we can pray for you anyway!

I am counting the days down to spring but it is going to be awhile although the Lenton season is already starting in a few weeks which will lead us straight to Easter! My favorite holiday of the year! I have been thinking about that. Christmas is when we celebrate a birth and Easter is when we celebrate a death & resurrection and my favorite is the celebration of death/resurrection. Not what we do normally as a society but if history teaches us anything, you have to be born to die and it is in death that a person is defined. It is when someone spends a few short minutes trying to capture your life before life goes on without you. Makes you hope that whatever it is that is said is something really spectacular! We had a very dear friend that unexpectently died this month and there were many wonderful things shared from his time on earth and every one of them were true! We will miss him!

This coming month holds a special holiday in it for those that have that special person to say "I love you" to! For those that have never found that love, I pray that you do some day! For those that have had that love but no longer have that person here to physically say those words to, I ache for you because I know you are missing him/her and I pray that it was enough to have known that type of love! For those of you that still have it, don't waste it…relish it and cherish it.…it has a value that you won't know until it is gone! All that being said though, it is also a holiday to say "I love you" to friends and family…so to each of you, *"we love you and we thank you for all you have done and continue to do for us!"*

Your friends,
Cindy and Doc (Darwin)

Doc has a PS: He wants to remind everyone that pitchers and catchers report on the 14th of this month! Baseball season is almost upon us!

Doc with Fredbird

Doc and Cindy with Tony LaRussa

Doc with Chris Carpenter

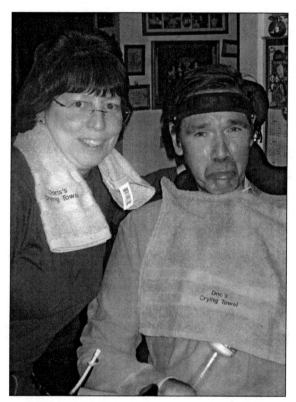

Doc and Doris with their Crying Towels

February 2009

I thought we were going to start this update off with some exciting news of owning a better vehicle but instead we are in a waiting pattern. We did do some shopping for the van and although they didn't have anything on the lot that would work for us, they had something that they had recently purchased that would be perfect and it was at the location where they make the lift modifications. It only had 13,000 miles on it and guess what? It was Cardinal red! Imagine that-like destiny! They told us that it would be delivered on 2/20 and we could pick it up the first part of the week of 2/23 so we sat back and waited 2 weeks with excitement and great expectations! On 2/26 we received a call that the delivery date had been posted on the internet page incorrectly and that would have to wait at least another 3 weeks. That was a big bummer for Doc because ever since we located this van, he has been less and less in love with the bouncy ride that Porky dishes out! He has been really counting the days down to a better ride! Now he has to wait another 3 weeks but it will pass soon enough and I am sure it will all work out because it always does! One way or another, it always falls into place and life goes on. So as soon as we get the van, we might have to send out a special update just to let everyone have a look at it and find out the new name....Doc said he has to experience it before he can name it, although I think he is secretly already leaning toward something special! Hehe! He thought he was going to get some light colored van that would work well on gravel road so he was thinking he was going to have some "female" name for it but now that it is a Cardinal red, he says that is for sure a "male" name! There isn't anything sissy about red! Hehe! Anyway, it will all work out because we are still finalizing the funding and waiting on the check for our loan (which we should get any day!) and I am sure it will all come together in the end. It still seems surreal to me that this type of dream could even come true! Thanks to all of you!

The day we went van shopping, we decided to grab a bite to eat and as we were entering the restaurant, the wind caught the door and slammed it into Doc's wheelchair shearing off a plastic bolt that connects his puff and sip straw to the control box. I tried to hold it while he drove but too much air leaked out and he could not control his chair. I cut a small pc of tubing off something else and threaded that into the straw and connector and that worked as long as I held it in place because there was no support for his straw. I did rig something up when we got home that worked for the rest of the evening but when I got him up for church the next morning, it fell apart and we were just stuck at home because I cannot push him and his chair very far…it is way too heavy! I wanted to call for help but Doc said he knew what tool I needed and was pretty sure no one would have that type of tool just lying around—we would have to wait and call our wheelchair support company on Monday. When our Sunday evening helper came by to help me put Doc to bed, he took a look at it and decided he had a tool at home (for those of you that are tool savy…I think it was a 1/8" pipe tap-nothing I had in my tool box!) that would fix it. So he went home, did some quick work, brought it back and it worked so Doc was mobile again! Doc is still talking about the odds of someone having that type of tool but we were excited and we really appreciated Ted's help! The silver lining in all of that was that Doc thought if I grabbed the drill to try and work out the plastic that was stuck in the threads, it might help. When I went to pull the battery for the drill off the charger, I noticed it was really hot and when I moved the battery charger (it was in the corner on our bathroom floor), we had a hole about the size of a quarter that was already burnt into the floor and the charger was hot…probably a good thing we discovered that before it was a full blown fire! God does work in mysterious ways….(our charger has since been replaced!)

Our friends Brandon and Amanda took us to the Blue Note in Columbia one Saturday night. They had a couple of bands playing and they were awesome! We so enjoyed that and although the bands played until 1, we left around midnight! We must be getting older because that is about our limit anymore! By the time we drove home and got Doc tucked in, we were pushing 1 a.m.! It was a great evening though! We love listening to good music and some of this was better than good!

Then we went to see the movie Pink Panther 2. It is exactly the kind of humor that we enjoy so it was a great movie for us! Doc said that we probably couldn't recommend it because it wouldn't be something that everyone would like but we sure enjoyed it. We were actually the only two persons in the theater and I tried to tell him that was my Valentine gift to him…that I reserved the entire theater for a private premier of it for him but I am not a very good liar and he saw right through me! He still expected a surprise on Valentine's Day! Hehe!

We saw some good basketball this month and Doc is totally excited about the spring baseball season getting in the swing of things! We also had a day or two this month that reminded us that we could get out on the golf coarse in the near future too!

We spent some time in KC attending a Trace Adkins concert. Our friends Howard and Ellen went with us and as always, we make a ton of great memories when we travel together! We spent the night at the motel where our son is the director of the attached waterpark and got a special tour and special treatment…that was a bonus on the weekend! Whenever we travel together, we usually end up with a good story or two and this time was no exception. We were on one of our state's great highways and there was a major dip in it and when Porky hit it, a piece of Doc's equipment bounced off the back seat and came down on the side of Doc's vent shearing off a plastic connector that stopped the air flow to Doc. For the 2nd time this month, I was looking at a broken plastic connector with no way to fix it! The vent started alarming and Doc was clicking but luckily, Howard was driving and I was in the back with Doc. I first thought to grab the ambu bag and have Howard pull off at the next exit so we could try to work it out but then I remembered the pacer so I just turned the vent off and turned the pacer on and Doc was breathing on his own without the vent. He can't do it for long periods of time yet but it held him over while I figured out what to do. I happened to have the extra vent on the seat next to me that I usually take just in case the vent on the chair quits and there is an emergency so it was as simple as changing the connections and turning it on. In a matter of a minute or two, that scare was over and we were ok…it is amazing at all the thoughts that flood through you mind though in a short period of time while you are thinking about how to react quickly to something that is scaring you! I could blame that on the monkey but I know that it was just a bad Missouri highway!

I have to write that there was one more highlight of our trip and that was that we spent a little time in Bass Pro and even though it wasn't on our list, Doc found some river waders that were 50% off and wanted to know if I wanted them for trout fishing. I tried them on and just fell in love with them! It will be so much nicer standing in that cold stream water with those on instead of shorts. What it did though, is give me trout fishing fever and I cannot wait to try them out! Doc said it was hard enough to get me out of the river the way it was and now I would probably never want to come out…he is probably right BUT he is the one that found the waders and then talked me into buying them! (told me it was his St Pat's day present to me! Hehe! Like anyone gets a St Pat's day present!) We have always shared almost all our hobbies and interests and we sometimes talk about what activities we would do if we didn't have each other anymore and I told Doc that there was one thing that I would never give up and that was trout fishing.

Doc wants me to include that one of the highlights of his month was a Sunday afternoon when several of his former work buddies and friends showed up to play some cards for the afternoon. AND I think, if Doc is telling me the truth, he even came away a winner! But that is with a table of 7 or 8 guys as competition…he seems to have more problems beating the gals…(the things that make you go hmmmmmmm!) That is all I am going to say on that subject unless he makes me add something else after he reads through it!

We took a big road trip on today (Sunday, 3/1) to visit our kids in St. Joe! We met up with Adam/Laura and Jaymi/Joey for lunch and then we went over to Jaymi's for some games and cards. What a great time we had! We really were expecting it be our first road trip in the new van but Porky had to make that trip one last time! It is probably a good thing too because about ½ way there, the van lost all power going down the highway and I was already preparing to slide over to the shoulder and figure out what to do…my stomach was turning at the thought of going through that again (especially in the middle of no where on a Sunday and in bitter temperatures!) but then the engine picked back up and we were off again! The only side effect from it was that the check engine light came on and remained on the rest of the way so I am not sure what happened but we made it home and we don't have anything planned for the next couple of weeks that will take us very far from home! Hopefully, it was something silly and the light will go back off in a few days!

Our pacer update this month is exciting...Doc was breaking records one after another...he currently stands at a little over 32 minutes as his longest single time off the vent and on average, I would say his is pushing over 10 minutes! We are still looking forward to being vent free and although it is a slow process, we are still making progress and that is what is important! Whenever his head fills up (either from a little cold or from sinuses) we have little set backs but when he is feeling good, I can see improvement with each passing day!

We spent some time working on wedding preparations with our youngest daughter, Carrissa and her fiancé, Brian. We also spent some time looking at some real estate with them as they are in the process of finding a place to live after they are married. For now, it looks like they are going to settle somewhere close to the area and that will be nice for us. They have had a lot to be excited about this month and it is fun to watch them take those steps to independence!

I do have an update on the puff and sip fishing pole...we have been working on the little final touches and have actually put together a few more and are very close to sending them out. We are currently working on a one with a joystick control so that if someone has a little arm movement, they can control it without the puff and sip. We are also waiting on some aluminum tags to arrive so we can attach those with a phone number on it in case someone that is using it runs into a problem and needs a contact. Our goal is to have those distributed to a few of our pre-designated places by the time the weather is nice enough to enjoy them! (Dominic, Jason, and Craig Hospital… you are on the list!)

Our March calendar looks a little less full for now but we will probably fill it up. By the time the weekends arrive, Doc has usually come up with a plan if I didn't already have one. March is the month that I usually take a day to spend with one of my cousins to just have a girl's day and we have a date planned for that. We also have the National Wild Turkey Federation Banquet that we are attending on the 7th in Moberly that we are both looking forward to. It gives Doc a little taste of the outdoors and he enjoys the discussion of hunting and turkeys! There is once again another Terry Redlin print in the live auction that he has his eye on so I would imagine he might bid that up a little bit. Most of my family, if not all of it, show up for this event so it is a great family bonding time for all of us too! That just doubles the pleasure! If you look past March, Doc has tickets to 2 Cardinal games in April so he is already looking forward to traveling to those! We also are taking advantage of having season tickets to Silver Dollar City and making an extended weekend trip to Branson. We received an offer from the motel that we usually stay out down there and they have a special of 60% off their rooms so it was too tempting to pass up! It will add up to an inexpensive mini-vacation!

Doc and I have several things that we do each day to expand our faith and our knowledge but one thing we have is a devotional that has a morning and evening reading in. One day several weeks ago, there was one that has just not left my mind. It was saying something along the lines that our life is like a garden....the things that are in it are sown by us....and if you look at your garden, you will see healthy fruitful plants and you will find some weeds...it is up to each of us to maintain our garden and pull out those weeds and try hard to sow more healthy plants and less weeds! It reminded us that the grace of God is what allows us to choose to plant the good things! We have been so blessed by God with grace because even though our garden isn't what we thought it would be but there are not many weeds in it! AND when weeds do appear, so does the help to assist in pulling them out! So we have been looking at our "garden" since then and trying to remember to sow good things and weed out the bad...it has been a good experience and I invite you to do it too!

The Lenton season started this week and it is a great time leading up to Easter to reflect on things and make positive changes. I am excited about the challenges that our faith imposes on us during the season and the opportunity to grow in our faith! Easter will be here before we know it!

One more big day that is coming up this month is 3/21 and that is the first day of spring! Who doesn't love spring? Once more, thanks to all of you for your friendship and prayers and whatever else many of you did for us this month! May God bless each of you with all the blessings that you bestow on others!

Your friends,

Cindy and Doc (Darwin)

March 2009

We didn't have any exciting outings on the calendar this month so most of our excitement was close to home. Doc had a couple of buddies that he worked with bring their wife's out for an afternoon of cards and supper…I think he was desperate for a "male" victory and although it was by the skin of their teeth, they pulled it out right at the very end! They wanted to make sure that I included that little tidbit in the update this month…I don't think they trusted me to make sure that it was put into print! BUT, here it is—right at the front! Of course, that only means a rematch and I am not sure if they can pull that stunt two times in a row….time will tell! I also have to publicly apologize to one person who attended…mostly because it makes for a great story…so sorry, Lori and here is the story…it was the first time for Lori to visit our house and there isn't much to her small frame. They knocked on our door and Buck, being our meet and greet committee, rushed to the foyer area ready to express his gratitude in seeing them. I could tell by the speed of his wagging tail that he was going to be even more exuberant than usual so I grabbed his collar to hold him back as I opened the door. The collar was brand new though and I hadn't tightened it quite enough so he managed to pull his head out of it and bound toward the open door while I stood with collar in hand. Lori, not knowing that we really didn't care if he bounded out the door, tried to stop him from escaping without the collar on and Buck in turn, did a quick turn about to officially welcome her. What happened next is a little bit of blur in my mind but I remember thinking that when Buck is on his 2 back legs, he was much taller than she was and then as she fell backwards onto the steps leading upstairs and into the door that swings there, I can remember the bang of the door. I really could only see the golden color of Buck and not much of Lori! Buck was only concentrating on giving as many smooches as he could fit in while the rest of us were all trying to rescue her from his affections! Needless to say, it isn't how you want to make a first impression but she was very gracious about it, told us it was the first time she was totally bowled over when visiting someone, and once things settled down and Buck was reprimanded (although not nearly as harshly as he would have been if Doc had been able to administer the punishment!), he did pretty much behave the rest of the visit! I am pretty sure that memory might stick around for awhile! We probably need a "beware of dog" sign on our front porch but it isn't because our dog is so vicious…it is because he would love you death!

We thought we would be sending an update and picture out to welcome the new van sometime earlier this month but we had to wait longer than we wanted too for our van to arrive. We just now arrived home with it and we stopped on the way to take a couple of pictures so the daylight would not fade away. I couldn't resist capturing one of Doc's smiles so I put that one in too! Like all things that are good…it was worth the wait! So many of you helped us get Porky when the accident happened and Doc & I wanted to make sure that all of you knew how much we enjoyed Porky and how much he meant to us! He served his purpose and Doc & I were both very grateful for him and he served us well....Porky has been having several problems though and it is nice to have this replacement! You cannot know how great it feels to be driving something so much easier to handle and so much more like a "normal" vehicle....how Doc feels to be able to see out of the window and to not be bouncing around like he used to be! How the convenience of power locks and doors makes life so much easier! How nice it is to fill it up with gas and not break the bank and know that we are going to so much better gas mileage than we got with Porky! I think it sort of sums it up with one thing that happened on the ride home. Doc was looking out the window and he saw a wild turkey in a field...he was so excited to see that-he said that was the first time he saw anything like that for 4 and ½ years! I could go on and on with our excitement of what this means to us because it really is thrilling but our updates are long enough without me going on and on about the same thing! All we can say to all of those that helped this become a reality is thank you, thank you, and thank you! Doc named the van on the way home from Columbia but I think he was already thinking about it before we picked it up...he just had to make sure his name suited it and I think it does! As you can see in the pictures, the van is a beautiful red and so all our fellow Cardinal fans will understand when you hear that Doc's name for the new van is Stanley (Stan for short)....

so the future stories of our outings are for sure going to have messages about Stan!

Doc's only horror story this month was only that he had to visit Hobby Lobby with us to do some wedding shopping! As this was his first visit in a long, long time though, I didn't allow him too much whining about it! He just had to suck it up and then as a reward, he got to pick out where we ate supper! That should have been an even trade-off. Well except, that we also went dress shopping and then of course, there were the white shoes to match the wedding dress that we had to look for! As long as we gave him time to nap though, he gave us as much time in every store that we wanted! It was a good shopping day and we marked a bunch of stuff off our list! I just keep reminding him that not very many dads get to the opportunity to be such an in-depth part of their daughter's wedding plans. A remark that he usually just frowns on. (I think he is missing the point!) All he keeps saying is that at least it is the last one!

My horror story came when I made a HUGE mistake this month and I have no excuse for it except that I just overlooked something critical! Doc's wounds were making such great strides and were well on the way to actually healing....I would have guessed them to be at least ½ of what they were before we located the alternating pressure wheelchair seat and looking like they were healing at a good pace (at least for the way sores heal!...nothing is speedy about that at any time!). Anyway, a Saturday comes along and I decide to get up early and spring clean the house and let Doc sleep late. It was all good and it worked out nicely until I get ready to put him back to bed that night and realize that deviating from my usual routine caused me to forget to turn the wheelchair seat on. That meant he was flat on his bottom for the whole day and needless to say, I probably set his wounds back about a year's worth of healing. Isn't it amazing that it takes a year to get to the point we were at and then a few short hours to set us back that far? I was upset at myself for forgetting some critical like that but it was already water under the bridge and I can only go forward. At least I know what works and what doesn't so I started the routine all over again and it took a few days to wear away the dead skin and tissue and now I am treating it with what I know will help it and we will eventually get back to where we were at! As always, Doc just goes with the flow and tells me not to worry about it…he has to be one in a million!

Doc broke another record on the pacer (over 47 minutes at one attempt!) and while that is exciting, it is confusing to us why we can't gain any consistency in it. Every month, it seems like we have a day or two that he does really good on it and then other days that he struggles to have much success at all! I would think it is a good sign though that he tops his best time each month at least once. That is what is giving us some hope anyway! The Cleveland facility calls and discusses our progress though and usually has something else for us to try so they are only a phone call away!

We had a good time at the Wild Turkey Federation Banquet but Doc did not win the bid on the Terry Redlin print that he was hoping to attain! Instead it is decorating someone else's wall. It was fun being there and being part of the fun though!

"The Fishing Doc" (the fishing pole officially has a name now!) is coming along nicely. We have mastered the joystick version and have designed a way to quickly go from a puff & sip or a joystick, depending on your needs. What that means is that places like rehab facilities can use the same outfit for either need and if someone had one of the setups and either improved or his needs increased, it would be easy to replace one type of control with another. It is just a matter of unplugging one control box and plugging in the other! We have built 3 but in the process of making our finishing touches and adding our last minute improvements, we aren't quite ready to distribute them yet. Plus, we want to try them out and make sure they all cast well...that is our R&D department's job...a.k.a.-Doc Blackmore! If the weather holds some this month, they might be shipped out before the next update! We have had some shirts made up for our team and are hopeful to be making some more units and traveling to some upcoming outdoor expos to shed some light on our innovative way of fishing. It has been a long time coming but our finished result looks to be worth the wait!

As quiet as March was, April is not! We have at least 2 trips to St. Louis to watch the Cardinals! That is probably going to be the highlight to Doc's month! We have a trip to Branson for a 3 day weekend to catch some action at Silver Dollar City and maybe a show or two. We have a couple of days set aside to try and fit in some spring fishing. And finally, last but not least, we have Easter to celebrate. There is never enough time of the "perfect" weather.... it is usually either too hot or too cold for Doc's temperature control but while spring temperatures last, I will try to fit in as much "outdoor" stuff as we can do! IF those April showers hold off!

One thing I wanted to make sure to say is that I decided to send these updates out from our home e-mail address instead of using my work address starting next month. I have our address book updated (at least I hope I have) but just in case any of you do not receive an update next month and you still want to get them, you might let me know because I might have made a mistake in transferring the addresses.

Our last thought for this month is something we heard in church a few weeks back. The word Pal was broken down to what a real pal is and it has stuck in my mind and I thought I would share it....

PAL: what is a Pal?
P: Pray for each other
A: Attend to each other
L: Love each other

Isn't that cool? We have a ton of "pals" and we are so thankful for each and every one of them! That is exactly what you do for us... pray for us, attend to us, and love us! AND vice-versa...we hope we are "pals" to each of you too! Thanks for all that each of you continue to do for us and may each of you be blessed with a very good month!

Your friends,

Doc (Darwin) and Cindy!

Stan the Van

Doc Loading into Stan the Van

Cindy, Doc and Stan the Van

Doc Saying Thank You
for Stan the Van

April 2009

Doc was speaking at a church the Sunday after we picked up Stan and the pastor there told Doc that he thought his play on Stan the Man with Stan the Van was clever…I have to admit that I hadn't put that together but Doc was grinning that someone got it! So the weekend after that, we took Stan the Van on his first roadtrip. Doc said the only problem with traveling in Stan was that now that he can see out of the windows, he finds it hard to take any naps! ☺ We did have a few wrinkles in our trip but none of them involved Stan… most of them I would have to blame on the monkey because they were just freaky things! Twice, it involved problems with Doc's vent and/or tubing and he wasn't breathing so I had to pull over on the side of the road immediately and try to find the problem and then fix it. Both times, I was giving thanks that I was able to access him from the driver's side because Porky did not have a side door on that side but Stan does. I was also giving thanks for the pacer because even though Doc isn't vent free on any type of consistent long length of time, he can breathe for awhile on it and I was able to turn that on and not worry about him not breathing while I worked to fix the problems. That was a "life-saver" in the real sense of the words!

Our first road trip was to Branson and what a beautiful weekend we had! The weather was absolutely made to order except it was cold, rainy, and windy on the way home but that didn't bother us because Stan kept us warm and dry. We had gotten a postcard from a motel that we had stayed at previously with an offer of a good rate for the off-season so we used it and our season passes to Silver Dollar City to have an inexpensive weekend. It was the International Festival at Silver Dollar City and we chose to catch the performances from the countries of Russia, China, Peru, and Ireland. We could have fit another country in but Doc & I both so enjoyed the Irish performance that we did a double dip on that one! Besides Silver Dollar City, we also spent some time at Landing (a neat new shopping/restaurant area right on the lake) so Doc could visit the Cardinal store. We found a big Cardinal magnet for Stan so now he is dressed for the ballgames!

Speaking of Cardinal games, the very next weekend was another road trip and what could be more appropriate than our first Cardinal game of the season? Again, the weather was almost made to order and I have to admit the atmosphere at the stadium was almost tangible. Doc and I were both soaking up the sounds, sights and smells and just celebrating being there! Of course it helped that we had something to cheer about! We won by a large margin, partially thanks to 2 homeruns by Albert Pujols-one of them a grand slam home run! Then we followed that up with another trip to the ballpark on the last weekend of the month but it wasn't as perfect of a day. It was much hotter so we ran into a little "over-heating" issue and then we had to take our first loss of the season too! We still enjoyed it though and Doc had a great visit with Fredbird...those two are starting to be quite the pair! So we are starting off 1 for 2 this year and overall for the past 3 years, we can brag we have seen 17 victories in 20 visits!

That is a pretty good winning margin. Hopefully, we can keep it up. Unfortunately, after our games in April, we don't have any tickets to any games until August. That might be too long but by the time you fit in the Bluegrass & Bar-B-Q Festival in Branson in May, graduations, wedding showers and preparations, some golfing, and of course, fishing, there isn't much time for trips to St. Louis. You can bet Doc will be listening or watching to every one of the games though via radio or television!

Speaking of fishing, I am soooo excited to report that our fishing pole project is finally complete and we are actually sending the poles out into the field. Now there are "Fishing Docs" being used in other parts of the country! It took us longer to get to this point than I was expecting or hoping for but the finished product is so much better than I imagined that it could be that the wait was worth it. The ability to open fishing back up to those that thought they might not fish again is, as the commercial says, priceless. I want to make sure to say thanks to the company that I work for that sponsored it and continues to sponsor it and to the team that spent the hours on it perfecting it. Now our next goal will be to attend some recreational shows, put the information on the web, and find other ways of communicating that this is available for those that need it. We are also going to research sponsorships to support the costs so that those that need one but cannot afford one will be able to obtain one!

Doc broke record after record after record this month on the pacer. He finally went over an hour and then continued to even break that record, doing a little better each day after that. His current record is 70 minutes. What still doesn't make sense to us is that although we did seem to do better day after day, we still had times within these days that dropped back down to 5 minutes or less. It would be great to figure out why we can't turn the pacer on and know for sure we are going to go at least an hour. Maybe I am just impatient because when I look back on our updates, I can see how much we improve each month and how far we have come since we first had this pacer added (40 seconds). Hopefully, these new times are an indication that the best is yet to come and it isn't so far off! ☺

Easter was a wonderful holiday, as it always is. We had a wonderful service at church and our choir was magnificent. I think I could just sit in church all day on that day and be content. Actually, that might work for any day of the year though. Doc and I have often talked about how no matter what is going on in our lives, when we get to church, it is just all about a feeling of peacefulness that descends on both of us. Anyway, after church we headed over to my moms and had a wonderful meal and then we played a game and had some old time family fun! It is hard to believe how grown up our nieces and nephews are getting but they are actually young adults now and instead of running around and playing their own games, they are joining in with ours and I totally enjoy that!

We did have one weekend that we didn't have anything planned but that didn't last. I happened to be browsing through a magazine and saw that Doc's 2nd favorite bluegrass band was going to be in

Columbia. I happened to mention it to one of my brothers and the next thing I knew we were on an all day outing and it ended up being another great adventure.

May isn't quite as crazy at April was but it is still busy, busy. I think the majority of it is close at home with graduations and a few other school events. If the weather permits, we are going to spend our anniversary/Mother's Day trout fishing for a few days and I cannot tell you how excited I am about that....I finally get to try out those waders! Doc is looking forward to that also, so I hope the weather is perfect for fishing on the weekend of the 9th! Then we are closing the month out with the Bluegrass and Bar-B-Q adventure in Branson. That is quickly becoming one of our favorite annual outings!

In conclusion, we wanted to make sure to say our continued thanks for all that each of you do for us! For all the prayers that are lifted up for us! We appreciate all the wonderful e-mails and the many, many other things that are supplied to us to make our life a little easier. Then finally, the best is for last....Happy Mother's Day to our mom and to all the mom's out there! I know it might not be a national holiday but it is recognized on a Sunday, which is a day of rest so may each of you have a day of enjoyment, peace, and little work! May your month be filled with wonderful spring events until we write again!

Your friends,

Doc (Darwin) and Cindy!

May 2009

This month was jammed packed full of exciting and wonderful tales to tell but I have to admit that the one that meant to most to me is sort of selfish. But it was so exciting that I just have to start off our update with the story! It was the weekend of Mother's Day and our 29th anniversary. Doc and I had planned on me taking a day of vacation on Monday and going trout fishing at Bennett Springs State Park for 3 days. Then we get an invitation to share our story with a local church that we have not previously visited and they wanted us to do that on Sunday evening. The Sunday that is right in the middle of our 3 days off...The Sunday that was Mother's Day and our 29th anniversary...The Sunday that we really didn't want to! BUT we didn't say no right off because there was something tugging at us not to say no! Doc suggested that we return the call and offer to come any other time but that didn't feel right either. So I put off returning the call while we struggled with it and prayed on it until there was less than a week to go before the date arrived. I figured I had put it off long enough that they probably didn't even need us to do it any-more. (I didn't do that on purpose-it just crept up on me!) So it was the Sunday evening before that date and we were heading to church where Doc was a closing speaker for a women's retreat that had been going on. I told Doc that when we got home, I would just call and offer to come another weekend and apologize for not calling back sooner. BUT then we get to church and at the very end of the service, they had a prayer that went as close to this as I can remember, "Lord, give me the strength to choose to be your servant when the opportunity arises rather than to choose my personal pleasures." Doc and I just looked at each other because even though it was hard, God had just hit us over the head with a message that couldn't be any plainer! So as soon as I got home I returned the call and unbelievably they had not filled that slot for us to speak yet. We simply rearranged our schedule and left a little earlier on Friday and fished Friday evening, Saturday, and then part of Sunday morning before we packed up to come home. Now, for this next part, I can only think that God was smiling on us because I said a prayer that even though we were going to cut our trip short, maybe God could see his way clear in letting Doc catch (and net) his first trout with the new pole and if it wasn't too selfish, I would sure like to catch a big one for the wall. Doc was teasing me when I shared this with him because he said we didn't have room on our wall for a big fish but to catch it first and then we would talk about it. Doc not only caught his first trout with his puff and sip pole (that the netter actually secured before it got off the line-which is a totally different story that is soooo funny that I think I will type it up exactly as Doc quotes it to me because I was the clown in this story and Doc was just sitting in his chair watching me try to help him land this fish and his account of this is pretty much true and the story will brighten your day!—but that is later!)-back to my story…God also sent me the biggest rainbow trout that I have ever dreamed of catching! If you are familiar with river trout fishing, the term is called a "lunker". I could not believe it when this monster of a trout showed up at the end of my pole and was rolling on the river top! I was so scared that I would break the line or he would spit out the hook before I netted him. I got him close enough to net but he would not fit in my net head first so I had to let him have another swim around me until I could net him from behind! My heart was pumping so fast that I could hardly breathe and Doc said that while he was fishing away from me and could not see me, he could hear me, as could everyone else in the county! ☺ He knew I had a nice one but he wasn't prepared for the one that I popped in front of him with! For those that want specifics, I caught him on yellow powerbait, he weighed in at almost 5 lbs and I was in zone 3 at Bennett Springs State Park. I had to attach a copy of the picture that they took at the state park office and then one of Doc & I with it! I won a lunker patch for my fishing vest, a lunker pin, and as redneck as it sounds, Doc is having it mounted for me as an anniversary present! I just know it was heaven sent and every time I look at it, I will remember that God given fish and the opportunity to share our story with the Carpenter Street Baptist Church!

You will also see that I attached a copy of Doc's first "official" trout catch and it was a really nice sized trout! Bigger than a lot of them that is pulled out of the river! So for the rest of this paragraph, you will get Doc's rendition of how "we" caught his fish…. "About the time I realized I had a fish, Cindy saw it too and came running in her big waders, fishing pole under the arm, and trying to get her net up to net my fish! When she got out to where she thought my fish was, she tried to net my fish but it jumped out of the water about 4' away from her in a different direction. So she moved where the fish was and tried to net it but the fish jumped about 4' away from her again in the other direction. So then she tried to net it in yet another place but once again, it jumped somewhere not anywhere close to where she was at. The next thing I know she had fallen onto her knees, onto my line and was using her net to try and push the fish up on the rocks. About this time, I told her, "just let it go and I'll try to reel it in myself." She was determined to get it in her net though, so she struggled to her feet and the trout swam between her legs. She took the net from behind her and got the trout in the net from behind, in between her legs. If it hadn't been for the fish swallowing my hook, it would have been long gone! It drew the attention of about a dozen other fishermen, who I am sure had the biggest laugh of the day...☺ But we got my fish and later Cindy was complaining about being sore and said it was from fighting her fish but I told her, "no, it was from dancing with mine."-it would have made some classic video.".......Doc didn't even write that the current was running hard and the water was dark brown because the river was flooded but he said we have a space restriction...I found the space!

All of that excitement out of the way, I can tell you that Doc having the opportunity to share his faith at the end of a great retreat with those women that were floating on the holy spirit was very, very special! It was special to him to be able to do it and it was special to me (and probably every one that heard him) to hear the message! I have heard him speak many, many times and I still could just sit in a chair and listen to him talk all day when he testifies! There is something about the way that he lights up and always has the perfect words to say. I cannot explain it but if you have had the opportunity to listen to him, you will understand. If you haven't heard him share his testimony, I hope some day the opportunity arises for you to hear it. Then to turn around and the very next weekend, have the opportunity to share some of our experiences again was a great blessing to both of us. We continue to thank those that welcome us into their space to share.

If you can't tell, poor Stan hasn't had much rest this month. Besides those journeys, we also spent a day exploring with my mom as a Mother's Day treat to her. I have discovered that it isn't the things in boxes or bags that mean the most to moms but rather the time it takes to make memories that are the greatest gifts of all! Those are the best presents....I remember how busy we were when we were newly married and then had young children so I appreciate the time that my kids give back to us now and I understand how precious time is. So that is what we did too...we gave my mom a day to do whatever she wanted and in the process it was a gift of a great memory for her and for us too! Give and you should receive was exactly what that day was about!

We had one weekend that we stuck close to home because we had a high school graduation and a junior high school graduation to go to and then celebrate. Milestones like those that gather the family around always makes for such a wonderful day! Our best wishes go out to both our nephews and for all of those that are reaching those milestones this month and starting a new adventure in their worlds! Whether it be junior high, high school, or college!

I guess spending one weekend at home was too much because the next weekend was Memorial weekend and we were off again! This time to Branson to head to the Silver Dollar City Bluegrass & Bar-B-Q Festival! It is always a highlight of our year! I took a couple of days of vacation and we were able to stay down there for almost a week. We squeezed in a cowboy Chuckwagon Dinner Show, a Broadway production of Peter Pan (which was a favorite with both Doc & I), and a Springfield Cardinals minor league baseball game while we were there too. It rained on us every day but we managed to switch our schedule around and fit in some indoor stuff so we still filled our days! Weather permitting, we spent as much time as we could at Silver Dollar City taking in as much of the bluegrass scene as we could fit in each day! Doc is the lover of bluegrass music but I can appreciate it and enjoy it also. AND I once again, enjoyed wayyyy too much of the bar-b-q-but it was awesome!

We caught the ballgame with some friends that live in the area and that visit was special to both of us also! We were sharing our story of our fishing/speaking engagement weekend when he said something along the lines of "you can sure tell that God is driving your bus". I have thought a lot about that and it is so true. God is driving our bus. I used to be sitting right behind him trying to tell him how to drive but in the past few years, I have learned to move to the back of the bus and stretch out more. There is a peace in letting someone else do the driving through life. Occasionally, I get off for a stop and when I get back on, I forget to move on back and find myself once more right behind the drivers seat trying to give directions but then I remember that he knows where we are going so much better than I do. Do you know what's it's like when you are on a long drive and you fall asleep while someone else is driving and when you wake up, you have covered so much ground and are so much closer to your destination? That is how I feel most of our days are....just another day closer to our destination! It is a wonderful feeling to learn to let go and realize that life should be lived one day at a time and in the end, we won't be part of this world. That is ok and there is absolutely no sadness in knowing that. Doc has been pushing me to visit our funeral home to go ahead and make some final arrangements for both of us so that those would be taken care of and I kept putting it off for this reason and that reason. I finally set up an appointment and we walked through the arrangements together and planned things that each of us wanted for ourselves and we are in the process of finalizing those plans. It wasn't so bad....it was actually a great memory that we made that day. There was also the peace in knowing that if something would happen to either one of us, the other one would not have to deal with the normal stresses of the moment. Doc will tell you that he was not pushing me to do it but he was....the thing is that I am glad that he did!

I ended the month participating in the Orscheln golf tournament and what a fun day that was although I could tell that I need to get out and practice more! Our eldest daughter, Jaymi, volunteered to come home and spend the weekend so she and our youngest daughter, Carrissa, could get Doc up for me that morning so I wouldn't have to try and work out how to accomplish that and be at the tournament by 6:30 in the morning! I am still not sure how I would have pulled that feat off but luckily, I didn't have to worry about it. I think Doc really enjoyed his father/daughter time too. They loaded up Doc and headed off in Stan to go out for lunch while I enjoyed a few hours of just having fun. I think it was another one of those win/win situations! ☺

You can tell that other than the minor league game, we weren't able to attend any Cardinal games in person but Doc didn't miss many of them. Have radio, will travel is a good motto for him! They put the stations on their schedules so you can find the town you are close to and it will tell you exactly where you can pick the game up on the radio. That is something that we use often!

Doc's monkey is still around and causing trouble but then his Wednesday night card partner made a trip to Hawaii and came home with a "special" bikini clad monkey that we have named Lola. It's not like he doesn't have enough monkeys to cause trouble but now we have another one that I suspect could cause a little more. They thought it was going to be their good luck charm and that they were in line for a winning streak BUT…hehe…it didn't work! It will take more than a lucky monkey! To be honest though, I have to admit that we did take the crying towels for a couple of weeks this month but currently, they have them back!

Doc was so busy doing and going that I thought for awhile that he had forgotten to concentrate on his pacer. He didn't have a great month with it but he ended up squeezing in yet another new record of 73 minutes. I do know that when we travel it is nice because not only is it a safety feature to fall back on, but it also makes it easier to do transfers from the chair to the motel beds. I used to have to fight with the tubing and make sure everything stayed hooked up to the vent but now, I just unplug all that and turn the pacer on until I get him settled and then I reattach the vent for the night. That makes things so much easier!

June, for right now anyway, is much calmer than May. I can honestly say that other than we know that we want to return to do some more trout fishing (AND maybe pick up our mount because they said they might be done by June), there isn't much on the calendar. I am going to join my mom and sister is a town wide yard sale on the first weekend and as I haven't done any type of preparation for that yet, this week will be busy, busy! I have already warned Doc that he isn't going to get as much attention as he usually does this week so I hope there are a lot of Cardinal night games! He doesn't notice that I am unavailable if that is on television! ☺

We hope that this coming summer month brings some time off work to enjoy the many outdoor activities there are to do and that the memories that each of you make are good ones! I pray that each of you remember to let God drive your bus this month! We want to say again this month, as we do every month, how much we appreciate anything that each of you do for us! We wish each of the fathers out there a very special Father's Day! I like it that we have the opportunity to say thanks for our moms and dads & that each of them get a special day for it! Doc & I have both lost our fathers and we miss them. If you still have yours, make sure you get that hug in! May God bless you as he continues to bless us!

Your friends,
Doc (Darwin) and Cindy!

Cindy with Lunker

Cindy and Doc with Lunker

Doc with his Trout Catch

June 2009

There are so many things that stick out from this month that I hardly know what to put in this update and what to leave out. I guess all in all, most of the month's activities centered around The Fishing Doc! The first weekend, had us gathering all the completed fishing units, loading them up in Stan, and heading over to a friends house to test them out on some catfish. Doc tried out all the puff and sip controls and Howard tested out all the joystick controls while the gals went for a walk. I think that sounded like a wonderful plan and it worked well. We even had a campfire to roast some hot dogs and marshmallows when we got back from our walk! I think we all enjoyed our time. All the units caught some fish and although Howard thought it was unfair that the puff and sips were catching more fish than the joystick version, the joystick version was still catching a fair share! It was exciting to know that we had completed our first 5 units and they were actually ready to be distributed. We thought we would distribute the local ones first but the weather sure hampered that idea. It seems like every time the ground would get close to being dry enough to try them out and give them away, it would rain again!

Our first big adventure was to head back to Bennett Springs to try our hand at catching some trout again. We were hoping that our mount would be done but it wasn't. The only good thing about that is that we will have to travel back there again to pick it up and that just means a little more fishing! Once again, we both caught some trout and even though it wasn't a lunker, Doc's was the largest this time. It is always good to catch a meal or two in trout....I like to keep finding new ways to cook it and so far, I haven't found any that we don't like. We did have some excitement that started before we even got there! I had taken a day of vacation to meet our son in Columbia to play a round of golf. We totally enjoyed that and as we chose to walk it, we were able to get in some quality visiting time. The paths were all paved and other than getting a little warm, I think Doc managed fairly well. After we finished and Adam headed back home (which is Kansas City), we decided to cool off in a matinee movie before we drove all the way to Bennett Springs. By the time the movie was over, I noticed that Doc was having a problem with some of his equipment so I had our daughter meet us with a replacement so that I wouldn't have to worry about it all weekend. That put us a little later heading out than I was hoping for but it was still going to put us at the motel by 10 and I didn't think that was too bad for a Friday night...we aren't that old yet! Hehe! Plus, Doc was feeling much better after he cooled off so his ride would be better too! At least I thought so! We stopped for gas about halfway there and Doc asked me to pick up a cappuccino for him to have for breakfast. I guess from what we can figure that was about all he can remember about that day! I knew he was a little quiet but I thought he was asleep so I sat back to enjoy some music. About 20 minutes later, I heard a noise that I thought was a scratch on my cd but instead it was a gurgle from Doc. It was dark so I had to pull over on the side of the road and open the side door so I could see what was going on and I have to say that most times, I can about handle any situation but this time, it really scared me. I saw that he was completely passed out and he was gurgling up secretions and blood through the mouth. I think it was the blood that scared me and the fact that no matter what I did, I could not get a response from him. I cleaned him up the best I could and then reclined him back as far as I could in case it was blood pressure and then I unhooked his wheelchair straps so I could position the wheelchair to leave him reclined and get the doors shut. I thought that I had better keep going forward because I knew we were a long way from a town if I turned back. Luckily...I wrote that word on purpose...do you ever wonder about what really is going on when you get to use that word? Is it fate, destiny, luck, coincidence or a planned purpose? All I know is that whenever I need something, I am provided for...something that I give thanks for every day! Anyway, "luckily", I only went a few hundred yards when I passed a hwy patrolman on the shoulder of my side of the road. I stopped and explained my situation to him and he was able to let me follow him directly to the hospital...as I had no idea where I was going, this was a pretty big thing! Plus, just having him in front of me gave me the feeling of not being alone in the dark because I wasn't sure what was in the immediate future. Also, "luckily", we had some great friends that happened to mention they were taking a short vacation weekend at the lake, which was less than an hour away so I gave them a call and they started off to meet me at the hospital. During that call, I regrouped myself and remembered that whatever happened was in God's hands and that brought me more calming moments. When we arrived at the hospital, Doc was still unconscious but shortly after we arrived, he opened his eyes....that let me know he was at least alive! You could tell he wasn't seeing or comprehending anything but at least he was awake. From that point on, he slowly came around. At first he didn't know me or where he was at but then he comprehended that much but he still wasn't able to speak so we could understand him. He indicated to the doctor that he knew what he wanted to say but he just couldn't form the words. Because he was so confused and his speech was messed up, they were guessing he had a stroke so they decided to transport us to the hospital in Springfield, MO...about an hour away...I never road in the back of an ambulance before and I have to note here that the EMT's we had were like gold! Jim and Tim...I don't think I will ever forget them! As we approached the end of our destination, Doc continued to improve until he was pretty much completely recovered by the time we got there. Our friends followed the ambulance with Stan the Van so I would have it if we needed it. By this time, it was well into the morning hours of Saturday and I can only imagine that our friends were as tired as we were so I truly will never forget what they did for us! They ran all kinds of tests when we arrived in Springfield but they could find no confirmation that he had a stroke....they did see that the blood was a result from Doc biting about a 1" gash in his lip and his tongue was bitten into also. That made them suspect a seizure but once again, they couldn't confirm that. So around 3:30 a.m., they told us that they could admit him or release him....you can imagine which he chose...release! Doc told them, "I have some fishing to do!" So we headed back towards Bennett in the thickest fog I have had to drive through in a long time! It was hard to see anything! I did manage to see deer on the side of the road about every mile or so (I felt like I was a float in a deer parade!) and I was just praying that after everything else the night had held, if we could just arrive at the motel without having a wreck in the fog or hitting a deer..... that prayer was answered and it might have taken awhile to get there but we arrived safely! By the time I unloaded the van and got Doc tucked in, it was almost 6 a.m. and the horn was sounding for the fishing to start! I didn't think I could sleep but once my head hit the pillow I was out just as Doc was! We slept until noon and then we decided to get up and go fishing! We had the perfect weather and the perfect time! There is something refreshing and soul soothing fishing for trout. The river was so pretty and quiet! (I've attached a picture just so you can see how beautiful it was!) Some might say that after our experience, I should not have taken Doc fishing but it was exactly what we both needed and without knowing for sure what even caused our little problem, it didn't seem right to just go home and wait for it to happen again! So we spent the rest of the weekend resting up, fishing and enjoying our time together! By the time we arrived home Sunday evening, the rumors were running hot and heavy with some of them even having Doc in a coma….that one wasn't true! We had about 6 hours of being me being frightened (Doc says he isn't scared of nothing!") but we had over 48 good hours so I think we came out ahead! I am just thankful that we had another fishing trip memory because on that Friday night, I didn't know if we would ever get another memory like that! Looking back on it, I think of something that we read in the chapter of Mark where Jesus tells someone to feel a little less fear and a little more trust. There was a part of me that had complete trust in what that night might have held but the fear was outweighing it for awhile!

Father's Day held a surprise for Doc. We got him to Kansas City and he knew the kids were all going to meet him for lunch but what they really had planned was tickets to the Royals/Cardinal game so after lunch, he was treated to his surprise and I think there isn't anything that would have pleased him better! To share a Cardinal game with the kids was something really special! I am attaching a picture of Doc (actually 2 pictures..one of him coorperating and one of him being the goofball he is!) and the kids at the game…umbrellas and all…we had a 2 hour rain delay in the start of the game but it only created the perfect temperature for the game when it started! It wasn't a storm…just a nice steady drizzle and I don't think anybody minded the wait. Of coarse it was better because the Cardinals won! So now our record is 2 for 3 this year and overall for the past three years we are 18 wins for 21 games!

We had a fund raiser at church that we participated in to raise some money for a family facing a medical challenge and that was an enjoyable evening. So many persons joined together to help us when we needed it that it felt good to be doing it for someone else. Knowing how much it means to have that many people gather together to support you...some of them knowing you and some of them just knowing the situation...it is heart warming and while the funds do come in handy when you are struggling through some situations, that isn't the most important part...it is the support and the prayers! Anyway, the fund raiser was a trivia contest and each table had 8 players. Considering that there are some that say Doc is the smartest man in the world, you would have thought that we had secret weapon because we made Doc our team captain. However, he either underplayed his knowledge or was saving it for another day because we were not victorious. We saved face though because we were just slightly behind with a 3rd place finish.

Doc once again set a new record on the pacer going over 75 minutes. He still has his good days and his bad days but Cleveland Clinic is working with us and trying to help us over this hump! We still hope for the day to be vent free! Our new schedule is doing it for a set amount of minutes but doing it constantly throughout the day. They started us at 4 minutes and I think they are hoping that Doc will tolerate it better this way. I think they wonder if that one record breaking time each month isn't actually doing more harm than good.

We will see how this new process works! So far, I think Doc prefers the way he was doing it but he is up to trying anything.

The highlight of my month would have to be when we delivered the first Fishing Doc. It went to a young man living in our area that has some use of his arms and hands so he received a joystick version. The day we delivered it was a very hot day and I wasn't sure how the fish would be biting and I thought that even if they weren't biting, at least we could show him how it works and let him try another day. I was wrong though and the fish were biting like crazy....actually there was a little girl that was also present and she asked if it was an instant catch fishing pole because every time Jason cast it, it seemed like he had a small perch or bass on it! I asked Jason if it was exciting to be able to fish again and he said he had a better word for it..."extremely thrilled"....I have watched how much fishing means to someone that has little control over other things in their life and it is a great blessing to share this opportunity! So, "Jason Patrick Tindle, standing tall and quite the stud muffin" as he likes to be called, good luck fishing!

Probably the highlight of Doc's month was when we were approached by my company to see if Doc and I would be interested is taking a company expensed trip to Denver, CO, to deliver the Fishing Doc's to Craig Hospital in person instead of mailing them! How exciting to think that Doc could do his own in-service training! That will be really special! I am actually sending this e-mail out a little early because of that...we will be in Colorado visiting with old friends and probably making a few new ones. Of coarse we will try to fit in at least one hike in the mountains while we are there because I think Doc and I both feel like our souls live there! If heaven is anything like the mountains, we would both be happy! I am sure that a 12 to 14 hour trip one way and a few days in Colorado will have its share of adventures…seems like wherever we go, we come home with some story but that will have to be part of our July update.

July has an exciting weekend planned in St. Louis. This year the all-star game is being hosted by St. Louis so we are heading that way for some of the festivities. We were not able to secure all-star tickets (although my son and his wife were able too.…Doc calls them "lucky little turds") we did get tickets to the Fun Fest and Taco Bell Sunday so we get to participate in some of the events. It will just be nice to share in the atmosphere…if you are a baseball fan; the all-star break is a wonderful thing to participate in! Then we have a bridal shower coming up and there is plenty of wedding to-do things left to do! That is sneaking up on me more quickly that I am ready for it!

In closing, we wish each of you a safe and wonderful 4th of July! Living in our country is a privilege and an honor and celebrating its birth date and what it stands for is special! Having the freedom to worship is a powerful thing! We should also remember to say a special prayer for those that are celebrating it outside the boundaries as they fight to protect it! Doc and I want to say thanks to all of you that continue to remember us in your prayers. To all of you that helped us out in any way! Especially to Dana and Chad for giving me some late night hours in Springfield and to my family who helped me out of a pickle or two this month!

Your friends,
Doc (Darwin) and Cindy!

PS: We have had some persons inquiring about Buck....Our wonderful puppy is still around and makes us laugh every day! He is a fantastic dog that keeps Doc entertained daily! He still is a little too exuberant with our visitors and he loves to make his rounds every day with all our neighbors but I think he spreads smiles all around.... He will turn 2 in August so all too soon, he will be growing out of his puppy stage! I have a neat picture of him all curled up and being a good dog for a change...I have attached that for those of you that were wondering!

Bennett Springs, MO-Trout Fishing

Father's Day at the Cardinal Game
Doc, Jaymi, Adam, Laura, Carrissa, Brian

Doc Messing up the Picture but Being Doc!

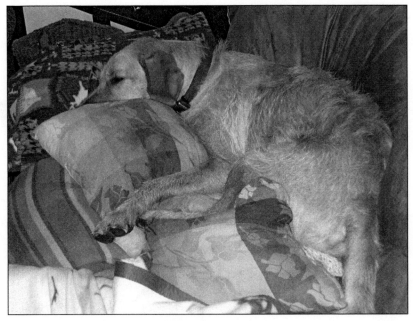

Buck Resting

July 2009

I almost sent out an update just on our trip to Colorado to deliver the Fishing Doc's to Craig Hospital because it was great story just in itself and I knew that we had other adventures on the July horizon but I decided to wait and put it all in one. Doc & I got up early on a Sunday morning and were able to make our trip to Denver in one day. It was a long day but we sure enjoyed the ride and having Stan was a blessing we gave thanks for more than once during this trip! Our first moment of awe happened right after we crossed over into Colorado. The sky was an unbelievable canvas that God was painting right before our eyes. I was driving close to 80 mph (almost legal in Colorado as their speed limits are faster than ours and I always shade a mile or two-can't help it and I can always blame it on my big feet! ☺)..So, I was driving with no exits in sight and wishing that I could have taken some pictures but the way it ended was just being photographed in my mind. My dad used to tell me that was the best way to remember something…take a photograph with your mind and you could hold onto it that way. Anyway, this is what it was like….to the south of us as wide as we could see and from the ground to the heaven was a huge storm. Walls of black clouds that almost resembled a huge tornado touched down that extended for miles! In front of us were the bluest, clearest skies you can imagine. Then right in front of us, a tiny bit of rainbow appears in the middle of the blue sky…a park ranger once told us they call them a sprite but I have never been able to find it in a dictionary so either I am not spelling it correctly or they really don't have that name…anyway, it was there when a long, skinny, gray cloud-almost like a line- comes floating across under it in through the blue sky…it wraps around the sprite and then forms a perfectly shaped heart with the sprite right in the center of it. The cloud stayed like that for a long time and eventually the colors left the middle and blue surrounded the inside and outside of that perfect heart. I have never seen anything like it but before I could really let my breath out from that experience, I looked back to the south and in front of the storm were the 2 largest, brightest rainbows that I have ever seen! From that point on, the sky changed as fast as the minutes with colors and it was like watching a light show. I finally did reach an exit where I pulled off and took some pictures of one of the most beautiful colored skies I have seen in my lifetime. Doc was enjoying it also as he was able to see out of the windows. Some of you might find this hard to believe but we probably rode along through this beauty for an hour of more just speechless. By the time we arrived in Denver, there was an over-whelming sense of peace and spirituality that Doc & I were both feeling. Doc put it well when he asked me if I didn't feel like we were right where God wanted us to be. We didn't know what was to lie ahead of us in the next few days but there is no doubt in our minds that we were on that trip for more reasons than to deliver a couple of fishing poles!

We spent the first day hiking in a canyon that I had found with handicap trails and although they were a little challenging, it was the closest thing to actually hiking that Doc & I had done since the accident. Poor Stan actually had to do some mountain driving and I am not sure that the van was made for mountain off-roads but he made it through it unscathed! Then that afternoon we had set up a time to deliver the poles and do a little one on one in-service on them. We were then scheduled to come back on Tuesday to do a more lengthy in-service with the entire rec team. To say The Fishing Doc was a smash hit would be putting it lightly. It put on a show like it was strutting itself and rose up to the occasion. Our only hope is that some patients find it to be as satisfying as Doc does and that some persons can use it to find a quality in their life again! After we were done with that in-service we made our way upstairs to visit with some of Doc's former caregivers while we were there. In the process of that, we were asked to visit some of the patients that were in a similar situation as Doc and we spent many hours making new friends, answering questions, and encouraging persons to hang in there. We also visited with the respiratory group and when they found out Doc had a pacer and was still on the vent after all these months, they encouraged us to try and set up an out-patient visit with the pulmonologist group while we were there. So we went downstairs and they were able to squeeze us in on Wednesday. We were looking forward to having some good advice on how to win the battle of getting off the vent! Then the rec department tracked us down again to come back on Wednesday and do one more in-service of the pole for publicity purposes and Doc was delighted to do that.

By the time we left the hospital, we had time to catch a quick supper before we headed downtown to a play. It was called Quilters and I think Doc thought it might be a chickflick thing but to tell you the truth, we were both surprised at how professional and entertaining it was.

Wednesday started off with the in-service and then we met with pulmonary and they had so many ideas on how to improve our quest to get off the ventilator. They prescribed some equipment and some supplies that we hadn't heard of before. Then they changed the type and size of trac that Doc was using. All in all, when it was all put in place, it has been amazing! The changes have all been to the good and although we are truly excited about how things have improved, it is sorta frustrating to think that no one has told us about any of these things before now. We have a cough assist machine which clears Doc's lungs out 2 or 3 times a day and it has taken care of our filter issue that we have been fighting for years. Instead of going through 6 or more a day, we are down to one or two. Doc's pacing has been much more consistent and we can finally see where he might be rid of the ventilator for longer periods of time. He is taking it slow and increasing it a minute or two a day each time he paces but he hasn't had anything less than 5 minutes for a long, long time.... he can pretty much reach the upper teens to 30 minutes every hour. That means that in an 8 hour period, he might be off the vent for close to 3 or 4 hours of it. That is amazing to us. He continues to tell me that it is getting more comfortable and that he could probably go longer but he wants to take his time and work into it gradually. He can also now talk while he is pacing and that is something new too. We are working on trying to get a portable oxygen machine approved through insurance and once that happens (hopefully this week), things will even get better because as long as we have a small oxygen tank with us, we can use it wherever we are and will be able to use the pacer while we are out and about. As Wednesday evening approached, I asked Doc if he wanted to chill one night at the room and maybe regroup but he said that would be wasted time and surely we could find something to do. I remembered reading about this place called Red Rock Amphitheater so I plugged it into our Garmin and away we went. When we got there, the Celtic women were going to perform in a couple of hours and they just had 2 handicap seats left so we bought them and ended up enjoying an outdoor performance that was awesome. The best part was that at intermission, we heard someone say, "Is that Doc and Cindy?" and it was some friends of ours from Wyoming. I still think it was great that they could make us out because it was pitch black by this time but what a joy running into them! It is a small world that we live in!

We took a day off on Thursday to head up to the mountains. Craig Hospital loaned us a portable tank of oxygen so we could keep Doc hooked up to oxygen while we were at the higher altitude and still get out and hike some and that made a huge difference. We both totally enjoyed that day. (I have attached a couple of pictures of the mountains) We had such a beautiful morning but as we climbed higher into the mountains the weather took a change for the worse. By the time we reached the divide, a fog was rolling in and it was starting to rain. We decided to stop at a little shop/restaurant that they have at the top and hoped that the weather would pass so I wouldn't have to drive down the mountain in total whiteness! It was the type of fog that didn't allow you to see much past the hood of your vehicle. This is where another neat experience happened... a young couple were sitting at a table across the room from us and we were watching them thumb wrestle and they just glowed...they were such a young and beautiful couple....after awhile, we had sorta forgotten about them being there when they got up and came over to our table to ask our names because they wanted to pray for us. How inspiring to see such young people of faith! They visited with us a little bit, told us they were from San Antonio and that this was their first trip to the mountains and how much they loved them. Then they said they had to go and the guy put his hand on Doc's shoulders and said, "Doc, you and Cindy hang in there, keep up with your ministry, and we will see you both when you get to heaven." It just sent chills up and down both our spines and as they disappeared into the fog, Doc asked me if I thought we had just met a pair of angels and I can't say for sure if they were heavenly angels but they were for sure earthly angels...anyone that has hearts of love and the compassion that they shared with us have halos and wings somewhere! The fog hadn't lifted by the time we started down the mountain but it wasn't scary to drive I in after an experience like that!

Friday found us doing something that was a little sad but I was so thankful we were in Colorado to be able to do it! My Uncle Jim passed away while we were in Colorado and that just happened to be where he and his family lived. I have many, many wonderful memories of visiting and traveling with them so it seemed so right to be able to drop in and give my aunt and cousins a hug and let them know that we cared. I know that he is at peace now and I am happy for him although he will be missed by those that are left here for awhile longer! We made it about ½ way across Kansas after we left there and managed to make it the rest of the way home on Saturday. It was a long week and we were tired but I can't explain how perfect that week of our life was. We are so grateful for Orscheln's sponsoring the trip because it was so fruitful!

We stayed home 4 days and then we were off again for 5 days in St. Louis. We had tickets to some of the events at the all-star activities. What a fun time we had there….not only was it all about baseball but it centered around the Cardinals with it being hosted by them this year. We met several former Cardinal players and got autographs but the highlight of all of them had to be meeting Lou Brock. (I am attaching that picture)…I am also going to attach a copy of us with Fredbird trying to eat Doc's Taco hat. It was Taco Bell Sunday and they were giving these hats away at the fan-fest and we had fun with them! I know they aren't much to look at but we had several persons trying to get us to give them up…I think it might be the next fashion statement..or not! While we were in St Louis, we met up with several of my cousins and made some memories! Good memories!

After that, it was mostly about fishing and wedding stuff. I spent several hours working on invitations and flowers. I still have more to do but I am making headway! By the next time I update you, the wedding will be only a week away. Amazing at how fast this summer is going. Doc got a lot of fishing in although I have to call and see if my trout is mounted because we plan on making another trip back to pick it up and squeeze in at least one more attempt at catching a few more trout! We were able to fish with a young boy, Dominic, from the Macon area that is paralyzed and on a vent, much the same as Doc's condition. He is 12 years old and has quite the sense of humor. He was smart too…I think we were with him for less than 30 minutes when he looked at me and said, "Cindy, I haven't known your husband very long but he's trouble isn't he?"….hehe…I think he meant it in a nice way because I think he could be "trouble" too…that is where that sense of humor comes in. (I attached a copy of Doc and Dominic so you can see for yourself how onery they look! :))He made a comment that he had gone fishing several times in his life but he had only watched and never got to fish. He was pretty excited about getting to fish on his own. I think the one thing that was burnt in my mind is when he said, "Cindy, here I am just fishing with my dad." I looked over there and his dad was sitting in a chair beside him and they were fishing and there was such a wonderful look of joy on Dominic's face. Dominic ended up landing a

6 lb catfish and you can imagine his excitement! We didn't realize until it was almost dark that he didn't know he was going to keep his pole…until he knew that, I think he would have fished all night! What an evening that was! If any of you want to see The Fishing Doc in motion, I think you can find it on youtube.com.…just search for disabled fishing and several come up but Doc is in the picture on the one that talks about the fishing doc and it isn't hard to spot it.

Doc was a good sport because I had to make a trip to Hobby Lobby for some wedding supplies and he was wonderful about it! I think I was in there for over 2 hours and he actually was even helping me find things! Sometimes he finds a hole and takes a nap but this time, he kept right up with me. As a reward, he got to go to Mernards and do some "manly" shopping too! Then we went out to eat and while we were eating a flock of turkey and a herd of deer were in a field across the road from the restaurant and we were seated so that Doc had a perfect view of them while he was eating. I can't imagine that he thought it could get any better than that! If he could watch that view every time, we would probably be eating at that restaurant more!

Carrissa, our daughter, had a bridal shower and I had to laugh at how slick Doc was about finding his own "Doc" sitters so he wouldn't have to go to that! It was almost funny at how he lined up some guys to come sit with him and play cards so he would not have to go to that shower! It all worked out though and I think we all had a great time that evening.

Buck had a rough month because last week, someone shot him with a rifle…he was only outside for about 15 minutes and he was pawing the front door that he wanted to come back in. I let him in but he didn't try to play with me like he usually does and then I saw all this blood. So I took him to the vet and he said he was just really lucky because it appeared that someone had stood over the top of him and shot down into the back of his neck and there was a good sized hole. We could feel the bullet on the side of his body under the skin. The vet thinks the bullet hit a rib and slid down it instead of entering a lung or organ. He thought that he would be ok without taking it out and he is already getting back to normal. For a day or two, he was a little slow at getting around but he is back to wanting to play again. The vet said he was one tough dog. My heart just broke for him though and I had to say several prayers for the person that would take a gun to a dog like that. Buck isn't the type of dog to chew or bother anything so I am almost positive that Buck came up to this person thinking that he was a friend with his tail wagging as fast as it would go only to have a gun put to his back.

So that was the highlights of our month. Some good, some bad, some happy, and some sad…isn't that what life is like? We had a substitute at church this past weekend and he said something that has stuck with me. He said that our earthly lives are made up of spiritual things and material things. What we should think about is that if we give away some of our spiritual things, we only gain more back for it but if we give away our material things, we have less.

So isn't it much better to have more of what grows when you give it away? It put our material possessions into perspective for me... it is all just stuff. This brings me full circle to say thanks for all the prayers and kindness that have been shed for Doc & I this month. Those are the types of things that are the most precious to us and that we never take for granted. I hope that the upcoming month has many highlights for all of you! I think that we are pretty busy....besides the last minute wedding activities, we have tickets to 2 Cardinal games, a family reunion, my mom's birthday, not to mention that we have upcoming shower and wedding activities planned for other dear friends that we know that are getting married also. As August is frequently a vacation month we pray for a safe journey for all that are traveling!

Your friends,

Cindy and Doc (Darwin)

PS: I always write this with Doc and I told him this was already too long to add this next note but he insisted that you would all be interested in knowing that for 4 weeks in a row, he has given away his crying towel to me and my partner in our card games. I am on a losing record but hopefully, we will change that trend soon! ☺

Cindy, Doc, and Fredbird on Taco Bell Sunday

Doc with Mr. & Mrs. Lou Brock

Doc, Cindy and the Craig Rec Dept with The Fishing Doc

Doc and Dominic Fishing

View Hiking in the Rockies

Doc and Cindy Hiking in the Rockies

August 2009

This month has flown by fairly uneventful with the exception of a few outings and the upcoming wedding preparations. Doc is counting down the days until we don't have ribbons, bows, flowers, and piles of wedding stuff smothering him in the living room. I think it is over-shadowing his items and he just wants his room back! To tell you the truth, I am looking forward to having wedding clutter out of the house too! Less than a week now and we are in countdown mode. The only thing that is bothering me a little bit is Doc's health because he hasn't felt just real perky for awhile and he slips just a little more each week and I have been trying to turn a blind eye to it until after the wedding and I sure hope he can hang on or whatever it is that is bugging him will go away! He is not sleeping very well and even though I have to get up every hour or two to attend him, I think he sometimes goes for the entire night without sleeping. Whenever he starts to have oxygen problems along with other symptoms, you can bet there is an infection in there somewhere and the doctor never seems to want to try to solve it as an out-patient so if I call, I know exactly what road we will be on and that is to the hospital for tests and the next thing I know, they will be dragging him to a room for admittance. So far, I have put it off knowing that he hasn't had a fever and the infectious disease doctor once told us that without a fever, he would never treat an infection anyway because the fever was the indication that it was active. Tonight was the first night that I saw an increase in his temperature and although it wasn't much over 100, it still is concerning me. I have prayed hard the last few days for God to allow Doc to attend his daughter's wedding but sometimes, as we well know, our plan is not God's plan. I will just trust that however this week pans out, it will be the way it is supposed to be! Doc and I have a motto…one day at a time and that is how we take life….so, I will hope that our one day at a time gets us to Saturday!

We did have some fun times this month….we went to 4 Cardinal games…we just arrived home tonight from an entire series with the Washington Nationals and we managed to pull off a sweep so that was great! Doc did really well Friday night and not too bad yesterday but he struggled to get through the day today. I could tell that he would have given up on about anything else the way he was feeling but it is hard for him to leave a Cardinal game! Yesterday was a promotion they call photo day and the players, coaches, and managers come out and walk around the field and let persons take pictures of them. The gates open early and the fans are allowed on the outer edge of the field so they are very close. What I didn't expect was that everyone in a wheelchair is taken to a special gate and they are wheeled down to the field right behind homeplate. The announced that they would only be taking pictures and no autographs were going to be given so I was surprised that when they got to the wheelchair section, every single player, coach and manager autographed something for the fans in that section. It was a really special moment that they all took the time to sign and to visit with each person in that area. Doc came home with more collectables for his "Cardinal" collection but I think what he really enjoyed was just visiting with them and talking to them. It was especially great that Chris Carpenter (a Cardinal pitcher) that we met in January at the Winterfest actually remembered Doc and they had a nice visit. I think that was Doc's highlight! So we saw 4 victories this month and our record is now 22 wins in 25 games....he is definitely on a winning track! We don't have any games in Sept as it is pretty booked with other activities but he has a couple the first weekend in October. He is already telling me that I should be prepared to try to get some playoff tickets if we win our way into them and they way they have been playing, it looks promising!

We also went to the State Fair and watched a concert by Little Big Town. They did a tremendous job and even though it was a week night and we were really late in getting to bed, it was a wonderful time. I think both of us would choose to do that again!

We got to do a little fishing and the weather was wonderful! What a perfect August...it was mild although a little wet...I don't think we reached 100 degrees one day this summer and that is very unusual for Missouri! The only thing that is sad about it is that summer is almost over and it doesn't seem like we had one! We actually had blankets and jackets this past weekend at the Cardinal games and I was wishing I had brought heavier jackets!

Doc's pacer is doing much better! It is unbelievable at the headway he is making. His current one time record is over 2 hours now and he can consistently go at least an hour or two a day at one time with several other decent pacers to go along with it. During the course of a day, he spends about 25% of it or better without the ventilator. Those little 4 or 5 minute pacers are a thing of the past! We were finally outfitted with some portable oxygen containers that will work with his chair so now we should be able to pace even when we are out and about. That was a bottleneck until now but it shouldn't be anymore! That is one thing that I have noticed....without the ventilator, he is going to have to be on oxygen full time but I would rather deal with that than to the vent destroying his lungs!

This next part is a secret from Doc....It is an invitation to anyone that wants to come out and wish him happy birthday or send him a card for his 50th birthday....His birthday is actually 9/22 but I am planning a surprise b-day party at the Moose in Moberly, MO on Saturday, 9/26, from 6-10 p.m. It is an open invitation because I am not sending out personal invitations. Please no gifts!! What we are doing instead is just asking everyone that wants to, to bring a finger food of some type. I had no idea how many to prepare for with an open invitation so I thought this would work. For those that can't make the party and would like to send a card, his address is 3301 CR 1330, Moberly, MO 65270. He thinks he is going to a co-ed bridal shower for a friend of ours and he is NOT happy about it....I think if it were for anyone else but her, he probably would just say a flat out NO! hehe! It is bothering him so bad, that I don't think he can see past it to suspect a party even though I know he doesn't trust me! Remember, it is a surprise!!!

In between the wedding and the birthday party, we are heading to Branson for a few days to meet up with his brother and wife for a week of shows and fishing and whatever else we throw in there. It will be nice to get away after the wedding and just chill! I just want to forget about "planning" things for a day or two!

The first part of October is already full of plans too and I keep telling him that there just isn't a good time to get sick so hopefully, he will pull out of his current slump and we will be back in shape to enjoy all of the upcoming activities!

I read something that has stuck in my mind all month and I have tried hard to remember it on our hard days. It was "The will of God will not lead you where the grace of God cannot find you." That is my thought of the day as I saved the best part for last and that is to say thanks for all of you that have lightened our days in any way and/or continue to lift us up in prayer. There is nothing more consoling than to know that someone is remembering to pray for you or that whenever I need help, I have a friend only a phone call away! Doc and I never take that lightly and we are both very grateful for the prayers. We do believe in the power of prayer and even though the answers might not be the way we would like to perceive them, we do believe that prayer is always answered!

As fall ushers in, we wish all of you the best of days and the opportunities to make some lasting memories!

Love,

Your friends,

Doc (Darwin) and Cindy

PS: I could update you are that status of the card playing but I think I will just let it go as it will be my b-day present to Doc not to mention it! Hehe…oops, I think I just did! ☺

September 6-2009

It is with mixed feelings that I have to write this update....When you have something that you really love but you have to give it up for something better for them, it is hard to let go. Whether it is a kid going off to college or a child getting married or letting someone that you love go to heaven. In my case this morning, it is letting a love one prepare to go to heaven.

On my last update, I knew that after our almost "perfect" weekend with an entire Cardinal series with the Washington Nationals, Doc wasn't feeling well. For those that haven't known, I spent that entire night up with Doc trying to figure out why his oxygen levels were slipping. By morning, I knew I needed to check him out with a doctor but the sats slipped too fast for me to even get him out of bed and I had to call an ambulance. Since that time, we have been on a roller coaster....trying to establish what was wrong, trying to follow all of Doc's ups and downs, and trying to fit a "perfect" wedding into the scheme of things.

The verdict was that Doc has had acid reflex, unknown to either of us and stomach acids have filled his lungs, causing aspirated pneumonia. At first, we were hopeful that they could treat it and that there was a slight chance that he would even still make it to walk Carrissa down the aisle. Monday afternoon and Tuesday were pretty good days...Doc felt pretty bad but he was able to communicate and he had his sense of humor still in tact! By Tuesday night, he drifted into a more comotose type of state and occasionally he would rouse himself out of it and pucker his lips for a kiss or give someone a smile that popped into the room. He has remained in that state for the rest of the week.

On Monday, while he was still alert, he looked at me and told me he was sorry that he was making me spend hospital time on the week that I had everything going on with the wedding. He said, "Cindy, we are in a tight spot!"—one of his sayings that he picked up out of one of his favorite movies 'Oh Brother Where Art Thou'. Then he made me promise that whatever the week held for us that I would be at the rehearsal and the wedding and that the wedding would go on. He said that if we couldn't both be there, at least one of us should be...we are the parents after all! So, the wedding went on and our son took Doc's place as proxy for Carrissa and it was almost like he was there because if any of you have met our son, he looks an awful lot like his dad! Just a little younger! :) Sorta like when I married him!

The doctor had told me on Wednesday that he wasn't sure that Doc was going to pull out of this one and that he felt that he might be holding on for something before he gives in. I think that it might have been the wedding because as of this morning, the prognosis is that he has less than a 5% chance of pulling through. I am going to have to make a decision soon as to whether to keep fighting the pneumonia or to just keep him comfortable. At this point, they are telling me that we probably have a couple or three days but that no one knows for sure. As his kidneys and liver are starting to fail, usually his heart will give out. I have already communicated to them not to revive him from a heart failure and put him on life support because I know that he has been tired for a long time and maybe his reward is due!

Doc has had an amazing life and we have shared over 30 years of mostly happy times and happy memories. We have been able to experience things in the past 5 years that I have never imagined! God has driven our bus to locations that I never expected to be a part of. Now he might be parking it to let Doc get off and when he does get off, he will walk off. I can only imagine how wonderful it is going to feel to him to be able to run and jump! My thoughts go back to a little 4 year old that once came up to Doc to tell him not to be sad about being in the wheelchair and not walking because when he gets to heaven, he will be good again. Doc often shared that story and how he gained so much comfort in the wisdom of that little boy!

Our daughter that was married last night has been a wonderful support in the past week and her wedding last night was the most blessed occasion. They are now headed to Colorado for a honeymoon in the mountains and I spoke with her before she left so that I would know that if Doc took a turn for the worse, if she would want to return early or if she would want me to hold off a funeral. It was her decision that she would want to know what was going on but that she would finish her honeymoon because IF something happened to her dad, being in the mountains would be exactly where he would want her to be...and that is true...Doc's spirit soars when he is in the mountains! So if something would happen to Doc before then, I am not making any plans for anything until the first part of next week.

My last coherant and lengthy discussion with Doc was on the ride home from St Louis Sunday evening and he told me that he wondered who was going to take his place. At first I thought he meant with me but he told me he wasn't meaning that...he meant in life....he said, "I wonder who is going to take my place and bring all those to heaven that I haven't got to yet because I have alot of persons that I wanted to bring to heaven with me that aren't going yet. Who is going to take my place and bring them?" At the time I just told him that I didn't think God would take him until he had gathered up everyone that he was supposed to. I never suspected that less than a week later, I would be writing this e-mail but maybe he knew something that I didn't!

Please keep Doc in your prayers and we do believe in miracles but to be honest, I know that greatest gift in life for both Doc and I has always been the promise of dying! The hard part is not doing it together at the same time. So if you have a moment to add me to your prayer list too so that I might have the strength to stay focused on the gladness for Doc and not the sadness for me, I would appreciate it! I know Doc would be saying the same thing if he were proofing this like he usually does!

With love from your friends,

Doc (Darwin) and Cindy

September 15-2009

I first want to say a special thanks to ALL of you that sent such heartwarming responses and memories to my last update from about 9 days ago. I was not accessible to my e-mail during that time so I have just sat down to read them and they have all lifted me up! It is amazing at how God uses us to serve each other and I am blessed for the opportunity to do what so many of you have testified that Doc and I have done but to also have received those same blessings back!

At 11:30 this morning, Doc exited this world and I am sure has won his reward! I cannot imagine the sights and feelings he must be encountering today! He has put up a valiant battle although he was never really conscious, I feel like he wanted to make sure that Carrissa returned from her honeymoon and for my birthday to come to pass. After that, I think he could comfortably move on. My grief that I am experiencing at thoughts of not seeing his smiling face every day or having his wisdom when I have a problem, is over-shadowed by the joy that I know that he is experiencing! We have spent many hours talking about this day so it doesn't come with any questions for me...only a plan to put into action. He was adamant that we make these plans and now I know why. It is making today and tomorrow much easier for the knowledge of just implementing what he had already planned out.

I asked my kids to gather in Doc's room on my birthday and we shut the door and spent 4 hours just digging up wonderful memories of Darwin and laughing (because not many memories of Doc does not bring up a smile or two!) and I feel in my heart that Darwin found as much comfort in those memories as I did. After that they took me out to eat and I felt comforted to know that they were all married, happy, and living a Christian life....what more could a parent ask for? I returned to Doc's room and whispered to him that I thought he had done what his mission was and that he could be proud of the dad and husband that he had been. I truly have been blessed to have shared his life and to have had the family and friends that we have.

Please do not find sorrow in this news but rather a reason to rejoice! That is what we both have always wanted! The fact that Darwin goes before me only leaves him "waiting on his woman".... something that we often smiled about!

Your friend,
Cindy

October 12-2009

For awhile, my life was broken into two sections.....before Doc had his accident and after he had his accident but now there is another piece...after Doc died. My daughter doesn't like that word...died... it sounds harsh and permanent to her. I am not sure that any other word really softens the emptiness and loneliness though, so to say passed or no longer with us or however you want to say it doesn't really change anything. It is just part of this world anyway because Doc is saying "I have arrived!"..."at last!" I can just imagine his smile on his face as he walked into heaven. I used to tell him that if he died before me, that he better be watching over me and keeping me on a path to heaven....while he was in the wheelchair, I was so busy taking care of him and God had his own purpose for our life during that time and we were constantly squeezing in more in a day than most do in a week so it wasn't hard to stay focused on that path! I think my biggest fear is that I somehow get to sunnier days and I forget what is the most important thing in this world... which is actually something outside of it! When times are tough, you are always aware of it because leaning on it is the only thing that gets you through some days! I pray hard that I remember to let God continue to drive my bus...through good weather and bad! Just like many of you have said that reading these e-mails each month kept you in touch with the important things, being around Darwin did that for me! I can look back on things now and am amazed at all God did with us during 5 short years! I think he worked us hard so

Doc didn't have to wait any longer than he needed to in order to earn his reward. He was ready for that reward too!

I wanted to say thank you to every single one of you that took the time to come to the visitation and/or funeral…what a tribute to Doc (and to me!) to see so many persons that cared. If that outpouring wasn't enough to warm a heart, I also received so many cards, e-mails and calls expressing the most wonderful sentiments. The funeral was exactly the way Doc wanted it to be…uplifting and spiritual. I don't think I have been to one that was more suited to the deceased than this one was for Doc! From the standing ovation that he received to the bluegrass music that he had picked out to the orange flowers that he wanted to the many Cardinal touches! The most awesome parts were the tribute to his life and the eulogy that our son delivered! It was just perfect! He is buried in a place in the cemetery that is close to the trees and in the shadow of a huge cross. I would bet that you would find a deer or turkey that wonders near him on a daily basis. I stop in and talk to him occasionally but only his earthly body is actually buried there so I don't haunt it incessantly. It is a quiet place to reflect on life though and I find peace there.

There were all kinds of things to take care of during the first couple of weeks after the funeral. Paperwork, name changes, insurance, social security, equipment, supplies, and the list could go on and on…I know that I am still not finished with it….I have at least one new issue that pops up every day! Besides those things, my daughter went with me and we ordered a headstone that looks like a block right out of the side of a mountain cliff and it is perfect for us! They told me they would set it after the grounds settles.

As many of you can guess from all the e-mails you received in the past that told you where we went and what we did, that we didn't spend much time at home. That was good for us but not so good for the house. Our house has many bedrooms and closets and they became a stashing place for "stuff" as we went and went and went. Now I have to pay the price for that and I have dived into chores. In the past 5 yrs I haven't had the ability to spend much time upstairs, in the basement or in the garage because I had to stay close to Doc's vent. Now I am starting to clean the closets out one at a time. I am trying to clean the bedrooms upstairs one at a time. I have the attic, garage and basement to get to also. I have already made 2 trips to Goodwill with a car full of donations and I am sure that I will make many more! On top of that my poor trash man has to be wondering if I am going around collecting garbage from others just to put it out to make work for him! I have stacked huge piles for weeks and I know I am not done yet! I got their bill this week and they raised their prices and I was afraid for a minute that they were going to tell the world that it was because Cindy Blackmore had too much trash! (just in case you were wondering, I was not the reason!) :)

What else have I been up to? Well, let's see…I found someone that I could donate the wheelchair to and it will be put to a good use! I found someone that needed most of the rest of Doc's equipment and many of his supplies so those were donated to them. I still have a few supplies to dispose of and as hard as it might be to just throw them away, it is probably what I need to do! When I think what they cost to buy though it is soooo hard to just ditch them! It is hard to throw things away that I conserved in order to be financially smart when they would have made our life easier to use them! I am in the process of changing the room that we were using for a bedroom into a nice family room. I am doing it in the Cardinal theme so I can keep our many treasures and happy memories on display. I even bought a red sofa and loveseat combo and a Cardinal rug to finish it off. It will make a nice gathering place for all of us when the kids are all home together. Then I am in the process of remodeling our old bedroom upstairs into something special for me. It is good to have great memories but they can sometimes be painful too so it helps to change things a little bit and not be forced to relive the past so much. I am finding that there needs to be a good balance between new and old....I don't want to live in the past but I don't want to forget it either!

So that means a lot of cleaning and painting and mending! Luckily, Doc trained me well in the past 5 years so I am pretty handy with tools. He tried to teach me some electrical stuff too but I still don't have the confidence to try my hand at it solo! As many of you know, anything that has any type of association to possible fires should probably be something that I leave alone! The person that took many of Doc's supplies also had need of a better ramp so

I donated the one out the back door. (I am keeping the front one though in case any of our wheelchair bound friends come to visit!). Our family at AECI built the ramps and they did a tremendous job! The paralyzed boy and his family that I passed the back ramp to were very excited about it! After we moved it I saw that someone had to break up my back steps to put in the ramp though so now I am going to have to build a deck or a patio out the back but that will be a spring project. I stacked some bricks to make a temporary fix so I can still use the back door and it works ok. I am actually looking forward to fixing up a special place outside next year! We have a beautiful shade tree right where it needs to be planted to allow me to actually enjoy the area!

I have decided to join a couple of groups. One is a club in our community that does some community service and I am excited about participating in that and maybe giving just a little something back. Then I joined a group at church and I think that is going to be rewarding too! They will meet once a week starting this week.

I find myself with my weekends booked clear out into December and so even with Doc not coming up with ideas on how to spend our Saturdays and Sundays, I managed to fill them myself. Well, actually many of them are as a result of persons calling me to invite me to somewhere so maybe those are my angels to keep me busy until I adjust to this new style of living alone. It is a first for me because I have never lived alone. I know a lot of persons do but it is an adjustment if you have never done it before and you reach my age and are trying it for the first time! Like everything, it has its pros and cons! Having my daughter get married and moved out during the same time frame as losing Darwin has been a double whammy but she still stops by frequently.

The hardest thing that I have done to date is sell Stan the Van. That was a crushing day and I still have a hard time when I think about it or try to talk about it. I am not sure exactly why that was so hard compared to other things but it was. I think it was a combination of how much it meant to Doc & I, how everyone pulled together to help us get it, how much fun we had with it and finally, how many plans we had made that were unfulfilled. In selling the van, it was like it made it a certainty that those dreams would remain unfinished! That was my heart talking though. The head was telling me that the license was due on it and the insurance was due and I already had another reliable vehicle. It was telling me that I had a loan that I needed to pay off and that someone else out there in a similar situation just might be waiting for the same opportunity that we had in getting a more reliable vehicle. We only had it for 6 short months but we put over 10,000 miles on it and it took us to the mountains for one last hike together and I will never, never forget that trip!

I could tell Buck was missing Doc but as the days pass, he is quickly adapting to another routine. He searched for Doc for awhile and one night I woke up to him whining and found him under Doc's chair. That was a little bit sad for both of us! He was used to someone being home all day and giving him attention but now he has to survive on his own until I get home from work. He is probably getting a little spoiled right now as Doc was always the one that made me reprimand him (although I never was as rough as Doc wanted me to be! ☺) He loves to go on walks and so I try to fit them in while the weather is nice. I sorta like walks too! ☺

I am not planning on continuing these e-mails but I wanted to send out one more to say one final thank you! As I finish up some of my many projects and I can relive some the past years without the pain of missing Doc so much, I plan on writing a book about our experiences. The wonderful support, the earthly angels, and miracles that we have seen! The way God used both of us to witness to others…the way Doc's face just lit up when he was sharing his story and how the holy spirit just radiated off of him! I am not sure how to even start it or how to fit all the material into just one book but I am sure with the grace of God, it will all come together just as it should! I have kept a journal through this entire experience and it is full of wonderful stories that are going to make some awesome chapters!

So many persons have asked and I wanted you all to know that I was doing ok…."ok" is a weird word but I have found myself using it a lot. What does ok mean and why do people use it when on the inside they feel anything but ok? I think I mean my life is ok and I am staying busy and the days still go by one by one. There are still things that need to be done and others that aren't so important. There is a hole in my heart that is like an open wound and over time, it will probably heal a little bit but how could it be anything less? When you love someone with your heart and soul and God joins you to be "one", then all of a sudden half of your being is gone, it is going to hurt. But those are just earthly pains that many before me have experienced and many after me will experience. The heavenly joys that are yet to come will wipe every tear away! I feel like I am being remolded into something else as God tenderly pushes me in a new direction in life. I am sure I have no idea where I am going but I am just as sure that God does know! That is all I really need to rely on!

I will close this as Doc and I always did…with a huge, heartfelt thank you for all of the wonderful and thoughtful deeds that each of you did for my family in the past month! I had so many thank you notes to write after the funeral that I was unable to write what was really in my heart in each of them so without meaning to leave anyone out, I want to say a special thank you to our AECI family… what an awesome display of love you guys shared with me! For my Orscheln family…you guys were also wonderful! For the Cairo community and the ballteams that took the time to come by and give me a hug! For our church community and the many that came from the churches that we had visited! For our families and the love they wrap around me! For the wonderful outpouring of support for The Fishing Doc Memorial fund, which officially has a banking account now. We raised over $5,000 to help others fish and I can't think of anything, other than his faith, that Doc would have wanted to share more! He was truly a fisher of men!

A few of us are working at an expo in Atlanta, GA in November where Orscheln's has a booth reserved to promote the fishing doc.... hopefully, we will obtain enough interest in it to be able to make our first production run soon! I am looking forward to that weekend! I know that Doc really was looking forward to attending that show but instead of being there physically, he will there in spirit! He was a huge part of the development of the fishing doc and his story will live on through it!

Thanks for the many prayers that you have offered for me in the past month and if I could just remain in them for a little longer, it would probably be a good thing! This isn't a final good-bye or anything....many of you have offered me help if I need it and if you haven't figured out from the past 5 years, I do ask when I need help so some of you will probably get a call now and then. I love to get and answer e-mail so keep me in your address book! My daughter is trying hard to get me signed up on facebook so I might be doing that soon too! Thanks for sharing these past 5 years with us and God Bless!

Your Friend,
Cindy

PS: Just in case anyone is wondering, I am thinking that when you get to heaven God must keep you really, really busy because Doc did not have time to help his Cardinals! They went down fast and hard! I know that if Doc could have sprinkled some wake up and play dust on them, he would have done so! As it was, I hope he didn't get to witness any of it! The last weekend he was healthy, we watched a 3 game sweep and after he went to the hospital, they didn't play well for the rest of the season! Maybe they were just missing one of their greatest cheerleaders!

December 2009

Christmas greetings! I have had so many persons asking me if I might just send out an update and let everyone know what is going on that I thought I would take the opportunity of updating everyone and to wish you all a very blessed Christmas-sort of like the price of 2 for 1! ☺ For those that enjoy these updates, it is my gift to you!

Speaking of 2 for 1 reminds me of one of the activities that I have been doing a lot of lately and that is shopping. I always am ready to shop but especially at Christmas time. It always feels good to give and Christmas time is a wonderful time to share. Not only with family and friends but with someone that you might be able to help that might not even know you are doing it. Or maybe through a church program or through a tag off a tree in a department store or through a toy for tots drive or a food pantry donation... there are so many ways to help others. I know that for some, times might be hard but I don't believe that donations have to be big to be helpful-or for that matter, even financial. Sometimes it might be just a donation of a kind deed or an afternoon of service or something as simple as cleaning out your closet and finding something that you really don't use anymore that might just be what someone else needs. I also know that you can get wrapped up in all the stress of having to be here or there and do this and that and the list almost goes on past the 25th except that is the deadline so it can't! I don't know if I am still in what feels like a bubble on most days or what, but I can tell you that I look differently on life. Things that used to be important really aren't all that big of a deal. Walking around shopping, it isn't so important that I end up having bags of stuff in my hands…it is sharing a smile with someone that looks like they really need it, it is letting someone step in line in front of you, it is being able to tell someone to go ahead and add their little handful of stuff onto your bill because it isn't going to make that much difference to your total but it will add a little joy to their day…how do you put a price on joy? It is letting someone have a parking spot that you might have been waiting for to park further back on the lot and then to be able to say a prayer of thanks that you can walk from your car to the store with two working legs!

If you ever are in need and have to be humbled to accept help, it sure makes you appreciate the persons that give it and it makes you understand how it might be hard to be on the receiving end too! Doc and I were blessed to never be in a financially strapped position, mostly because of his good insurance and benefits from his employment but also through the generosity of those we worked with along with our family and friends that always seemed to be there when a need arose. BUT, we were often in need of help in other ways that maybe money couldn't buy, even if I had wanted to! Things like a card or a call when we needed it…knowing someone was saying a prayer for us on a hard day.. a visit or an invitation out when things seemed to be a private battle which reminded us that we weren't battling anything on our own! What I am trying to say without writing an entire page (which I have almost already done) is that so many of you did so much for us without you even knowing how much it meant (and continues to mean) that I am trying to pay it forward and I hope that you find a way to continue to treat others like you treated us! This might be my first Christmas without the physical presence of Doc but his spiritual presence and his effect on my life (and probably on many of your lives) will never be gone. When someone molds your character into something better, that person is never really gone…he continues to live in that part of you that is better for having known him!

I still cry for missing Doc…I still laugh at memories of him…I still ache for the memories we didn't finish and give thanks constantly for the ones that we were allowed! I see his smile.. the ornery twinkle in his eyes.. I have days that I long for his wisdom and conversation. I don't miss the battles of insurance, wheelchair mechanical issues, home health care issues, supplies and the battle to obtain what he needed to get the most from life! I don't miss getting up every hour to care for him almost every night and I don't miss the look in his eyes for him having to ask me to get up! Even after 3 months, I still haven't gotten used to the fact that if I need to run to the store, I can…If I want to be away from home longer than 9 p.m., I can without calling anyone to tell them I will be late.. if I want to visit one of my children and spend the night, I can.. and only by packing one small overnight bag and getting in the vehicle and going! Things are much easier and yet harder. Nothing is ever perfect… I wrote that line on purpose because I hope there are a few of you that are thinking, "Doc is where it is perfect!" because that is what I believe...there is one place that is perfect and that is what gets me through each day...knowing Doc is there and that I know in my heart that I am going to be there too one day. That is what makes this season of Christmas what it really is...the birth of Jesus that gives us that promise to allow us to know that we can be perfect through him! That we can have an eternal "perfect" home!

Now, about my present home...I have changed the room we were using as a bedroom into a family room with a Cardinal baseball theme...it is pretty cool to sit in it and look around at things that Doc found joy in and to remember our many Cardinal outings! It is the room that I put up our Christmas tree in this year and when the kids come home for Christmas, we will have joyful memories to make in there! I have renovated part of the upstairs and I have a beautiful master bathroom and bedroom, complete with a walk-in closet, which has always been a dream of mine! Doc often said that if he could give me two things, it would be a jetted tub and a walk in closet and now I have them and I know he is saying "finally!" I could just sit in my new surroundings upstairs and never leave them and be happy...what a wonderful and peaceful haven it turned out to be. The kitchen floor had been carpet and as Doc's wheelchair could not take its boots off at the door so there wasn't much I could do about the flooring except clean it as best I could but now I replaced it with something newer and easier to clean and I am pleased with how it turned out too. Now I am working on one more room which I want to change into a media room and then I will be done with most of what I wanted to do. The house was in need of some attention and it is amazing at what a little facelift can do! It has kept me busy whenever I was home but I have to admit that my friends, children and family have been keeping me pretty busy away from home.

I had a long weekend with my cousin in St. Louis. I attended a play of 'It's a Wonderful Life' with some friends at a theater. I had a weekend with my daughters for some "girl" time. "Girl time" reminds me that I also have a group of girls that make Wednesdays "girls night out" and we have come up with some creative things to do. This past Wednesday, we went to see Big Bad Voodoo Daddy (it's fun just to say that outloud..go ahead and try it a few times... it will make you smile!), which was a swing band and they were putting on a Christmas concert-they were great! I am not sure what we are doing this week but it is not my turn to plan it! This one, I will just be along for the ride! I have been hitting some local basketball games when I can. This past weekend, I was in Branson and Silver Dollar City. Back in July, Doc said that instead of buying my mom a present, maybe we could take her to Branson and show her the lights at Silver Dollar City so that is what I did...I took her to see the lights, catch some shows, and we had a wonderful time celebrating the season and eating wayyyy too much food but I enjoyed every bite! As usual, Doc had a wonderful idea and I am glad that I followed through on it! Now I have to tell a story here though...I made my mom rent a little go-cart type thing to wheel around Silver Dollar City on because it was too hilly for her to walk and get around for a whole day…by nightfall, the park had become unbelievably crowded… to the point of having people packed in like sardines and my mom was trying to work her way to the exit without much luck (as was about 1,000 other folks…to be honest, I have never seen it so crowded in all the times we had visited before) so we patiently tried to weave through an inch at a time as we saw openings… well, she missed an opening and the next thing I knew someone was singing, "Grandma ran me over with her go-cart.." then others starting joining in and you can have one guess as to who "Grandma" was…hehe…I just acted like I didn't know her until we got passed that part of the crowd..hehe…it makes for a great story though!

We had a night last week in our community that was like a Hallmark movie moment… at least it seemed like it to me…they had a downtown event where different folks were the living Christmas window displays in the shops…some were singing and there was acting and puppeteers…there were persons giving away hot choco- late (which was a good thing because it was frigid temperatures that night) and they had a fire on one corner to roast a hot dog or warm your hands… I went to it alone just to walk along the streets..mostly because I knew one of the groups singing and I wanted to support them.. I watched couples strolling along hand in hand and I thought how blessed they were.. I watched parents with kids and I wondered if they knew they were making memories in what might be the best part of their life but most of all, as I walked the streets and met person after person that I knew and gathered hugs and well wishes and shared a moment or two with them, I thought how blessed I was to live in a community that cared. To be able to know almost everyone that walked up and down the street and have their friendship is a wonderful gift! When I headed home, I was cold from the temps but warm in the heart! There are pros and cons with living in a smaller community but on that night it was all pros!

A group of us were able to attend the Expo in Atlanta, GA, to promote The Fishing Doc and it was a success. We have our first orders for it and we are working on a distribution plan. It was so great to let persons try out the fishing unit and see the smiles on their face as they made a cast and reeled it in…and that was without a fish… I could only imagine how it would be with a fish-(actually I know because I have seen it on Doc's face)! I hope it continues to grow and that many persons gain joy from using the fishing doc!

Speaking of fish, guess what I did this weekend? I got to pick up my lunker on the way to Branson that I caught back in May that Doc had mounted for me as an anniversary gift. Remember that? It is awesome and I think it was my favorite anniversary gift I ever got! I just know Doc is smiling down on that! I wish I could have seen his face when I picked it up but I can imagine it! I was so excited and I know he would have been excited for me too! Now I get to hang it in just the right spot! Right on the wall so you can see it when you come in the front door…isn't that where everyone hangs a big fish mount?

Buck is still going strong…I was a little scared last week as he disappeared for over 24 hours and he never wanders from home but he finally made his way back and since then, he lost a little of his freedom. At the same time, he is a country dog and I am not going to be walking him around the yard when it is zero degrees while I am waiting for him to do his thing! So he is going to have to learn to stay where he belongs or remember how to get back…he is a smart dog so I am sure we will work it out somehow if he can keep from getting shot. I also put a new rule in place that he is not allowed to sleep up on top my bed anymore. He has he own little bed at the side of my bed and he has already figured that one out! I think we enjoy each others company but I do know he is a dog…I just have to remind him once in awhile!

Well, it is getting late but I wanted to get this put together while I was thinking about it. The holidays are a little hard but to tell you the truth, sometimes the "plain" days are harder. I told my cousin that sometimes it seems like I am the loneliest when I am in the biggest crowds if that makes any sense. Doc LOVED Christmas.. he loved decorating, he loved my snowman (we call them mine but to tell you the truth, he probably picked out half of them), he loved the trees and he loved to Christmas shop (as long as it wasn't for clothes or in Hobby Lobby! Hehe), he actually had done all his "special" shopping before he passed away so there are several persons that are going to get to enjoy a "Doc" gift just one more time! Most of all, Doc loved Christmas because of what it really is…the celebration of the birth of Jesus! Because of the love we shared for this holiday, it would be remiss of me not to continue to enjoy it and so my house is decorated, my snowmen are out and soon, mine (and his) gifts will be wrapped! Christmas Eve, I will go to church and even though there might be a tear in my eye that he is not sitting beside me, I know my kids will be there and we will all be missing him together but smiling at the memories we have! To not enjoy life to the fullest for each day we are given would be against everything that Doc preached..both in words and actions! So that is my gift this year for each of you… a reminder to enjoy each and every minute of each day you are given…each is a gift from heaven to be made the most of…. Remember to find a way to give this season because it really is in giving that you receive!

Have a Blessed Christmas,
Your friend Cindy

February 10-2010

It might be that it is the still the season of winter but my heart is slowly mending and my life is slowly finding direction and I sense that spring is coming. In the past 5 years, I have learned a few things about letting go and trusting in God's plan, even if it is really foggy and unclear. I set to working on the house and I worked hard too! I was able to get a lot accomplished in a short amount of time. I learned to adapt to an empty house. I was going to write of adapting to being alone but that isn't necessarily true. I wrote that in one update and I was quick to get responses that I should not think that I was alone because there were so many of you out there that wanted to make sure that I wasn't! I also have my faith and when I pray at those hard moments, I don't feel "alone" for long!

The holidays came and went and along the way it seems like there has been direction in my life. I was really worried that without Doc to guide my path that I might forget how we walked together with Christ through almost every minute of every day but then I found a gift. I found a box of letters stashed under my bed...I have no idea when I put them there but from the evidence of dust on them, I would say it had been awhile. I know that I am getting older and my mind does forget things but this one still baffles me. What I found in that box was letters that I had written to God...starting from about 7th grade and going through when I met and married Doc... they stopped soon after that-probably because things got busy and I went to verbal prayer...I cannot remember writing these letters but

I do recognize my handwriting and I see that I signed them all with my name. I sat for hours on the floor in bedroom and the cleaning stopped while I read those letters. I was looking at myself as a third person and I was so happy that I had written them and that I found them back when I needed to be reminded that I loved God before I met Doc...my faith was strong before I even knew him and I know God allowed me to find those letters to reassure myself that my faith was not dependant on Doc. It grew because of my relationship with him but it was not rooted in him. It is rooted in me and it is between me and my savior. I am sure Doc was in the same situation...we had a relationship that we shared with each other, a relationship that we shared together with Christ, and yet another private relationship with Christ that just belonged to each of us individually—as each of you either have or can have. That one is the most important of all because it is not based on anything that can be lost....it is something that will last through eternity.

So it became my first step of many, with many, many more to yet come, that I have had to take on my own, without Doc by my side! Do I still cry over not having him by my side? Absolutely and I hope I never lose that pain. I hope that when I die, someone misses me too! If not, we missed something very important during our time on earth. We missed the chance to love others and allow them to love us. Whether it be a son, daughter, spouse, parent, friend, grandparent, cousin, or other family member...your mission in life should be that when you die, you have lived your life in such a way that they can celebrate the beginning for you and mourn the end for themselves. That they hear a song, see something or even get that wiff of a smell that brings back a memory… a special moment or an ordinary moment…a moment with you in it. To live life and leave that tear in someone's eye occasionally is a story of a life success-fully lived.

My next step took me towards some retreats. The first was a woman's retreat in my own church. It was another step in the healing process. It was marching forward in my own faith relation-ship. There was a moment that others shared what we meant to them and their faith and although there were so many that had many, wonderful, kind and generous words for me, I felt empty because the one person that I wanted to hear words of encouragement from was obviously missing. The one opinion that would matter the most to me couldn't send me that message…that was my thought…but then a calming feeling came over me as I read what so many others wrote and I realized that they were telling me what he would have said too….I can just see him sitting there and me asking him, "well, sweetheart, aren't you going to say anything?" and he would say, "babe, I have been married to you for all these years and you don't already know what I think about your faith, your beauty, your love? You are my angel and I see you through the heavenly eyes of love-you are perfect." I think that is called unconditional love because I am not perfect and I am not a beauty but I was in Doc's eyes and I am in God's eyes too. This I know! I didn't realize this until after I had time to reflect on the weekend but I did see it. I felt another little bitty part of me heal. I knew I was one day closer to my promised date with heaven too. I will wait patiently for it to arrive and will treasure every day until it gets here as another gift from heaven to make a difference in this world.

So the following weekend, I stepped into a teen retreat. To be surrounded by the love and faith of young people is unlike anything else that you can experience. The wisdom and enthusiasm of youth is so powerful. I hope that I can serve in this capacity again but I trust that I will find my path and if this is not it, at least it was a stepping stone towards it.

I was invited to speak at 2 events in March which allowed me to continue to share the faith and the story. It was my first time to share in an organized gathering without Doc but his presence was there in the changes in me for having known him and in spirit. It wasn't difficult to share our story without him because it was about him! He was there almost as if he was still sitting there right beside me.

I have given a lot of thought lately to my dad too. My dad died of cancer when I was only 19. He had just turned 40 and Doc & I had to move our wedding date up-twice- to insure that he could attend and even at that, he almost didn't live long enough. Through the grace of God, he was able to make a turn for the better just as he appeared to be at his worse and even managed to walk me down the aisle and give me away. I have no sad stories of my childhood...it was great! We didn't have a lot of money but we had a ton of faith and a ton of love! Things that money can buy really don't add up to what faith and love can give you. So we had the best of what was offered. Shortly after our wedding, God took my dad home and he passed the torch of earthly care and love over to Darwin. Darwin did that for almost 30 years until finally, at the age of almost 50, God knew that I could stand and survive on my own. He put a good foundation of friends, children and family under me for support and he lights my way and I follow. I am not trying to swim upstream anymore. I am simply floating along and God allows me to go to the shore every now and do something in his name. That gives me great peace to serve him and have a purpose. All of us need a purpose and we all have one...sometimes we just have to open our eyes to see it. I am blessed to be loved by God and so are you. If you haven't opened your arms up to that love yet, I encourage you to search it out because it isn't hard to find! Your life will be "perfect" when you find it!

Your Friend, Cindy

Conclusion

I didn't write any more updates at this point because I started to work on my book to fill in all those blanks. Things that happened in our life that weren't included in these updates. Things that I wanted to share to give hope to others that might be wondering how they will make it through some huge struggle in their life! I titled the book "Remember to Laugh... The Story of Doc and Cindy Blackmore".

I still speak at churches and events when invited and it always feels good to share our story. I know some do not believe me and have to wonder at the things I say but I know them to be true and it is easy for me to believe because they happened to me.

I will always love my Darwin because he was my soulmate. God gave us the greatest gift of love when he gave us each other! I do not know what my future holds but I do know that my past has been blessed. It hasn't been without its tears, because there have been many, but the blessings have been greater. I had a wonderful father that gave his children a wonderful childhood but God took him home when I was only nineteen and he was only forty years old. Then he gave me Darwin but took him home when he was only forty-nine. I keep hearing that old phrase in my head though that goes, "it is better to have loved and lost, than to never have loved at all." How blessed I was to have someone love me for me…just the quirky way I am….he did not expect, nor want, me to change in any way. I was able to love him the same way back. We did not wear blinders and we were aware that we were not perfect but we loved the good and the bad…the sweet and the weird…and we were lucky enough to still be on our honeymoon as death did part us-just 29 short years after we said, "I do".

I dedicate this book to him, to our three wonderful children whom continue to be my blessings, and to all of you that know that kind of love, that seek that love, or have lost that love! Remember to honor marriage and to love our Lord. I will end this collection of memories the same way that I tried to remember to end each e-mail that I sent out….with a heartfelt thanks to those that served us, prayed for us, and/or in any way enriched our lives….this collection of adventures goes out to each of you. You were as much a part of this story as Doc & I were! God Bless and Amen!

9 781613 790090